Ancient Mesopotamia

New Perspectives

ABC-CLIO's
Understanding Ancient Civilizations

The Aztecs
Ancient Canaan and Israel
The Ancient Greeks
The Ancient Maya
The Romans

Forthcoming

The Ancient Celts
The Ancient Egyptians

Ancient Mesopotamia

New Perspectives

JANE R. MCINTOSH

A B C ● C L I O

Santa Barbara, California • Denver, Colorado • Oxford, England

Library of Congress Cataloging-in-Publication Data
McIntosh, Jane.
  Ancient Mesopotamia : new perspectives / Jane R. McIntosh.
    p. cm.—(ABC-CLIO's understanding ancient civilizations)
  Includes bibliographical references and index.
    ISBN 1-57607-965-1 (hardback : alk. paper)—ISBN 1-57607-966-X (ebook)
    1. Iraq—Civilization—To 634. I. Title. II. Series: Understanding ancient civilizations.

DS69.5.M385 2005
935—dc22

2005014930

08 07 06 05 / 10 9 8 7 6 5 4 3 2 1

This book is also available on the World Wide Web as an e-book.
Visit abc-clio.com for details.

ABC-CLIO, Inc.
130 Cremona Drive, P.O. Box 1911
Santa Barbara, California 93116-1911

This book is set in 10 pt. Palatino.

This book is printed on acid-free paper.
Manufactured in the United States of America.

Production Team:
Acquisitions Editor   Simon Mason
Submissions Editor   Peter Westwick
Senior Media Editor   Giulia Rossi
Media Manager   Caroline Price
Media Resources Coordinator   Ellen Brenna Dougherty
Production Editor   Anna R. Kaltenbach
Editorial Assistant   Cisca Schreefel
Production Manager   Don Schmidt
Manufacturing Coordinator   George Smyser

For Patrick
1931–2004

Contents

Series Editor's Preface

In recent years there has been a significant and steady increase of academic and popular interest in the study of past civilizations. This is due in part to the dramatic coverage, real or imagined, of the archaeological profession in popular film and television, and to extensive journalistic reporting of spectacular new finds from all parts of the world. Because archaeologists and other scholars, however, have tended to approach their study of ancient peoples and civilizations exclusively from their own disciplinary perspectives and for their professional colleagues, there has long been a lack of general factual and other research resources available for the nonspecialist. The *Understanding Ancient Civilizations* series is intended to fill that need.

Volumes in the series are principally designed to introduce the general reader, student, and nonspecialist to the study of specific ancient civilizations. Each volume is devoted to a particular archaeological culture (e.g., the ancient Maya of southern Mexico and adjacent Guatemala) or cultural region (e.g., Israel and Canaan) and seeks to achieve, with careful selectivity and astute critical assessment of the literature, an expression of a particular civilization and an appreciation of its achievements.

The keynote of the *Understanding Ancient Civilizations* series is to provide, in a uniform format, an interpretation of each civilization that will express its culture and place in the world, as well as qualities and background that make it unique.

Series titles include volumes on the archaeology and prehistory of the ancient civilizations of Egypt, Greece, Rome, and Mesopotamia, as well as the achievements of the Celts, Aztecs, and Inca, among others. Still others are in the planning stage.

I was particularly fortunate in having Kevin Downing from ABC-CLIO contact me in search of an editor for a series about archaeology. It is a simple statement of the truth that there would be no series without him. I was also lucky to have Simon Mason, Kevin's successor from ABC-CLIO, continuing to push the production of the series. Given the scale of the project and the schedule for production, he deserves more than a sincere thank you.

JOHN WEEKS

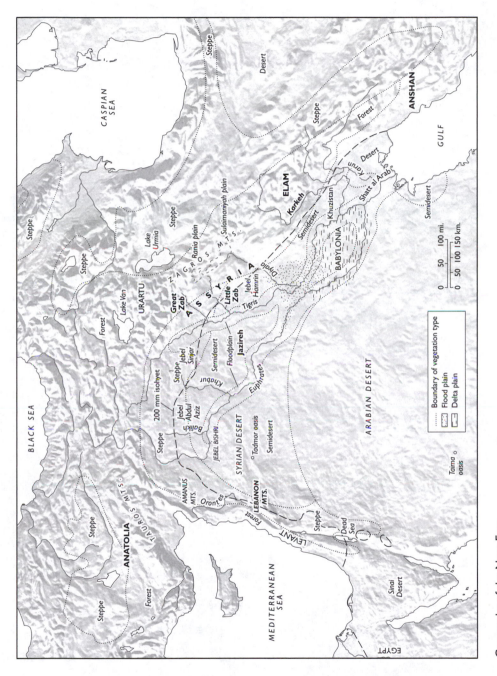

Geography of the Near East

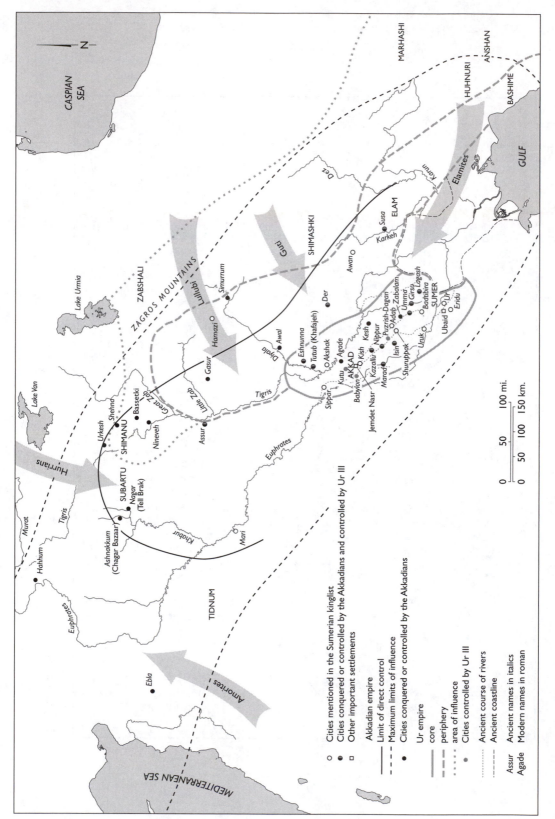

Sumer and Akkad in the Third Millennium

Legend:

Cities mentioned in the Sumerian kinglist ○
Cities conquered or controlled by the Akkadians and controlled by Ur III ●
Other important settlements □

Akkadian empire
Limit of direct control
Maximum limits of influence
Cities conquered or controlled by the Akkadians ●

Ur empire
core
periphery
area of influence
Cities controlled by Ur III ●

Ancient course of rivers
Ancient coastline

Assur   Ancient names in italics
Agade   Modern names in roman

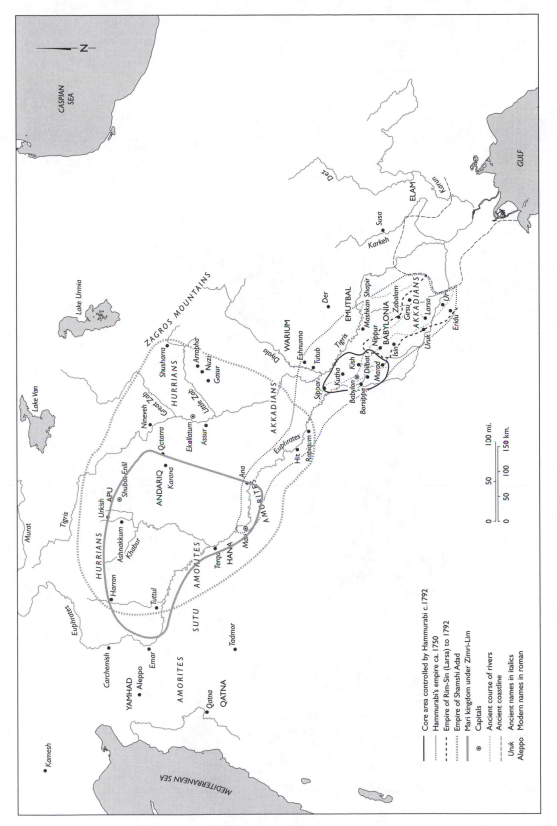

Early Second-Millennium Empires

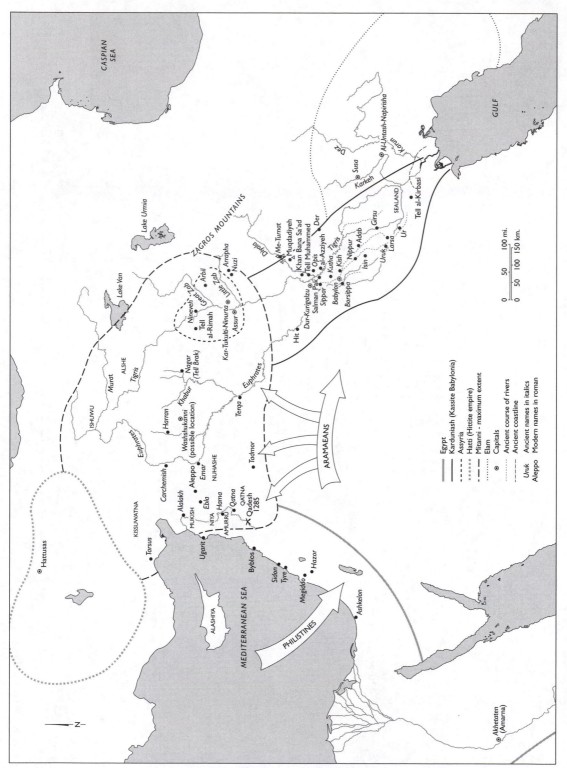

Later Second-Millennium Empires

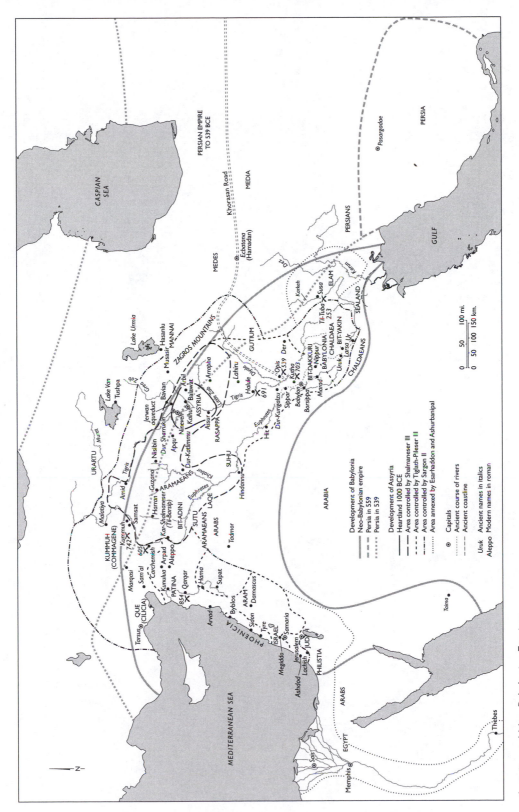

Assyrian and Neo-Babylonian Empires

PART I

Introduction

CHAPTER 1

Introduction

MESOPOTAMIA IN THE NEAR EAST

Mesopotamia—the land between the rivers—is the Classical name for the ancient land that lies along the Tigris and Euphrates, ancient Assyria and Babylonia. Most of it is now within present-day Iraq, but it also includes parts of eastern Syria and small parts of Turkey and Iran; conversely, the modern state of Iraq includes areas that in antiquity were outside Mesopotamia. To the west lies the Syrian Desert, home in the past to seminomadic groups—Amorites, Aramaeans, and Arabs—and the foothills and mountains to the east held other tribal groups, including Guti and Lullubi. Beyond them the Iranian plateau nurtured city-states and empires: in the west Elam by the fourth millennium, and Media and Persia in the first, by turns enemies, friends, and trading partners of the Mesopotamians. Mountainous regions also set a northern limit to Mesopotamia, as the Zagros swung west to join the Taurus range: Here the kingdom of Urartu grew up in the first millennium B.C.E., with Mannai to its southeast in the northern Zagros. Further west lies Anatolia, where towns and cities eventually united into the great Hittite Empire. City-states and kingdoms also sprang up in the Levant; their inhabitants included the seafaring Phoenicians and their enterprising predecessors, and the peoples of the Bible. The region is today the scene of strife and hostility among states and would-be states; in antiquity it was no less turbulent, fought over by local states but also frequently a battleground between the empires of Mesopotamia, Anatolia, and Egypt, and beyond them Iran and Europe. At their greatest extent, the empires of Mesopotamia ruled not only the Levant and all the lands between but also Egypt itself. The Persians added this entire region to their empire, which already controlled the lands from Thessaly to northern India; and Alexander the Great united these briefly with Greece and its dominions before the region was carved up by his successors.

THE CRADLE OF CIVILIZATION

The Near East and Egypt had been the cradle of Western civilization; after Alexander, Europe increasingly played a dominant role. By the nineteenth century C.E., Europe was a world power and the Near East was in decline under the decaying Ottoman Empire. Memories of its former greatness were kept alive through the distorting lens of the Bible, but investigations of its past, at first by amateur antiquarians, giving way to progressively more skilled and competent professional archaeologists, gradually revealed the true magnificence of its history.

Southern Mesopotamia—ancient Babylonia—and more particularly Sumer, its southern part, first saw the emergence of many of the developments that transformed the world into the urban society of today. Intensive agriculture, industrial production, state-controlled religion, complex stratified society, and the city itself had their beginnings here, as did many key innovations—including writing, without which we could neither share nor preserve our cultural and technological heritage. Sumer's achievements were built on developments elsewhere in the Near East, where millennia earlier agriculture had had its beginnings, providing a way of life able to sustain large and densely packed sedentary communities. The Near East and Sumer were not the only regions of the world in which these developments took place, but they were the first, and many of the lands beyond them were to adopt their innovations and build upon the foundations they had laid.

REVEALING MESOPOTAMIA'S PAST

The cruel picture of merciless Assyrian armies and Babylonian despots painted in the Bible was given substance by the discoveries in the nineteenth century in the ancient Assyrian cities and palaces—but a far richer and more varied world was also revealed. Alongside the enthusiastic but often destructive activities of the excavators, whose finds richly furnished the Oriental departments of major museums in Europe and the United States, the painstaking efforts of linguists and epigraphers enabled the writings of the ancient Mesopotamians to be deciphered and read once more. The deeds of kings, the exploits of heroes, and the acts of the gods were now laid bare, alongside the smug achievements of schoolboys, the angry actions of litigants, the careful calculations of engineers, and the devotions of priestesses. The clay that was the medium for writing for most of Mesopotamian history ensured the survival of huge numbers of texts, and the process of reading and publishing them occupies a major part in uncovering the story of Mesopotamia's past, which is still far from complete. Monographs and journals are now being supplemented and will perhaps one day be superseded by the Internet, which offers modern scholars the opportunity to share their discoveries swiftly, universally, and cheaply. The modern world is less helpful in the opportunities it affords for investigation in the field, since most of ancient Mesopotamia lies in Iraq, virtually closed to scholars since 1991, shifting excavations and survey work to adjacent but often still troubled regions like Syria. The Iraq War has made Mesopotamia's past even more inaccessible and has enabled looters to obliterate many of the remaining sites.

PART 2

Mesopotamian Civilization

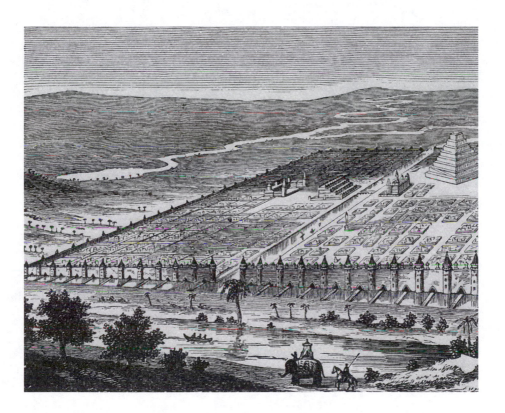

CHAPTER 2

The Location of Mesopotamian Civilization and Its Environmental Setting

INTRODUCTION

Surrounded by mountains in the north and east and desert in the west and bounded in the south by the Persian Gulf, ancient Mesopotamia was shaped by its two rivers, the Tigris and Euphrates. These provided water for agriculture and daily life and were the main highways for communication. Major environmental differences divided Mesopotamia into two distinct regions, the northern plains of Assyria and the southern Babylonian alluvium. Further differences split Babylonia into a northern river plain (Akkad) and a more southerly delta plain (Sumer). These geographical contrasts were mirrored by cultural, political, and economic distinctions. Marshes divided Babylonia from Elam, the eastern alluvial plain and adjacent Zagros Mountains, a land whose history frequently intertwined with that of Mesopotamia. At times, cities and states beyond the desert and the mountains were also involved with Mesopotamia, while mountain and desert fringes were home to tribal groups who frequently raided their settled neighbors.

The surface geology of the Near East is mainly sedimentary limestone and sandstone, but volcanoes have also created outcrops of basalt and obsidian. Pressure from the Arabian shield in the west forced the adjacent lands to fold, forming the Zagros Mountains and depressing the intervening area, creating a trough in which the rivers deposited alluvium.

THE CHANGING SEACOAST

At the height of the last Ice Age, global sea levels were some 100 meters lower than they are today. The whole Gulf was dry land, through which flowed the Tigris and Euphrates Rivers. Global sea levels began to rise from around 14,000 B.C.E., rapidly drowning the shallow Gulf, which reached its present shores by 5000–4000 B.C.E. By 3000 B.C.E. waters in the Gulf may have risen a further 1–2 meters, bringing the coast some 150 kilometers farther northwest and reaching nearly to Ur, which is recorded in early texts as a port.

When and how did the Gulf achieve its present shoreline? Alluvium deposited by the rivers may gradually have enlarged the delta, causing the head of the Gulf to retreat, although an important study by Lees and Falcon (1952) suggested that this alluviation was balanced by subsidence caused by continued tectonic activity. There is some evidence that the present shoreline had been reached by around 1500 B.C.E., but other data suggests that this did not happen until around 1000 C.E. Since the region at the head of the Gulf is very flat, slight changes in the levels of sea and alluvium can cause significant changes in the line of the coast, and flooding can create new areas of swamp. It is therefore difficult to determine when and in what way the shape of the region developed over time.

Deep-sea core evidence may indicate that before 4000 B.C.E. extensive annual flooding made southern Mesopotamia mainly marshland and that during the later fourth millennium this region became drier, at first creating a land crisscrossed by waterways but by 3000–2800 B.C.E. becoming similar to the way it is today. The dearth of evidence from the region itself, however, means that not all scholars accept this scenario.

THE ENVIRONMENTAL SETTING

Sealand

The extreme southwest was until very recently a region of marshland; forcibly drained by Saddam Hussein, it is now being restored again to marshland. Around Qurnah the Tigris and Euphrates combine to form the Shatt al 'Arab, joined by the Karun from the east before discharging their waters into the Gulf. In antiquity, however, the rivers flowed independently into the Gulf. South of Nasiriyah on the Euphrates and Amara on the Tigris, the waters of the delta spread out to form a huge area of perennial marsh, lakes, and waterways. Reed beds and rushes cover the area, and date palms grow along the waterways. There is abundant wildlife—fish, shellfish, turtles, and waterfowl—and fowling, harvesting dates, and fishing have always offered a productive way of life in the area. In times of political unrest, the marshland has also served as a place of refuge for defeated soldiers, escaped slaves, and other fugitives.

Babylonia

Between the marshlands and the latitude of modern Ramadi and Baghdad, where the Tigris and Euphrates come within 32 kilometers of each other, lies the alluvial region of Babylonia. Its agricultural prosperity depends on irrigation, since the scanty rainfall is quite inadequate to water crops and the rivers' annual inundation unhelpfully occurs around harvest time. The deeply incised and fast-flowing Tigris was difficult to harness for irrigation, and settlement along its course was largely eschewed. Farming therefore concentrated along branches of the slow-moving Euphrates, which watered a wide expanse of plain. The land to the east along the Diyala, a tributary of the Tigris, formed an extension of the Babylonian political and economic sphere; here both dry farming and irrigated agriculture were possible.

Chaldaeans hiding from Assyrian soldiers in the reed beds of the southern Mesopotamian marshland. Sennacherib's palace, Nineveh, ca. 630–620 B.C.E. (Zev Radovan/Land of the Bible Picture Archive)

The alluvial river plain is almost flat, decreasing from a gradient of 30 centimeters per kilometer to just 10 centimeters, producing a landscape in which the river divides into several meandering watercourses, and farther south in the delta plain below Hilla, it decreases still further to 3 centimeters per kilometer. The meager gradient causes the Euphrates's branches to run sluggishly through the plains, depositing silts that gradually raise their beds and the surrounding banks so that the rivers flow on levees, which can reach 2–3 kilometers in width, raised above the surrounding plain. These provide a fertile and well-drained environment ideally suited for cultivation. Irrigation channels can be cut through the levee banks to divert water onto the surrounding land, using gravity flow. Willow, poplar, licorice, and tamarisk, grasses and rushes, form dense thickets along the watercourses, providing food and shelter for wild boar and fallow deer.

Spring melting of snows in the distant Taurus Mountains, where the Tigris and Euphrates rise, swells the rivers in April and May, causing them to flood their backslopes. Every few years they burst their banks and inundate a wide expanse of the alluvial plains, encouraging the Euphrates to change its course and multiply its channels. The arrival of floodwaters just when the crops are

The alluvial plains of the river Euphrates furnished the agricultural wealth of Babylonia. (Zev Radovan/Land of the Bible Picture Archive)

ready to harvest means that drainage and flood control are as important as irrigation.

Away from the narrow fertile strip along the rivers and canals, the land is dry, semidesert mud. Here the perennial vegetation consists of scrubby, xerophytic species such as camelthorn and artemisia (wormwood), which in antiquity were more abundant. Overexploitation has resulted in erosion and desertification in many places. During the hot, dry summer and early autumn (May to October), this is a bleak region inhabited by small, elusive fauna—birds, burrowing creatures, and their predators, jackal and fox. The rains, although generally slight (rarely exceeding 150 millimeters per annum), transform this landscape in the winter and spring, producing fast-growing grasses, flowers, and other herbaceous plants that provide seasonal grazing for domestic sheep and goats and for gazelle and, in antiquity, onager, preyed on by hyenas and lions. In places, low-lying hollows and relics of former watercourses allow water to collect, creating shallow lakes or seasonal swamps that attract wildlife, particularly birds, including sandgrouse, teal, pelicans, geese, cranes, and sometimes flamingos and ibises.

Towns and cities clustered along the watercourses, each surrounded by fields and gardens, and the adjacent desert provided grazing. But the contrast between waste and fertile land hung on the availability of water. Prosperous settlements could suddenly be stranded in newly formed semidesert, as their life-giving river moved elsewhere. The Babylonian landscape is littered with abandoned settlements, great tells rising in what is now the middle of nowhere. And the greater the investment in irrigation works, the more catastrophic the change.

Although often politically divided, the city-states of Babylonia were united by their environment, common problems, and solutions, promoting the growth of a common culture. Sharp ecological contrasts and significant geographical barriers divide this region from the surrounding lands—marshes to the east and to the west a low rocky escarpment marking the frontier with the desert.

The Western Desert

Not far west of the Euphrates lies the vast desert that runs continuously from southern Arabia through the southern part of the Near East, shading off into semidesert where rainfall increases well north of Babylonia. Its fauna included ostrich, cheetahs, and hartebeest, as well as onager. All but its fringes were virtually impenetrable until use of the domestic camel developed around 1000 B.C.E. The Near Eastern portion, the Syrian (Shamiyah) Desert, therefore, effectively separated Mesopotamia from the well-watered lands of the Levant, although a route ran from the middle Euphrates (an area closely associated with Babylonia) west to the oasis of Tadmor (later Palmyra) where it joined routes through the Levant. Farther north, the Euphrates bend brought the Mesopotamian plains within 160 kilometers of the Mediterranean, linked to it via a well-used route.

The desert fringes were home to many pastoral tribes who raised sheep, goats, and donkeys. Some lived in permanent camps and also grew some crops; others practiced transhumance. The vagaries of climate made their existence precarious. A succession of dry years would drive them into the fat lands of their settled farming neighbors to the east and west, whose writings portray them as uncouth, alien, and often hostile.

While the southern Shamiyah Desert is flat and uniform, farther north it is broken up by wadis. In the hilly semidesert in the northeast, the Jebel Bishri, settlement was denser and often more settled; here petty Aramaean kings established towns and fortified strongholds.

Assyria

The desert follows the western edge of the Euphrates. Above Ramadi the alluvial plain ends, and for around 200 kilometers the Euphrates runs through a narrow valley, tightly constrained by cliffs on either side. Low rainfall and very limited arable land mean there are few settlements of any size along this corridor. Near the modern border between Syria and Iraq, the valley broadens out, but rainfall is still too low for rain-fed cultivation, and settlement remains sparse up to the Euphrates bend. Cultivation is confined to the alluvial banks of the Euphrates and occasional wadis where fields and orchards flourish.

Though slower to develop cities and political complexity than Babylonia, by the first millennium B.C.E. Assyria was the dominant power in the Near East. The Assyrian king Sennacherib built this "Palace without a Rival" around 700 B.C.E. when he moved the Assyrian capital to Nineveh. (Bettmann/Corbis)

Control of river trade and communications supported the few major ancient centers, such as Mari, set in a broader stretch of valley, and Terqa, near the confluence of the Khabur and Euphrates.

East of the Euphrates lies a region of semidesert steppe stretching to the foothills of the Zagros. The Jazireh ("Island"), the plain enclosed by the northern reaches of the Tigris and Euphrates, is a relatively flat region with a gentle gradient, broken by low, rolling hills, once forested, and deep wadis carrying seasonal water. Winter rainfall coats the steppe in a carpet of grasses that provide seasonal grazing for domestic flocks, wild cattle, gazelle, fallow deer, and, in antiquity, onager. Alluvial soils occur in small patches, but the dissected terrain inhibits the construction of simple irrigation channels, so agriculture is dependent on rainfall. The 200-millimeter isohyet marks the southernmost limit of potential dry cultivation; this curves around in a great arc from the Levant, passing above the Euphrates bend to cross the Tigris just south of Jebel Sinjar and run south between the Tigris and the Zagros; the 300-millimeter isohyet farther north, however, represents the boundary of really reliable rain-fed agriculture. Numerous tells marking ancient settlements in the steppe to the south of Jebel Sinjar indicate that the situation was more favorable in the third and second millennia B.C.E., with adequate rainfall available farther south than to-

The Taurus mountains where the Euphrates rose were the source of many of the minerals exploited by the people of Mesopotamia from early times. (Holy Land Photos)

day. The area probably also had a better water supply in the past, flowing in wadis from the Jebel Sinjar.

The Euphrates and its tributaries, the Khabur and the Balikh, and the Tigris and its tributaries, including the Greater and Lesser Zab, also water cultivable areas. Springs and wells contribute to the local availability of water, which supports parkland vegetation outside the cultivated areas. Between the low ranges of the Jebel Sinjar and Jebel Hamrin and the foothills of the Zagros lay the heartland of Assyria, centered on the Tigris. To the north, a fertile corridor lay between the low but difficult hills of the Jebel Sinjar and the Zagros, which swings westward to join the Taurus Mountains of eastern Turkey. Heavily wooded in antiquity, these mountains were the source of many desirable raw materials.

The mountains set a natural limit to Assyria, inhibiting expansion into Iran and Anatolia, although the Assyrians undertook trading expeditions into the mountains and periodic raids against their hostile tribes. No such natural barriers separated Assyria from regions to the west. From the Euphrates bend, where the river turns almost straight north to its mountain source, the land is a fertile rain-fed plain, running continuously into the Assyrian corridor to the

Susa, the capital of Elam, was a great city that rivaled those of Mesopotamia down the ages. (Ridpath, John Clark, *Ridpath's History of the World*, 1901)

east and the Levant to the west. Here lay the heartland of the Mitanni Empire in the mid–second millennium B.C.E., and in earlier and later times, the Assyrians expanded from the east to control this region, eventually moving south through the Levant as far as Egypt.

Although the uncultivable southern steppe marked a sharp ecological divide between Babylonia and Assyria, the two were linked by their shared rivers. Southerners expanded north along the rivers, often incorporating Mari and Assur within their cultural sphere or dominions, while Assyrian empires likewise repeatedly enlarged their political control southwards into Babylonia.

Elam and the Zagros

Babylonia and Assyria were also linked by an eastern overland route. This passes through prosperous villages along the Zagros foothills, a region of open woodland and grasses enjoying warm, dry summers and mild, wet winters. It skirts the low ranges that jut out from the Zagros; of these the most formidable is the Jebel Hamrin, a steep and rugged range rising to 200–300 meters that presents a major barrier dividing the lands of the north from the plains of Babylonia. The Diyala River cuts a pass through Jebel Hamrin, and from here the route follows the Diyala to its confluence with the Tigris some 180 kilometers to the southwest. South of the Diyala, marshes divide the Babylonian plain from Susiana (Khuzestan).

Although Susiana is geologically part of the southern plain, it was culturally and economically quite distinct from Babylonia. Apart from marshes in the extreme south and an arid zone south of Ahwaz, the region lies within the area where rain-fed agriculture is possible. Five rivers rising in the Zagros, of which the Karun and the Karkheh are the most substantial, allow productivity to be increased by irrigation.

Cultivation was only a part of the farming economy of Susiana, where transhumant sheep and goat pastoralism has great antiquity. In winter, flocks grazed on the plains and foothills, covered in tamarisk, pistachio, jujube, and grasses, and in summer in upland pastures of the Zagros, where in antiquity there were widespread open forests (now largely denuded), mainly of oak and pistachio, interspersed with abundant herbaceous vegetation, home to herds of red deer, roe deer, wild sheep, and wild goat.

Susiana and the adjacent Zagros region became known to the Mesopotamians as Elam. Through history, Elam varied in extent, at times including Anshan, the mountains and coastal plain along the eastern side of the Gulf. From the Zagros, Elam looked east across the Iranian plateau with which it often had close economic and cultural ties. To the west, routes around the northern and southern edges of the marshes gave access to Babylonia, by turns friendly or inimical to Elam; the northern passage also joined routes into Assyria, with whom Elam often had hostile relations.

The Diyala River, Elam's northern boundary, was one of the main access routes into the Zagros Mountain chain, which rises to 3,600–4,000 meters in a series of steep terraces, well watered and lushly vegetated in antiquity. In places, patches of grass-covered soil along valleys or on hillside terraces give the opportunity for small communities to practice cultivation, although pastoralism has always provided the main way of life. The high Zagros offers rich summer pastures, and in the bitter winters grazing is found on the lower slopes or foothills on either side of the mountains. Three larger intermontane valleys—the Shahrizur, Rania, and Rowanduz plains—offer scope for more dense settlement, but the difficulty of movement through the Zagros meant that they were always home to tribal groups rather than larger political entities. From the Zagros, Assyria and Babylonia were frequently raided by groups speaking many languages, such as Hurrians, Guti, and Kassites.

THE CHANGING LANDSCAPE

Since 8000 B.C.E. the Near Eastern environment overall has been much as it is today, but there have been many changes in the detail, owing both to natural factors and to human activity, sometimes affecting individual settlements, at other times impacting entire regions.

Changes in the Course of the Rivers

As rising postglacial sea levels progressively flooded the Gulf, the changing location of the coast affected the gradient of the rivers, causing the upper reaches to become more deeply incised and therefore generally stable in their location, but slowing their flow across the plains so that an increased volume of alluvium was deposited there. Just north of Sippar, the plain broadens out and its gradient declines, causing the rivers to become far less stable. The Euphrates in particular has split into a number of major and minor branches, and in years of heavy flooding these can change their course, with devastating effects for their dependent settlements. Before 3000 B.C.E., the Euphrates flowed in three channels, passing through Kutha, Kish, and Jemdet Nasr; by the third millennium, the Kish branch had become the principal one. Around the end of ED

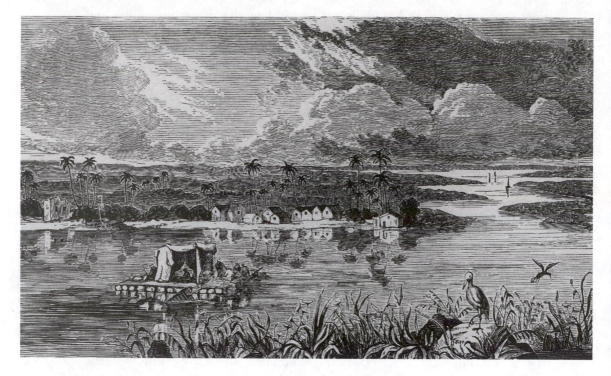

In early antiquity the Tigris and Euphrates Rivers flowed separately into the Gulf, considerably north of its present shoreline. The rivers, and particularly the Euphrates, have changed their course many times. The copious volumes of silt they deposited created a delta within which the two rivers eventually met. This nineteenth-century engraving shows their confluence in recent times. (Ridpath, John Clark, *Ridpath's History of the World*, 1901)

(Early Dynastic period) I (ca. 2750 B.C.E.), the main flow of the Euphrates farther south moved eastward to run down a previously minor branch, reducing water in its former main channel. Uruk, on the latter, though still a major city, declined from its earlier preeminence, while cities on the eastern branch, including Umma, grew in importance. During the later third millennium, a minor branch developed though Babylon, growing to become the principal branch by the late second millennium B.C.E. Today the principal bed of the Euphrates lies farther west.

The Euphrates is not alone in changing its course. Below Kut, the Tigris is also unstable and is known to have shifted at least three times. In antiquity, it flowed directly into the Gulf, having followed a much more direct course than that of today. The Diyala anciently joined the Tigris considerably south and east of their present confluence near Baghdad. And until around a millennium ago, the Karun and Karkheh in Susiana formed a joint estuary.

Evidence from pollen cores and oxygen isotope profiles from mountain lakes gives some indication of variations in vegetation, rainfall, and temperature, although many uncertainties remain. Temperatures exceeded those of today by 1–2 degrees C around 5000–2000 B.C.E. This, combined with higher rainfall, allowed trees to grow at higher altitudes and in regions of steppe that today have sparse vegetation. A period of reduced rainfall in the northern mountains from 3800 B.C.E. may have caused the marshes of southern Babylonia to become progressively drier. Further evidence suggests that the years around 2900 B.C.E. saw particularly severe inundations, giving rise to the story of the Flood (see chapter 11). During the third millennium B.C.E. river levels may have fallen, particularly around 2350–2000 B.C.E., necessitating increasing investment in irrigation works. Later episodes of fluctuating river levels included peak volumes of water in both the Tigris and the Euphrates around 1350–1250 B.C.E., followed by a reduction that lasted until around 950 B.C.E.

The Consequences of Human Activities

Many changes in the Mesopotamian environment were the result of human activity. The creation of canals and dams could significantly alter drainage patterns, often unwittingly, although at times the interference was malicious. Upstream communities sometimes channeled water to serve their own needs at the expense of communities farther downstream, a catalyst to conflict. Several kings diverted the Euphrates to starve hostile cities of essential water supplies, or to destroy them by flooding, often with devastating long-term effects.

Even more damaging was the impact of millennia of exploitation of upland forests. Trees were cleared to create arable land or to provide timber for building and wood and brush for fuel. Grazing also took its toll, preventing the regeneration of trees and scrub. The lowlands similarly suffered degradation and destruction: Originally the northern plains were covered by savannah with small trees, while the steppe was densely vegetated. The destruction of plant cover caused further changes, promoting desertification of the steppe and producing erosion in the mountains, which increased runoff, swelling the rivers and causing aggravated flooding downstream. However, the effects of these activities were probably not significant before the later first millennium B.C.E.

Prolonged irrigation had another significantly detrimental effect—salinization. Small amounts of salts carried down by the rivers from the sedimentary rocks of the north have over the millennia accumulated in the groundwater of southern Mesopotamia. The deposition of salts is greater in periods, like that between 2350 and 2000 B.C.E., when the volume of water in the rivers is reduced. Intensive irrigation raises the water table, bringing this saline water close to the surface, where it is drawn up by capillary action, causing salts to accumulate in the subsoil and on the surface where water spread for irrigation also contains salts. When moisture is removed by evapotranspiration, the salts are deposited on the land, progressively reducing fertility. Many scholars believe this can be seen during the earlier second millennium B.C.E. when land once suitable for wheat was sown with the more salt-tolerant barley (although scholars opposed to this theory argue that barley was selected for its higher yields rather than its salt tolerance). Eventually the land became too saline for cultivation. Many southern cities were abandoned, and their inhabitants moved north or turned to pastoral nomadism.

TEXT REFERENCES

Buccellati, Giorgio, and Marilyn Kelly-Buccellati. 1997. "Terqa." Pp. 188–190 in *The Oxford Encyclopedia of Archaeology in the Near East*. Edited by Eric M. Meyers. 5 Volumes. Oxford: Oxford University Press.

Butzer, Karl W. 2000. "Environmental Change in the Near East and Human Impact on the Land." Pp. 123–151 in *Civilizations of the Ancient Near East*. Vol. 1. Edited by Jack M. Sasson. Peabody, MA: Hendrickson Publishers. (Reprint of 1995 edition. New York: Scribner.)

IUPUI (Indiana University Purdue University Indianapolis) Geography Department. 2001. "Sea Level Change." http://www.iupui.edu/~geogdept/g305/sealevel.htm (cited October 2, 2002).

Lambeck, K., P. Johnston, C. Smither, K. Fleming, and Y. Yokoyama. 1995. "Late Pleistocene and Holocene Sea-Level Change." *Extract from RSES Annual Report 1995*. Geodynamics. http://www.rses.anu.edu.au/geodynamics/AnnRep/95/AR-Geod95.html (cited October 2, 2002).

Lees, G. M. and N. L. Falcon. 1952. "The Geographical History of the Mesopotamian Plains." *Geographical Journal* 118: 24–39.

Lloyd, Seton. 1980. *Foundations in the Dust*. Revised edition. London: Thames and Hudson.

Margueron, Jean-Claude. 1997. "Mari." Pp. 413–417 in *The Oxford Encyclopedia of Archaeology in the Near East*. Edited by Eric M. Meyers. 5 Volumes. Oxford: Oxford University Press.

Meyers, Eric M., ed. 1997. *The Oxford Encyclopedia of Archaeology in the Near East*. 5 Volumes. Oxford: Oxford University Press.

Millard, Alan. 2000. "Aramaeans." P. 28 in *Dictionary of the Ancient Near East*. Edited by Piotr Bienkowski and Alan Millard. London: British Museum Press.

Nissen, Hans J. 1988. *The Early History of the Ancient Near East*. Chicago: University of Chicago Press. (Paperback edition 1990.)

Nutzel, Werner. 1976. "The Climatic Changes of Mesopotamia and Bordering Areas." *Sumer* 32: 11–24.

Oates, Joan. 1986. *Babylon*. Revised edition. London: Thames and Hudson.

Oppenheim, A. Leo, and Erica Reiner. 1977. *Ancient Mesopotamia. Portrait of a Dead Civilization*. Revised edition. Chicago: University of Chicago Press.

Pillsbury, A. F. 1981. "The Salinity of Rivers." *Scientific American* 245(1): 54–65.

Pollack, Susan. 1999. *Ancient Mesopotamia. The Eden that Never Was*. Cambridge: Cambridge University Press.

Postgate, J. Nicholas. 1994. *Early Mesopotamia*. London: Routledge.

Potts, D. T. 1997. *Mesopotamian Civilization. The Material Foundations*. London: The Athlone Press.

———. 1999. *The Archaeology of Elam. Formation and Transformation of an Ancient Iranian State*. Cambridge: Cambridge University Press.

Reade, Julian. 2000. *Mesopotamia*. 2d edition. London: British Museum Press.

Roaf, Michael. 1990. *Cultural Atlas of Mesopotamia*. New York: Facts on File.

Roux, Georges. 1992. *Ancient Iraq*. 3d edition. Harmondsworth: Penguin.

Saggs, H. W. F. 1995. *Peoples of the Past. Babylonians*. London: British Museum Press.

Wilkinson, T. J. "Indian Ocean: Cradle of Globalization. Scholar Voices." http://www.accd.edu/sac/history/keller/IndianO/Wilkin.html (cited October 2, 2002).

CHAPTER 3

Historical and Chronological Setting

HISTORY OF THE INVESTIGATION OF MESOPOTAMIA'S PAST

Investigations into Their Past by the Assyrians and Babylonians

The people of Mesopotamia had great respect for their traditions. Many practices that evolved in the fourth millennium B.C.E. or even earlier were still being followed by the Assyrians and Babylonians of the first millennium. For example, the word lists that were being compiled almost as soon as writing began were still standard scribal exercises under Hammurabi and are found in Ashurbanipal's library. Ashurbanipal recorded with pride that he could not only read ancient texts, but that he had read "obscure and confused inscriptions on stone from before the flood" (Leick 2001: 241).

Respect for tradition permeated official life. Kings rebuilt and restored the monuments of their distant predecessors as works of pious merit, often adding their names to those of the original founder. When Ashurbanipal sacked Susa he gained great satisfaction from restoring to its original home the statue of Inanna that had been looted from Uruk 1,635 years earlier.

Pride in their past went along with considerable interest and curiosity. Ashurbanipal created a great library of more than 5,000 cuneiform tablets in his palace at Nineveh, in which he collected copies of all the surviving texts that his agents could lay hands on: Some went back to before the time of Hammurabi. But Ashurbanipal's library was only the most spectacular of its kind; many others were enthusiastically accumulated by kings, priests, and private citizens alike.

The Neo-Babylonian kings were particularly enthusiastic in their restoration of earlier temples and cities, often excavating to recover details of the original foundation. Nebuchadrezzar II (r. 604–562 B.C.E.) dug at Ur and restored the Nabu temple and ziggurat at Borsippa. Nabonidus (r. 555–539 B.C.E.) investigated and restored many sacred places in Sumer and Akkad, including the ancient Akkadian capital Agade. Here after some three years of fruitless searching he at last discovered the remains of the temple of Ishtar: A heavy rainstorm cut a trench revealing the temple.

Nabonidus was a devotee of the moon god Sin (Nanna), whose temples at Ur and Harran he restored. While excavating the residence of the *entu*-priestess of Sin at Ur, Nabonidus was thrilled to find ancient inscriptions. One belonged to Enanedu, who, following earlier custom, had been dedicated as *entu*-priestess by her father, Kudur-mabuk, a ruler who predated Hammurabi.

The Assyrian king Ashurbanipal, shown in traditional pose, carrying a basket of soil to initiate the restoration of Esagila, the temple of Marduk, in Babylon. (Zev Radovan/Land of the Bible Picture Archive)

Nabonidus revived the ancient practice, finding details of the appropriate costume for an *entu*-priestess on an inscription of Nebuchadrezzar I (1124–1103 B.C.E.) and dedicating his own daughter, En-nigaldi-nanna, to this position.

Nebuchadrezzar and Nabonidus housed the ancient relics that they found in a museum within the North Palace at Babylon. Interesting in their own right, such objects also served to emphasize the kings' status as heirs to Babylonian traditions. Nabonidus and En-nigaldi-nanna also housed a collection of antiquities in a special room in her residence at Ur; these included a statue of the Ur III king Shulgi (2094–2047 B.C.E.).

Knowledge that the things of the past lay buried beneath the buildings and mounds of the present was not new. More than a thousand years earlier, a young Babylonian wrote to his father asking for a bead headdress; he suggested that, if his father could not get new ones, he should dig in an ancient site to recover some antique beads.

Historical Information Preserved in the Bible and Classical Writings

The influence and prestige of Mesopotamia ensured that its myths, legends, and history were widely disseminated in the Near East and beyond. Many elements of Assyrian and Babylonian legal institutions and laws, science, astronomy, mathematics and medicine, calendar and the division of time, as well as magical and ritual beliefs and practices such as divination were widely adopted, as can be seen in Classical and Hellenistic Greek literature and in the Bible.

Whereas the early Greeks knew of Mesopotamia at one remove, the Israelites had direct and often painful experience of the Mesopotamians. Mesopotamian myths and history are interwoven with biblical accounts of the early days of the world: for example, the story of the Tower of Babel in Genesis 11. From the mid-ninth century B.C.E., the biblical kingdoms of Israel and Judah suffered from Assyrian expansionism, and revolts against Assyrian, and later, Babylonian, rule led to the sack of their cities and the deportation of many of their citizens. The climax came in 588–587 B.C.E., when Jerusalem was put to the torch, the Temple destroyed, and its notables exiled to Babylon.

Although a substantial Jewish community flourished in Babylon for many centuries, becoming familiar with Babylonian traditions, it is the purple prose of the traditionalists who returned to Judah that formed the picture of Mesopotamia that passed into Western consciousness via the Bible. Centuries of conflict had produced a very hostile biblical view of Mesopotamian culture and civilization, especially of Babylon "the mother of harlots and of the abominations of the earth" (Revelation 17:5), ruled by supposedly corrupt and decadent rulers like Belshazzar, who was "weighed in the balance and found wanting" (Daniel 5:27).

Although the Greeks had no such political axe to grind, they also gave the Mesopotamians a bad press, contrasting their alien practices with the civilized behavior epitomized in the Greek mind by the Greeks. Thus, for example, Herodotus draws attention to the practice of sacred prostitution. He also gives

The hostile view of Assyria and Babylonia in the Bible colored European perceptions of Mesopotamian civilization, as in this nineteenth-century engraving of the Babylonian Captivity of the Jews. (Ridpath, John Clark, *Ridpath's History of the World*, 1901)

an anecdotal and fanciful account of Mesopotamian history. In contrast, his descriptions of the cities of Babylonia, and particularly Babylon itself, are both accurate and informative. Nevertheless, contemporaries came to doubt his accounts, which conflicted with those in the twenty-three-volume *Persica* of Ctesias, a Greek doctor at the Persian court in the fifth century B.C.E. In fact, Ctesias's account is far less reliable than that of Herodotus, being filtered through the attitudes and knowledge of Mesopotamia's Persian conquerors. Unfortunately, it was upon Ctesias's work that later Classical scholars based their writings about Mesopotamia.

This was despite the existence of a far better account, a three-volume work by the third century B.C.E. Babylonian scholar Berossus. A native of Babylon, Berossus wrote in Greek but had access to many cuneiform texts that provided detailed and accurate information on Mesopotamian history and culture. Berossus's *Babyloniaca*, which ran from the Creation to Alexander's conquest, was copied and circulated for a few centuries but by the first century B.C.E. had been largely superseded by a digest in which a Greek scholar, Alexander Polyhistor, uncritically assembled material from a number of different and conflicting texts, including Berossus and Ctesias. Information was drawn from Berossus's work to calculate chronology, particularly the dates of the Creation and the Flood, but his original was otherwise neglected. Little of it survived the Classical period.

The Hellenistic Greeks took an active interest in the visible relics of Mesopotamia's past. Alexander the Great began reconstructing the ziggurat of Marduk (the Tower of Babel), although work ceased upon his death. His successors carried out restorations in the precinct of Marduk and of the temple of Nabu in Borsippa. The Hanging Gardens of Babylon, reputedly built by Nebuchadrezzar for his Median queen, Amyitis, were regarded as one of the Seven Wonders of the World, their fame long outlasting their physical existence. Some versions of the list of Seven Wonders also included the great walls of Babylon, said by Herodotus to be wide enough to turn a four-horse chariot on.

Early European Travelers

While Egypt's enduring monuments inspired perennial interest, little survived to provoke similar curiosity in Mesopotamia after the fall of its great cities. Local people preserved some ancient names for the mounds that lay around them but mercilessly plundered them of baked bricks for building. Knowledge of the ancient Mesopotamian world was filtered through the hostile lens of the Bible and the Classical works known to Medieval Europe. More information survived in the educated Muslim world, but its literature was largely unknown to Europeans.

The Bible, however, ensured an enduring interest in the great and, from the biblical perspective, wicked and decadent cities of Babylon and Nineveh. Medieval pilgrims and travelers, both Jewish and Christian, visited the mound that was still known as "Babil" covering part of Babylon. They searched for, and often believed they had found, the prison in which the prophet Daniel was confined and the burning fiery furnace. They looked also for the notorious Tower of Babel, which some visitors identified with the ziggurat at Birs Nimrud (ancient Borsippa) or that at Aqar Quf, both at some distance from the mounds of Babylon. Among them was Rabbi Benjamin from Tudela in Spain, who visited Babylon and Nineveh between 1160 and 1173 and whose account of his travels was published in 1573.

Pietro della Valle, a widely traveled Italian nobleman, visited Birs Nimrud and Babil in 1616, making an accurate description of the remains he observed, which included glazed bricks, and removing "some square bricks on which were writing in certain unknown characters" (quoted in Lloyd 1980: 8), the first cuneiform inscriptions to reach Europe. Babylonian cuneiform inscriptions at Persepolis were transcribed in 1686 by Englebert Kaempfer, who

This basalt statue of a lion trampling a man was discovered by local villagers in 1776 in the North Palace at Babylon, where it had formed part of the collections in Nebuchadrezzar's "museum." (Library of Congress)

coined the term *cuneatae* to describe them, thus narrowly anticipating Thomas Hyde, professor of Hebrew and Arabic at Oxford, to whom the honor of inventing the word *cuneiform* is usually ascribed.

The Danish scholar Carsten Niebuhr also studied the Persepolis inscriptions, recognizing the presence of three different scripts and making accurate copies, which enabled scholars, notably Georg Grotefend, to begin the decipherment of these scripts. Niebuhr also visited Babylon in 1765, making a detailed study of the visible remains; he observed that the use of fragile mudbrick and easily reused baked brick as building materials explained the lack of "magnificent monuments such as one encounters in Persia and Egypt" (quoted in Lundquist 2000: 70).

Abbe de Beauchamp, the Pope's vicar-general in Babylonia, visited Babylon in 1780 and 1790. His accounts of the inscribed cylinders, statues, and walls decorated with glazed bricks that were exposed by brick robbers sparked considerable interest among the European public, and the East India Company commissioned their Resident in Basra to obtain some inscribed material from Babylon. This was duly dispatched to Britain, the first of many consignments of Mesopotamian antiquities to find a new home there.

In 1807 the East India Company created a new post of Resident in Baghdad, appointing Claudius James Rich, a young man already enjoying a formidable reputation for his knowledge of Oriental languages. Rich threw himself enthusiastically and skillfully into his official duties but, fascinated by the country, devoted much of his free time to collecting and studying manuscripts and antiquities and visiting sites. In 1811 he explored the ruins of Babylon, making a detailed survey with measured topographical plans and drawings, which he published in a memoir describing the visible remains. He also obtained antiquities from the locals' brick diggings and tried his hand at a little digging in the Babil mound.

Rich's many visitors also took delight in exploring the region, among them the painter Robert Ker Porter, whose admirably readable account of his visits to Babylon, Birs Nimrud, Kish, and Aqar Quf, illustrated with his fine romantic engravings, fired popular interest. In 1818 Rich published a second memoir on Babylon and its relics. Rich's enthusiastically amassed antiquities was purchased in 1825 by the British Museum for £7,000, the beginning of Britain's impressive collection of Western Asiatic antiquities. But by this time Rich himself was dead, victim of a cholera epidemic; his widow, Mary, brought out a third volume on his finds in 1839.

The Scramble for Antiquities in the Later Nineteenth Century

European interest in the Near East was growing. By the 1850s decipherers were making it possible to understand the ancient cuneiform texts. The names of kings and places familiar from the Bible began regularly to appear, whetting public appetite for further investigations. Intrepid explorers like Robert Mignan and J. Bailie-Fraser observed and described southern Mesopotamian mounds that hid the remains of other major cities, including Ur. In the late 1840s and 1850s, serious excavations began at Babylon and in the Assyrian cities around Mosul. The impressive results sparked considerable international rivalry, especially between Britain and France, and substantial public funds began to be committed to the investigation of ancient Mesopotamian cities.

Nimrud, Nineveh, and Khorsabad. Rich's find inspired the French to initiate their own investigations. They therefore created a post, consular agent at Mosul, for Paul-Emile Botta, who in 1842 began digging in the Kuyunjik mound, part of ancient Nineveh. The finds here were unpromising, and Botta was easily seduced away in 1843 when sculptures were discovered at nearby Khorsabad, which he took to be more of Nineveh. In fact it was Dur Sharrukin, the creation of Sargon II, who in 707 B.C.E. transferred the capital here from Nimrud. Here Botta soon discovered Sargon's palace, its walls resplendent with carved reliefs and gateways guarded by monumental human-headed winged bulls and lions. This success led the French to provide greatly increased funds for further excavations and the services of Eugene Napoleon

Engraving from the nineteenth century of the palace built by Sargon II at Dur Sharrukin, rediscovered by the French scholar Paul-Emile Botta in the 1840s. (Ridpath, John Clark, *Ridpath's History of the World*, 1901)

Flandin, a distinguished painter, to record the finds. Despite tremendous difficulties, some maliciously created by the local Pasha, Botta managed to ship a number of the sculptures and other finds to France, where in 1847 they were displayed in the newly founded Musee des Antiquites Orientales in the Louvre. And in 1849 Botta published an impressive account of the excavations, including four volumes of Flandin's superb illustrations.

The novelty and splendor of the sculptures took Europe by storm. One of those most fascinated was Austen Henry Layard, already an experienced Oriental explorer familiar with the region. Privately sponsored by Sir Stratford Canning, British ambassador in Istanbul, in 1845 Layard began excavating Nimrud, another mound near Mosul, and soon discovered inscriptions and sculptures from two palaces. Like Botta, Layard believed that he was investigating ancient Nineveh but had in fact struck an earlier Assyrian capital. This was Kalhu, center of the empire from 878 B.C.E. until Sargon's move to Dur Sharrukin.

Like Botta, Layard experienced hostility from some local officials and problems owing to the fragility and vastness of the remains, but in addition he was severely handicapped by lack of funds. In 1846 the trustees of the British Museum were induced to offer official sponsorship, but their £2,000 was a pittance compared with the generous French excavation funding. As a result, the inevitable destruction wrought by excavators, who were pioneers in a discipline where there was no accumulated knowledge and experience to draw upon, was compounded in Layard's case by the need to acquire the maximum yield of exhibitive objects using minimal resources. Later archaeologists have looked severely on the results, and one can only regret the vast quantity of information lost and of antiquities destroyed as a consequence of these constraints and of the fierce competition among excavators sponsored by rival national governments.

A confrontation developed almost at once between Layard and Botta's successor. Layard believed the French had abandoned their claim to Kuyunjik when Botta transferred to Khorsabad, and in 1846 he conducted a trial investigation there himself. The French representative maintained his nation's primary right to the mound and also started work on it, leading to an unedifying race and mutual recriminations.

Layard's excavations at Nimrud, on a grander scale than before, yielded magnificent

A portrait of Austen Layard, whose investigations at Kalhu and Nineveh inspired popular interest in ancient Assyria. (Library of Congress)

results. Among the ruins of twenty-eight halls and rooms, Layard recovered antiquities ranging from thirteen pairs of enormous winged bulls and lions to a series of exquisite carvings in ivory. One of the most impressive finds was the Black Obelisk, a four-sided stone carved with a long inscription and twenty reliefs showing vassals bringing tribute. The drama of the exponential growth of knowledge in these years is epitomized by this monument. Its author was unknown and unknowable in 1846, but by 1850 Henry Creswicke Rawlinson was able to identify him as Shalmaneser III (858–824 B.C.E.) and give a rough version of the inscription; by 1851 Edward Hincks could identify one of the vassals as the biblical king Jehu of the line of Omri, and by 1853 he had accurately deciphered the entire inscription.

In 1847, Layard also dug briefly in the ruins at Qal'at Sharqat, the site of Assur, the original capital of Assyria. Here he was puzzled and disappointed to find virtually nothing: The architecture was of mud brick, a material that, to the inexperienced eye, blends imperceptibly with the surrounding soil, and Layard and his team dug straight through it. Layard returned to Mosul and took a final hack at Kuyunjik: With remarkable good fortune, his diggers discovered the palace of Sennacherib.

Back in Britain Layard's application for further funding was met with characteristic reluctance and parsimony by the British Museum trustees; but his account of the excavations, *Nineveh and Its Remains,* sold like hotcakes, 8,000

A winged lion with a human head, one of the monumental stone guardians of the palace of Ashurnasirpal II brought to light in Layard's excavations at Kalhu (Nimrud). (Library of Congress)

copies being purchased within a year. The obvious popular interest may have moved the trustees, who in 1849 came up with £3,000 to fund a further two seasons. They also sent out artists to record the discoveries, a vital necessity at that time when conservation was still in its embryonic stage and many items "fell to pieces as soon as exposed" (Layard quoted in Lloyd 1980: 116). At

Kuyunjik Layard revealed many reliefs from the walls of Sennacherib's palace, some depicting the siege of the biblical town of Lachish. Layard also found a huge library of cuneiform tablets, providing decades of work for the newly emerging band of Assyrian scholars. Layard reopened his excavations at Nimrud and conducted preemptive strikes on a number of other mounds to secure the right to explore them for Britain. By the end of 1851, however, Layard had had enough of the unequal struggle to operate with limited funds.

A period of heightened activity followed his departure. Captain Felix Jones of the Indian Navy surveyed the region between the Tigris and the Great Zab, producing a map of Assyria that is still in use. Rawlinson, by now a considerable Assyriologist, excavated the ziggurat at Borsippa, finding inscriptions of Nebuchadrezzar in its foundations. William Kennett Loftus investigated Warka (Uruk) and Senkereh (Larsa) while other British and French archaeologists made soundings at Eridu, Ur, and Kish. The lack of spectacular architecture and impressive sculptures in these sites disappointed their investigators, however, so Babylonia was abandoned in favor of the magnificent sites of Assyria. Rawlinson and the new French consul at Mosul, Victor Place, agreed to divide the disputed Kuyunjik mound into French and British areas. The British section was entrusted to Hormuzd Rassam, a Chaldaean Christian who had been Layard's assistant. Among his discoveries—in an area assigned to the French, where he initially investigated secretly at night—was the palace of Ashurbanipal, complete with magnificent reliefs of the king hunting lions.

Over the next two years Place excavated in Kuyunjik, Assur, and Sargon II's palace at Khorsabad. In 1855 disaster struck when the fleet of rafts carrying around 300 cases of antiquities and records from the French excavations was attacked and capsized by bandits. Only twenty-six cases survived to reach Paris, a terrible loss. The outbreak of the Crimean War made this the last year of European involvement in Mesopotamia for several decades.

Chasing the Bible.   Although official attentions were now turned elsewhere, strong popular interest in Mesopotamian antiquities continued, fueling a flourishing trade in material looted by local merchants from the ancient cities of Assyria. Scholarly plundering had already caused considerable destruction. Now the situation reached its nadir, with the retrieval of saleable pieces being the only aim, very much at the expense of the ancient remains.

Scholarly activity had not ceased, however, although it was no longer concentrated in the field. By the end of the 1850s the successful decipherment of Akkadian cuneiform meant that inscriptions and texts recovered from Nineveh and elsewhere could now yield a vast amount of information on the ancient Mesopotamian world. One of the most surprising discoveries was the great time depth of the civilization. Biblical and Classical sources had painted a picture of the wealth and grandeur of Assyria in the first millennium B.C.E., and this had been confirmed by the excavations at Nineveh and adjacent cities. The library uncovered in Ashurbanipal's palace included texts written in the second millennium B.C.E., shedding light on the period of the Old Babylonian Empire and the early history of the Assyrians, the time of the biblical patriarch

Abraham, native of the Mesopotamian city of Ur. But there were also copies of even more ancient texts that revealed the existence in the third millennium B.C.E. of the southern Mesopotamian civilization of Sumer and Akkad.

The later nineteenth century was a time of great intellectual upheaval. The developing science of geology was revealing the immense age and gradual formation of the earth, while Charles Darwin was showing how life had evolved in all its diversity. This new knowledge undermined the certainties of the Bible, according to which the world was created in immutable form at a date calculated by biblical scholars as 4004 B.C.E. In this epoch of challenge to established traditional views, many found it reassuring that archaeological research in the Near East was uncovering cities and records of individuals familiar from the Bible, thus confirming and buttressing its authenticity.

It was therefore electrifying news when George Smith, who had spent many years quietly studying cuneiform texts, announced in December 1872 that he had found part of a tablet recounting the story of the Flood. A serious-minded man, he amazed his colleagues at the moment of discovery by leaping to his feet, rushing round the room, and beginning to tear off his clothes. In less than two months he found himself en route to Mosul to look for the missing pieces of the tablet, lavishly sponsored by the *Daily Telegraph* of London—a measure of the immense popular excitement that his discovery had generated. Once Smith had accomplished the tedious and time-consuming task of extracting a permit from the Ottoman authorities, he achieved his objective in just five days of digging, finding among the debris left by previous excavators a piece of tablet that accounted for the major part of the missing section.

Smith later returned to excavate further at Nineveh, but in 1876 he contracted a fatal illness. As his replacement, the British Museum appointed Hormuzd Rassam, veteran of the 1850s excavations.

Telloh, Nippur, and Other Sites.   Arriving in 1878, Rassam went to work with a will. Over a period of four years he opened excavations not only at Nineveh but at sites ranging from eastern Anatolia to southern Iraq, leaving the day-to-day excavation to his assistants and rarely visiting the sites. His discoveries included panels of embossed bronze sheeting that had originally covered the great gates erected by Shalmaneser III at Balawat near Nimrud, and around 50,000 cuneiform cylinders and tablets in the Shamash temple at Sippar near Babylon. But times had changed since the cavalier days of the 1850s. Considerable advances had been made in excavation techniques and recording methods. It was no longer enough to plunder sites for antiquities; buildings and other contexts had to be carefully investigated and recorded, and objects had to be recovered with care, without allowing them to "crumble to dust." Rassam was seriously criticized by other scholars in the field, and his departure largely saw the end of crude excavation methods in Mesopotamia—until the wanton destruction by bandits with bulldozers following the 2003 invasion of Iraq, which threatens utterly to obliterate a huge number of sites.

As a native of the region, Rassam was very aware of the threat to the ancient cities from treasure hunters and brick robbers. When he left for Britain, there-

The bronze decorations of the gates erected by Shalmaneser III at Balawat were excavated in the 1870s by Hormuz Rassam. This detail shows the people of Tyre bringing tribute to the Assyrians. (Zev Radovan/Land of the Bible Picture Archive)

fore, he hired guardians to prevent future plundering in the important sites, including Kuyunjik and Sippar. Over the following decade, however, antiquities, and particularly tablets, that seemed likely to have come from these sites appeared in some numbers on the international market. The British Museum sent out Wallis Budge to investigate.

Budge arrived in Baghdad in 1888, armed with a permit to excavate Kuyunjik as a cover for his detective work. Within days, he purchased many tablets from local dealers, most of whom he found to be the very people appointed to guard the ancient sites, and skillfully foiled a plan to prevent him from exporting them. Later in the year he reopened excavations at Kuyunjik, recovering some 200 tablets from the spoil of previous excavations. His luck turned the following year, however, when he excavated at ed-Der, part of ancient Sippar. The procedures involved in obtaining an excavation permit were long-winded and public: By the time Budge could start work, ed-Der had been thoroughly "examined" by the Vali of Baghdad, with the result that 10,000 tablets had found their way into the hands of dealers.

A similar fate befell the Frenchman Ernest de Sarzec, who excavated Telloh (ancient Girsu) in 1877–1881 and 1888–1900. This was the first serious investigation of a site belonging to Mesopotamia's original Sumerian civilization, and

The terra-cotta head of a deity recovered from the important Sumerian city of Girsu (Telloh). Investigations here by the Frenchman Ernest de Sarzec in the 1880s gave the western world its first glimpse of the third-millennium Sumerian civilization. (Zev Radovan/Land of the Bible Picture Archive)

the objects found here created great excitement in Europe, where they were displayed in the 1880s Paris exhibition. The powerful and austere art style typified by the diorite statues strongly impressed European art critics, and a sculptured slab, dubbed the "Stele of the Vultures," sparked great interest, because it showed for the first time in history an organized army going to war.

Telloh also yielded numerous tablets, some relating to border disputes with neighboring Umma, the fascinating first contemporary account of warfare—but most of them were not recovered by de Sarzec. During de Sarzec's frequent absences, local people, often sponsored by Baghdad dealers, abstracted around 40,000 tablets from one of the mounds. These provided the first substantial body of works in the Sumerian language, whose very existence had been doubted in earlier decades.

The first U.S. expedition to work in Mesopotamia experienced an even more dramatic mixture of success and failure. Sponsored by Pennsylvania University, a team headed by John Peters arrived in 1887 to excavate Nippur, the holy city of ancient Sumer. Hopelessly out of their depth in the complexities of dealing with the local villagers and authorities, their first season ended in an all-out attack in which their camp was set on fire, half their horses perished, and they lost $1,000 in gold—although they saved their antiquities. Work resumed in 1890, under more auspicious circumstances, and continued intermittently until 1900. Among the 30,000 tablets recovered from Nippur were around 2,100 whose subject matter was literature, in contrast to the ubiquitous economic texts: These opened a window onto the fascinating world of the Sumerians and to this day form the bulk of known Sumerian literature.

Advances in Archaeological Techniques in the Earlier Twentieth Century

Koldewey and Babylon. An important new scholar entered the field of Mesopotamian excavation in 1899. Robert Koldewey, a German archaeologist, architect, and art historian with considerable prior excavation experience, was commissioned by the newly formed Deutsche Orientgesellschaft (German Oriental Society) to investigate and select sites in Mesopotamia for excavation. Because of "the singular beauty and the art historical value" of glazed tiles that Koldewey found when visiting Babylon, he selected the city for investigations that were to last for the rest of his field career (Koldewey quoted in Leick 2001: 246).

His work was to revolutionize Mesopotamian archaeology. Unlike his predecessors, Koldewey, who had considerable experience uncovering baked-brick buildings, had also developed techniques for recognizing and excavating mudbrick architecture. The workmen trained by Koldewey were to become the first in a long line of professional diggers, whose skills have been appreciated on Near Eastern excavations ever since. Furthermore, Koldewey was one of a new breed of archaeologists, particularly Germans, for whom tracing and recording architecture rather than collecting antiquities was the main priority. In addition to exposing the plans of ancient settlements, Koldewey and his colleagues studied stratigraphy to establish the sequence of construction. By these means it now became possible to reveal the historical setting of the material that previously had been removed haphazardly from ancient cities.

Koldewey began his excavations in the area where he had previously found glazed tiles. He was rewarded with the discovery of one of Babylon's greatest glories, the Ishtar Gate and Processional Way erected by Nebuchadrezzar in the sixth century B.C.E. Their towers and walls were decorated with shining blue glazed bricks with yellow and white figures in relief—bulls and dragons on the gate and lions along the processional way. Only the lowest exposed portions of the walls and gate survived; in 1927 these were taken to Berlin and incorporated into a reconstruction of the Ishtar Gate in the Pergamon Museum.

Between 1899 and 1914, Koldewey surveyed the whole city of Babylon, establishing its plan, and excavated most of its principal buildings, including palaces, the massive walls surrounding the whole city, and the sacred precinct of the city's patron deity, Marduk. Here he located the ziggurat that was probably the Tower of Babel; unfortunately, after the departure of the German team the local people totally destroyed it, using its bricks for construction. Koldewey also believed that he had located the famous Hanging Gardens, although this is now disputed (see chapter 11). Unusually for his time, he also excavated a substantial residential quarter of the city, rather than concentrating exclusively on monumental structures.

Koldewey was something of an eccentric, but totally dedicated and a meticulous scholar. His work at Babylon was interrupted by World War I, but he remained there as long as was possible, leaving in 1917. By 1924, when he died, he had completed and seen the publication of his excavation reports on the city.

Andrae and Assur. Among the archaeologists working with Koldewey was Walter Andrae, who in 1903 was entrusted with the excavation of Assur, capital of the Assyrian state until the ninth century B.C.E. Andrae's highly trained team brought to Assur the skills in tracing mudbrick buildings that they had learned at Babylon; over a period of twelve years they surveyed the plan of the city and uncovered many temples and houses, water channels, a palace, and the city walls. Andrae went one step further, expanding the study of

The magnificent Ishtar Gate at Babylon erected by Nebuchadrezzar was rediscovered in the meticulous excavations of the German scholar Robert Koldewey. (Corel Corp.)

A basalt altar dating from ca. 1240 B.C.E. from the temple of Ishtar in Assur, painstakingly excavated by the German archaeologist Walter Andrae. (Zev Radovan/Land of the Bible Picture Archive)

stratigraphy by excavating one structure, the temple of Ishtar, from its latest form in the Neo-Assyrian period right back to its earliest beginnings as a small shrine in Sumerian times. Each rebuilding of the temple was meticulously excavated in full, described, planned, and photographed before being removed to reveal its predecessor. Andrae produced detailed and thorough reports, which he enlivened with vivid reconstruction drawings and watercolor paintings of ancient buildings and vistas.

Koldewey and Andrae were the major innovators of the prewar period, but there were many other excavations, most still unaffected by the advances pioneered by the Germans. A U.S. team was working at Bismayah (ancient Adab, a Sumerian town), the British were still investigating Kuyunjik, and the French had initiated work at the important Sumerian city of Kish. At the same time the French had secured a monopoly on archaeological work in Persia, where they

Ruins of the great Sumerian city of Ur. Excavations here by Leonard Woolley revealed the early development of urban life in ancient Sumer, cradle of civilization. (Nik Wheeler/Corbis)

excavated the great city of Susa, capital of Elam, the neighbor and great rival of Babylonia. Starting in 1884, over a period of many years they removed vast quantities of soil and recovered a huge amount of interesting material, including many important Mesopotamian inscriptions and works of art looted during Elam's wars—but because of their crude excavation techniques, they recovered very little information about the context of their pre-Persian finds. It was not until Roman Ghirshman took over the excavations in 1946 that mudbrick architecture began to be recognized and excavation techniques here improved.

Woolley and Ur.   After World War I, Iraq came under British mandate, and Gertrude Bell was charged with creating an Iraqi antiquities service and museum. She took steps to control and monitor the conduct of archaeological work in Mesopotamia. Permits were now issued for strictly specified investigations, and teams were required to meet current standards in excavation and to include relevant specialists, such as an epigrapher. A proportion of the remains excavated in Mesopotamian sites was now to become part of the new national collections in the Iraq Museum, although foreign expeditions were still allowed to export many of their finds. Neighboring countries made similar provisions.

The outline history of Mesopotamian civilization as far back as the Third Dynasty of Ur (Ur III–ca. 2100 B.C.E.) was by now well known, and attention could be focused on acquiring a more detailed knowledge of individual parts of it. A shadowy period preceded the Ur III dynasty, known from texts with a strong legendary component, such as the *Epic of Gilgamesh;* archaeologists sought to shed light on this period and on the historicity of individuals like Sargon of Akkad. New excavations began to reveal the antecedents of the world's first urban society.

From 1922 to 1934, Leonard Woolley led joint British and U.S. excavations at Ur "of the Chaldees," familiar from the Bible as the reputed home of Abraham. Archaeology by the 1920s was becoming a well-established discipline with recognized standards and competent professionals. Woolley was an experienced excavator who was not only careful, observant, and thorough but also inspired in his interpretation of buildings and imaginative in dealing with fragile or poorly preserved objects. Time and again he recovered the form of long-perished artifacts of wood and other organic materials by judicious use of plaster of Paris and wax. He followed stratigraphic principles, using differences in the pottery found in the different layers to allocate them to periods, an idea that was only just coming into vogue.

Having a strong theological background, Woolley was particularly fascinated by the biblical connections of Near Eastern sites. In the deep soundings that he opened at Ur he found a 3-meter-thick layer of clay devoid of archaeological material and apparently deposited by water. Woolley commented that "this could only have been the result of a flood. . . . the Flood of Sumerian history and legend, the Flood on which is based the story of Noah" (Woolley 1950: 22–23). Woolley investigated a number of areas in Ur, uncovering houses of all periods from the Ubaid period (before the "Flood" deposits) to fourth century B.C.E., as well as harbors and city walls. But his work was concentrated in the city's sacred heart, the temenos of the city's god, Nanna. Dominating the precinct was the great ziggurat built by Ur-Nammu of the Ur III dynasty and enlarged by the Neo-Babylonian king Nabonidus.

Early in the excavations the workmen came upon graves containing gold objects. Woolley had the good sense and self-discipline to postpone investigation of this area for four years until he and his workmen had developed the skills necessary to deal competently with the material. They finally uncovered a cemetery of some 2,000 graves, including sixteen richly furnished "Royal Graves." The honored dead were laid to rest in large pits with their magnificent objects, such as harps and gaming boards ornamented with gold, silver, mother-of-pearl, and lapis lazuli and accompanied by guards, grooms, female attendants, and musicians—as many as seventy-four in the "Great Death Pit"—devoted servants who had, it seems, willingly accompanied their masters and mistresses into the other world.

Leonard Woolley brushing earth away from 4000-year-old records in the temple of the Moon God Nanna in Ur. (Bettmann/Corbis)

Searching for the Antecedents of Mesopotamian Civilization. In 1923–1924 Woolley also excavated at al 'Ubaid, a small site 6 kilometers west of Ur, where he found "a primitive settlement . . . of huts constructed of mud and wattle or slight timber ramming filled in with reed mats" (Woolley 1950: 15). The villagers used distinctive painted pottery of a type that Woolley also found in the early deposits at Ur.

Since Andrae's pioneering excavations at Assur, it had become common practice to investigate the stratigraphy of long-occupied settlements by making deep soundings in major buildings, cutting down to the natural soil through the material accumulated over hundreds and sometimes thousands of years to reveal the settlement's history. Pottery and other distinctive material enabled the deposits to be assigned to successive periods. Deep soundings at Ur, Uruk, and Kish produced the same three distinctive styles of prehistoric pottery, of which that found at al 'Ubaid was the earliest. Following this in time was unpainted pottery characteristic of the main occupation at Warka (ancient Uruk). Here a team from the Deutsche Orientgesellschaft was uncovering temples decorated with spectacular cone mosaics, written tablets and seals, and beautiful sculptures. Clearly this period had seen a major transformation in society. A small site near Kish proved to have been occupied mainly when the most recent of the three pottery styles, painted with geometric designs, was in vogue. At a conference in Leiden in 1931, international scholars agreed to name the periods characterized by these pottery styles after these sites: Ubaid, Uruk, and Jemdet Nasr, leading into the Early Dynastic period that preceded the historically known era. Mesopotamia's past was beginning to acquire a framework on which to hang the data gradually accumulating from the many excavations now taking place—nineteen in 1930, for example, run by teams not only from Europe and the United States, but from the Soviet Union and Japan as well.

These excavations showed that as yet archaeologists had only found the tip of the iceberg of prehistory. As new data accumulated it became possible to define earlier periods in northern Mesopotamia. Max Oppenheimer had been digging at Halaf from 1899 to 1929, revealing beautifully decorated and finely made pottery (see photo p. 57). In 1931 Max Mallowan dug a sounding 21 meters deep in the Kuyunjik mound of Nineveh where the stratigraphy revealed that this Halaf pottery belonged to the period immediately preceding the Ubaid period.

At the beginning of the century, Ernst Herzfeld had uncovered a cemetery at Samarra on the middle Tigris whose graves contained a fine style of painted pottery. When Mallowan excavated a settlement at Chagar Bazar in Syria he discovered that this Samarra ware belonged to the period before Halaf. Finally in 1943, Seton Lloyd and Fuad Safar from the Iraqi Antiquities Department found the final piece of the chronological jigsaw when they dug at Hassuna southwest of Nineveh. In the upper deposits of the settlement, locally made Hassuna ware was used alongside imported Samarra ware; below this were the houses of people who used only Hassuna pottery.

Other Sites. The 1930s saw further major innovations, many the work of the Oriental Institute of Chicago's lavishly sponsored team, led by Henry (Hans) Frankfort. Their main objective was to excavate Tell Asmar, the ancient Sumerian city of Eshnunna. Here they uncovered a series of superimposed temples, within which a cache of early limestone sculptures was found, providing a glimpse of the artistic achievements of the Early Dynastic Sumerians. Many inscribed tablets were recovered in the excavations of the city. Rather than risk transporting them in their fragile condition, the Eshnunna team baked them at the site, making them sturdier. For the first time, too, it was thought important to record both the findspot of each individual tablet and the level from which it derived. This information enabled Thorkild Jacobsen, who was studying the tablets as they emerged, to establish the complete sequence of Eshnunna's rulers.

The Chicago team also investigated other nearby sites. Pinhas Delougaz excavated in the city of Khafajeh where preliminary investigations had revealed very slight traces of a mudbrick building. With infinite care, using the techniques pioneered by the Germans of delineating such architecture brick by brick, pecking away the soil and removing it with compressed air, the team of highly skilled workmen gradually uncovered an oval structure only one, two, or at most three courses of bricks high that had been an oval temple of the Early Dynastic period—a remarkable feat.

In 1933 Lloyd and Jacobsen followed literary clues and the report of inscribed blocks to discover the remains of an aqueduct at Jerwan constructed more than 2,500 years ago by the Assyrian king Sennacherib to bring "clean water to Nineveh from the distant mountains" at Bavian (Sennacherib, quoted in Lloyd 2000: 2736). The sophisticated skills of the ancient Mesopotamians were gradually being revealed.

As the work of the Chicago team came to a close in 1936, Jacobsen and his wife embarked on one last innovative project, a survey of the Diyala River basin, where Eshnunna lies. Unlike earlier more haphazard surveys, the Jacobsens worked systematically through the area, locating and examining all the tells (mounds) that marked ancient sites and dating them by the pottery exposed on their surface.

The Chicago Institute was not the only important foreign expedition working in the interwar years. The Germans, for example, had been excavating at Uruk since 1912 and continued to do so into the 1990s. This magnificent site was to reveal more about the crucial period of transition to city dwelling and civilization than any other; it is considered the world's first city and the home of the written word. Here also, in the following Early Dynastic period, dwelt king Gilgamesh, hero of the world's first epic poetry.

In 1932 the director of the Iraqi Antiquities Department considerably tightened the rules governing the export of antiquities from Iraq, causing most foreign expeditions to move to neighboring Syria, where the regime was more relaxed. One of the most exciting results was that the French, under Andre Parrot, began excavating Tell Hariri, soon identified as ancient Mari, capital of a small independent kingdom in the third and earlier second millennia B.C.E. Among the remains of the palace, whose plan was admirably well preserved, Parrot recovered an enormous archive of letters and official documents, shedding enormous light on the world of the time.

More Recent Work in Mesopotamia

After World War II, there was a great revival of activity in Mesopotamia. The invention of radiocarbon dating by Willard Libby in 1949 now made it possible to date excavated organic remains (and therefore the contexts in which they occurred) without reference to historical material. This was a revolution. It changed both the picture of the past and the objectives of archaeologists, who could now look beyond chronology (*when* things occurred) to ask other questions about the past, such as *how?* and *why?* The result was a broadening of archaeological fieldwork, which began to involve the techniques and methods of other disciplines and to evolve related archaeological approaches, such as paleoethnobotany, archaeozoology, and ethnoarchaeology. The Near East was the main focus for investigating the beginning of farming, a subject that required full use of these new techniques and approaches.

Discovering Early Farmers. One of the most important projects was led by Robert Braidwood, who argued that the earliest traces of agriculture would be found in what he referred to as the "hilly flanks of the Fertile Crescent," where the plants and animals exploited by the first farmers occurred in the wild. Convinced of the value of combining the skills of many specialists, in 1948 Braidwood brought a multidisciplinary team to investigate Jarmo in northern Iraq, selected as a site likely to span the period of the transition to farming: an example of the problem-orientated research that was now coming into vogue. Rather than the spectacular artifacts once sought, Braidwood and his team looked for material that could answer their questions about how and why people began farming. Plant remains and animal bones shed light on the beginnings of domestication. The team also gathered evidence from which to reconstruct changes through time in the climate and environment of the region. Radiocarbon dates revealed that Jarmo had been occupied from around 7500 B.C.E., when the inhabitants were hunter-gatherers; in the upper levels, dated around 6500 B.C.E., the inhabitants not only farmed but also made pottery. The settlement and its material at this time bore many similarities to sites like Hassuna farther west; this linked Jarmo into the established sequence running back from historic times into the days of well-established village farming.

Further evidence of the transition to agriculture was uncovered by another U.S. team under Frank Hole, who between 1961 and 1963 excavated Ali Kosh in southwest Iran. They concentrated particularly on the recovery of carbonized seeds, using flotation, a technique for recovering plant material pioneered by Hole, revealing the growing importance through time of wheat and barley cultivation over the gathering of wild plants. Animal bones documented the increasing importance of herded animals. New ways of studying the artifacts from the site, including quantitative analysis, yielded more information about the inhabitants' way of life. The team also studied the ecology of the region and its influence on the way of life of the settlement's inhabitants, chronicling the interrelationship between ecology, population, subsistence, and settlement patterns.

In the 1960s, nomadic pastoralists still occupied the region for part of the year. Hole came to appreciate the value of studying contemporary traditional societies for the light they could shed on societies of the past (ethnoarchaeology). In 1974 he returned to the area to travel with these pastoralists, sharing and observing their way of life, thus gaining many insights that enabled him better to understand and interpret the material remains of pastoral communities from antiquity, and indeed to recognize traces of their very insubstantial settlements.

Interdisciplinary studies have continued to be valued in more recent excavations, new techniques such as microwear analysis, chemical analysis of human bones, and the study of residues on tools and pottery being constantly added to increase the recovery of information about many aspects of life, including subsistence practices and the development of agriculture. The picture built up in Mesopotamia was a part of wider investigations in the Near East, where the steps taken toward the adoption and spread of agriculture were charted.

Landscape Studies.   Braidwood and Hole focused attention on the ecology of the area surrounding their sites; another expedition, led by Robert MacCormack Adams, undertook a full-scale survey of the Diyala region, studying not only the ecology but also settlement patterns, ethnography, and history. This was the region in which Eshnunna, scene of the intensive Chicago investigations of the 1930s, was located; it had been an important focus of settlement throughout Mesopotamia's past. Jacobsen had systematically surveyed the region to locate sites in 1937; Adams's survey went further, studying all aspects of the environment and human geography. From this he was able to set the ancient sites in their context, deducing their relationship both to each other and to the environment and charting changes through time in the patterns of settlement distribution, density, and nature, and in economic exploitation. Jacobsen returned to the region with an eminent team in 1956 to investigate the salination of the soil. This study had important implications for the study of Babylonia, revealing the key role of overirrigation in the process of salination and consequent environmental degradation, responsible for the major northward shift in the political and economic focus in the mid–second millennium B.C.E.

Survey now became a regular part of archaeological investigations, its focus depending on the objectives of the investigator. Much has thus been learned about agricultural and other economic activities, settlement patterns, changes in the course of rivers, the construction of network of canals, communication routes, trade, and many other aspects of life.

Major Excavations and Discoveries.   Work in Mesopotamia in the postwar years was not confined to studying the origins of agriculture. New excavations were undertaken in important historical cities, and conservation also became a priority. For example, at Babylon millennia of plundering for bricks were halted by the Iraqi Antiquities Department, which has conducted major works of conservation and restoration here, alongside continued excavations.

In 1948 Samuel Noah Kramer and Thorkild Jacobsen began uncovering the scribal quarter of the city of Nippur, recovering many tablets. These they baked to preserve them but also took latex casts as an added precaution to ensure the survival of the information they contained. Almost all known works of Sumerian literature were represented among these tablets, which numbered tens of thousands.

Work was resumed at Uruk and Mari, and in 1949 Mallowan began new work at Nimrud where he laid bare palaces and temples, including "Fort Shalmaneser," the royal palace and arsenal in the southeast corner of the city. Here was stored much of the tribute and war booty accumulated by Assyrian kings, including exquisite pieces of carved ivory, particularly plaques that had once decorated furniture. Since 1963, Nimrud has been investigated by Polish, Italian, British, and Iraqi teams. In 1990 the latter discovered the richly furnished burials of four Assyrian royal ladies.

The Kassites, who had ruled Babylonia for much of the later second millennium B.C.E., were poorly known until 1942–1945 when Seton Lloyd and Fuad

Safar excavated Aqar Quf, exposing the remains of a short-lived Kassite palace and town, Dur-Kurigalzu, which yielded numerous texts. They also excavated a much earlier town in southern Iraq—Eridu, the original settlement created by the gods, according to legend. Here they uncovered a shrine to the benevolent god Enki, god of wisdom, which was in worship for some 2,000 years, beginning in the Ubaid period around 5000 B.C.E.

In addition to the problem-orientated excavations that were the norm by the 1960s, Mesopotamia saw a number of major rescue (salvage) excavations from the 1960s to 1980s at sites threatened with imminent destruction by major construction projects, particularly hydroelectric dams on the Tigris and Euphrates. These rescue projects involved the fruitful collaboration of the Iraqi government and Antiquities Department with international teams from many countries, and uncovered many interesting and important sites, including a well-preserved early village house at Tell Madhhur on the Diyala.

Political developments have taken their toll in recent years. Although work continued throughout the Iran-Iraq war of the 1980s, the Gulf War and subsequent sanctions seriously curtailed international work in Iraq, although the Iraqis themselves continued some archaeological activity, particularly rescue excavations on sites in the south. As a consequence, work has focused in adjacent regions, investigating sites that were part of ancient Mesopotamia, such as Tell Brak in Syria, or were involved with the Mesopotamian world, including Bahrain (ancient Dilmun), where a major project was undertaken by Jane Moon, Robert Killick, and Harriet Crawford in the 1990s. Plans in 2001 for a dam to be built near Assur focused Iraqi and international attention on salvage work in the area to be flooded; this and everything else has been brought to a halt by the coalition invasion that toppled Saddam in 2003 and the massive security problems that have followed; tragically the breakdown of law and order has greatly facilitated the plundering of archaeological sites by looters feeding the huge international trade in illegally acquired antiquities and has allowed them with impunity vastly to increase the scale of their operations.

STUDYING ANCIENT MESOPOTAMIA'S PAST

The Languages and Scripts

In the third millennium B.C.E., the people of southern Babylonia spoke Sumerian, while farther north Akkadian was the main language; speakers of both languages, however, were to be found throughout Babylonia. By around 1800 B.C.E., Sumerian had died out as a spoken language but was still used in many inscriptions and literary contexts. Sumerian was unrelated to any other known language.

Akkadian, in contrast, was one of the widespread group of Semitic languages. Old Akkadian was spoken in southern Mesopotamia until around 2000 B.C.E. After this date, two dialects developed, Assyrian in the north and Babylonian in the south. Akkadian was to become the lingua franca of the Near East in the second and earlier first millennia B.C.E.

Semitic languages were also spoken by many of Mesopotamia's western neighbors. People referred to collectively as Amorites ("westerners") are mentioned in texts from the late third millennium. From the ninth century B.C.E., Aramaic, a North Semitic language, is attested; this was later to replace Akkadian as the lingua franca.

Elsewhere, various other languages were spoken: Hattic in Anatolia, Hurrian by the people of Mitanni, Urartian in Urartu, and Elamite by Mesopotamia's traditional adversaries, the Elamites. Indo-European languages made their appearance in the Near East in the second millennium, when they included the language of the Hittite Empire.

Writing began in Sumer, logograms appearing in the fourth millennium B.C.E. During the early third millennium, a full syllabic script developed, using logograms, phonetic signs, and determinatives to record the Sumerian language. Some adjustments were made to record the very different Akkadian language, but the force of tradition meant that, throughout the script's history of use, there were some awkward accommodations in which spelling did not match pronunciation.

The Mesopotamian script was written with a reed stylus on clay tablets. The straight edge of the stylus, more deeply impressed and therefore wider at the end, created wedge-shaped strokes that give the script its name, cuneiform (from the Latin *cuneus*). The script was written in horizontal rows read from left to right and top to bottom.

This script became widespread in the Near East and was modified to record texts in a variety of languages, including Elamite, Hittite, and Levantine languages. Around the mid–second millennium, a rival script emerged in the Levant. Conventionally known as the first alphabet, it in fact recorded consonants as individual signs, but did not mark vowels. The alphabet was in widespread use in the Levant by the eleventh century B.C.E., but did not replace cuneiform until after the fall of Mesopotamia to the Persians.

Archaeological and Historical Methods of Age Determination

Dating is an essential precondition to studying the past, as it is impossible to analyze and understand past developments until the order in which they occurred is known. Archaeological and historical dating go hand in hand in establishing chronology; each has advantages and drawbacks. Archaeological dating depends to a large extent on relative dating by stratigraphy and typology; precise dates, within certain limits, are offered by a number of scientific dating techniques, which can, however, be used only on certain materials.

Historical sources may provide precise dates within a local chronology or tied to particular external phenomena, such as astronomical events, but these can be hard to pin down. The subjective and biased nature of many historical documents also makes the use of historical dates far from straightforward.

Archaeological Dating. Within an excavated site, stratigraphy indicates the sequence of deposition of the cultural remains that represent past occupation and activities, creating a relative chronology. Fixed points within the sequence come from typology: dating the deposits on the basis of the material found in them. Changing requirements and technology and the dictates of fashion cause some types of artifact to change frequently in form and appearance: Pottery is an excellent example. Initially fixed in relative time by stratigraphy or dated by historical or scientific means, characteristic artifacts can be used thereafter to provide a relative date for the deposits in which they are found. Pottery styles provide much of the dating for early Mesopotamian sites.

An armory of scientific dating techniques is now also available. Dendrochronology offered precise dates in rare special circumstances by the 1920s; in 1949 radiocarbon dating was the first of many scientific dating techniques to be developed. Often these do not date archaeological material but only the context in which it is found, and therefore depend on the quality of the link between them. Nevertheless, scientific dating techniques are an invaluable tool, producing dates that are quite independent of historical or cultural assumptions that can be subject to bias or misinterpretation. Most have some built-in imprecision, owing to statistical limitations on accurate measurement, and so are generally too imprecise for dating historical events, but they can date material to a particular period, they might help in determining the relative merits of alternative dates reached by other means, and they are essential in the prehistoric period.

Radiocarbon dating is used to date organic material such as bone, wood, and carbonized plant remains. It relies on the principle that radiocarbon (C-14), the radioactive isotope of carbon, present in the atmosphere in tiny but constant amounts, is continuously being taken up by all living things. After death, the radiocarbon decays at a known rate; measurement of the residual radiocarbon in ancient organic substances therefore allows the time elapsed since death to be calculated. Fluctuations in the past in the proportion of radiocarbon present in the atmosphere mean that there is a discrepancy between radiocarbon dates (conventionally written "ce" and "bce") and calendar dates, which becomes significant before 1000 B.C.E. and increases further back in time. Dendrochronology has been used to construct a calibration curve by which radiocarbon dates can be corrected to calendar dates, conventionally written "B.C.E." to distinguish them from uncalibrated dates.

Variations in the width of annual growth rings in certain ("sensitive") species of tree allow their timber to be dated by comparing the sequence of rings in the timber to a master sequence built up from living and dead trees growing in the region. Although the method provides precise dates for the age of the wood, this may not date the structure in which it was used, since there is often an interval for seasoning between felling and use, and timbers are often reused, particularly in a region like Babylonia where timber had to be imported and was therefore valuable. Most of the regional master sequence for the Near East has not yet been worked out, although there are a number of floating chunks that reach back into the fourth millennium B.C.E. Recently a floating sequence in Anatolia has been pinned down to 2220–718 B.C.E., offering precise dating for Near Eastern timbers felled during this period and thence for the contexts associated with them. The rarity of surviving timbers in Mesopotamia makes it of limited utility here.

A large range of other scientific techniques are used by archaeologists, many of which are dependent, like radiocarbon and thermoluminescence, on the decay of tiny amounts of radioactive material: These are known as radiometric dating techniques. Thermoluminescence can be used to date pottery and is therefore of great potential use to archaeologists. Decades of research, however, have failed to overcome the limitations on its precision, running at around 10 percent of the age of the sample, so it is currently something of a blunt instrument.

Historical Dating.   Dates for the 2,500 years of Mesopotamia's literate past come from written material of many kinds, including lists of rulers, official inscriptions, annals, and correspondence. From these varied historical materials a chronology covering much of the time span has been pieced together, some parts of it with more certainty than others. Sections of the chronology are generally anchored to real calendar dates only by a few fixed points. The resultant chronology represents only a best fit to the data and is subject to revision whenever new material appears.

Information from inscriptions, chronicles, and other texts enables a chronological framework to be built up, establishing the length of individual rulers' reigns and events within them. These can be given absolute dates by tying them in with the precisely dateable astronomical phenomena that are referred to in the texts. The Babylonians kept daily records of the heavens and produced a summary of these at intervals, linking them in with other occurrences of various kinds: These provide reliable dates for the first millennium B.C.E. The Assyrians used an eponym system, naming each year after an annually chosen official, the *limmu*. A fixed point for the sequence comes with the record of an eclipse in the year of one *limmu*: This took place in 763 B.C.E. Lists of these eponyms were meticulously kept. For the period from 910 to 649 B.C.E., these records are complete and dates can be given with precision, with at most an error of one or two years.

Things become less certain in the second millennium B.C.E., and in the third millennium there is even more uncertainty, including a gap of unknown duration between the Akkadian and the Ur III Empires. The chronology has been built up from a variety of sources, including the king lists, which were compiled around 1800 B.C.E. but which cover the period back to the early third millennium B.C.E. In the early part of the list, corresponding to the Early Dynastic period, the list consecutively chronicles the reigns of kings of different cities: These were often actually concurrent. It also gives early reign lengths of hundreds or even thousands of years, which clearly cannot be taken at face value; some later reigns are of a more credible length but still provide plenty of scope for debate. A sequence of annually named years from the time of Sargon of Akkad to the end of the First Dynasty of Babylon provides a chronology for the subsequent period. Later king lists were also produced, including a Babylonian King List running from the First Dynasty to the reign of Nabopolassar (early second to mid-first millennium) and an Assyrian King List covering a similar time span (see photo p. 269). Although there are debatable elements, after 1300 B.C.E. it is possible to give dates to within twenty years.

The chronology for most of the second and the third millennia is floating and is anchored to an actual date by the "Venus Tablet of Ammi-saduqa." This records the first and last appearance of the planet Venus each year during the early part of the reign of King Ammi-saduqa of the First Dynasty of Babylon. Since the movements of Venus are known, Ammi-saduqa's accession date can theoretically be deduced, but there are three dates that may fit the data. That most frequently chosen is 1646 B.C.E.: This date produces the Middle Chronology, adopted in this volume. Since the relative chronology is reasonably sound, the Middle Chronology provides a conventional means of applying notional dates to events in the second millennium, while accepting that these dates en masse may be out by more than a hundred years. An earlier date of 1702 B.C.E., associated with the High Chronology, is favored by some scholars. This best fits independent evidence from the Babylonian lunar calendar and gives a good match for a pair of lunar eclipses that took place late in the Ur III dynasty. Others argue the merits of the Low Chronology, with Ammi-saduqa's accession dated 1582 B.C.E., and recent work on dendrochronology gives strong support to this. It is clear from the contradictory nature of these pieces of evidence that providing true calendar dates for the chronology of early Mesopotamia is fraught with difficulty.

Sources for Studying Mesopotamia's Past

Chronology provides the essential framework for studying the past. Archaeology and history again combine to provide the material from which what happened in the past becomes known, allowing it to be analyzed and attempts made to understand how and why what occurred did so. For the prehistoric period, before the existence of written records, archaeology is virtually the only source of data, although there are aspects of other disciplines that might also shed some light on what happened. For example, some linguists believe that it is possible to reconstruct the prehistory of languages, revealing links between people and places that may support or call into question claims made by archaeologists about movements of people in the past.

With the emergence of literacy, we gain completely different information about the past—a detailed insight into events, associated with named people, and into their thoughts and beliefs, instead of the anonymous picture of life provided by archaeological data. There has been something of a tendency among those investigating historical times, in Mesopotamia as elsewhere, to rely primarily on written sources in their reconstructions and analyses, relegating archaeological investigations to the study of art and architecture and to gilding the historical picture, instead of recognizing historical and archaeological sources as complementary. Although many aspects of life can only be known from historical sources, this is equally true of archaeology, especially in finding out about the mass of the population generally ignored by the elite who ordered or produced the written sources.

Archaeological Sources.   Archaeology provides an abundance of information about the daily lives of ancient individuals and communities and about the development of humanity in general, drawing on the techniques and approaches of many disciplines. Artifacts, including pottery and jewelry, and artwork, such as the Sumerian statues and Assyrian reliefs, allow one to appreciate the aesthetic sense and artistic abilities of the ancient inhabitants of Mesopotamia. Artistic representations can provide a detailed picture of many aspects of life, from clothing to siege engines, often showing artifacts made of perishable materials that have not survived. Analyses of tools give details of ancient technological achievements; wear patterns and residues on them reveal the uses to which they were put. Relating artifacts to the contexts from which they come can shed light not only on past activities, from food preparation to grave robbing, but also on social organization and ritual practices. Aspects of artifact typology such as shapes and decoration can provide a similar range of information and, linked with physical analyses, can reveal patterns of communication and trade between communities, often over very long distances. Focused observation of modern ethnographic groups operating under similar environmental and other constraints to people in the past can often provide additional insights into tool use, economic activities, architectural function, and so on.

Much can be learned from the layout of houses about domestic organization and activities, while public architecture provides an insight into religion, political organization, and economic practices. Within the historical period and to a lesser extent in late prehistory, excavations in Near Eastern sites have tended to concentrate on the more impressive and spectacular edifices, such as royal palaces and temples, at the expense of studying private housing or industrial areas, although these have attracted far more attention in recent years.

On a wider scale Mesopotamia has seen a number of regional surveys studying the pattern of settlement in the landscape through time and relating it to potential land use, changes in the course of the rivers, and other natural features and alterations. This aspect of archaeological fieldwork has contributed significantly to understanding the historical period. Plant and animal remains, including carbonized seeds and animal bones, also contribute a major source of data on the economic subsistence practices of the past and provide much of the information from which the environment of the past is reconstructed: from the vegetation and climate of the region and the immediate environment to conditions within the home.

The remains of people themselves may reveal minute details of their lives—what they ate, what diseases and injuries they suffered, how their health related to their environment and diet, and even, with DNA testing, to whom they were related. Large cemeteries can yield fascinating information about ancient populations—the patterns of birth and death, the gap between rich and poor, the activities performed by men and women.

Historical Sources.   Ancient Mesopotamia's historical documents have been brought to light by archaeology and, like other artifacts, they can yield far more information if they are related to their context. For example, modern excavations of archives in which the exact position of individual tablets is recorded sheds light not only on the significance of individual tablets but also on the whole organizational system behind the records. Earlier excavations and looting, where retrieval of tablets was the only objective, destroyed this contextual evidence. Tragically, in the wake of the 2003 invasion of Iraq, looting is now taking place on an unprecedented scale.

Some sites have yielded large archives, such as the library of Ashurbanipal at Nineveh and the palace records at Mari. At the other end of the scale, individual tablets and inscriptions have been found in most historical sites. Most are economic records, useful for reconstructing many aspects of Mesopotamian life, such as the economy of the palace or temple and the organization of trading activities.

Other documents cover a wide range of subject matter. Inscriptions record the deeds of priests and kings, particularly military victories. Many texts deal with astronomical observations, mathematics, and other scientific subjects, or record hymns, omens, rituals, and incantations. Legal records include law codes, court records, and contracts. In addition there is a rich mythological literature, including the Creation and the Flood. Other literature describes the legendary deeds of rulers or recounts tales of humbler individuals. Many of these survive among the copybook tablets of schoolboys. These also contain their complaints and boasts of their skills, along with many of their exercises, such as bilingual lists in Sumerian and Akkadian and mathematical problems. Some letters survive, mostly those exchanged between members of the Near Eastern royal families but also including the correspondence of lesser folk, such as the merchants of eighteenth-century B.C.E. Assur.

Although documents are often thought of as "true" records, there are many aspects that need to be carefully assessed by experts before judgment is passed on their value. In documents written at the time of the events they record, there is an ever-present possibility of propagandist bias—the hidden agenda. Other documents were compiled long after the events they record, using extant contemporary records. Clearly some selection had already operated to determine which records were preserved and which not, providing the ancient writer with a set of data already biased by omission, and he then made his own selection and added his own slant. Careless scribes could introduce errors during copying, which would then be perpetuated by later copyists.

Despite the difficulties, historical documents combine with archaeology to present a detailed, though still far from complete, picture of the past. In addition to their intrinsic interest, these data can assist in answering what Lewis Binford calls "the Big Questions," such as how and why civilizations arose and declined, questions that have an enduring importance to understanding and coping with the world in which we live.

TEXT REFERENCES

Amiet, Pierre. 1983. "Susa." Pp. 14–23 in *Vanished Civilizations.* Surry Hills, NSW: Reader's Digest Services Pty Ltd.

Baird, Douglas. 2000. "Alikosh" and "Jarmo." Pp. 12 and 159, respectively, in *Dictionary of the Ancient Near East.* Edited by Piotr Bienkowski and Alan Millard. London: British Museum Press.

Bienkowski, Piotr. 2000. "Chronology," and "Nippur." Pp. 73–74 and 214, respectively, in *Dictionary of the Ancient Near East.* Edited by Piotr Bienkowski and Alan Millard. London: British Museum Press.

Bienkowski, Piotr, and Alan Millard, eds. 2000. *Dictionary of the Ancient Near East.* London: British Museum Press.

Cryer, Frederick. 2000. "Chronology: Issues and Problems." Pp. 651–664 in *Civilizations of the Ancient Near East.* Edited by Jack M. Sasson. Peabody: Hendrickson Publishers, Inc.

Curtis, John. 1982. "Arpachiyah." Pp. 30–36 in *Fifty Years of Mesopotamian Discovery.* Edited by John Curtis. London: British School of Archaeology in Iraq.

Daniel, Glyn. 1981. *A Short History of Archaeology.* London: Thames and Hudson.

Daniels, Peter T. 2000. "The Decipherment of Ancient Near Eastern Scripts." Pp. 81–93 in *Civilizations of the Ancient Near East.* Edited by Jack M. Sasson. Peabody: Hendrickson Publishers, Inc.

Geller, Markham J. 2000. "The Influence of Ancient Mesopotamia on Hellenistic Judaism." Pp. 43–54 in *Civilizations of the Ancient Near East.* Edited by Jack M. Sasson. Peabody: Hendrickson Publishers, Inc.

George, A. 1999. *The Epic of Gilgamesh. A New Translation.* London: Allen Lane, The Penguin Press.

Harris, Roberta L. 1995. *The World of the Bible.* London: Thames and Hudson.

Hole, Frank Arnold. 2000. "Assessing the Past through Anthrolopological Archaeology." Pp. 2715–2727 in *Civilizations of the Ancient Near East.* Edited by Jack M. Sasson. Peabody: Hendrickson Publishers, Inc.

Jacobsen, Thorkild. 2000. "Searching for Sumer and Akkad." Pp. 2743–2752 in *Civilizations of the Ancient Near East.* Edited by Jack M. Sasson. Peabody: Hendrickson Publishers, Inc.

Klengel-Brandt, Evelyn. 1997. "Babylon." Pp. 251–256 in *The Oxford Encyclopedia of Archaeology in the Near East.* Vol. 1. Edited by Eric M. Meyers. Oxford: Oxford University Press.

Kuhrt, Amelie. 2000. "Ancient Mesopotamia in Classical Greek and Hellenistic Thought." Pp. 55–66 in *Civilizations of the Ancient Near East.* Edited by Jack M. Sasson. Peabody: Hendrickson Publishers, Inc.

Kuniholm, Peter Ian, Bernard Kromer, Sturt W. Manning, Maryanne Newton, Christine E. Latini, and Mary Jayne Bruce. 1996. "Anatolian Tree Rings and the Absolute Chronology of the Eastern Mediterranean, 2220–718 B.C.E." *Nature* 381: 780–783.

Leick, Gwendolyn. 2001. *Mesopotamia. The Invention of the City.* London: Allen Lane, The Penguin Press.

Lloyd, Seton. 1980. *Foundations in the Dust.* Revised edition. London: Thames and Hudson.

————. 2000. "Excavating the Land between the Two Rivers." Pp. 2729–2741 in *Civilizations of the Ancient Near East.* Edited by Jack M. Sasson. Peabody: Hendrickson Publishers, Inc.

Lundquist, John M. 2000. "Babylon in European Thought." Pp. 67–80 in *Civilizations of the Ancient Near East.* Edited by Jack M. Sasson. Peabody: Hendrickson Publishers, Inc.

Meyers, Eric M., ed. 1997. *The Oxford Encyclopedia of Archaeology in the Near East.* 5 Volumes. Oxford: Oxford University Press.

Millard, Alan. 2000. "Annals and Chronicles," "Eponyms," and "King Lists." Pp. 21–22, 106–107, and 169–170, respectively, in *Dictionary of the Ancient Near East.* Edited by Piotr Bienkowski and Alan Millard. London: British Museum Press.

Oates, Joan. 1986. *Babylon.* Revised edition. London: Thames and Hudson.

Pittman, Holly. 1997. "Susa." Pp. 106–110 in *The Oxford Encyclopedia of Archaeology in the Near East.* Vol. 5. Edited by Eric M. Meyers. Oxford: Oxford University Press.

Reade, Julian. 2000. *Mesopotamia.* 2d edition. London: British Museum Press.

Renfrew, Colin, and Paul Bahn. 2000. *Archaeology.* 3d edition. London: Thames and Hudson.

Roaf, Michael. 1990. *Cultural Atlas of Mesopotamia.* New York: Facts on File.

Robinson, Andrew. 1995. *The Story of Writing. Alphabets, Hieroglyphs and Pictograms.* London: Thames and Hudson.

Saggs, H. W. F. 1995. *Peoples of the Past. Babylonians.* London: British Museum Press.

Sasson, Jack M., ed. 2000. *Civilizations of the Ancient Near East.* 4 Volumes. Peabody: Hendrickson Publishers, Inc. (Reprint of 1995 edition. New York: Scribner.)

Scarre, Chris. 1999. *Seventy Wonders of the Ancient World.* London: Thames and Hudson.

Summers, Geoffrey D. 2000a. "Susa." Pp. 281–282 in *Dictionary of the Ancient Near East.* Edited by Piotr Bienkowski and Alan Millard. London: British Museum Press.

Woolley, Leonard. 1950. *Ur of the Chaldees.* Harmondsworth: Pelican. (Revised reprint of 1929 edition.)

————. 1982. *Ur "of the Chaldees."* The final account, *Excavations at Ur,* revised and updated by P. Roger and S. Moorey. London: Book Club Associates / Herbert Press.

IV

CHAPTER 4

Origins, Growth, and Decline of Mesopotamian Civilization

EARLY MESOPOTAMIA (CA. 7000–2900 B.C.E.)

Early Farmers in Northern Mesopotamia

Introduction: The Beginnings of Farming. For most of human existence, people have lived by foraging, a way of life that generally necessitates some mobility, whether following migrating herds or seeking out seasonally available plants. After the most recent glacial maximum around 16,000 B.C.E., the ice sheets retreated and changes took place around the world, resulting by around 8000 B.C.E. in approximately the climate and environment that we know today. In parts of the Near East, nut-bearing trees (such as pistachio, almond, and oak) and cereals (wheat and barley) gradually became more widespread, allowing some communities to settle permanently in their vicinity, supported year round by stored grains and nuts, along with hunted game, fowl, and fish. Some archaeologists argue that the key role of cereals was not as a staple for everyday consumption but rather as a resource for feasting, an important social activity: In this case they may have been used to make beer.

Between 11,500 and 9500 B.C.E. sedentary communities became more numerous. Sedentism brought major changes. It was now worth investing labor in constructing substantial houses of wood or clay, often with stone foundations. Storage facilities—pits, bins, or baskets—became important. Previously all possessions had had to be portable or disposable; now there was no limit on their number or weight. New tools proliferated, including sickles and heavy equipment such as grindstones. On the other hand, reduced mobility meant that intercommunity relations needed to be cultivated and intensified in order to obtain essential or desirable raw materials that were not locally available.

Sedentary communities were also liable to grow. Some scholars argue that population growth was a constant feature of human development, held in check only by those natural constraints for which a solution had not yet been found; others believe that humans have generally acted to keep their population size just below the carrying capacity of their territory. In either case, sedentism in an environment rich in resources offered new opportunities for population growth. Larger communities brought with them the need to develop new ways of regulating social interactions, to avoid conflict, and to manage people and resources.

A Neolithic Hassuna jar decorated with incised motifs. Such vessels were among the earliest pottery produced in Mesopotamia. (Gianni Dagli Orti/Corbis)

As communities expanded, some people moved out and founded new settlements, eventually reaching areas lacking the cereals upon which they depended. Reliance on wild cereals was not merely a passive matter of harvesting ripe grain. Ethnographic studies show that hunter-gatherers also actively encouraged useful plants by planting and transplanting, weeding, and manuring. It was a small step from tending wild cereals to deliberately sowing them in areas where they did not naturally occur.

It is thought that a period of colder drier conditions set in around 9000 B.C.E., reducing the abundance of the natural vegetation and encouraging people to sow cereals in suitable locations. It is in this period that we see the emergence of agricultural communities in the region between Palestine and the northern Zagros; and as conditions improved these increased in size and number. Between 8500 and 7000 B.C.E., farming communities were established throughout the Near East in the zone where rain-fed agriculture was possible (roughly delineated by the 200 millimeter isohyet), from the Anatolian plateau and the Levant to the Iranian plateau and the southern Zagros. In northern Mesopotamia settlements grew up at sites in the Zagros, like Jarmo in the foothills and Ganj Dareh at a higher elevation, and on the steppe, such as Tell Maghzaliya. Agriculture made it possible also to establish settlements on the northern plains where only sparse wild foodstuffs were available, such as Bouqras on the upper Euphrates. Settlements varied in size but some were as large as 10 hectares, housing perhaps as many as 1,000 people.

Initially these early farming communities continued to hunt, but gradually wild game was superseded by domestic herds of sheep and goats; pigs and cattle were domesticated somewhat later. Typical material from northern Mesopotamian sites included clay figurines, small objects of native (pure natural) copper, and vessels of stone, lime, or gypsum plaster ("white ware") and clay, sometimes lightly fired.

Early Farmers of Mesopotamia. By around 7000 B.C.E., agricultural communities were widespread. This period saw two major technological innovations, foreshadowed at Ganj Dareh and other early sites: the manufacture of pottery and of metalwork.

Pottery was independently invented in many parts of the world, the earliest being Japan around 11,000 B.C.E. By 7000 B.C.E. in the Near East, roughly modeled but sturdy pots, sometimes painted red, were being made of clay tempered with chaff. Domed kilns were being used to fire the pottery before 6000 B.C.E. The growing understanding of pyrotechnology also led to the first smelting of lead and copper, previously worked by cold hammering; but metal objects, mainly ornaments, were still small and rare.

Distinctive pottery marked broad cultural provinces. In northern Mesopotamia, painted and incised proto-Hassuna and Hassuna pottery was found in the farming settlements now widespread on the steppe and in the western foothills of the Zagros. Houses in villages like Hassuna and Yarim Tepe I were constructed of pisé (packed mud—known locally as *tauf*) and were generally rectangular, with a main room, small storerooms, and a courtyard. Farming was well established, with pulses, developed varieties of wheat and barley, and domestic sheep and goats, although hunted animals still contributed to the meat supply. Alongside pottery, the villagers continued to use attractive stone vessels, which were among the goods they traded for nonlocal materials such as turquoise, shells, and obsidian. Stamp seals were perhaps used to imprint designs on linen textiles; Jarmo produced an impression of woven fabric, and widespread spindle whorls provide evidence of spinning.

The importance of leather, for clothing, containers, and other equipment, is demonstrated by the settlement at Umm Dabaghiyah in marginal steppe land

A view of the early farming settlement of Tell Hassuna, in northern Mesopotamia. Archaeologists Seton Lloyd and Fuad Safar dug through this level to reach the lowest at the site, the walls of which protrude slightly through the floor of the level shown in this photo. Finds here included a sickle made of flint chips set in bitumen, still sharp enough to cut grain. (Bettmann/Corbis)

beyond the parkland and fertile steppe where farming communities flourished. Umm Dabaghiyah's inhabitants relied at least in part on grain and other food brought in in exchange for hides and dried meat from the local onagers (wild asses), which they hunted in great numbers using nets and slingshot. The existence of a specialist settlement of this kind gives some indication of the developing economic complexity of the period; undoubtedly there were other examples of economic specialization.

The Beginning of Irrigation.   Initially farming was confined to regions where rainfall was adequate to water the crops. But between 6500 and 6000 B.C.E., settlements began appearing beyond these limits, in the central regions of Mesopotamia. In a number of sites the presence of thirsty crops like flax shows that irrigation was essential, and the large size that the grains attained points toward the abundant provision of water, using simple irrigation techniques. The inhabitants of Choga Mami constructed water channels for simple fan irrigation, and at Sawwan use was probably made of the waters of the Tigris. The distinctive Samarran pottery found at these sites occurs over a wide area, from the central Euphrates to the foothills of the Zagros; although partially contemporary with Hassuna pottery, it also follows it in some northern Mesopotamian settlements. Like Hassuna settlements, Samarran villages had multiroomed houses with substantial storage facilities and contained objects made of exotic raw materials. Among their finest products were beautiful alabaster vessels and figurines.

Further south, the site of Tell el-'Oueili (Tell Awayli) provides a solitary hint of the contemporary existence of communities far into the alluvial plains of southern Mesopotamia (see Farming Communities in Southern Mesopotamia).

An example of the fine Halaf pottery painted with intricate geometric designs. (Archivo Iconografico, S.A./Corbis)

By about 6000 B.C.E., a new pottery style was becoming widespread in northern Mesopotamia, replacing Hassuna and Samarran pottery at many sites and spreading farther to the east and west. Fired in double-chamber kilns, decorated with meticulously arranged zones of fine geometric designs, the Halaf pottery is considered by many scholars to have been made by specialist potters, in contrast to the domestic production of earlier wares. Analyses of the clay used for these vessels indicates that some settlements, such as Arpachiyeh on the middle Tigris, produced pots that were traded over a wide area.

Farmers like their ancestors, the Halaf people built beehive-shaped circular houses with a rectangular annex (*tholoi*). Late in the Halaf occupation at Arpachiyeh, a large rectangular building was erected and later burned down, preserving a quantity of material, including pottery, figurines, jewelry, flint and obsidian tools, and stone vessels, which had originally stood on shelves. This may have been a storeroom, belonging either to the community as a whole or to a village chief; clay sealings found here suggest the beginning of some degree of administrative control within the settlement.

By around 5000 B.C.E. the Halaf people had begun to interact with their neighbors in the south, known as the Ubaid culture; after a transitional period when the pottery showed both Halaf and Ubaid features, the Ubaid style of pottery became dominant.

Farming Communities in Southern Mesopotamia

The southern region of Mesopotamia is a land of waterways and marshes, and in prehistory these were probably more extensive, providing a rich livelihood for hunter-gatherers. Although their settlements (elusive even in ideal conditions) have not been found, it is probable that hunter-gatherer groups lived here well before the introduction of agriculture.

The first farming villages were established here by 6200 B.C.E., if not earlier. Deep alluvium masks the earliest settlements in the region: Hajji Muhammad, for example, lies beneath 3 meters of alluvium. Like the Marsh Arabs of recent times, the inhabitants of southern Mesopotamia often built their houses of reeds (see photo p. 236). Such perishable structures leave little trace for archaeologists to find, so only a tiny number of early settlements is known.

The earliest is Tell el-'Oueili: Visible as a small, low mound near the later city of Larsa, it was not occupied after the prehistoric period and so did not present the problem encountered in many sites, where massive deposits accumulated over millennia make it virtually impossible to investigate prehistoric levels.

The people of 'Oueili farmed but also made use of fish and shellfish and probably date palms, as did their successors. Built of mudbricks, their houses had flat roofs originally supported by wooden pillars. Each was divided into three sections and within them were found ovens, granaries, and substantial storage vessels.

Their pottery was similar to that of the Samarran culture, suggesting that they represented a southern extension of the farming communities belonging or related to the Samarran culture, who had already mastered the simple irrigation techniques essential for agriculture in this region.

The first farmers in southern Mesopotamia are known as the Ubaid culture, the earliest occupation at 'Oueili being assigned to a newly defined Ubaid 0 phase. During Ubaid 1, dated to the earlier sixth millennium B.C.E. at 'Oueili, dark painted pottery was made: This has been found on only a few sites, whereas the characteristic pottery of Ubaid 2 is far more widespread. The increase in known sites must reflect the expansion of farming communities within the region, where irrigation agriculture is highly productive and could support dense occupation. Settlements range from Eridu in the south to Ras al 'Amiya and Uqair in the region of Baghdad and possibly as far north as the Hamrin. Model boats found at Ur and Eridu show the settlers had mastery of the waterways that crisscrossed their land; communications between settlements were mainly by water, then and later. Cattle were the main domestic animals, although sheep, goats, and pigs were also kept. Six-row barley was widely cultivated: It required irrigation but produced yields around double those of the more primitive two-row barley previously cultivated.

By Ubaid 3, in the late sixth and early fifth millennia B.C.E., the Hamrin was certainly part of the Ubaid world. Ubaid 3 and 4 pottery was made using the tournette or "slow-wheel," a device turned by hand that allowed pots to be shaped (though not thrown) and horizontal decoration applied. The tournette was a labor-saving innovation that made possible the rapid production of fairly standardized pottery. Its development indicates that craft specialization was growing among the Ubaid people, which implies that communities were becoming larger and more numerous. Small villages and their inhabitants were largely self-sufficient, and families made their own tools, pottery, and other domestic objects. Larger communities, however, could provide sufficient demand for such objects to enable some individuals to work part time or full time producing them, developing specialist skills. Pottery, which preserves well, provides a marker for the growth of craft specialization; other craft products, now vanished, could also have been made by specialists in these communities.

Ubaid 3 pottery is found far outside southern Mesopotamia, replacing the fine painted Halaf ware in northern Mesopotamian settlements. Halaf ware was probably also produced, or at least decorated, by specialists; its

An Ubaid period painted vase. Ubaid pottery became popular over much of the Near East in the fifth millennium B.C.E. (Archivo Iconografico, S.A./Corbis)

replacement by Ubaid ware reflects the widespread adoption of the tournette, which allowed potters to produce more pots in a given time. This innovation shows that northern Mesopotamia, too, was by this time moving toward greater craft specialization, reflecting greater social complexity and larger, more numerous communities. By Ubaid phase 4, similar pottery was made over a vast area, from Bahrain, Qatar, UAE, and Saudi Arabia in the south, to eastern Anatolia in the north, and Susiana (Khuzestan) in the east.

Contacts between these regions and southern Mesopotamia were encouraged by the need to obtain raw materials. Southern Mesopotamia, although richly productive for agriculture and stock raising, generally lacked many materials required for a comfortable existence. Mud, reeds, and date palms could supply many needs—their ingenious use included sickles, sling stones, and pestles ("bent nails") of baked clay, and mansions of reeds—but timber, stone, gold and copper ore, and many luxury materials had to be brought in from outside. Exchange networks had been carrying materials over long distances for millennia, and these intensified through time. The distances over which materials could move is exemplified by the presence at Tepe Gawra in the northern Tigris plains of lapis lazuli from Afghanistan.

Tepe Gawra is a particularly interesting site. It was occupied first in the Halaf period; Ubaid 3 pottery appears alongside Halaf ware in somewhat later levels, still associated with characteristic Halaf *tholos* houses. At the same time a substantial building was erected on a slight platform, the first in a sequence of structures that had affinities with the temples found in Ubaid villages, notably Eridu. These attained monumental proportions in the Ubaid 4 period, with niches and buttresses. Stamp seals bearing linear patterns or

Early Mesopotamian houses had flat roofs of mud and reeds supported by wooden beams. (Zev Radovan/Land of the Bible Picture Archive)

designs of people and animals have been interpreted as evidence of administrative control.

Eridu was traditionally the first Mesopotamian settlement created when the world was brought into being out of the primordial waters. Situated on a small island among the pools and marshes of the southern Euphrates, it was settled early in the Ubaid period. At this time a small mudbrick single-roomed building with an offering table and pedestal was constructed on a platform, the first in a series of increasingly elaborate structures that from the start were probably temples to Enki, the god of the waters and of wisdom. Later versions consisted of a central nave flanked by side chambers—the tripartite plan that was to become the standard temple design. Although later abandoned as a settlement, Eridu was long respected as a holy site.

In contrast to the mudbrick temple, Eridu's houses were built of reeds, as were those at Ur, Uruk, and other Ubaid sites in the south. Farther north, mudbrick was the preferred building material, leaving much more substantial traces that give a clearer picture of domestic life. One house in the small village of Tell Madhhur in the Hamrin was exceptionally well preserved. It was burned down and abandoned around 4500 B.C.E.; its residents removed their valuables but left their workaday pottery and tools behind in the building's shell. The house, home to an extended family of perhaps twenty people, had a large rectangular central room with a hearth, probably the focus of domestic life. Small rooms opened off both sides: These included a kitchen, storerooms, and other rooms, probably the private apartments of individual nuclear families. A ramp beside the kitchen led up to a flat roof supported on wooden beams, where further domestic activities took place.

A large cemetery was found at Eridu, containing 800–1,000 plain or brick-lined pit graves. Individuals were buried with a few domestic items such as pots, tools, and personal jewelry, and sometimes with a dog: One lay across its owner's pelvis, with a bone in its mouth. Each grave contained one or sometimes two adults, with or without children: presumably family graves, reopened as required. No individuals seem to have been singled out for special treatment, reinforcing the picture suggested by villages like Tell Madhhur of a largely egalitarian society. Professor H. W. F. Saggs argues that Mesopotamian religious myths reflect the social setup at this time: Decisions were made by the whole community of gods in council together, and the voices of goddesses were equal to those of gods—a mirror of a society run by village assemblies, in which men and women had equal status (1995: 34, 51). Nevertheless, there are also signs of the growing importance of the temple as the center of the community's economic and social life: the repository for its accumulated wealth, the focus of communal endeavor in its construction and of communal worship, and the home of the priest responsible not only for the relations between the community and the gods but also for the management and administration of community affairs. Already at Eridu, the increasingly monumental shrine was probably the center of worship not only for the resident community but also for neighboring settlements—a situation that was to develop in the enormous expansion of the following Uruk period.

The Uruk Culture

During the fifth millennium B.C.E., settlements had been increasing in number and size across the plains of northern Mesopotamia and Susiana. Since arable agriculture could support considerable population density, settlements were now to be found in close proximity to each other. This greatly increased inter-action between communities, both friendly, exchanging commodities and mar-riage partners, and unfriendly, competing for access to land and resources. These interactions combined with those within communities to bring about other changes: promoting craft specialization as the pool of potential con-sumers for specialist products increased and encouraging the development of social mechanisms to regulate interactions and the proliferation of officially sanctioned individuals to administer them. At the same time, a hierarchy of settlements was also developing, settlements in more favored situations grow-ing more rapidly and larger than their neighbors and providing a range of ser-vices for the communities of the wider region, such as the more specialized crafts, a religious focus, and leadership.

Southern Mesopotamia had been settled later than the areas to its east and north. Its farming settlements were initially few and widely separated, al-though prosperous and enjoying easy communications by boat. But during the fourth millennium B.C.E. (the Uruk period) southern Mesopotamia not only reached the levels of settlement density and hierarchy of its neighbors but sur-passed them. It is suggested that a considerable increase in aridity caused much of the marshland of southern Mesopotamia to dry out, leaving a land-scape of richly fertile land dissected by small waterways tributary to the major rivers. This vast increase in arable land, provided with abundant water for simple irrigation, would have attracted settlers from outside as well as en-abling indigenous communities to grow rapidly. Over the course of the fourth millennium southern Mesopotamia was transformed into the most densely settled region of the Near East, becoming by its end an urban landscape—the first in the world.

The fifth and fourth millennia in southern Mesopotamia were a period not only of exponential population growth but also of great inventiveness. The plough was devised to improve cultivation, increasing arable productivity. Animals began to be exploited for more than their meat: Cows were milked and oxen used to carry goods and draw ploughs and sledges, as were don-keys, domesticated at this time. The wheel was also invented, initially for mak-ing pottery but soon added to sledges to create carts, facilitating land trans-port. Water transport was boosted by the invention of sails to harness wind power. Sheep were bred for their wool, which superseded flax for making tex-tiles. These innovations together form the phenomenon Andrew Sherratt (1981) dubbed the "Secondary Products Revolution," a quantum change in economic productivity and efficiency. Developed in the fertile environment of southern Mesopotamia, these innovations rapidly spread throughout the Near East and beyond.

Among the innovations of the early Uruk period, but not so widely adopted, was the potter's wheel. This device vastly increased the speed of pottery man-

Dairying became an important economic activity in Sumer during the fourth millennium. This stone frieze from the temple at Tel al-Ubaid, dating around 2500 B.C.E., depicts the preparation of dairy products. Here milk is being churned to produce butter. (Zev Radovan/Land of the Bible Picture Archive)

ufacture and facilitated the mass production of uniform wares, because it was independently driven, allowing the potter to use both hands and centrifugal force to draw up and shape the rotating clay. The Uruk wheel-thrown pottery was distinguished by its fine fabric and highly burnished surfaces but was largely undecorated.

While handmade pottery could be made with relatively coarse clay, that used for wheel-thrown pots had to be very well worked and homogeneous. In addition to the potter, the ceramic workshop now needed assistants to prepare the clay. Hans Nissen (1988: 43–48, 61–62) highlights this development as an example of the increasing specialization within many occupations, individuals now becoming engaged in small parts of production processes rather than creating objects from start to finish, and argues that this division of labor necessitated the emergence of a new class of specialist—the supervisor or overseer, who coordinated the activities of all those involved in the manufacture of particular goods. Metallurgy was another field where intensification is attested: A series of pits and trenches from Uruk have been interpreted as a copper foundry in which around forty people worked together.

An Uruk-period cylinder seal engraved with a design of animals and a modern impression taken from it. (Gianni Dagli Orti/Corbis)

Whereas the tournette had readily been adopted in northern Mesopotamia, the potter's wheel was not—a phenomenon that Nissen used to argue for a growing rift in social complexity between the regions, owing to differences in the size and density of settlements. Recent excavations at Tell Hamoukar and Tell Brak in the north, however, indicate that the picture was more complex: These were large settlements, with monumental structures and signs of social complexity, developing at the same time as the earliest urban centers known in the south.

In southern Mesopotamia Uruk itself provides the best evidence of the changes that took place, particularly in the Late Uruk (ca. 3400–3100 B.C.E.) and Jemdet Nasr (3100–2900 B.C.E.) periods. It was occupied by around 4800 B.C.E., probably beginning as two villages centered on shrines that later became Kullaba, the precinct of the god An, and Eanna, the precinct of the goddess Inanna. By the Uruk period, these villages had coalesced into a single town that continued to expand, reaching around 250 hectares by 3100. Excavations at Uruk have concentrated on the sacred precincts, so it is the public aspects of life that are best known. Throughout the fourth millennium Kullaba was focused on a single tripartite shrine; built from the start on a slight platform the shrine took the form of a tripartite building with a central hall flanked by side chambers, an altar and an offering table, and external niches and buttresses.

Temple and platform were repeatedly reconstructed, increasing in size and reaching their final version in the Jemdet Nasr period with the White Temple, raised on the 13-meter-high "An ziggurat."

Eanna ("House of Heaven"), in contrast, housed a complex of diverse buildings during the Uruk period, including several tripartite buildings but also square structures, courtyards, and semisubterranean buildings that were probably storerooms. Some buildings were decorated with cone mosaics, a technique also employed at other sites such as Uqair. Whereas mudbrick was by now the usual material for public buildings, in Eanna a variety of different materials were used, including limestone, rammed earth and bitumen, and a type of concrete made of gypsum and ground-up fired brick. Gwendolyn Leick (2001) sees this whole period in Eanna as one of ebullient experimentation and argues that the public spaces between the buildings, epitomized by the Mosaic Court with its cone-mosaic walls and pillars, were as much the focus of public activity (such as festivals and religious ceremonies) as were the buildings' interiors. Frequent demolition and reconstruction and the reverential burying of objects from demolished structures have made it difficult to interpret the function of Eanna's buildings: They must have included shrines, storerooms, workshops, and administrative buildings, and probably priestly residences as well.

The most significant finds from the Eanna complex are written tablets. Recording systems have a long history in the Near East (see chapter 10), and several sites of the early Uruk period have tokens, bullae, or tablets bearing numerical marks—but at Uruk around 3300 B.C.E. these systems took a great leap forward with the beginning of writing. Tablets of this period cannot be read but apparently recorded quantities of commodities such as sheep and grain that passed through administrative hands here—whether brought in as taxes or offerings or given out to temple employees. Their existence gives the first glimpse of the administrative organization of Mesopotamian society based around the temple. By the end of the millennium, the writing on these tablets became more comprehensible as the symbols used were refined and increasingly stylized, approaching the form they were to take in the third-millennium cuneiform script. From this period comes the first example of the Standard Professions List, a text that lists the professions practiced at the time, arranged in rank order. Although this cannot be read, its similarities to later examples allow much of its contents to be surmised. This text shows not only various ranks within society in general but also within many of the professions themselves.

In the Ubaid period stamp seals had probably been used by officials to seal jars or packages of commodities and the doors of storerooms and other communal facilities; these were now superseded by the more practical cylinder seal. The majority were used to represent officials or institutions. Their presence in large numbers in the Eanna precinct bears witness to the existence here of warehouses and administrative buildings even though these have not been identified.

A further clue to the growth of state control comes from a particular class of pottery vessel—the beveled-rim bowl. These bowls, crude and unattractive,

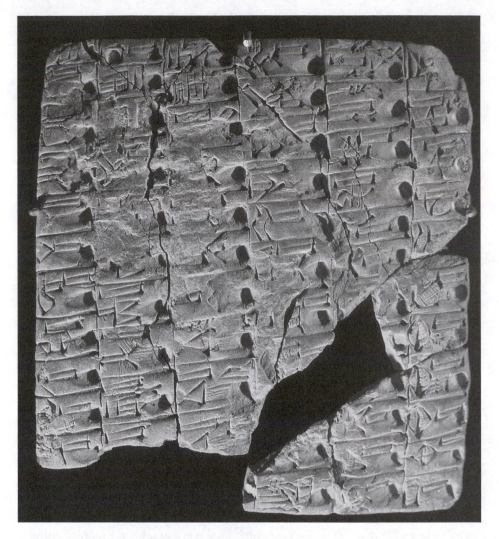

An archaic tablet bearing early cuneiform signs. Such early tablets were divided into boxes, each of which contained a short text, such as an inventory item and a number. (Gianni Dagli Orti/Corbis)

were made in vast quantities in moulds. They are of a standard size, their volume closely matching that of the daily food ration issued in later times to officially employed workers; it seems logical to view these bowls as containers for such a daily ration of grain or other foodstuffs to individuals working for the authorities in Uruk and other contemporary Mesopotamian towns. These would have included spinners and weavers of textiles, mainly women, potters and metallurgists, as well as herdsmen and farmers tending the flocks and cultivating the lands directly controlled by the religious authorities. Rations were also issued to residents of the city and its dependent settlements when they undertook public works such as the construction and maintenance of irrigation canals and the building of temples as corvée labor.

Beveled-rim bowls, cylinder seals, wheel-made pottery, and the beginning of writing are found outside southern Mesopotamia in adjacent Susiana, indicating a close link between these regions. Although some authorities see this as Sumerian domination of Elam, significant differences make this unlikely: In particular, the script of the early Elamites employs different signs to those of southern Mesopotamia and records a different language. By the early third millennium, the close similarities had disappeared and Elam developed along different lines, increasing its links with the trading towns springing up across the Iranian plateau to its north and east.

Different again is southern Mesopotamia's relationship with the north. While southern Mesopotamia was becoming more densely settled, the numbers of settlements having increased tenfold during the millennium, most of the north remained less densely populated, economically less developed, and politically more fragmented, although the excavations at Brak and Hamoukar show that the towns were emerging in the Khabur River basin; Hamoukar had a city wall before 3500 B.C.E.

In addition, there were a handful of settlements that are regarded as southern Mesopotamian colonies. The best known is Habuba Kabira South, a small town on the northern Euphrates. In this well-planned settlement, many houses have been uncovered, giving a welcome insight into Sumerian domestic life not furnished by early towns in southern Mesopotamia itself, where excavations have largely concentrated on the monumental religious architecture. The houses generally comprised a central hall flanked by smaller rooms, similar to the Ubaid houses at Tell Madhhur and elsewhere. A few larger houses probably belonged to the community's leaders. The settlement also contained workshops, making pottery and working lead, among other things. Habuba Kabira was initially unfortified, but a substantial wall was later erected.

Various theories have been advanced to explain the existence of these colonial settlements. They could represent an expansion of people from the densely populated south into the less settled north. One suggestion is that the great increase in sheep pastoralism for wool production encouraged communities to settle in areas like the northern Mesopotamian steppe where suitable pastureland abounded. Another is that increasingly heavy-handed bureaucratic control, perhaps brutally backed by force, made life burdensome in some southern cities and their dependent territories, causing some groups to emigrate to regions like northern Mesopotamia where they could lead a freer existence.

Another theory relates to trade. The Uruk period saw a change in the pattern of trading relations. Instead of depending on the transmission of raw materials through many hands before they finally reached southern Mesopotamian settlements (down-the-line exchange), the Sumerians were now actively involved in the procurement of materials and their transmission via Sumerian trading outposts established along trade routes or near sources. One example is the native northern Mesopotamian settlement of Hacinebi in Turkey, where an enclave of southern Mesopotamian traders was planted. It is possible that Sumerian colonies like Habuba Kabira were also established to control trade.

Features of the Eye Temple at Tell Brak show that there were contacts between the Uruk colonies and local settlements at this time.

In the Jemdet Nasr period (3100–2900 B.C.E.) trade links developed with lands in the Gulf, including Oman, an important source of copper. Jemdet Nasr pottery and weapons have been found in graves both here and in Abu Dhabi. The active promotion of Sumerian interests outside southern Mesopotamia is a reflection of the qualitative changes that were occurring in the society of southern Mesopotamia and the growing developmental distance between this region and its neighbors.

The political order in this period is still uncertain, but documented titles and artistic representations indicate the existence of both priests and kings, the latter probably elected by the citizen assembly. Cities were regarded as the personal property of individual gods, and the city's leaders acted in their name. Uruk was the home of Inanna, the goddess of fertility. A delightful legend recounts how she promoted Uruk's welfare by approaching Enki, patron god of Eridu, the primeval settlement, and making him drunk so that she could steal the *ME* (the attributes of civilization) that he was jealously monopolizing. The triumph of Inanna over An as patron of Uruk is probably reflected in the massive redevelopment of the sacred precincts during the Jemdet Nasr period. Earlier structures in Eanna, Inanna's precinct, were replaced by a massive platform 2 meters high, supporting a temple. Groups of houses and administrative buildings, courtyards, and sacrificial rooms surrounded it. By the end of Jemdet Nasr, the buildings of Kullaba, precinct of the sky god An, were also razed and incorporated into the platform.

The managerial role of the authorities increased exponentially in the Late Uruk period—organizing the construction and maintenance of irrigation channels; undertaking the delicate task of maintaining the vital good relations with other communities capable of disrupting the flow of essential water; supervising the production of commodities, notably woolen textiles, metal tools, and pottery, and the accumulation of reserves of grain; and promoting and sponsoring trading expeditions. To the authorities must also have fallen the task of leading the internal affairs of the vastly growing community, although even in the subsequent Early Dynastic period, community decisions were made in an assembly representing all the citizens. An alabaster jar (the "Warka vase") found within the Eanna precinct in Uruk vividly captures details of the relationship among community, ruler, and gods. Three registers of relief decoration run around the vessel. In the lowest are depicted a band of water, the lifeblood of the region, surmounted by date palms and ears of barley, the foundation of Sumer's agricultural prosperity, and above them, a frieze of alternating rams and ewes, source not only of meat but also of milk, leather, and wool for textiles. Around the center of the vessel, a procession of naked men bears offerings: bowls, baskets, and jars full of produce such as grain and fruit. In the top register (unfortunately incomplete) these offerings are being brought before the cloaked figure of the deity, identified as Inanna by the pair of reed pillars behind her. One man holds up a jar of fruit to the goddess; behind him (in the broken portion) stands a robed figure, presumably the officiating priest,

A detail of the famous "Warka Vase," an alabaster jar from Uruk, showing individuals bearing offerings to the city's goddess Inanna. (Gianni Dagli Orti/Corbis)

wearing a sash held up by an attendant. He may be the *en*, partner of the goddess in the Sacred Marriage. Behind the goddess are piled the offerings already made: These include a pair of jars identical in shape to the Warka vase itself, animals, and plates of food, as well as two statues borne on the back of a ram, a type of artistic creation familiar from Eanna in this period.

Over the course of the fourth millennium, the population of southern Mesopotamia increased tenfold. Uruk itself grew to around 60,000 people and around 600–700 hectares during the Jemdet Nasr period, emerging as the world's first city, a place not only of massive size but of corresponding complexity, home to farmers, herdsmen, artisans, traders, priests, and service personnel. In the Uruk region, there were now four levels in the settlement hierarchy: hamlets, villages, and towns, dominated by the city of Uruk.

Good relations within the community and between adjacent polities were vitally important but not always successfully maintained. From this period come the first signs of warfare: seals and other inscribed material depicting warriors armed with spears and prisoners bound and humiliated or worse. The increasing need to defend the community is reflected in the beginning of fortifications, seen at Habuba Kabira in the north and at Abu Salabikh, and attested in legend at Uruk, where the original city walls are attributed to the Seven Sages, belonging to the legendary period preceding the Early Dynastic period of the early third millennium B.C.E.

THE RISE OF KINGS (CA. 2900–2334 B.C.E.)

Early Dynastic Sumer

The centuries from ca. 2900 to 2334 B.C.E. are known as the Early Dynastic (ED) period, divided into three phases: ED I, ED II, and ED III. A time of great change, it saw the transformation of southern Mesopotamia into a historical civilization. Although ED I is shrouded in legend and almost entirely dependent on archaeological evidence, by the end of ED III we are dealing with an albeit fragmentary historical landscape in which known individuals performed historical deeds. The intervening centuries are a mixture of legend, history, and archaeological information, coming slowly into focus.

Surveys in various parts of southern Mesopotamia suggest that major landscape changes occurred around 3000–2800 B.C.E., reducing the number of minor water courses and concentrating water in the main river channels. Although water was still abundant, considerable work had to be put into building and maintaining canals to irrigate the crops during the growing season. Disastrous floods seem likely periodically to have swept through southern Mesopotamia, destroying fields and villages, breaking down dams, and overflowing canals. Such inundations, either overtaking different areas at different times or accumulating into a catastrophic flood that inundated the whole region around 2900 B.C.E., as some scholars suggest, are marked archaeologically by thick accumulations of sterile silt in cities like Kish, and entered the memory of the Mesopotamian people as the great Flood recorded in later literature.

The Flood legend also reflects the substantial growth of population in southern Mesopotamia. Settlement was concentrated in the fertile land along major waterways, creating the city-states familiar from later Mesopotamian history. By about 2500 B.C.E., around 80 percent of the population of southern Mesopotamia dwelt in cities "threaded like pearls along the main watercourses" (Nissen 1988: 141)—largely branches of the Euphrates and the Diyala, rather than the Tigris. Cultivation focused within the lands surrounding major settlements, their high productivity able to support cities with populations reckoned in tens of thousands. These provided a focus for services, industry, and political control, and, increasingly, defense.

Legend places the building of the first cities' walls in the Late Uruk period, as does archaeological evidence, the earliest coming from Abu Salabikh. Each city controlled its surrounding territories; beyond them lay the *edin,* land that was not cultivated or settled, a buffer zone between the territories of individual city-states that provided grazing for the animals of pastoral groups, either affiliated to the cities or independent.

Increasing evidence of warfare appears in ED II. As cities increased in size, inevitably conflicts developed between them over land, water rights, and political power. Archaeological and historical sources combine to suggest the increasing importance of secular authority within the cities as the need for defense put power into the hands of war leaders—probably originally appointed by the council to lead individual defensive or aggressive military actions against hostile neighboring cities but through time becoming a permanent authority, although still governing in the name of the city deity and backed by his or her authority.

A Sumerian votive statue, probably depicting a priest. (Zev Radovan/Land of the Bible Picture Archive)

The Sumerian King List and the epic literature surrounding Gilgamesh and the house of Uruk reflect developments in this period, although they were written down at a later date and were influenced both by propaganda and by anachronisms from the time of writing and compilation (Ur III to Old Babylonian times). One series of poems recounts attempts by King Enmerkar of Uruk and his son Lugalbanda to control trade with distant lands in essential and luxury goods. By military threat and religious intimidation, Enmerkar persuades the king of Aratta (somewhere in eastern Iran, now being identified with the recently discovered civilization of Jiroft on the Halil River in the southwestern province of Kerman) to exchange precious metals and "mountain stones" for grain. In another poem, Enmerkar's grandson Gilgamesh, who may have lived around 2600 B.C.E., comes into conflict with Agga, king of Kish, emerging triumphant.

Ruins of the important Sumerian city of Kish, whose king may have exercised some authority over other Sumerian rulers. (Corel Corp.)

Gilgamesh is credited with refurbishing and extending Uruk's city walls, traditionally built earlier by the Seven Sages. Plano-convex bricks, typical of the ED period, were used in the sections of Uruk's walls and towers that have been excavated, confirming their claimed age.

Gilgamesh and Agga are among the kings listed in the Sumerian King List. This enumerates each city's rulers as if they had ruled consecutively, the gods dictating that one city should hold supreme authority until divine sanction backed human conflict to transfer hegemony to another city-state. This is an anachronism from the later period when the region was united under a single imperial line; in reality many of the dynasties of these cities ruled concurrently. Although the length of individual kings' reigns cannot be taken at face value—many are immensely long, particularly in the period before the Flood—its genealogical information is often borne out by scraps of contemporary written material. For example, Agga of Kish is the son of Enmebaragesi in the King List. A bowl with a dedicatory inscription attests to the historical existence of Mebaragesi (*en*—a title meaning ruler—having been erroneously attached to his name by a later scribe). Several other kings who appear in the King List have also had their existence substantiated by the discovery of their inscriptions, including a number in the Royal Cemetery at Ur.

The "Peace" side of the Standard of Ur, probably the sounding box of a lyre, found in the largest tomb in the Royal Cemetery at Ur. It shows goods and animals being brought to furnish the royal banquet depicted in the upper register. (Bettmann/Corbis)

A number of cities have yielded seals bearing the names of several other cities, from ED I onward, and it has been suggested that these indicate the existence of cooperative leagues of cities. Texts recovered from Shuruppak, apparently written within the last six months before its violent destruction early in ED IIIa, repeatedly refer to the cities of Adab, Lagash, and Umma on the eastern branch of the Euphrates and Uruk and Nippur on the same, western, branch as Shuruppak. They also mention huge numbers of *gurush,* men and officials from cities outside Shuruppak, apparently drafted in to undertake various services, both military and civil. Although we do not know the form that cooperation between these states took, it probably included joint military expeditions and collaborative work on major public enterprises, such as erecting temples and other major public buildings, digging canals, and building dams. When Shuruppak was sacked, it was probably by Ur, not a member of this league.

Ur, situated on the Euphrates at the head of the Gulf and therefore ideally placed for trade to the south and east, was occupied from the Ubaid period and in ED times was developing into a major city. By early ED IIIa, its wealth and power were reflected in a series of sixteen spectacular graves within a large cemetery south of its sacred precinct. Several of these graves have yielded inscribed material, linking them to the tenuous historical information of the King List. A remarkable golden helmet in the form of a wig bore the name of King Meskalamdug; a large grave pit, richly furnished, contained a seal belonging to a queen, Puabi, and in the tomb below lay the remains of a king identified as Akalamdug, Meskalamdug's successor. All belong to the period before the kingship passed to Ur, according to the King

List. The First Dynasty of Ur listed here begins with Mesanepada, son of Meskalamdug, and his son A-anepada, both known from contemporary inscribed material. The spectacularly furnished graves included exquisite jewelry and fine artifacts such as wooden lyres with bull or cow heads ornamented in gold and lapis lazuli, reflecting well-developed and wide-ranging trading links extending as far as Badakhshan in Afghanistan and Gujurat in India.

Mesanepada, king of Ur in the King List, is identified on his seal as King of Kish. Kish was a major city in the third millennium B.C.E., ruled in ED II by Mebaragesi and Agga. A number of third-millennium rulers bore the title "King of Kish"—in addition to Mesanepada of Ur, these included Mesalim who may have ruled Der, Eannatum of Lagash, and the late Early Dynastic king Lugalzagesi of Umma. The existence of the title should provide some insight into political organization. Did it represent physical conquest of Kish and political hegemony over much of Sumer, or, more probably, acknowledgment of the preeminence in some other sense of the ruler who bore the title? The King of Kish was evidently respected by other city rulers and on at least one occasion acted as arbitrator in a border dispute between rival cities. The Gilgamesh poem that deals with Uruk's conflict with Kish implies that Gilgamesh had originally accepted Agga as his overlord. The ensis of Adab and Lagash acknowledged the authority of Mesalim, lugal of Kish, and the presence of a bowl at Khafajeh dedicated by Mebaragesi also implies that Khafajeh recognized Kish's hegemony. Although military action took place between states from early ED times, for most of the period these seem to have been skirmishes rather than full-scale conquest, with the victor receiving the submission rather than the allegiance of the vanquished. City-states retained their territorial independence, although, like Shuruppak, they might be sacked. It is not until late ED III that there is evidence for the carving out of more substantial domains.

A final power point in ED times was the city of Nippur, which exercised spiritual rather than secular authority. Opinions are divided on how early this developed, ranging from 3000 B.C.E. (e.g., Reade) to late ED III (e.g., Leick). Each Sumerian city identified itself as the property of its tutelary deity—Uruk of Inanna, Ur of the moon god Nanna (Sin), Eridu of Enki. The prosperity of the city depended on the presence and favor of the city's god, and in turn the god or goddess depended on the service of the citizens. Nippur was the city of the god Enlil, acclaimed as chief of the gods by the end of ED III. By this time, or possibly earlier, Nippur was regarded as the seat of the council of the gods, where early kings also met in council, and Enlil's temple at Nippur, the Ekur, was the acknowledged religious center of Sumer. The approval of Enlil was a prerequisite for success for any city's ruler, and his backing was invoked by kings anxious to extend their domains or attack their enemies. The priesthood of Enlil therefore exercised a powerful role in power politics in the region by the twenty-fourth century B.C.E., although an apocryphal story from the reign of the later king Naram-Sin suggests that Nippur was not immune from attack if the god's decree was found unacceptable.

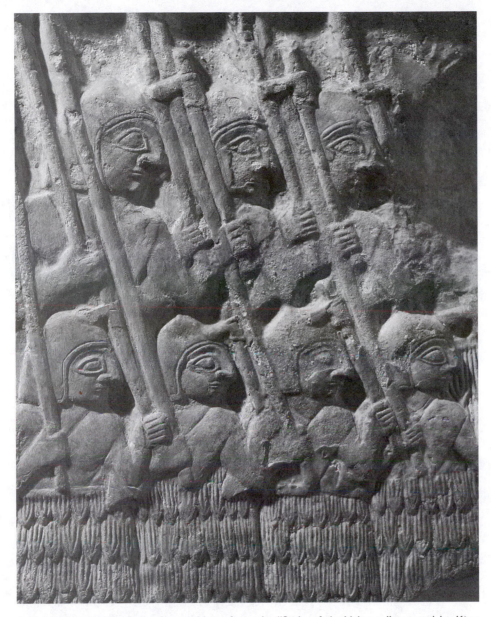

A detail showing Sumerian foot soldiers from the "Stele of the Vultures" erected by King Eannatum of Lagash around 2450 B.C.E. to celebrate his victory over the rival state of Umma. (Bettmann/Corbis)

Aggrandizing States

Toward the end of the Early Dynastic period, the historical sources become more informative, revealing that some states were developing territorial ambitions.

The first substantial contemporary text reflecting the political situation comes from Lagash. The city of Lagash was the capital of an eponymous state on the

Euphrates: By the mid-third millennium B.C.E., another city, Girsu, had over-taken Lagash city as the major center within Lagash state. Girsu was located only 30 kilometers south of Umma, capital of another state on the same branch of the river, and as the cities grew in size and increased their areas of influence, inevitably they came into conflict over the ownership and usufruct of lands along their mutual border. The problem was brought to arbitration by Mesalim, King of Kish around 2550 B.C.E.: He erected a stele marking the boundary line and awarded farming rights on the disputed lands to Umma, with an annual payment to Lagash from the produce. Border disputes broke out again during the reign of Ur-Nanshe of Lagash (ca. 2494–2465 B.C.E.), who also built temples and city walls: He became King of Kish and claimed to have defeated not only Umma but also Ur. His grandson Eannatum (ca. 2450 B.C.E.) also became in-volved in the dispute: He defeated Umma and also claimed to have defeated Uruk, Ur, Mari, and Akshak, as well as Elam and Susa in the east and Subartu in the north. The monument he erected, known now as the Stele of the Vultures, vividly depicts his stoutly armed and disciplined infantry and their doughty leader, the slain enemy attacked by vultures, and prisoners held in a net by Ningirsu, god of Girsu. The conflict between Umma and Lagash rumbled on for more than a century, with several attempts at arbitration.

Eannatum is unlikely actually to have conquered distant lands, but his victo-ries nearer home may represent an early attempt to gain control over neighbor-ing states rather than merely defeating them—such endeavors were to become increasingly common over the following century. Eannatum's nephew Enmetena made a pact with Lugal-kineshe-dudu, king of Uruk, who also gained control of Ur and Umma and held the title King of Kish. Around 2350 B.C.E. Uru-inim-gina became king of Lagash and brought in a series of domestic reforms aimed at improving the lot of the ordinary citizen, eliminating abuses practiced by officials, and restoring the eroded power of the temple. He fell foul of Lugalzagesi, governor (ensi) of Umma, who sacked Girsu, a disaster bitterly recorded by Uru-inim-gina. According to his own inscriptions, Lugalzagesi subsequently became the ruler of Ur, Uruk, and the other cities of southern Mesopotamia and gained control of the lands "from the Lower Sea" (the Gulf) "along the Tigris and Euphrates to the Upper Sea" (the Mediterranean). He commemorated his victories by dedicating more than fifty stone vessels at the Ekur (Enlil's shrine) at Nippur. In his inscription, he glorified the peace and prosperity he had brought the lands under his rule.

But this was not to last. Some years later, Lugalzagesi found himself again at the Ekur—but this time in a neck-stock, the humbled and defeated prisoner of Sargon of Akkad, who united the region into the first enduring territorial empire.

THE FIRST EMPIRES (CA. 2334–2000 B.C.E.)

Sargon and the Akkadian Empire

Sargon (Sharrum-kin—"true king"), the founder of the Akkadian Empire, epit-omized the successful king, beloved of the gods, becoming the role model for later dynasts keen to demonstrate their continuity with the glories of the past.

Many inscribed monuments set up by Sargon and his successors were assiduously copied by later scribes, and a few inscribed objects still survive. These contemporary records provide genuine historical information through which a picture of the Akkadian dynasty can be reconstructed. A body of legend was also accumulating around the Akkadian kings by the time of the next empire, Ur III: This reflects later propaganda more than historical truth.

Sargon's origins are unknown; he was probably from the northern part of southern Mesopotamia and from a humble background. According to legend, he was the son of a priestess and a man from the eastern mountains. After his birth, the priestess cast him adrift on the river in a reed basket; he

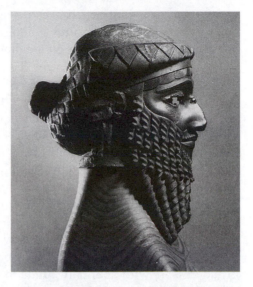

A cast copper head probably depicting the great Akkadian king Naram-Sin, found at Nineveh. (Time Life Pictures/Getty Images)

was rescued by Aqqi, a water carrier, who raised him as a gardener. In his youth he served Ur-Zababa, king of Kish, whom he succeeded in circumstances the details of which are now lost.

Sargon went on to win thirty-four battles, gaining control of the southern Mesopotamian cities by defeating Lugalzagesi. Parading Lugalzagesi before the Ekur in Nippur in effect demonstrated the transfer of authority from him to Sargon. Sargon also conquered Elam and towns to the north and west including Mari and Ebla. His inscriptions claim that he controlled areas as far afield as "Silver Mountain" (the Taurus range) in Anatolia and that his dominions stretched from the Upper Sea to the Lower Sea, in which he symbolically washed his weapons.

Like Lugalzagesi, who had made similar claims, Sargon's authority was probably closely linked to control of trade and of centers on trade routes rather than involving large-scale territorial conquest. Nevertheless in southern Mesopotamia at least, Sargon established a unified state that exercised hegemony over all the traditionally independent city-states: a new political form for all that it was couched in the traditional language "King of the Land, King of Kish" and, like Lugalzagesi, "King of the four rims of the world."

Sargon established a new city as his capital: Agade, whose name may mean "ancestral town," a minor settlement until Sargon brought it to prominence. A later poem, "The Curse of Agade," describes its architectural and cultural splendors, commercial success, and prosperity. Its glory did not survive the Akkadian period, and today its location is unknown. It was probably situated somewhere between Babylon, Kish, and Sippar.

Authority was centralized and life regimented. The Akkadian kings standardized weights and measures and the script, made Akkadian the official language, and probably introduced the practice of keeping a calendar by naming each year after a particular event. Trade flourished. An inscription records Sargon's dealings with Dilmun (Bahrein), Magan (Oman, a major source of copper), and Meluhha (the Indus civilization, at that time at its height). Sargon's grandson Naram-Sin boasts of a punitive military expedition to Magan in which he personally took part. Imports came from all quarters: from the Levant and Anatolia, from towns across the Iranian plateau, and from lands controlled or exploited by Meluhha; and they even included copal from Zanzibar (found at Ebla). Merchant ships docked at Agade from where imported goods were dispatched to other cities as payment to supporters of the regime or as temple offerings to win the favor of the gods. Agade was the hub of the empire, where crafts and industry were also concentrated.

Trade and military success, bringing booty and tribute, provided Sargon and his successors with abundant funds to support the substantial military machine that ensured their supremacy and their power to extract further taxes or tribute. Sargon claimed that 5,400 people ate daily in his presence, suggesting that he maintained a large standing army as well as other personnel. The army included levies from the various cities and other recruits, some from nomad groups on the periphery such as the Guti and Amorites. These soldiers received rations but might also be paid in grants of land. Sargon built fortresses such as Tell Brak (ancient Nagar or Nawar) in Syria to defend outpost regions but slighted the defensive walls of conquered cities and installed Akkadian governors. He appointed members of the royal family to senior religious posts; his daughter Enheduanna became the entu-priestess of the moon god Nanna at Ur. Supporters of the regime might be rewarded with grants of land, purchased cheaply or acquired by the Akkadians when they conquered hostile cities. Inscriptions claim that tens of thousands of the enemy were slain in battle or made prisoner. Some were used as forced labor (*karashim*); a camp inhabited by these laborers, probably engaged in quarrying, is recorded on the route between Agade and Susa.

Sargon reigned fifty-six years and was succeeded by his son Rimush, who was murdered in a palace conspiracy after nine years; his successor was Manishtushu ("who is with him"), probably his twin brother. Both extended the empire, campaigning in Iran as far as Marhashi and Sherihum, mounting expeditions to the south and west, and controlling Assur and Nineveh to the north. Manishtushu's son Naram-Sin, who succeeded in 2254 B.C.E., left inscriptions recording his campaigns as far north as Pir Hussein in southeast Turkey. All three rulers had to contend with both internal revolts and raids by tribes along their borders. A fine stele of Naram-Sin depicts his victory over the Lullubi, a mountain tribe to the northeast. Rebellions were ruthlessly put down—Rimush records the death or capture of around 50,000 people from one city alone.

Naram-Sin's defeat of nine hostile kings in a series of battles won him the gratitude not only of the citizens of Agade but even, he claimed, of the gods, who invited him to become the patron deity of Agade. His elevation to divine status then allowed Naram-Sin to lay claim to the temple lands and revenues of the city and thence of the empire it controlled. Traditionalist outrage at this impiety was later rationalized in the story of the *Curse of Agade.*

According to this tale, Ishtar (Inanna) gained permission from Enlil to take up residence in Agade as the city deity, bringing wealth, prosperity, and joy. Later, however, Enlil took offense at some action of Naram-Sin and withdrew his favor. Naram-Sin attempted unsuccessfully to change the god's mind, and in his anger and despair sacked Enlil's temple, the Ekur ("He set spades against its roots. . . . He put axes against its top . . ."—Electronic Text Corpus of Sumerian Literature 2002 "The Cursing of Agade"), demolishing the buildings and carrying off the temple treasures to Agade. The gods fled the city; Enlil brought down the savage hordes of the Guti upon it, and it was utterly destroyed.

There is no truth in this story—Naram-Sin made pious offerings at the Ekur, where he was held in honor long after his death; he refurbished the temple, at great expense, a work completed by his successor, Shar-Kali-Sharri, who ruled for quarter of a century before the Guti made a significant impact on Akkadian affairs.

The empire began to fall apart under this king. Amorite and Gutian raiders proved troublesome, and after his death there was a period of three years' anarchy in which four rulers claimed the throne. The last Akkadian kings, Dudu and Shu-durul, controlled a much-reduced realm. The city-states of Sumer broke away from the empire during the period of anarchy: These included Uruk, credited in the Sumerian King List (compiled some centuries later) with the kingship of the land for thirty years after the fall of Agade, followed by 124 (or 91) years when the Guti were supposedly in control.

The chronology of this period is not clear. The Guti, probably hill tribes from the east, had probably menaced the settled lands for a considerable time. Pastoralists without permanent settlements, they would have been hard to defeat outright. However, the period when they ruled in Mesopotamia was probably relatively short, around thirty to seventy years, and they dominated only a part of the region—Lagash, for instance, seems to have been totally unaffected by them.

These years saw a revival in the south. Dynasties were reestablished or reemerged, their ideology consciously recalling earlier days when each city was independent and existed as the estate of its tutelary deity. Best documented is the state of Lagash, with its capital at Girsu. Its pious king, Gudea, is well known from the many fine diorite statues that he dedicated in its temples, of which he rebuilt fifteen. On the temple of the city's god, Ningirsu, Gudea lavished foreign imported materials such as cedarwood, silver, and carnelian—an indication that trade still flourished after the fall of the Akkadian dynasty. Complete reversion to the status quo of more than a century earlier, with numerous independent city-states, is unlikely to have occurred. Gudea is recorded as having campaigned against Elam, where a native dynasty had replaced the Akkadian governors, and Lagash may also have influenced Ur,

One of the many diorite statues dedicated by Gudea, King of Lagash 2142-2122 B.C.E. (Zev Radovan/Land of the Bible Picture Archive)

where King Ur-Bau installed an entu-priestess. Utu-hegal of Uruk, Gudea's partial contemporary, appointed Ur-Nammu, probably his son or brother, as governor of Ur, which must therefore have been under Uruk's control—and around 2112 B.C.E., seven years after Utu-hegal drove out the Guti, Ur-Nammu succeeded him and began to forge a new empire, that of the Third Dynasty of Ur (Ur III).

The Third Dynasty of Ur

Soon after his accession as king of Uruk, Ur-Nammu defeated Lagash, taking the title "King of Sumer and Akkad," and within a few years he had gained full control of the south. He devoted much time and effort to reestablishing stability, particularly by restoring and building canals for irrigation. In the eighteenth year of his reign he died in battle against the Guti. His son Shulgi led several campaigns to avenge his father but for the first twenty years of his reign devoted himself largely to domestic matters, consolidating the empire and establishing its bureaucracy. He then instituted major reforms, creating a standing army and reorganizing the economic system, greatly increasing royal power, and decreasing the role of the priesthood. Thereafter he embarked on a series of campaigns that continued throughout the rest of his long reign, mostly in the east and northeast where groups like the Hurrians threatened important trade routes. He extended the lands under Sumerian control as far as Assur and Susa. International diplomacy and dynastic marriages also consolidated his dominions.

The result was an empire smaller in extent than that earlier under Akkadian control or influence but far more close-knit. The Ur III rulers expressed their authority in traditional terms, the king controlling city-states on behalf of the gods and standing between them and the people of the land—the accepted role of the city-state's ruler writ large, the whole empire being the estate administered by the king. The relationship between the ruler and the gods became closer when Shulgi proclaimed himself a god. Temples to his cult were maintained in every city. The Ur III dynasty traced a family relationship to the First Dynasty of Uruk, whose deeds they glorified by committing to writing the traditional stories of Gilgamesh and his forebears. Uruk was the spiritual home of the dynasty, and Ur was their capital. Their close involvement with the goddess Inanna, patron of Uruk, was particularly emphasized by Shulgi, who performed the traditional sacred marriage with the goddess.

The state created by Ur-Nammu and Shulgi was highly bureaucratic. Sumer and Akkad formed its core, divided into around twenty provinces, centered on the traditional city-states. These were often ruled by members of each city's original royal house or elite—now governors (*ensis*) instead of independent rulers, charged with supervising the running of the temple establishments and personnel, still the state's main source of revenue. To ensure their loyalty and cooperation, each province also had a military governor (*shagina*) appointed by the king and coming from outside—either from the royal extended family or from a foreign land. His role was not only to keep an eye on the civil gover-

The ziggurat of Inanna erected at Uruk by the founder of the Ur III dynasty, Ur-Nammu. (Time Life Pictures/Getty Images)

nor but also to oversee both the army and crown land with its dependents and employees.

The conquered lands east of the core region were also formally included within the state. These were ruled by military governors who reported to the *sukkalmah* (grand chancellor), the most powerful individual after the king. Among these was a province governed from Assur. Outside the empire were other smaller states that retained their independence but enjoyed a close relationship with the Ur III state—these included Mari, Ebla, Tuttul, and Byblos.

Tributes of livestock, grain, and manufactured goods were accumulated at Puzrish-Dagan (Drehem) near Nippur and at Dusabara; from these major depots they were distributed to the temples in Nippur, Ur, and Uruk, or issued as supplies to officials and members of the royal household and sent to the capital, Ur.

Ur-Nammu and his successors undertook extensive restoration and new building in the traditional religious centers. Ur received particular attention. The buildings constructed in its sacred precinct included a magnificent royal mausoleum, the *E-nun-mah* (probably the sacred treasury), and the *giparu*, a palatial structure that incorporated the residence of the entu-priestess of Nanna (a position still held by a royal daughter) and the parallel residence of Nanna's consort,

Ningal. But the chief glory of the temenos was the ziggurat to Nanna erected by Ur-Nammu (see photo p. 201). He also built ziggurats at other major centers—to Enlil in the hallowed city of Nippur, to Inanna at the dynastic capital Uruk, and to Enki in the ancient city of Eridu, now abandoned except as a holy place. At Eridu, the Ur III kings refurbished and restored the sacred buildings.

The Ur III state was theological in principle, giving the king control over all of the temple estates, their revenues, produce, industries, and personnel. But it was also secular in its reach, controlling many aspects of citizens' lives with a bureaucracy that probably became increasingly stifling. Shulgi promulgated one of the first law codes, laying down rules of conduct and punishments for crime: Apart from a few very serious crimes like murder, which were capital offences, crimes generally attracted financial penalties, a more civilized approach than the many "eye-for-an-eye"-style punishments laid down in the later and more famous code of Hammurabi.

Labor gangs organized by the state undertook public works, constructing and maintaining roads and canals for irrigation and communications. The state also regularized many aspects of life, from the calendar and the use of Sumerian as the language of officialdom to the standardization of weights and measures. Foreign trade, which expanded, was state controlled, merchants being issued with goods for exchange and returning appropriate quantities of foreign goods at the end of their expeditions, although they were also allowed to trade on their own account. Industry was generally in the hands of the authorities, particularly the all-important production of textiles, in which thousands of women and young people were employed. Shulgi founded a number of huge industrial establishments producing particular commodities under government supervision.

Such a bureaucratic state required many scribes to deal with its administration—which was so meticulous that the death of a single sheep was recorded in three separate places in the archives. To ensure an adequate number of literate individuals Shulgi founded schools at Ur and Nippur where scribes were trained in all necessary skills, including reading, writing, and mathematics, along with more specific knowledge such as accounting procedures and the new format devised by Shulgi for archival documents. Excellent communications were also essential to the smooth running of the state. Shulgi built and maintained roads with regular caravanserais, in which official travelers might stay, and employed a network of messengers.

Shulgi's sons, Amar-Sin and Shu-Sin, continued his military activities, but already the tide was turning. Outsiders were proving troublesome in border regions, particularly in the west where the pastoral and seminomadic Amorites raided settled areas. Even as early as year 35 of Shulgi, the problem was becoming so grave that Shulgi constructed a wall to keep them out, and Shu-Sin built another, called "Fender-off of Tidnum," 200 kilometers long, stretching between the Tigris and Euphrates across the northern edge of the alluvial plain. Shu-Sin also campaigned against the Amorites, action that by now was more defensive than offensive. The situation deteriorated further under his son, Ibbi-Sin. As central control weakened and defenses became less effective, some regions broke away. The decline of Ur III control of even the core provinces can be traced in the administrative documents issued under Ibbi-Sin, which failed to appear in cities as they seceded—Eshnunna in Ibbi-Sin's year 2, Susa in year 3, Lagash in year 5, Umma in year 6, and Nippur in year 7. Natural disasters may have played an important part in the decline of the empire, including major floods and drought, reducing pasturage and therefore putting pressure on the pastoral peoples of the west, notably the Amorites. Amorite attacks disrupted communications and the movement of goods, especially food. Ur was completely dependent upon the efficient maintenance of bureaucracy and communications for essential supplies: Soaring inflation and attendant famine are painfully chronicled in the last days of the city. Ur's plight was exacerbated by Ishbi-erra, governor of Isin, who failed to deliver essential supplies, pleading a problem with transport shipping. When the Ur III dynasty fell in 2004 B.C.E. to an attack by the combined forces of Guti and Elamites (who had thrown off the Ur III yoke after years of hostilities), it was Ishbi-erra who was the first to reap the benefit, soon creating his own state centered on Isin: This was to become one of the key players in the following period.

"The very foundation of Sumer was torn out" (Electronic Text Corpus of Sumerian Literature 2002 "Sumerian King List," lines ca. 353–354).

THE RISE OF BABYLON (CA. 2000–1600 B.C.E.)

Isin and Larsa

The Ur III Empire broke up into a number of autonomous smaller states, controlling and fighting over other ancient cities. Initially the most important was Isin, whose lands stretched from Mashkan Shapir and Kazallu in the north to Uruk, Eridu, and other southern cities. These included, crucially, Nippur, which gave Isin nominal legitimacy as the successor of Ur III, theoretically appointed by the gods as the ruling state of Sumer. Ishbi-Erra of Isin regained control of Ur and eventually defeated the Elamites, avenging Ur's fall. He restored many of the buildings of Ur and other cities and deliberately followed many of the practices and norms of the Ur III Empire. A number of kings in this period have left law codes, following the earlier example of Shulgi, and consciously upholding and imitating ancient values. Sumerian continued to be the language of scholarship but was no longer spoken; Akkadian, in contrast, was used for international communication from Anatolia to Elam.

But times were changing. Whereas king and temple had generally controlled the state economically in earlier times, private enterprise now began to flourish, the government receiving taxes from the success of privately financed ventures rather than the profits of publicly controlled enterprises. The temple authorities, while still of great importance, now gave way politically to the king, who had full control of the state's administration, as is vividly shown in a number of surviving archives. Frequent records of the construction or restoration of city walls reflect the instability of the times and the need for constant defense. No ruler was strong enough to control all of southern Mesopotamia.

Many of the independent kingdoms, here and further west, had rulers with Amorite names, now clearly integrated into Mesopotamian society, while in northern Mesopotamia many of the dynasties were Hurrian. These successor states included Susa, Assur, Eshnunna, Yamhad, and, most significantly, Larsa, which by the reign of Lipit-Ishtar of Isin had thrown off Isin's authority and was challenging Isin's primacy.

Gungunum of Larsa claimed descent from earlier kings of the city, but his forebears were in reality Amorite sheikhs. He and his father had probably been governors of Isin's province of Lagash, which included Larsa. Under Gungunum, Larsa probably came to control Nippur, Susa, and perhaps Uruk, and in 1925 seized Ur from Isin, thereby gaining control of the still lucrative Gulf trade, especially in copper, now conducted through the trading entrepôt of Dilmun. Political changes did not affect other, traditional aspects of life. For example, Ibbi-Sin's daughter remained entu-priestess of Nanna at Ur until her death, when she was replaced by Ishbi-Erra's daughter; similarly the Isin incumbent continued in office when Larsa took Ur. Maintenance of canals and irrigation works were crucially important for the well-being of the state. Neglect of irrigation works outside Isin's heartland probably contributed to the decline of Isin's power, and when Sumu-El of Larsa was thought to be neglecting his duties in this field, he was overthrown in a popular revolt and replaced by a commoner, Nur-Adad.

For several centuries, political power was very volatile. States expanded and contracted and from time to time new ones gained a foothold. Uruk briefly controlled Nippur and under Sinkashid (an Amorite) for a while held the balance of power between Isin and Larsa through its control of the middle Euphrates. In 1834 B.C.E., Kudur-Mabuk, Amorite ruler of Emutbal on the eastern flank of Mesopotamia, gained control of Larsa, giving the throne to his son Warad-Sin who reigned until 1823 when he was succeeded by his brother, Rim-Sin I. Their sister became entu-priestess in Ur. The family embarked on an ambitious restoration program in the southern cities, including Ur and Nippur. Rim-Sin defeated Uruk, Isin, Rapiqum, and Babylon, along with Sutu nomads from the west, in 1804 and conquered Isin in 1794, a triumph that he celebrated in his annual year-names throughout the remaining thirty-one years of his reign; he was to dominate the south until 1763.

Elam, freed of Sumerian domination, was entering a period of expansion and affluence. Its control of a major source of the important and scarce metal, tin, must have played a substantial part in its prosperity and power. Until defeated by Hammurabi in the eighteenth century B.C.E. it was a major player in Mesopotamian politics, closely involved with the states on its borders, particularly Eshnunna, which enjoyed considerable power through its control of trade routes into the Iranian plateau. Competing for power with Der and Kish, Eshnunna's territories fluctuated in extent. It expanded in the later nineteenth century B.C.E. under Ipiq-Adad II, coming into conflict with neighboring Babylon, Assur, and Larsa. Under his successor, Eshnunna gained control of the middle regions as far east as Mari and as far north as the source of the Khabur, conquering Assur, capital of the small city-state of Assur (Assyria).

Babylon, seen here in a nineteenth-century C.E. engraving, became the capital of Babylonia under Hammurabi and remained the principal city of the region until replaced by the Seleucid capital Seleucia-on-the-Tigris in the fourth century B.C.E. (Ridpath, John Clark, *Ridpath's History of the World*, 1901)

Assur city was easily defensible and was strategically situated to control trade and communications along the Tigris and the eastern foothills, making it a major trade center. But its cultivable land was limited, so it was unsuitable as the capital of a major territorial state: When Assur expanded, its capital was moved elsewhere. A major town in the north that had been controlled by both Akkadian and Ur III governors, Assur became the focus of a growing state after the fall of Ur. Early in the nineteenth century B.C.E., its king Ilushuma probably began Assur's role as a major trading entrepôt when he established favorable free-trade conditions to attract merchants from the south. A large archive of commercial documents preserved at Kanesh (modern Kultepe) in Anatolia gives a detailed insight into Assur's trade and other aspects of life in the nineteenth century B.C.E. Smaller archives show that Assur was not alone—other major trading centers included Emar, Mari, Carchemish, Sippar, and Babylon. Assur's trade with Anatolia flourished until around 1820 B.C.E. when Kanesh was sacked; it was briefly revived in the eighteenth century, under Shamshi-Adad.

Shamshi-Adad and Assur

Shamshi-Adad's father was apparently an Amorite sheikh operating in the town of Terqa north of Mari, though the region of Ekallatum (north of Assur) may have been their ancestral kingdom. Shamshi-Adad succeeded him around 1836, but around 1818 an invasion by Eshnunna forced him to flee to Babylon. Within a few years he had regained control of Ekallatum and expelled the Eshnunnites from Assur. Other areas followed, including Mari, Karana, Nineveh, parts of Elam and the Zagros region, and as far south as Rapiqum. Shamshi-Adad was a fine example of the charismatic ruler of the age, the force of his personality enabling him to carve out a state that disintegrated shortly after his death. Under him all northern Mesopotamia was united into a single state, with its capital at Shubat-Enlil (probably modern Tell Leilan) and subsidiary centers at Ekallatum and Mari, ruled respectively by the king's sons, the energetic Ishme-Dagan and his indolent and spineless brother, Yasmah-Addu. These subsidiary centers controlled the surrounding regions, Yasmah-Addu's being known as "the Banks of the Euphrates." The kingdom's influence extended as far as the Mediterranean, separated from it by a series of well-disposed states, including Qatna, whose ruler's daughter was married to Yasmah-Addu. While Yasmah-Addu achieved little but controlled a relatively peaceful area, Ishme-Dagan spent much of his viceroyalty fighting the Elamites and Eshnunna. The Elamites found many opportunities to intervene in regional affairs, for example in 1771 (after the death of Shamshi-Adad) when they combined forces with Eshnunna successfully to invade Assur, capturing Shubat-Enlil and penetrating into Syria but failing to establish lasting control over the region. At the same time, the king of Yamhad also attacked the crumbling state. His son-in-law, the rightful king of Mari, Zimri-Lim, now regained his throne and began a prosperous reign, details of which are well known from the palace archive preserved when the city was sacked in 1757. Like other lesser rulers of the period, he trod a skillful path between diplomacy and force, making alliances with neighboring rulers, often cemented by marriage with one of his daughters, and counteracting raids with his armies.

Around 1764 the Elamites attacked again, capturing Eshnunna and Shubat-Enlil, although again their occupation was short-lived. Ishme-Dagan, still tenuously maintaining his hold on the remnants of Assur, took refuge with Hammurabi in Babylon and probably remained Hammurabi's vassal for the rest of his reign. Defeating the Elamites and their allies encouraged Hammurabi to make his own bid for power.

Hammurabi and Babylon

Babylon had begun to grow in importance early in the millennium when a major westward shift in the course of the Euphrates deprived traditionally powerful states farther east of its waters. Babylon's First Dynasty, founded in 1894 by Sumu-abum, was like many others an Amorite royal house. Babylon began to play a major role in the region under Hammurabi's father, Sin-muballit,

Stela showing King Hammurabi, creator of the Babylonian empire. (Zev Radovan/Land of the Bible Picture Archive)

who spent much of his reign strengthening the kingdom's defensive city walls and who joined a coalition with Isin, Uruk, and others against Rim-Sin of Larsa, the most powerful ruler at that time. Babylon now controlled a small territory that included Sippar, Dilbat, and Kish. Hammurabi came to the Babylonian throne in 1792 and in 1787 was able to seize Uruk and Isin from Larsa's domains. For the next twenty years or so he quietly ruled Babylon, initially probably as a vassal of Shamshi-Adad. But by 1764 he had gained enough strength, in collaboration with others including Mari, to defeat Elam and its allies, and in 1763 he was able to challenge and defeat Rim-Sin. He conquered Eshnunna in 1762, completing its destruction in 1755 by diverting the Diyala to flood the city, an irreversible disaster. Hammurabi then turned on his longtime ally, Mari, possibly following the death of Zimri-Lim. Defeating Mari in 1759, over the following two years he stripped its palace bare and then set fire to it. Hammurabi now controlled a substantial empire, stretching from Nineveh in the north to Mari in the west and encompassing all of Babylonia. Hammurabi was a strong ruler who took most of the business of government into his own hands, delegating little. His conquests coupled with major programs of land reclamation and irrigation gave him control of substantial lands, which he exploited as a source of raw materials and manufactured goods and issued as landholdings in payment to public servants.

Hammurabi was succeeded by his son Samsu-iluna, who experienced revived difficulties with the south. Eshnunna rebelled and was crushed; Rim-Sin II of Larsa also revolted, occupying Nippur in 1742, although he was defeated the following year. Samsu-iluna's tactics involved diverting the Euphrates to cut off Nippur. This spelled economic ruin in an area already suffering decline due to salination. Within eighty years of Hammurabi's death, the state of Babylon was reduced to the region around the city that had been controlled by Hammurabi's predecessors. Larsa, Ur, and Uruk were deserted by 1738, Nippur and Isin by 1720, their populations often moving north to towns like Kish. Other southern cities were also abandoned or reduced to small settlements of little importance, ruled by the First Dynasty of Sealand. At the same time the towns of the north were also experiencing problems, possibly because of a succession of bad harvests. As frequently happened when climatic and environmental conditions deteriorated, the nomads of the periphery began to put pressure on settled lands. But it was from the Hittites, a developing kingdom in Anatolia, that Hammurabi's dynasty received its deathblow, when in 1595 they sacked the city of Babylon.

SHIFTING POWER BLOCS (CA. 1600–1150 B.C.E.)

Sealand and the Early Kassites

During the reign of King Samsu-iluna cracks had begun to appear in the Babylonian Empire. A new dynasty of Sealand gained control of the region from Nippur southward, a land that was now mainly marsh; its founder, Iluma-ilum, consciously revived Sumerian traditions. After the Hittites sacked Babylon, Sealand briefly gained control of the city itself. Little is known of the

A Kassite chalcedony cylinder seal from Babylonia. It bears a heraldic scene of two winged, rampant bulls resting their forelegs upon a small tree with a round crown belonged to an official of the Kassite king Burnaburiash, 1359–1333 B.C.E. (Zev Radovan/Land of the Bible Picture Archive)

dynasty but during its rule trade links between Babylonia and the Gulf were severed.

Samsu-iluna also came into conflict with the Kassites, who were known in Babylonia by around 1770. The Kassites' origins are unknown; currently they are thought to have come from the Zagros region, although an origin in the northwest was formerly favored. Generally they were nomads, but over the years many settled peacefully in Babylonia where they were employed as mercenaries and agricultural laborers.

According to the Babylonian Chronicle, the Kassite dynasty reigned for 576 years and 9 months; this figure takes the dynasty back to the time of Samsu-iluna. Gandash, the traditional founder, may have ruled a small Kassite kingdom on the middle Euphrates established around this time. Details of the dynasty's rise in importance over the following centuries are completely unknown, but around 1570 the Kassite king Agum II kakrime was sufficiently powerful to wrest control of Babylon from the Sealand dynasty. By this time the Kassites were probably thoroughly integrated into Babylonian society. Although they had their own gods, they paid devout attention to the Babylonian pantheon, and it was during their reign that Marduk, patron god of Babylon, gained the preeminent position of king of the gods. The Kassites took pains to preserve and encourage Babylonian traditions, restoring or building temples and other monuments and reinforcing Babylonian customs and practices.

Around 1475, Ea-gamil, king of Sealand, fled to Elam, where a little-known dynasty, the Kidinuids, ruled for about a century. Shortly afterward Ulamburiash, brother of the Kassite king Kashtiliash III, conquered Sealand, unifying the whole of southern Mesopotamia under Kassite rule. The conquest of the south reopened connections with the trade routes of the Gulf, and under the Kassites Dilmun (Bahrein) came under direct Babylonian control. Nearly a century later, Kurigalzu I constructed a fortress, Dur-Kurigalzu (modern Aqar Quf), to protect another important trade route that led east across the Iranian plateau to Afghanistan, source since distant antiquity of lapis lazuli, which now figured prominently among the diplomatic gifts sent to Egyptian kings who reciprocated with gold.

Although the Kassite realm seems to have enjoyed peace and prosperity, very little is known of the political history of the region beyond the names of the rulers and occasionally their achievements. The earliest known from contemporary inscriptions was Kara-indash, who ruled around 1415. He signed a treaty with Ashur-bel-nisheshu of Assyria establishing the line of their shared border, an action that had also been taken by an earlier Kassite ruler, Burnaburiash I. Thereafter Babylon began to play a more important role in the wider world. Kara-indash's son, Kadashman-harbe, had considerable trouble with nomads on his western border and strengthened a series of fortresses in the Syrian Desert as defense against them. At this time, around 1400, a new dynasty, the Igihalkids, gained control of Elam. Good relations between Elam and Babylonia are implied by successive marriage ties between their royal houses.

Assyria and Mitanni

Among the many peoples of northern Mesopotamia were the Hurrians, known from texts but impossible to identify in the archaeological record. They were concentrated on the northern and eastern margins, and by the early second millennium B.C.E. many of the small states of the north were ruled by Hurrian dynasties.

In the later seventeenth century B.C.E. when Babylonia was in decline, a larger Hurrian state began to develop on the north Mesopotamian plain, possibly coalescing as a response to aggressive moves by the Hittites farther to the west. By around 1500 this was becoming a major power, a state known as Mitanni, which came to control a huge swathe of territory from eastern Anatolia and the northern Levant through northern Mesopotamia to east of the Tigris. Assyria was swallowed up and for many years remained under Mitanni rule. Some linguistic evidence was formerly taken to indicate that Mitanni was ruled by an Indo-European-speaking elite, but this theory has now largely been superseded.

Glimpses of the early Mitanni state come from various sources. An inscription written around 1480 implies that Alalah in the northern Levant was a vassal of Mitanni by this time. The Egyptians were now seeking to control the Levant; Mitanni was the major power with which they came into conflict in the north. Thutmose I, Thutmose III, and Amenhotep II campaigned in this region,

A quartz cylinder seal, a product of the workshops of one of the principal Hurrian centers of the Mitanni Empire. Combined in this seal are elements from Egypt (the sphinx and the Hathor heads), from Mesopotamia (the master-of-animals motif and the winged disc), and from Anatolia (the double-headed creature). (Zev Radovan/Land of the Bible Picture Archive)

recording the defeats they inflicted and setting up stelae to mark their farthest successes. For example, around 1447 Thutmose III defeated Mitanni forces in a major battle near Aleppo and ravaged lands on both banks of the Euphrates. An embassy was sent from Babylon to congratulate him on his victory.

The Assyrian king Ashur-nadin-ahhe I also sent an embassy to Thutmose III. Possibly in revenge for this action, the Mitanni king Saushtatar, who flourished around 1430, sacked Assur, carrying off a gold and silver door from Ashur's temple to the Mitanni capital, Washshukanni (a city that has yet to be identified). Saushtatar extended the Mitanni dominions to include the region of Nuzi and Arrapha east of the Tigris and the kingdom of Kizzuwatna in southeast Anatolia. Kizzuwatna later made a treaty with the Hittites that reneged on its allegiance to Mitanni.

This period is brought more sharply into focus by the increase in surviving documents, particularly from Egypt. Letters survive from the reigns of the pharaohs Amenhotep III and his son Akhenaten (fourteenth century B.C.E.) in the latter's capital, Akhetaten (modern Amarna). This famous archive, the "Amarna letters," contains diplomatic correspondence between contemporary rulers, discussing diplomatic gifts and exchanges of courtesies, along with the sealing of ties by marriage. For instance, a daughter of the Kassite king Kurigalzu I married Amenhotep III. Some years later his son declined to send a princess to Egypt, on the grounds that he knew nothing of the current fate of his sister. The kings address each other as "brother," implying that they accorded each other equal status. The letters are mostly written in the cuneiform script and in the Babylonian Akkadian language, the lingua franca of the Near East at that time, used for example in letters to Egypt from its vassals in the Levant. By the end of the fifteenth century, the Egyptian pharaohs decided that their interests in the Levant would best be served by peaceful relations with Mitanni, with whom they shared a common enemy in the Hittites. According to the Amarna letters Thutmose IV married a daughter of Artatama I of Mitanni, and the latter's son Shuttarna sent his daughter as bride to Amenhotep III, who also married Shuttarna's granddaughter Tatuhepa. By now, however, cracks were appearing in the Mitanni kingdom. Shuttarna's heir was murdered by conspirators who enthroned his brother Tushratta, probably still a minor, as their puppet. Eventually Tushratta was able to rid himself of them and restore Mitanni's good relations with Egypt. His authority was disputed by supporters of a rival claimant, his brother Artatama II, who had the backing of the Hittites: Civil war ensued. Eventually the Hittite king, Suppiluliumas I, gained control of all the Mitanni lands in the west and plundered Washshukanni, ruling through his son-in-law Shattiwaza, a son of Tushratta who had taken refuge at the Hittite court.

At the same time, Assyria, for many years under Mitanni domination, took the opportunity to seize control of some of the eastern Mitanni territory, led by its strong and enterprising king, Ashur-uballit I. To underline its newly won independence, Assyria sent an embassy to Akhenaten. Initially a small state centered around Assur, Arbela, and Nineveh (the Assyrian heartland), Assyria under Ashur-uballit came also to control a considerable area to the north and east. A fragment of the old Mitanni state remained, a temporary buffer between the rising powers of the Hittites and the Assyrians and at the mercy of both.

Ashur-uballit also extended his influence southward by concluding a treaty with Babylonia, sealed by marrying his daughter to the Kassite king Burnaburiash II. When the son of the marriage, Karahardash, succeeded to the Babylonian throne, he was deposed and killed by the army. Ashur-uballit swiftly intervened, deposing the usurper, Nazi-bugash, and installing his own candidate, Kurigalzu II (another son of Burnaburiash), in place of his murdered grandson. Kurigalzu had a successful military career; a later chronicle asserts that he defeated Elam, Assyria, and Sealand, and he himself claimed to have conquered Susa, Elam, and Marhashi. During the Mitanni period Babylonia had encroached on Assyrian terrritory and several boundary engagements had been fought. After a battle between Kurigalzu and Ashur-uballit, the border was redrawn south of the Lower Zab.

Assyria, Babylonia, and Elam

The Egyptians and their rivals, the Hittites, signed a peace treaty around 1259. Babylonia and initially Assyria managed to enjoy good relations with both. However, Ashur-uballit's successors, Adad-nirari I and Shalmaneser I, further extended the Assyrian realms, sacking Washshukanni and taking control of the

A *Kudurru* (boundary stone) recording a grant of land from the Kassite king Melishipak (1186–1172 B.C.E.) to his son Marduk-apla-iddina. The symbols, which represent gods, include Marduk's dragon, the sun god Shamash, the moon god Sin and the planet Venus representing Ishtar. (Gianni Dagli Orti/Corbis)

tattered remnant of Mitanni. This brought them into direct conflict with the Hittites, whom Shalmaneser resoundingly defeated, taking, according to his claims, 14,400 prisoners. Shalmaneser also won victories in Urartu to the north (a region whose highland terrain made it virtually impossible actually to conquer) and fought off many nomad raids.

The next Assyrian king, Tukulti-Ninurta I, built extensively at Assur but also founded a new capital city, Kar-Tukulti-Ninurta, just to its north. He campaigned on all fronts, further extending the Assyrian Empire, now one of the major powers of the Near East. In the west he again defeated the Hittites, reputedly taking 28,800 prisoners. He also reopened the border dispute with Babylonia. The Babylonian king, Kashtiliash IV, misjudging his opponent's strength, invaded Assyria. Tukulti-Ninurta responded by conquering Babylonia in 1225, deposing Kashtiliash and initially taking the throne himself. The following year he installed a puppet king, Enlil-nadin-shumi.

Good relations had been maintained throughout the fourteenth and thirteenth centuries between the royal houses of Elam and Babylon, while both were often hostile to Assyria. In support of his ally, the Elamite king Kidin-Hutran III invaded Babylonia in 1224, capturing Nippur and deposing Enlil-nadin-shumi. Some years later he again invaded Babylonia and overthrew another Assyrian appointee. Tukulti-Ninurta was unable to respond because of domestic problems, and in 1207 he was assassinated.

Kashtiliash's son regained control of Babylonia, restoring the Kassite line and later defeating Assyria. Kidin-Hutran III of Elam died a few years later, and with him the Igihalkid dynasty. The new dynasty, the Shutrukids, also intermarried with the Kassite royal family. Conflict with Assyria was renewed when its king Ashur-dan I mounted a raid after the death of the Babylonian king Marduk-apla-iddina I in 1158. Babylonian relations with Elam now also turned sour. Shutruk-Nahhunte, king of Elam and grandson of the previous Kassite king, Melishipak, decided that he ought to be the next Babylonian king. When his "sincere proposal" was rejected, he invaded Babylonia, overthrew the new Kassite king Zababa-shuma-iddina, and sacked many Babylonian cities, including Babylon, carrying off a huge amount of booty, including precious objects like Hammurabi's law code. He installed his son Kutir-Nahhunte as ruler of Babylonia. Despite this, a Kassite king, Enlil-nadin-ahhe, managed still to rule Babylonia for three years. In 1155, however, Kutir-

The palace of Ashurnasirpal II (883-859 B.C.E.) at Kalhu was built with the wealth accumulated through aggressive military campaigns and the resultant plunder and extraction of tribute from the vanquished. It was inaugurated with a ten-day banquet at which there were nearly 70,000 guests. (Ridpath, John Clark, *Ridpath's History of the World*, 1901)

Nahhunte again invaded, sacking cities, including Babylon, and carrying off the city's precious image of its patron deity, Marduk. Thus after almost 400 years the Kassite dynasty was finally overthrown.

Kutir-Nahhunte was succeeded by his brother Shilhak-Inshushinak, who gained control of many cities within Babylonia and Assyria, taking advantage of Assyria's decline under the now aged Ashur-Dan, the fall of the Kassites, and their replacement by the much less powerful Second Dynasty of Isin. His son Hutelutush-Inshushinak came under attack by the fourth king of this dynasty, Nebuchadrezzar I, who defeated him. Elamite history at this point descended into obscurity that lasted around 300 years.

ASSYRIA RESURGENT (CA. 1150–780 B.C.E.)

Decline

The twelfth century was a time of international upheaval that saw the decline of some circum-Mediterranean states and the demise of others. Contemporary documents refer to crop failure and famine linked to drier climatic conditions.

The volume of water flowing in the Tigris and Euphrates was reduced and did not begin to rise again until around 950 B.C.E. Archaeological evidence confirms the information revealed in the documentary sources.

Large bands of marauders of diverse and obscure origins, including women and children as well as warriors, roamed the shores of the eastern Mediterranean, attacking anywhere that they could. These Sea Peoples were driven off several times by the Egyptians; some settled in coastal regions, including the group known as the Peleset (Philistines), and others were directly or indirectly responsible for the fall of the Hittites. Mesopotamia was shielded from direct attack by its inland location but suffered significantly from the disruption of its trade and international relations.

The region immediately west of the middle Euphrates had been home for some time to tribes known collectively as Aramaeans (Ahlamu). They spoke Aramaic, a Semitic language, which eventually replaced Akkadian as the lingua franca of the Near East. The Aramaeans were originally seminomadic, depending largely on sheep pastoralism supplemented by trading, but by 1200 B.C.E. some also dwelt in towns. The deteriorating climate drove Aramaean tribal groups into Mesopotamia, raiding and causing substantial destruction. They settled widely and carved out many small principalities, ruled by tribal sheikhs. Had the Aramaean tribes been united they would have been a major and formidable political force; as it was, each tribe acted independently and the Assyrians and Babylonians were sometimes able to secure the alliance of some Aramaean groups against others. By the end of the eleventh century, the disastrous Aramaean raids were largely over, but they had left a legacy of economic and political weakness in Mesopotamia, and Aramaean dominance of the middle Euphrates had cut traditional north-south trade routes.

After the Kassites fell in 1155, the political vacuum in Babylonia had been filled by a southern dynasty, the Second Dynasty of Isin. Under its first three rulers, Babylonia gradually recovered from the disaster of Elamite defeat, driving the Elamites from the eastern regions where they had established themselves. The fourth king, Nebuchadrezzar I, carried the fight into Elamite territory, eventually sacking Susa and recovering the venerated statue of Marduk. Nebuchadrezzar was a vigorous king, campaigning against eastern tribes and the Aramaeans and scrapping with the Assyrians. His youthful successor reigned only four years; he was succeeded by Nebuchadrezzar's brother, Marduk-nadin-ahhe, who made an ill-judged raid into Assyria, attracting defeat at the hands of Assyria's strong king Tiglath-Pileser I. Marduk-nadin-ahhe's reign ended disastrously in its eighteenth year with a severe famine. Thereafter the country went downhill. In the mid-eleventh century the major shrine of Shamash at Sippar was plundered and other cities were sacked. These disasters may be the inspiration behind the magnificent poem "The Epic of Erra" (see chapter 8). A succession of weak kings ruled before the country began to revive in the late tenth century B.C.E.

Assyria enjoyed relative prosperity under a series of rulers beginning with Ashur-dan I (r. 1178–1133). He and his successor successfully fought off Aramaean and Babylonian attacks and expanded Assyrian territory. Tiglath-

Pileser I (Tukulti-apil-esharra), who acceded in 1114, defeated Nebuchadrezzar and Marduk-nadin-ahhe of Babylonia, various Aramaean groups, and the Mushki (Phrygians), and successfully raided Urartu. Assyria controlled a substantial empire under his rule. He was murdered, however, in 1076, and after his death Assyria declined; territory was lost, particular to the Aramaeans, and by 1030 B.C.E. the Assyrians again controlled only their ancestral lands.

Ashurnasirpal II and the Assyrian Revival

Assyrian fortunes revived in the reign of Adad-nirari II (911–891), who began winning back lands lost to Aramaean tribes. He conquered areas to the north and west of the Assyrian heartland, acquiring substantial quantities of booty, and raided Babylonia on several occasions as well as promoting domestic enterprises, notably agriculture. His son, Tukulti-Ninurta II, further extended the realm, but it was his grandson, Ashurnasirpal II, who contributed most to the state's expansion, conducting successful annual campaigns in every direction, particularly to the west, where he defeated a number of Syrian and Levantine states. In 877 Ashurnasirpal "washed his weapons" in the Mediterranean, a traditional victor's gesture.

Initially the Assyrian kings had campaigned to defend their borders and keep open their trade routes, while also acquiring booty and captives. Defeated states had to pay annual tribute: Revolts and failure to honor tribute obligations were savagely dealt with in punitive raids. Ashurnasirpal acquired a reputation for cruelty that led some states to offer allegiance and tribute without previously being attacked. As the size of the empire and the distance from the heartland grew, local rulers tended to be replaced by Assyrian governors who administered the provinces for the Assyrian king. Vast wealth and manpower flowed from conquered states to enrich the Assyrian heartland; these enabled Ashurnasirpal to undertake major projects, in particular the construction of a canal from the Upper Zab river to Kalhu (Nimrud), and the transformation of the latter from a small administrative center into Ashurnasirpal's magnificent new capital city, a project that took fifteen years. To celebrate its founding, Ashurnasirpal held a ten-day banquet for 69,574 guests. Well defended and strategically located, it remained the capital until 707 B.C.E.

In Babylonia, the Dynasty of E had come to power in 978 B.C.E. For a number of years Aramaean raids made it impossible to celebrate the vitally important New Year festival on which the spiritual well-being of the Babylonian state depended. The fifth king, Nabu-shuma-ukin I, was defeated in battle by the Assyrians under Adad-nirari; thereafter, however, a treaty was made in which the kings exchanged daughters as wives and agreed the line of their frontier, inaugurating a peace that lasted for eighty years.

Shalmaneser III and Assyrian Conquests

Nabu-shuma-ukin's grandson, Marduk-zakir-shumi I, was aided by the Assyrian king Shalmaneser III to put down a rebellion. Shalmaneser then made a pious tour of Babylonian shrines, and a relief scene of the two kings

A detail from the relief decoration on the throne of the Assyrian king Shalmaneser III (right) (858–824 B.C.E.) at Kalhu showing him grasping the hand of the Babylonian king Marduk-zakir-shumi (left) (ca. 854–819 B.C.E.). (Gianni Dagli Orti/Corbis)

grasping hands as equals—an unprecedented honor—was carved on Shalmaneser's throne in his new palace ("Fort Shalmaneser") at Kalhu.

Like Ashurnasirpal, Shalmaneser undertook annual campaigns, although he did not always enjoy his father's success. Expeditions against Urartu ended in victories but did little to set back Urartu's growing power. In the first years of his reign Shalmaneser successfully fought the Aramaean state of Bit-Adini, capturing its capital, Til Barsip, where he constructed a fortress as a base for further operations in the west. In 853 he fought a coalition of Levantine states at the battle of Qarqar. Although some states were forced to become Assyrian tributaries, or chose to do so rather than risk further attacks, Shalmaneser's victory was not conclusive. He continued to campaign in the region until 838 when finally he turned his attentions elsewhere, fighting for ten years against Que (Cilicia) and its neighbors in the Taurus region. He also made expeditions into Iran, reaching the land of the Medes.

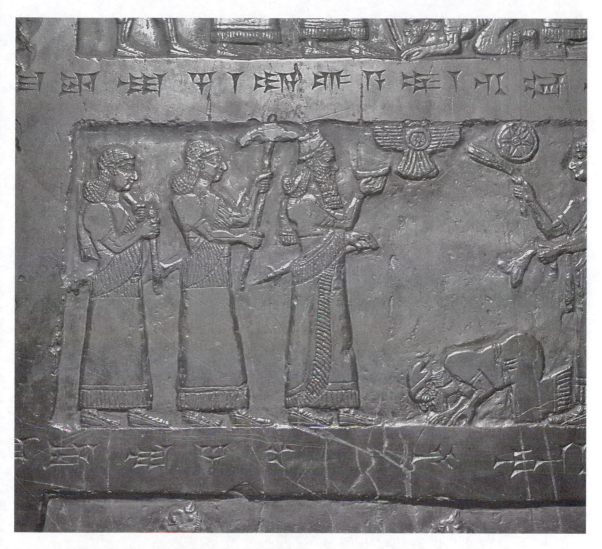

A panel from the "Black Obelisk" of King Shalmaneser III from Kalhu, carved in 825 B.C.E. It shows the king receiving tribute from the kneeling figure of King Jehu of Israel or his representative. (Zev Radovan/Land of the Bible Picture Archive)

Assyria's ally, Babylonia, did not control Sealand in the south. This was home to five Chaldaean tribes, of which Shalmaneser attacked three. The Chaldaeans' origins are uncertain but they were probably not related to the Aramaeans. They raised cattle, cultivated date palms, and engaged in trade; their prosperity is reflected in the enormous booty that Shalmaneser won from them.

Assyria's good relations with Babylonia were strained by events at the end of Shalmaneser's long reign. In 828 the king's son Ashur-danin-apla revolted and was joined by many Assyrian cities. The civil war lasted beyond Shalmaneser's death in 824, when he was succeeded by another son, Shamshi-

Adad V. Marduk-zakir-shumi of Babylon aided the latter but on terms that were humiliating to Assyria. Some time after their joint victory, and after the death of Marduk-zakir-shumi, Shamshi-Adad took his revenge, turning on the Babylonians and capturing first the new king Marduk-balassu-iqbi and later his successor. As a result, Babylonia descended into anarchy.

Adad-nirari III succeeded Shamshi-Adad in 810. His mother, Sammuramat (who appeared in later Greek literature as the cruel queen Semiramis), enjoyed an unusually high profile, her name appearing alongside his in some official records. Little is now known of this queen. Adad-nirari proved a vigorous monarch, campaigning to west, east, and south. The traditional view is that in his reign and that of his successors, powerful provincial governors began to act as independent rulers. A recent reinterpretation of the evidence, however, suggests that the provincial governors, though often exercising hereditary rule, did so as loyal deputies of the Assyrian monarchs. The period, nevertheless, saw a decline. Assyrian prosperity was undermined by revolts and plagues. Aramaean tribal leaders seized the opportunity to expand their territories, and Israel and Judah regained their independence in the early eighth century.

ASSYRIA'S HEYDAY (780–605 B.C.E.)

Tiglath-Pileser and Sargon

After 780 B.C.E. both Babylonia and Assyria were economically in decline. Sealand was controlled by five Chaldaean tribes whose territories varied in size depending on the might and charisma of their individual sheikhs. Several succeeded in seizing power in Babylonia; of these Eriba-Marduk, who ruled around 770, was regarded as the founder of the Chaldaean dynasty, although after his death Babylonia was plunged back into anarchy. North of Assyria, Urartu was becoming a powerful state, gaining control of its smaller southern neighbors. Several unsuccessful engagements showed the Assyrians the wisdom of avoiding direct conflict with Urartu.

In 746 there was an uprising in Kalhu, the Assyrian capital, from which in 744 Tiglath-Pileser III emerged as king. In his inscriptions he was reticent about his parentage, suggesting he was not royal. Tiglath-Pileser rapidly began rebuilding Assyria's empire, attacking and defeating its neighbors in all directions. His success was founded on many public reforms. The army now became a professional body with an elite cavalry core. A network of roads and an efficient messenger service kept the king in control of army and administration. Tiglath-Pileser created numerous small provinces, ruled by governors who were generally eunuchs: a strategy widely used to obtain a cadre of administrators without dynastic ambition. To promote stability and reduce the possibility of organized rebellion Tiglath-Pileser deported conquered peoples on a scale hitherto unknown. The deportees were often kept together as a community, frequently working as farmers or state employees, and were generally well treated.

In the second year of his reign, Tiglath-Pileser faced a powerful coalition of western states under Sarduri II, king of Urartu, and defeated them at the battle of Kummuh (Commagene). In subsequent years he brought many city-states in northwest Syria and Phoenicia under Assyrian control. By the end of his reign, Assyria directly ruled or received tribute from most of the region to its north and west, including parts of the Taurus. Rival states occasionally sought Assyrian backing in their wars and faithful allies of Assyria could expect generous and lasting support.

In 737–736 Tiglath-Pileser moved to the east, gaining control of the central Zagros region and advancing into Media. Returning via Urartu in 735, he besieged its capital, Tushpa. Although he did not capture it, the invasion discouraged further trouble from Urartu. Meanwhile a coalition of Israel, Damascus, and other states was threatening Judah, who appealed to Assyria for help. The Assyrians soon defeated the coalition and seized additional lands in the Levant.

Three years before Tiglath-Pileser came to power, Nabu-nasir (Nabonassar) acceded to the Babylonian throne. He was on friendly terms with Tiglath-Pileser, who aided him in dealing with internal problems. Tiglath-Pileser defeated the perennially hostile but generally fragmented Aramaean tribes in north and east Babylonia and Chaldaean tribes as far south as the Gulf, and followed this by receiving offerings in the temples of Babylon, Kutha, and Borsippa, a royal prerogative. Although he styled himself king of Sumer and Akkad, he did not displace Nabu-nasir or his successors. However, when a Chaldaean sheikh, Nabu-mukin-zeri, usurped the throne, Tiglath-Pileser intervened. After three hard years' campaigning, in 729 Tiglath-Pileser gained control. He played the key role in the New Year festival in 728 and 727 but generally ruled Babylonia through eunuch governors. Most cities in northern Babylonia were content to accept Tiglath-Pileser as king, while the Chaldaean south became a hotbed of dissidence, often actively supported by Elam—a situation that was to continue until the end of the Assyrian Empire.

In 726 Tiglath-Pileser was briefly succeeded by his son, Shalmaneser V, as king of Assyria and Babylonia. Israel seized the opportunity of Tiglath-Pileser's death to rebel, in alliance with Egypt, which had controlled Phoenicia until Tiglath-Pileser conquered the region. The Egyptians were not at this time powerful enough to attack Assyria themselves but actively encouraged revolts among Assyria's vassals. The Assyrians captured the Israelite capital, Samaria, after a three-year siege. Leading Israelites were deported and many people from other parts of the Assyrian Empire were settled in Israel.

In 722 Sargon II gained the Assyrian throne: He may have been the leader of a rebellion in Assur against Shalmaneser's taxes. The name "Sargon" means "legitimate king," a title frequently assumed by usurpers; and his inscriptions give no clue to his parentage. In alliance with Elam, Babylonia seized this opportunity to reassert its independence, led by a Chaldaean, Marduk-apla-iddina (Merodach-Baladan), sheikh of the powerful Bit-Yakin tribe. He succeeded in uniting the disparate factions within Babylonia and acted as a model king, restoring temples, maintaining irrigation systems, and piously following tradition.

Marduk-apla-iddina saw himself as Marduk's representative on Earth, charged with overcoming Babylonia's enemies. Chaldaea was solidly behind him in his revolt against Assyria, the cities of northern Babylonia less so. In

720, the third year of his reign, Sargon marched south against the rebels. Battle was joined between the Elamites and the Assyrians at Der; the Babylonians were not engaged, either because they arrived after the fighting or because their forces were held in reserve. Both sides claimed the victory; but for the next ten years Sargon turned his attention to other fields.

Many cities in the west had risen against Assyria after Shalmaneser's death. Sargon quickly put down this revolt, extending the area under Assyrian control as far south as the Egyptian border. In 712 Egypt encouraged a number of Levantine states to rebel, but after their defeat it established good relations with Assyria, paying it tribute, and Palestine remained quiet for the remainder of Sargon's reign.

Between 717 and 712, Assyria annexed a number of smaller states farther north, including Que, Kummuh, and Carchemish, and entered an alliance with Mida (King Midas of Greek fable) of Mushki (Phrygia). In 716 Urartu replaced the ruler of Mannai in western Iran with its own candidate, Bagdati. Mannai was crucially important as the supplier of horses for the Assyrian army's elite cavalry, so Sargon reacted swiftly, killing Bagdati and installing a sympathetic ruler. The war seesawed between Assyria and Urartu, with successes on both sides; in 714 Sargon sacked the holy city of Musasir in southern Urartu, gaining enormous booty. Cimmerian attacks on its northern borders made Urartu ready to accept a truce with Assyria: This endured for a century.

In 710 Sargon returned his attentions to Babylonia, where he won support among northern cities and was able to drive out Marduk-apla-iddina, who took refuge in his fortress of Dur-Yakin, seizing hostages from major disaffected Babylonian cities. The following year Sargon celebrated the New Year festival as ruler of Babylonia. Marduk-apla-iddina sought Elamite support, but this was no longer forthcoming. In 707 Sargon sacked Dur-Yakin, freeing the hostages but failing to capture Marduk-apla-iddina, who escaped to the marshes of the south (see photo p. 9). More than 100,000 Chaldaeans and Aramaeans were deported to western provinces of the empire, their place being taken by deportees from Kummuh (Commagene). Sargon appointed Assyrian governors throughout Babylonia and the kingdoms were again united.

In 717 Sargon had begun construction of a new capital, Dur Sharrukin ("Sargon's fortress"—modern Khorsabad), near Kalhu, and in 707 the city was officially inaugurated. But in the following year Sargon was killed in battle while campaigning in the northwest. His body was not recovered, a terrible and ill-omened disaster. His successor, Sennacherib, consulted oracles to avert the divine displeasure that this implied; Dur Sharrukin was abandoned and Sennacherib moved the capital to Nineveh.

Nineveh's Glorious Kings

Nineveh was a small but ancient and prestigious city with an excellent strategic location controlling both extensive arable land and a major crossing on the Tigris. Sennacherib rebuilt and enlarged the city, enclosing it with a massive wall and building a long canal and aqueduct to bring water to the city, which boasted orchards, fields, and a royal park. On the citadel he constructed his

Nineveh, located across the Tigris River from modern-day Mosul, was occupied from the Halaf period onward and was made the capital of the Assyrian Empire by Sennacherib (704-681 B.C.E.). (Ridpath, John Clark, *Ridpath's History of the World*, 1901)

"Palace without a Rival." He also sponsored building in many other Assyrian cities.

Sargon's death sparked off revolts in many parts of the empire. Judah and adjacent kingdoms formed a league with Egypt against the Assyrians. Sennacherib savagely put down this revolt, fighting the Egyptians in Philistia, defeating Sidon and Ascalon, and besieging and sacking Lachish in 701—as he vividly depicted on his palace walls (see photo p. 180). He sacked many other towns in Judah and besieged, but failed to take, Jerusalem. Defeated Judah was forced to pay massive tribute.

More problematic was Babylonia, where in early 703 a Babylonian official had seized power, to be quickly supplanted by Babylonia's veteran Chaldaean king, Marduk-apla-iddina, supported by Elam and Aramaean tribes. Sennacherib defeated one combined army at Kutha and marched on Babylon, where he captured Marduk-apla-iddina's family and court but again not the elusive king. Sennacherib pursued him into Chaldaea, seizing eighty towns and taking 208,000 prisoners. He installed a puppet king, replacing him in 700 with his own eldest son, Ashur-nadin-shumi, who proved an effective king under whom Babylonia enjoyed peace and prosperity.

Marduk-apla-iddina disappeared from the records after 700 and presumably died in exile. The Chaldaeans and Elamites still posed a threat, and in

The Assyrian king Ashurbanipal (668-627 B.C.E.) hunting wild asses, a detail from one of the reliefs decorating his palace at Nineveh. (Zev Radovan/Land of the Bible Picture Archive)

694 Sennacherib initiated a new campaign against them. He won substantial victories in Elam; at the same time, however, the Elamites launched an attack in the north, capturing Sippar. Rebels in Babylon handed over prince Ashur-nadin-shumi, who disappeared into Elam where he presumably died. The Babylonian throne was eventually seized by a Chaldaean sheikh, Mushezib-Marduk (Shuzubu). In 691 an enormous combined force of Babylonians and Elamites marched on Assyria. Sennacherib met them at Halule on the Tigris. The Assyrians won an indecisive victory, claiming to have killed 150,000 of their enemies but being forced to retreat afterward. The following year Sennacherib renewed his activities in the south, placing Marduk-apla-iddina's son on the throne of Sealand and campaigning against Babylonia's Arab allies. He then laid siege to Babylon, whose defenders held out for fifteen months, suffering terrible famine and disease. In November 689 they surrendered.

Breaking with the honor and pious respect traditionally accorded to Babylon even in defeat, Sennacherib exacted a terrible revenge, sacking the city and smashing or carrying off the venerated statues of the gods, including Marduk. For this sacrilege Sennacherib paid an awful price: His authority was undermined not only in Babylonia but probably even in Assyria, and after eight years he was murdered in an uprising by several of his sons.

Sennacherib had appointed his youngest son, Esarhaddon, the child of his favorite wife, as his heir, provoking family friction. When Sennacherib was assassinated, Esarhaddon was quick to march on the rebels. Many of their troops defected to him, and he soon defeated his brothers, although it was not until 674, seven years later, that he was able to pursue and execute them. Though implacable in righteous vengeance, Esarhaddon won popular support throughout his realms by his sympathetic and clement treatment of former enemies, including Arabs, Aramaeans, and Elamites. He reversed his father's harsh and impious approach to Babylon, rebuilding the city and its shrines. His fair administration eventually won over most Babylonians. He also encouraged the worship of Babylon's gods, Marduk and Nabu, in Assyria. Under his rule Assyria's trade reached its apogee and its empire its maximum extent.

Esarhaddon dealt effectively with the usual problems with subject and neighboring groups, putting down revolts in the Levant, mixing military action and diplomacy in handling attacks by the Cimmerians and Scythians, raiding on the Iranian plateau, making alliances with several Median princes and with the Aramaean people of Gambulu on the lower Tigris, and successfully intervening in Elamite domestic affairs. He carried the traditional hostility with Egypt onto Egyptian soil, repeatedly campaigning there between 679 and 671, capturing the city of Memphis, driving the pharaoh Taharqo far into the south, and seizing vast amounts of booty. Much of this wealth he spent on rebuilding Babylon.

Esarhaddon's many successes were offset by his perennially poor health and consequent addiction to omens. Although placing a temporary substitute king on the throne to circumvent a predicted threat to the real king was a time-honored Mesopotamian practice, it had actually occurred only a few times in the course of Mesopotamian history; Esarhaddon, however, invoked it six times during the twelve years of his reign. A number of planned military expeditions were canceled or postponed because of the king's bouts of ill health. Aware of his frail hold on life, in 672 Esarhaddon appointed his son Ashurbanipal to succeed him in Assyria and Ashurbanipal's elder brother Shamash-shuma-ukin (whose mother was Babylonian) as heir to Babylonia, obliging his nobles and officials to swear allegiance to the princes. When in 669 the king died on his way to deal with an Egyptian rebellion, the succession took place without a hitch.

Ashurbanipal

Ashurbanipal (see photo p. 20) attributed his peaceful accession to the good-will of Marduk, whose temple in Babylon was now ready for the god's return, in the person of his statue, which was reinstalled with great ceremony. After the New Year festival the following year, Shamash-shuma-ukin took up office as king of Babylon.

Ashurbanipal proved an able administrator as well as a great patron of the arts. He employed many people to trace and copy ancient texts, which he

Bas-relief sculpture from the palace of King Ashurbanipal depicting him hunting and killing lions, on horseback and on foot. (Library of Congress)

amassed in a great library, and constructed a magnificent palace at Nineveh, which is famous for its fine reliefs depicting the king in the royal sport of lion hunting and his many military successes. A year passed before Ashurbanipal was ready to tackle the situation in Egypt, defeating Taharqo, who again fled, leaving the Assyrians in control of Egypt. In 664, Taharqo's successor, Tanutamani, invaded the Assyrian-held lands and defeated Assyria's allies, but fled when a fresh Assyrian army arrived. The Assyrians recaptured Memphis and sacked the venerable city of Thebes, seizing a huge quantity of booty from the temple treasury. Psamtek (Psammetichus), an Egyptian prince in the delta region, was made king of Egypt as Assyria's vassal.

Trouble now appeared on a new front. Esarhaddon had made a treaty with Urtagu, king of Elam, which was honored in Ashurbanipal's early years. In 664, however, Urtagu invaded northern Babylonia, perhaps to divert attention from internal unrest. He was quickly defeated and died shortly afterward, whereupon a revolution took place. The families of both Urtagu and his predecessor Humban-haltash II fled to Assyria, and the throne was taken by an unrelated king (called Te-Umman in the Assyrian records—probably Tepti-Huban-Inshushinak). No further trouble came from Elam for a decade. In the intervening years, the Assyrians campaigned farther north against Mannai and the Medes and concluded alliances with the Scythians and Lydia.

The year 653 saw trouble on two fronts. Te-Umman had repeatedly demanded the return of the refugee Elamite princes, and Ashurbanipal had repeatedly refused. The Elamites made common cause with Gambulu and prepared to attack. Ashurbanipal made a preemptive strike, and the armies met at Til Tuba on the Ulai River. The Assyrians were victorious, many Elamites were slaughtered, and Te-Umman lost his life. A punitive raid on Gambulu was mounted, and Elam was divided between two of Urtagu's family, Humban-Nikash III and Tammaritu I.

Meanwhile, Psamtek used Greek mercenaries to expel the Assyrians from Egypt. The Assyrian army was tied up in the east and could not respond. Events now unfolding in Babylonia were to eclipse Egypt's loss.

Decline and Fall

For sixteen years, Shamash-shuma-ukin had accepted his brother's considerable interference in the affairs of his kingdom. In 652, however, his discontent, particularly with Ashurbanipal's failure adequately to protect Babylonia from attack, came to a head. Obtaining the support of other disaffected or anti-Assyrian groups, including Arabs, Egypt, and many Levantine states, as well, surprisingly, as Humban-Nikash, Ashurbanipal's appointee in Elam, Shamash-shuma-ukin rose in rebellion. Most Chaldaean and the two principal Aramaean tribes were firmly behind him, as were central and northern Babylonia, but Ashurbanipal found support among the cities of southern Babylonia and some Aramaean tribes. The war raged for four years, with successes on both sides, but by 649 Ashurbanipal controlled all of the south. Civil war had broken out in Elam, depriving Shamash-shuma-ukin of one of his principal allies. In 648, after a terrible famine in which cannibalism was attested, Babylon fell and Shamash-shuma-ukin perished. By the end of the year, Ashurbanipal controlled all Babylonia. He now turned his vengeful attentions on Elam, sacking around thirty cities, including Susa. After several savage campaigns, by 645 Elam was firmly subdued.

Babylonia now enjoyed twenty-one years of peace under the rule of Kandalu, a mysterious figure who may have been Ashurbanipal himself. A paucity of records means that little is known of Ashurbanipal and Assyria after 645. It is generally thought that he died in 627, but there is no record that he was still ruling after 630. If he and Kandalu were separate individuals, Ashurbanipal would have been succeeded on the Assyrian throne by his son Ashur-etil-ilani. Kandalu died in 627, and trouble at once broke out. Another son of Ashurbanipal, Sin-shar-ishkun, declared himself Babylonia's king, but his main concern was to wrest the throne of Assyria from Ashur-etil-ilani. This he achieved in 623. Meanwhile in 626 the Babylonian throne had been seized by Nabopolassar (Nabu-apla-usur), who had formerly ruled Sealand. War between Nabopolassar and Sin-shar-ishkun occupied much of the following decade, Sin-shar-ishkun being supported by Egypt, Mannai, and some pro-Assyrian towns in Babylonia, while Nabopolassar enjoyed widespread support in Babylonia and was aided by disaffection among the Assyrian vassal states in the Levant. By 616 Nabopolassar controlled Babylonia and was posing a threat to Assyria itself. In 615 he led an army up the Tigris and besieged Assur but was driven back and himself besieged in Tikrit. A timely invasion by the Medes, now the most powerful people in western Iran, forced the Assyrian army to withdraw. The Medes took Arrapha and the following year sacked Kalhu and captured Assur. The Babylonian army joined them there, and a pact, was made between Nabopolassar and the Median king Cyaxares, later cemented by a royal marriage. Domestic troubles forced both armies to withdraw before they could follow up the Median victories. The Assyrians seized the initiative, marching against Babylonia, but by the following year the tables had turned again and the Medes and Babylonians were laying siege to Nineveh itself. The city fell after three months, during which King Sin-shar-ishkun died.

This was virtually the end for the Assyrian Empire, so recently all-powerful. While most Assyrian cities fell by the end of 612, an Assyrian general, Ashur-uballit II, held out at Harran in the west until forced to abandon the city as the Babylonians advanced. The Egyptians had regained control of Palestine, either opportunistically on their own behalf or in support of the remnants of Assyria. The final blow came in 605 when Babylonia's crown prince Nebuchadrezzar twice defeated the Egyptians, at Carchemish and at Hamath on the Egyptian border, virtually annihilating their army. Assyrian resistance was at an end, and its lands became part of the rising Babylonian Empire.

BABYLONIA TRIUMPHANT (605–539 B.C.E.)

Nebuchadrezzar II

Nebuchadrezzar's campaign was interrupted by news of his father's death, necessitating a brief return to Babylon to be crowned. He then conducted a winter campaign in the Levant—an unusual action. Over the following four years he fought annually in the Levant where his main opponent was Egypt. By 601, Nebuchadrezzar had driven out the Egyptians; they were unable thereafter to confront the Babylonians directly but continued to incite rebellion among the Levantine states. A revolt by Judah in 598–597 was put down; ten years later Judah, encouraged by the mirage of Egyptian support, again revolted and was again defeated. Jerusalem fell after an eighteen-month siege; the temple was destroyed and the city put to the torch. Further unrest occurred the following year. The prophet Jeremiah, who had warned successive kings against contesting the might of Babylonia, claimed that 4,600 people were deported from Judah in the aftermath of these risings (Jeremiah 52:28–30). Tyre also resisted the Babylonians and withstood a thirteen-year siege, falling around 571.

Most of the lands formerly under Assyrian control were now ruled by Babylonia. Nebuchadrezzar conducted other campaigns, gaining control of Cilicia and possibly invading Elam in 596. In 595 he put down an internal revolt; otherwise it appears that he reigned over a peaceful and contented king-

Babylonians under Nebuchadrezzar II breach the walls at Tyre around 571 B.C.E. The prosperous Phoenician trading city was situated on an island off the Levant coast. (Ridpath, John Clark, *Ridpath's History of the World*, 1901)

dom. This impression may be false, however, since the Chronicles for the latter part of his reign are missing and only building records survive. These extol the major works that the king was undertaking in many cities of Babylonia, especially Babylon.

Nebuchadrezzar sponsored a complete refurbishment of the city, rebuilding the shrine and ziggurat of Marduk, constructing palaces, defending the city with magnificent walls, creating the majestic Ishtar Gate (see photo p. 34) and Processional Way, and possibly commissioning the legendary Hanging Gardens.

The Medes had been firm allies of the Babylonians at the start of Nebuchadrezzar's reign, but their increasing power may later have made him uneasy. He constructed two massive defensive walls, ostensibly to keep out the barbarians; these stretched between the Tigris and Euphrates, one just north of Babylon, the other between Sippar and Opis, which became known as the Median Wall.

The Writing on the Wall

Nebuchadrezzar died in 562 after a long and glorious reign. His son and successor, Amel-Marduk (Evil-Merodach in the Bible), was not popular; after two years, he was overthrown by his brother-in-law, Nergal-shar-usur (Neriglissar). After three years Neriglissar also died and was succeeded by his young son in 555 B.C.E. Within at most three months, he, too, was dead, victim of a conspiracy possibly led by a prominent courtier, Bel-shar-usur (Belshazzar). The leaders of the revolt invited Nabu-na'id (Nabonidus), Belshazzar's father, to become king. Although his selection was initially opposed by some cities, within a few months he had been generally accepted.

Nabonidus, by his own account a "nobody," was the son of a provincial governor and Adad-guppi, a devotee and possibly a priestess of the moon god, Sin (Nanna), patron of their hometown, Harran. She was perhaps related to the Assyrian royal house; during the reigns of Nebuchadrezzar and his successors, she and her son had been prominent members of the court. In 555 Nabonidus was already at least fifty and possibly in his sixties; his mother was to die eight years later at the remarkable age of 104.

Nabonidus was a learned man, steeped in Babylonian traditions, and he sought to uphold and revive ancient ways and practices. This frequently led him to investigate ancient structures, often by excavating them, and he and his daughter En-nigaldi-Nanna both created "museums" in which they treasured ancient objects they had uncovered. (See chapter 3.) In 554 Nabonidus appointed his daughter to the ancient office of entu-priestess of Nanna in Ur, which had lapsed many centuries earlier. Nabonidus was deeply religious and placed much reliance on dreams and portents. In a dream early in his reign, he claimed that Marduk or Sin had commanded him to rebuild the temple of Sin in Harran, at that time in territory controlled by the Medes; the god promised Nabonidus that this situation would soon change. Two years later, Cyrus king of the Persians began his revolt against his overlord, Astyages king of the Medes, and by 550 Cyrus was king of both Medes and Persians. It is possible he was allied with Nabonidus at this stage. Nabonidus now began restoring the temple in Harran although it was not completed until 543.

In the interim, however, Nabonidus had taken up residence in Taima, an oasis in northwest Arabia, where he remained for ten years. He had campaigned in Cilicia and the Levant in the opening years of his reign, reaching northern Arabia in 552. Here he remained, leaving Belshazzar as his regent in Babylonia. The reason for his decision to stay in Taima is much debated. One theory is that Nabonidus's adherence to Sin (whom he later made supreme deity in place of Marduk) had caused widespread opposition, particularly among the priesthood. Belshazzar, however, was an orthodox adherent of Marduk and may have been more acceptable. However, how much hostility Nabonidus's devotion to Sin aroused cannot be gauged: The texts claiming this postdate his fall and may have been Persian propaganda.

An alternative view is that Nabonidus was extending and enriching the empire, bringing under Babylonian control the gateway to the lucrative trade

A nineteenth-century engraving depicting the Persian king Cyrus the Great who in 550 B.C.E. became king also of Media, an event regarded as the founding of the Persian Empire. (Ridpath, John Clark, *Ridpath's History of the World*, 1901)

routes that carried northern Arabian gold and southern Arabian incense and linked Mesopotamia with Egypt, the Levant, and the Gulf, where Babylonia also controlled Dilmun.

During the decade of Nabonidus's absence the international situation changed dramatically. Under Cyrus the Persians had expanded their domains from an Iranian kingdom subject to the Medes into an empire stretching from western Anatolia to northern India. Now Babylonia lay in their path. Belshazzar had already become uneasy about Persian ambitions, leading the army north to defend his borders from potential attack in 547, when, however, Cyrus's objective proved to be Lydia. In 543 Nabonidus returned to Babylon, making it possible to resume the all-important New Year celebrations, which

Nineteenth-century engraving depicting the capture of Babylon by the Persian king Cyrus the Great in 539 B.C.E. (Ridpath, John Clark, *Ridpath's History of the World*, 1901)

required the king's presence; the ten-year suspension of the festival must have been a major source of dissatisfaction. According to the later, hostile documents, Nabonidus now became more fanatical in his worship of Sin. Rising inflation and, in some places, catastrophes like plague and famine also struck Babylonia, and these can have done nothing for the popularity of the ruler, responsible to the gods for the well-being of his state. Furthermore, Cyrus was a superb propagandist and laid the political groundwork for his invasion many months in advance.

Whatever the reason, it seems many welcomed the Persians when they invaded in 539. The governor of Gutium joined Cyrus and together they defeated Babylonian forces at Opis. Cyrus apparently then took Sippar and Babylon without further opposition; he was welcomed as a deliverer rather than a conqueror—and he took care in his merciful treatment of his enemies to reinforce this impression. Nevertheless, the fierce battle at Opis shows that

Cyrus's invasion was not unopposed, and the account of subsequent events is colored by his propaganda, so it is impossible to be sure how widespread was the acceptance of his seizure of power.

Cyrus proved a clement and benevolent ruler. According to one account, he did not kill Nabonidus, but installed him as governor of Carmania in southern Iran. Belshazzar's fate is unknown: He may have died at Opis. Babylonia was no longer an independent state, but in many respects life continued little changed under Persian rule. Cyrus encouraged Babylonian religion, claiming Marduk's sanction and support for his invasion. The administration was maintained as before. Cyrus's son Cambyses also looked favorably on Babylonia. But after more than three thousand years of preeminence, Mesopotamia was no longer the center of civilization.

TEXT REFERENCES

Akkermans, Peter M. M. G., and Glenn M. Schwartz. 2003. *The Archaeology of Syria. From Complex Hunter-Gatherers to Early Urban Societies (ca. 16,000–300 B.C.)*. Cambridge: Cambridge University Press.

Algaze, Guillermo. 2001. "The Prehistory of Imperialism." Pp. 27–83 in *Uruk, Mesopotamia and Its Neighbours. Cross-Cultural Interactions in the Era of State Formation*. Edited by Mitchell S. Rothman. School of American Research Advanced Seminar Series. Santa Fe, NM: School of American Research Press.

Baird, Douglas. 2000. "Ganj Dareh," "Hassuna," "Obsidian," and "Samarra." Pp 123–124, 141, 217–218, and 250, respectively, in *Dictionary of the Ancient Near East*. Edited by Piotr Bienkowski and Alan Millard. London: British Museum Press.

Beaulieu, Paul-Alain. 2000. "King Nabonidus and the Neo-Babylonian Empire." Pp. 969–979 in *Civilizations of the Ancient Near East*. Edited by Jack M. Sasson. Peabody, MA: Hendrickson Publishers. (Reprint of 1995 edition. New York: Scribner.)

Bienkowski, Piotr, and Alan Millard, eds. 2000. *Dictionary of the Ancient Near East*. London: British Museum Press.

Charpin, Dominique. 2000. "The History of Ancient Mesopotamia: An Overview." Pp. 807–830 in *Civilizations of the Ancient Near East*. Edited by Jack M. Sasson. Peabody, MA: Hendrickson Publishers. (Reprint of 1995 edition. New York: Scribner.)

Clayton, Peter A. 1994. *Chronicle of the Pharaohs*. London: Thames and Hudson.

Curtis, John, ed. 1982a. *Fifty Years of Mesopotamian Discovery*. London: British School of Archaeology in Iraq.

———. 1982b. "Arpachiyah." Pp. 30–36 in *Fifty Years of Mesopotamian Discovery*. Edited by John Curtis. London: British School of Archaeology in Iraq.

Danti, Michael D. 1997. "Hassuna." Pp. 483–484 in *The Oxford Encyclopedia of Archaeology in the Near East*. Edited by Eric M. Meyers. Oxford: Oxford University Press.

Electronic Text Corpus of Sumerian Literature. "The Curse of Agade." http://www.etcsl.orient.ox.ac.uk/ (cited January 30, 2002).

———."Enmerkar and the Lord of Aratta." http://www-etcsl.orient.ox.ac.uk/ (cited January 30, 2002).

———. "Sumerian King List." http://www-etcsl.orient.ox.ac.uk/ (cited January 30, 2002).

Frangipane, Marcella. 2001. "Centralization Processes in Greater Mesopotamia." Pp. 307–346 in *Uruk, Mesopotamia and Its Neighbours. Cross-Cultural Interactions in the Era of State Formation.* Edited by Mitchell S. Rothman. School of American Research Advanced Seminar Series. Santa Fe, NM: School of American Research Press.

Franke, Sabina. 2000. "Kings of Akkad: Sargon and Naram-Sin." Pp. 831–841 in *Civilizations of the Ancient Near East.* Edited by Jack M. Sasson. Peabody, MA: Hendrickson Publishers. (Reprint of 1995 edition. New York: Scribner.)

Gentili, Paolo. *"Sargon, re senza rivali."* http://www.helsinki.fi/science/saa/sargon.html (cited September 11, 2002).

Hansen, Donald P. 1997. "Samarra." Pp. 472–473 in *The Oxford Encyclopedia of Archaeology in the Near East.* Vol. 4. Edited by Eric M. Meyers. Oxford: Oxford University Press.

Harris, Roberta L. 1995. *The World of the Bible.* London: Thames and Hudson.

Huot, Jean-Louis. 1997a. "'Oueili, Tell el-." Pp. 191–194 in *The Oxford Encyclopedia of Archaeology in the Near East.* Vol. 4. Edited by Eric M. Meyers. Oxford: Oxford University Press.

Iranian Cultural Heritage News Agency. "Iranian Archeologists to Identify Jiroft Ancient Quarries." NetNative. http://www.payvand.com/news/04/jul/1134.html (cited August 9, 2004).

———. "Public Plunder of Jiroft Artifacts Resumes." http://www.chn.ir/english/eshownews.asp?no=2812 (cited August 9, 2004).

———. "Jiroft a Key Business Hub 5,000 Years Ago." NetNative. http://www.payvand.com/news/04/sep/1133.html (cited September 15, 2004).

Kirkbride, D. 1982. "Umm Dabaghiyah." Pp. 11–21 in *Fifty Years of Mesopotamian Discovery.* Edited by John Curtis. London: British School of Archaeology in Iraq.

Klein, Jacob. 2000. "Shulgi of Ur: King of a Neo-Sumerian Empire." Pp. 842–857 in *Civilizations of the Ancient Near East.* Edited by Jack M. Sasson. Peabody, MA: Hendrickson Publishers. (Reprint of 1995 edition. New York: Scribner.)

Kohlmeyer, Kay. 1997. "Habuba Kabira." Pp. 446–449 in *The Oxford Encyclopedia of Archaeology in the Near East.* Vol. 2. Edited by Eric M. Meyers. Oxford: Oxford University Press.

Kuhrt, Amelie. 1995. *The Ancient Near East. c. 3000–330 BCE.* 2 Volumes. London: Routledge.

Leichty, Erle. 2000. "Esarhaddon, King of Assyria." Pp. 949–958 in *Civilizations of the Ancient Near East.* Edited by Jack M. Sasson. Peabody, MA: Hendrickson Publishers. (Reprint of 1995 edition. New York: Scribner.)

Leick, Gwendolyn. 1999. *Who's Who in the Ancient Near East.* London: Routledge.

———. 2001. *Mesopotamia. The Invention of the City.* London: Allen Lane, Penguin Press.

Matthews, Roger. 2000. "Eridu," "Gawra, (Tepe)," "Habuba Kabira," and "Halaf, (Tell)." Pp. 107, 125–126, 135–136, and 137–138, respectively, in *Dictionary of the Ancient Near East.* Edited by Piotr Bienkowski and Alan Millard. London: British Museum Press.

Meyers, Eric M., ed. 1997. *The Oxford Encyclopedia of Archaeology in the Near East.* 5 Volumes. Oxford: Oxford University Press.

Millard, Alan. 2000. "Tiglath-Pileser." Pp. 289–290 in *Dictionary of the Ancient Near East.* Edited by Piotr Bienkowski and Alan Millard. London: British Museum Press.

Nissen, Hans J. 1988. *The Early History of the Ancient Near East.* Chicago: University of Chicago Press.

———. 2000. "Ancient Western Asia before the Age of Empires." Pp. 791–806 in *Civilizations of the Ancient Near East.* Edited by Jack M. Sasson. Peabody, MA: Hendrickson Publishers. (Reprint of 1995 edition. New York: Scribner.)

Northpark College. "Sumerian Inscription *Umma and Lagash.*" http://campus.northpark. edu/history//Classes/Sources/UmmaLagash.html (cited September 6, 2002).

Oates, Joan. 1982. "Choga Mami." Pp. 22–29 in *Fifty Years of Mesopotamian Discovery.* Edited by John Curtis. London: British School of Archaeology in Iraq.

———. 1986. *Babylon.* Revised edition. London: Thames and Hudson.

Oates, Joan, and David Oates. 2001. *Nimrud. An Assyrian Imperial City Revealed.* London: British School of Archaeology in Iraq.

Postgate, J. Nicholas. 1994. *Early Mesopotamia.* London: Routledge.

Potts, D. T. 1999. *The Archaeology of Elam. Formation and Transformation of an Ancient Iranian State.* Cambridge: Cambridge University Press.

Reade, Julian. 2000. *Mesopotamia.* 2d edition. London: British Museum Press.

Roaf, Michael. 1982. "The Hamrin Sites." Pp. 40–47 in *Fifty Years of Mesopotamian Discovery.* Edited by John Curtis. London: British School of Archaeology in Iraq.

———. 1990. *Cultural Atlas of Mesopotamia.* New York: Facts on File.

Rothman, Mitchell S. 1997. "Tepe Gawra." Pp. 183–186 in *The Oxford Encyclopedia of Archaeology in the Near East.* Vol. 5. Edited by Eric M. Meyers. Oxford: Oxford University Press.

———. 2001a. "The Local and the Regional. An Introduction." Pp. 3–26 in *Uruk, Mesopotamia and Its Neighbours. Cross-Cultural Interactions in the Era of State Formation.* Edited by Mitchell S. Rothman. School of American Research Advanced Seminar Series. Santa Fe, NM: School of American Research Press.

Rothman, Mitchell S., ed. 2001b. *Uruk, Mesopotamia and Its Neighbours. Cross-Cultural Interactions in the Era of State Formation.* School of American Research Advanced Seminar Series. Santa Fe, NM: School of American Research Press.

Roux, Georges. 1992. *Ancient Iraq.* 3d edition. Harmondsworth: Penguin.

Saggs, H. W. F. 1995. *Peoples of the Past. Babylonians.* London: British Museum Press.

Sanders, Seth. "New Discoveries in Syria Confirm Theory on Spread of Early Civilization." http://www-news.uchicago.edu/releases/02/020531.hamoukar.shtml (cited May 20, 2003).

Sasson, Jack M. 2000a. "King Hammurabi of Babylon." Pp. 901–916 in *Civilizations of the Ancient Near East.* Edited by Jack M. Sasson. Peabody, MA: Hendrickson Publishers. (Reprint of 1995 edition. New York: Scribner.)

Sasson, Jack M., ed. 2000b. *Civilizations of the Ancient Near East.* 4 Volumes. Peabody, MA: Hendrickson Publishers. (Reprint of 1995 edition. New York: Scribner.)

Schwartz, Glenn M. 2001. "Syria and the Uruk Expansion." Pp. 233–264 in *Uruk, Mesopotamia and Its Neighbours. Cross-Cultural Interactions in the Era of State Formation.* Edited by Mitchell S. Rothman. School of American Research Advanced Seminar Series. Santa Fe, NM: School of American Research Press.

Sherratt, Andrew. 1981. "Plough and Pastoralism: Aspects of the Secondary Products Revolution." Pp. 261–305 in *Pattern of the Past: Studies in Honour of David Clarke.*

Edited by Norman Hammond, Ian Hodder, and Glyn Isaac. Cambridge: Cambridge University Press.

Stein, Gil J. 2001. "Indigenous Social Complexity at Hacinebi (Turkey) and the Organization of Uruk Colonial Contact." Pp. 265–305 in *Uruk, Mesopotamia and Its Neighbours. Cross-Cultural Interactions in the Era of State Formation.* Edited by Mitchell S. Rothman. School of American Research Advanced Seminar Series. Santa Fe, NM: School of American Research Press.

Uerpmann, H. P. 1996. "Animal Domestication: Accident or Intention?" Pp. 227–237 in *The Origins and Spread of Agriculture and Pastoralism in Eurasia.* Edited by David R. Harris. Washington, DC: Smithsonian Institution Press.

Villard, Pierre. 2000. "Shamshi-Adad and Sons: The Rise and Fall of an Upper Mesopotamian Empire." Pp. 873–884 in *Civilizations of the Ancient Near East.* Edited by Jack M. Sasson. Peabody, MA: Hendrickson Publishers. (Reprint of 1995 edition. New York: Scribner.)

Wright, Henry. 2001. "Cultural Action in the Uruk World." Pp. 123–147 in *Uruk, Mesopotamia and Its Neighbours. Cross-Cultural Interactions in the Era of State Formation.* Edited by Mitchell S. Rothman. School of American Research Advanced Seminar Series. Santa Fe, NM: School of American Research Press.

CHAPTER 5

Economics

INTRODUCTION

The landscape of Mesopotamia was dominated, and indeed formed, by the Tigris and Euphrates Rivers. They provided highways for transport and communications and water for daily needs like drinking, cooking, and washing, and for industrial activities like dyeing and potting. In the south, their waters enabled barley, fruit, and vegetables to be grown on the alluvium they deposited, and elsewhere supplemented the rainfall on which agriculture depended. They teemed with fish and watered vegetation that supported wild and domestic animals—the versatile date palm, reeds, scrubby trees and bushes, and grassland, with forests on the hills and surrounding mountains.

The land's produce fulfilled other needs besides providing food. Herbs and spices were used for medicines and magic, hides for leather, oil in lamps and industrial activities like leather- and woodworking. Flax and wool were made into textiles, reeds and palm leaves into mats, baskets, and houses, and palm fibers into ropes. Timber from native trees and cultivated fruit trees were used to build houses, vehicles, and boats, and to make tools. Clay, also used for building, and for making pottery and tools, was universally available on the plains. Stone suitable for tools and building was plentiful in the north and in the desert to the west, and the rivers carried smaller stones into the south. Bitumen (natural asphalt), which wells up in several localities, was also used in building and for caulking boats. Salt could be gathered in Babylonia from saline lakes and marshes after the summer heat had evaporated their waters.

In preliterate times domestic necessities such as pottery, tools, clothing, and houses were generally created by family members, but well before the emergence of cities some individuals were specializing in the production of particular commodities, such as fine pottery, the acquisition of particular resources, or the provision of services, particularly intercession with the gods and the management of production. As society grew in complexity the importance of management also increased to ensure the efficient production and distribution of the resources upon which the people of the Mesopotamian cities, towns, and countryside depended.

Many essential or highly valued materials, however, were lacking. Nowhere in Mesopotamia were there metals—initially a luxury but regarded as a necessity by the later third millennium. Fine timber, volcanic rock for grindstones, attractive stones, and other materials like ivory were all absent from Mesopotamia itself, but many of these were to be found in adjacent regions, and distant lands held others of which the Mesopotamians became gradually aware, creating a demand. Trade was therefore a vital part of the economy. Some goods such as incense and lapis lazuli came only from single or restricted sources, and it was necessary to develop ways to acquire them. Others, such as copper and gold, were to be found in a number of locations: Political and economic factors determined which of these were exploited.

Royalty and temples were the major sponsors of trading expeditions, requiring materials to build and embellish palaces, temples, ziggurats, gardens, and other major works—quality building stone and timbers, gold, silver, and precious stones, and exotic plants and animals—as well as for more ephemeral luxuries. Public factories and private workshops had to procure the raw materials for their products—metal ores, timber, wool and flax, leather, and the like. And ordinary households needed to acquire basic necessities like salt. Mesopotamian trade was never either wholly state-sponsored or completely private. Even under tight state control, merchants could undertake some trading on their own behalf, while private expeditions often had some state patronage and were subject to state taxes and regulations.

PATTERNS OF SUBSISTENCE

The general environmental constraints and opportunities in Mesopotamia, such as the timing of the rivers' annual inundation and the seasonal availability of pasture, have remained unchanged for millennia. Many economic practices devised to cope with and exploit the region's different environments were established at an early date and have endured. Modern subsistence practices in the region, therefore, often provide an invaluable insight into patterns of subsistence in ancient Mesopotamia.

On the other hand, patterns of exploitation have been affected by natural and man-made changes, such as minor fluctuations in temperature and rainfall, alterations in the course of the rivers, salinization, and deforestation, as well as by technological innovations, the exploitation of new crops and animals, and the variable power of individual rulers to mobilize large workforces and control large areas. Increasingly sophisticated irrigation techniques, for example, expanded cultivated land, but misuse of water management also brought ruin to some areas.

The collection of faunal and plant remains and other direct economic evidence has concentrated mainly on sites from the early stages of agricultural development in Mesopotamia, and so for the historical periods most economic data come from written sources. Copious and detailed in some areas, they are reticent or silent in others, biasing the economic picture toward urban and public rather than rural and private aspects.

The Agricultural Year

One notable exception is a school exercise dating from Ur III times, *The Farmer's Instructions*, transcribed at Nippur around 1700 B.C.E., in which a farmer advises his son on the year's agricultural tasks. This and other less-detailed texts reveal traditional agricultural practices that changed little over the millennia.

The spring equinox marked the beginning of the Sumerian farmer's year. It was then that the rivers, swelled by melting snow in mountains far to the north, topped their banks, spreading water and silt over adjacent land and filling the canals and reservoirs. Water soaked into weed-strewn fields that had lain fallow since the previous year's harvest, softening the ground and leaching away salt. When the water had drained away, the land was surveyed to assess its cropping potential. Leases for the coming year were negotiated and settled.

The farmer now cleared the fields. An entertaining Sumerian literary disputation between plough and hoe contrasts their merits in fulfilling this and other tasks. The hoe claims:

"I clear the recesses of the embankment for you. I remove the weeds in the field for you. I heap up the stumps and the roots in the field for you." (Electronic Text Corpus of Sumerian Literature "The Debate between the Hoe and the Plough," lines ca. 84–88.)

The wooden ard, a simple type of plough, ideally with a metal share, did not turn the sod but broke up the ground, inhibiting the capillary action that brought salts to the surface. Hoes were also of wood but might have a stone head.

Under supervision by the *gugallum* (canal inspector), over the summer debris was cleaned out and silt removed from canals onto their banks and necessary repairs made. When the first autumn rains began, the fields were ploughed and harrowed, preparing them for sowing, generally with barley. Mesopotamian texts give the expected ratio of seed to finished crop as between 1:10 and 1:15, a surprisingly high yield, explained by the use of the seeder plough, a Mesopotamian invention attested from Early Dynastic times onward. This incorporated a funnel down which seed was dribbled, releasing it at regular intervals along the furrow the plough was cutting. This used less than half as much seed as sowing the same area by broadcasting.

Combined ploughing and sowing was an expensive and labor-intensive activity. The plough was drawn by two (sometimes four) oxen kept largely for this task. The expense of feeding them throughout the year made up a substantial proportion of the total cost of cultivating land. They were given barley during their working season, consuming around half as much grain as that needed to sow the fields. A team of three or four ploughmen, paid daily rations or a proportion of the final yield, were needed to lead the animals, feed grain into the seeder funnel, and manage the plough. Fields were usually long and thin, partly to maximize the number that could be supplied by a single canal or watercourse but also to increase efficiency since a field's optimum length was the distance that a team could plough before requiring a rest, food, and water, which were taken when the team was unhitched to allow the plough to be turned. *The Farmer's Instructions* recommends ploughing and seeding in furrows spaced approximately 75 centimeters apart (eight furrows in a field 1 *nindan* (6 meters) wide). In a day a team could plough 1–2 *iku*

(0.36–0.72 hectares) or harrow 6 iku. In Akkadian times an average holding was 4–10 iku (1.5–3.6 hectares), presumably enough to sustain a household, although in *The Farmer's Instructions* an individual's cultivated area was given as 18 iku (6.5 hectares).

After sowing, another survey assessed likely productivity. The fields were now flooded to the top of the furrow—this leached salts from the side of the furrows where the grain had been placed, reducing their salinity and thus increasing fertility. The winter months saw further maintenance of the irrigation canals and dykes—work essential to protect the growing crops from the annual floods arriving just before the harvest. Between sowing and harvest, the field was irrigated three or four times: If properly timed, there was little risk of crop failure. A final yield survey was conducted just before harvest.

Teams of three harvested the grain, one to reap, using a sickle, one to bind, and a third whose duties are unclear. Then "the orphans, the widows and the destitute take their reed baskets and glean" (Electronic Text Corpus of Sumerian Literature "The Debate between the Hoe and the Plough," lines ca. 47–48). Barley and onions were harvested in March or April, followed by other vegetables, flax, and emmer wheat, then fruit, the harvest generally being completed during June. Threshing began at once, using threshing sledges drawn repeatedly over the harvested grain by oxen (or sometimes donkeys). Finally the grain was winnowed with forks to separate it from the chaff. This postharvest work, including storing the grain, could take an additional three months, in the stifling summer heat. The harvested fields were turned over to the draught animals, often along with flocks of sheep and goats (see pages 124–127), to graze the stubble, at the same time adding nutrient-rich dung to the soil. This land was now left fallow until the following spring when the cycle began again; and fields that had been fallowing throughout the year were now prepared anew for cultivation.

Farther north the growing season came later in the year. Here rainfall supplied crops with water, supplemented where suitable by irrigation from rivers, wells, and springs, to raise productivity. In areas relying on rain-fed agriculture, seed was often broadcast and yields were correspondingly low—a ratio of around 1:5 seed to harvest. Sowing began after the autumn rains (the timing of which varied) had thoroughly softened the ground. The success of the harvest, around five months later, was at the mercy of rainfall during the winter, both the amount and the timing being important. As in the south, fallowing was essential to restore soil fertility between cropping years.

Crops and Their Cultivation

High-yielding hulled barley was the main cereal throughout Mesopotamia. It required relatively little water, tolerated relatively saline soil, and increased its yield under irrigation. It ripened earlier than wheat and was therefore less susceptible to rust, a dreaded fungal disease. Wheat came in a poor second. The primitive hulled emmer wheat was gradually replaced by bread wheat and club wheat, free-threshing wheats that were easier to process.

Cereals were the main staple of the Mesopotamian diet, but pulses, vegetables, and fruits also played their part. Pulses grown for human consumption comprised lentil, field pea, grass pea (*Lathyrus*), chickpea, and broad bean. Unlike the others, broad beans were frost tolerant but not drought resistant, making them more suitable for cultivation in the north. All the pulses yielded better if irrigated but differed in their water requirements. Because pulses fix nitrogen from the air, they were important in maintaining soil fertility and were therefore grown in rotation with other crops. Pulses, particularly chickpeas, were also tolerant of salinated soil. Other pulses—bitter and common vetch and clover, and later alfalfa—were grown in some quantity to feed cattle and draught animals (oxen and donkeys).

Both pork fat and plant oils were used for food and other purposes. *Linum usitatissimum* was cultivated widely and was probably used to produce linseed oil, although this quite rapidly became too rancid for culinary use. Most *Linum* was grown for its fiber, flax, from which linen was made. Other plant fibers were not important, and most textiles were made of wool.

The main oil-bearing plant grown in Mesopotamia was sesame, attested in texts from the reign of Naram-Sin (2254–2218 B.C.E.) onward. Its origins present an interesting puzzle. Some scholars claim that it was indigeneous to the Levant or imported there from Egypt and that *she-gish-ia*, the Sumerian equivalent of the Akkadian word *shamashshammu*, to which *sesame* is related, derives from an Eblaite word. Sesame is indigeneous to both Africa and India. Copal from East Africa is known at Eshnunna on the Diyala, a region renowned as a major producer of sesame, so some would argue that the sesame reached Mesopotamia originally from Africa. On the other hand, sesame was certainly cultivated in the Indus region by the later third millennium B.C.E., and the date of its appearance in Mesopotamia coincides with the beginning of direct seaborne trade with the Indus civilization. Furthermore, the Sumerian word *ilu / ili*, meaning "sesame oil" and its Akkadian equivalent, *ellu / ulu*, bear a striking resemblance to an early Dravidian name for sesame, *el, ellu*, reinforcing the likelihood that the plant and its name were introduced originally from India. Unlike most of the plants cultivated in Mesopotamia, sesame was a summer crop, sown in May or June and harvested in August or September. Despite being salt-intolerant it was the only oil-bearing crop grown in Babylonia. It needed very little water, and its yields were enhanced by the region's hot dry conditions and high sunshine hours.

Cereals, pulses, and oil seeds were grown on both the fertile soils of the levees and the poorer but more extensive areas of backslope and basin land, easily irrigated by gravity-flow canals. Vegetables were usually cultivated in gardens on the levees (often beside villages) where they could be watered frequently, either by hand or by lifting water from the river, canal, or reservoir using a shaduf. Often a highly efficient shade-tree garden system was used. The tall date palms that grew along the waterways of southern Mesopotamia provided daylong shade from the hot summer sun, creating a microenvironment of cooler temperatures and higher moisture. Shorter fruit trees such as apple and pomegranate were planted beneath the date canopy, and at ground level vegetables, herbs, spices, and other thirsty plants, and at times cereals, pulses, and oilseeds, too. Manure was sometimes applied to increase productivity. Similar gardens shaded by other trees were popular farther north, along the banks of rivers and canals, in the courtyards of palaces, in the suburbs and even within the city walls, and the great kings of Assyria and Babylonia invested much effort and ingenuity in creating pleasure gardens stocked with exotic trees and plants—the legendary Hanging Gardens of Babylon (see chapter 11) epitomize this practice.

A text describes one such garden, belonging to Marduk-apla-iddina II (Merodach-Baladan), the eighth-century Chaldaean king who ruled Babylonia in the face of Assyrian aggression. Here were grown garlic, onions, leeks, lettuces, cucumbers, radishes, beetroot, turnips, various herbs and spices, and a number of unidentified plants, sixty-one different kinds in all. Leeks, onions, and garlic were very popular, and onions merited special attention. A large twenty-third-century B.C.E. archive at Nippur dealt specifically with their cultivation: Seeds were issued by the Onion Office to specialist growers, and the harvested onions were sent to favored individuals.

Dates were the chief fruit grown in Babylonia: Rich in vitamins and high in carbohydrates (being three-quarters sugar), they were also easy to store and to transport. They were hand pollinated from at least the time of Hammurabi, allowing growers to raise mainly the fruit-bearing female trees. Many surviving legal texts are concerned with the leasing and rental of date palms, estimates of their expected yield, their allocation to officials as part of their salary, and so on. Their young sprouts could be eaten as a vegetable, and the palms yielded leaves for making roofs, baskets, and mats, bark fibers for making rope, and, at the end of their productive life, timber. Date palms represented a considerable investment because they did not bear fruit until their fourth or fifth year and reached full productivity only around twenty-five years.

Grapes were among the many fruits grown in shade-tree gardens, although vineyards were established only in the north—those east of Nineveh were reckoned the finest. Grapes were eaten fresh, made into wine, or dried. Dates, apples, and figs were also dried and packed in baskets, pottery jars, or wooden boxes; strings of dried apple halves actually survived in a grave in the Royal Cemetery at Ur.

Timber was also of great importance. The north was well provided with suitable trees, including oak, which grew both in parts of the steppe and in the adjacent regions. The trees of the south, including willow and poplar, could not produce massive beams but were perfectly adequate for building boats and smaller structures and for making tools. Forests of these timbers were carefully managed and tended by professional foresters and were legally protected.

Water Technology and Irrigation

Babylonia was a land of sharp contrasts, cultivation giving way to desert at the farthest point that water from rivers and canals could reach. Irrigation was essential, because annual rainfall was generally below 100 millimeters, but even in the zone of rain-fed agriculture farther north, irrigation was important to increase productivity. Success in water management was therefore a crucial part of a ruler's duties. Mesopotamian kings proudly recorded the creation of dams, canals, and reservoirs, and the failure to provide or maintain water facilities could bring down a monarch or regime. Landowners and cultivators were legally responsible for the proper control and maintenance of the canals that supplied and the dykes that protected their lands, as law codes and court records attest; there were stiff penalties for causing damage to a neighbor's crops or land by failing in these duties. Clashes over water rights provoked not only fights among neighbors, but also wars between neighboring states. Land was plentiful and could be taken into cultivation by creating new canals and dykes, but this was only worthwhile in politically stable times. The importance of water management is also demonstrated by numerous school math exercises concerned with such matters as calculating the volume of water that needed to be released from canals or reservoirs to irrigate fields of certain sizes.

Since the annual inundation came just around harvest time, flood control was as important as irrigation. Dykes and embankments were built to contain the river at flood level and to protect existing irrigation works, and immediately before the floodwaters arrived, sluices and regulators were opened. The flood waters spread out over an area several kilometers wide, depositing the coarsest silt, richest in nutrients, on the levees, which were raised above the watertable, encouraging good drainage; as the waters moved farther from the river, the silts deposited became progressively finer and more prone to waterlogging. Thus the fertility of the land fell with distance from the rivers.

For plants cultivated on the levees, water was drawn directly from the river, using lifting equipment. The simple shaduf devised by the ED period was widely used, both to obtain water for immediate use and to raise it from lower to higher canals, reservoirs, and watercourses. The lower reaches of the Tigris, which flows at a lower level than the Euphrates, defied use for such simple irrigation but began to be exploited in the first millennium B.C.E. when the Assyrians invented more sophisticated water-lifting equipment.

The backslopes and lower land were irrigated by canals, often several kilometers long, cut through the banks of the river levees. Regulators—brick-built structures that narrowed the watercourse and could be blocked or opened as required—allowed the water level in the river to be raised high enough to flow into these channels, through sluices and outlets. Their slight gradient meant the water flowed slowly along these channels and much was consequently lost to evaporation and seepage. Large networks of irrigation channels were constructed in the delta plain. Farther north in Babylonia's river plain the annual floods could sweep through with devastating ferocity, often damaging or destroying canals and breaking down the levees. The volume of silt carried and deposited by the river also tended to clog up the river and canals, exacerbating the problem. Much effort was therefore put into creating dykes to protect the land and its irrigation works from the force of the waters. Early settlement concentrated particularly on the delta plain, but by the early second millennium B.C.E., developing technology, enhanced by the larger workforces that could now be mobilized, enabled the Babylonians to cope better with the river-plain floods.

Irrigation exacerbated the naturally occurring problem of salt deposition on Babylonia's fields. Strenuous efforts were made to drain away surplus water to prevent the water table from rising. Fields were left fallow, and therefore unirrigated, in alternate years, and affected areas were flushed with large amounts of water, to leach out and carry away the salts. Ironically, since barley required only small volumes of irrigation water, its cultivation increased salinization.

Dams and weirs retained water in reservoirs until it was needed. An inscription of Enmetena of Lagash (ca. 2404–2375 B.C.E.) shows the scale of work involved in building and maintaining waterworks: He used 648,000 fired bricks and 1,840 *gur* (264,960 liters) of bitumen to restore the Lumagimdu reservoir built by his uncle Eannatum. The laborers' perspective is vividly conjured up at the beginning of *Atrahasis,* the epic story of the creation, when the lesser gods charged with canal work complain and go on strike, burning their tools and threatening their overseer, the god Enlil. Their problem is solved by creating humanity to do the work instead.

Animal Husbandry

The Mesopotamian farmer relied on oxen to plough a substantial area of arable land each year and thresh the grain raised on it. Cows were kept for breeding and for their milk. Cattle were rarely sacrificed or slaughtered for meat, although their hides were a valuable source of leather. Individual households kept only a few cattle, grazing them on vegetation at the edge of their cultivated land and on stubble in the summer, and feeding them on barley, reeds, and fodder crops, particularly when they were working. Only major state institutions could afford to keep large herds and move them to winter pastures.

Most cattle kept in Mesopotamia, as in the rest of West Asia, were descendants of the aurochs *Bos primigenius,* but during the later third millennium, the zebu, *Bos indicus,* was introduced from India, probable source also of the water buffaloes that were briefly present at this time.

Pigs were commonly kept throughout Mesopotamia and Khuzestan, mainly as a relished source of fat, at least until Akkadian times when sesame came under cultivation. Their skins were made into leather, and their bristles might also be used. Like cattle they were raised in small numbers by individual households, and larger herds were tended by professional swineherds.

In early times, fish were caught in rivers, swamps, lakes, and the sea, using nets of plant fiber with terra-cotta, stone, or lead sinkers, or hooks and lines, and, in shallow waters, traps. Their exploitation tailed off markedly from the mid-second millennium B.C.E., until in Neo-Babylonian times to be called a fisherman was an insult, signifying a person outside the law.

Game—deer, boar, onager, antelope, gazelle, hare, and a great variety of wild fowl—was plentiful. Falconry was an established sport by the second millennium; dogs were used in the chase, and nets employed to capture ani-

Detail of a stone mosaic frieze from the temple at Tel al-Ubaid showing a cow being milked. Its calf stands nearby so that the cow will let down its milk. (Zev Radovan/Land of the Bible Picture Archive)

mals, particularly when they were wanted alive for stocking parks or to be fattened for the table. Attempts to domesticate deer and antelope were unsuccessful, but wild fowl—ducks and geese and perhaps francolin—were kept by the third millennium B.C.E., for meat and eggs, and there are records of fowlers and birdcatchers, and of keepers fattening these birds on dough. Chickens were a late introduction—kept by the people of the Indus civilization, they had reached West Asia by the thirteenth century B.C.E., if not before.

Onagers, the native wild steppe ass (*Equus hemionus*), were also the subject of attempted domestication, but their intractable nature made them difficult to use. However, they were successfully crossed with domestic donkeys (*Equus asinus*) to produce a useful mule. Along with this mule, donkeys, locally domesticated in the fourth millennium, became the main pack and draught animals, used to pull carts, wagons, and war chariots. They were also ridden, the rider being seated on the animal's rump. The horse, domesticated in the European steppe around 4000 B.C.E. and introduced to Mesopotamia by Ur III times, gradually superseded the donkey for pulling war chariots and the vehicles of the elite. They were also crossed with donkeys to produce mules, replacing the earlier donkey-onager cross. By the ninth century B.C.E. horseriding was well established and the Assyrians exploited this to the full in their elite cavalry divisions and their royal mail: couriers entrusted with the rapid delivery of messages or small packages. Horses were highly valued and were often given as royal gifts.

Camels, native to the desert regions on Mesopotamia's western fringes, were domesticated during the third or second millennium B.C.E., probably initially for their rich and nutritious milk. By around 1000 B.C.E. they were coming into common use, opening up the previously inaccessible inner desert, where water and pasture are rare and widely scattered, to the Arab pastoralists who kept herds of camels for milk, blood, and meat. These herders also made a living from trading with and raiding their settled neighbors, from the eighth century conducting the valuable trade in incense and spices with southwest Arabia. The Arabs maintained close ties with the Babylonians and first came to Assyrian notice in 853 B.C.E. when an Arab contingent with a thousand camels formed part of the army that Shalmaneser III defeated at Qarqar. The Assyrians bought camels from the Arabs in large numbers and received thousands in tribute from their queens.

Sheep, Goats, and Pastoralism

The desert fringes had long been home to pastoral groups keeping sheep and goats, generally in mixed herds in which sheep predominated. Goats produced milk and hair and often led mixed flocks, but they were chiefly a source of meat. Flocks varied in size, small farmers owning a few animals, whereas full-time pastoralists might manage several hundred. Although they frequently had permanent homes in one area, full-time pastoralists were generally transhumant, moving seasonally to obtain pasture for their flocks—during the winter in the steppe or desert fringes or on the wasteland between areas of cultivation, in summer moving to camp in settled areas where their flocks grazed on stubble and in fallow fields, leaving dung as fertilizer. Grazing rights were negotiated and often established over long periods, both between different pastoral groups and between pastoralists and farmers. In the autumn the pastoralists returned to their own villages where they often planted some crops. Some of the group, particularly the elderly and women with small children, might live in the villages year round. Pastoralists also inhabited the Zagros and Taurus and the mountains of Lebanon, grazing their flocks in the rich upland pastures in the summer and returning to the foothills for the winter. As well as herding and cultivating, pastoralists engaged in trade and probably exploited wild plants and animals.

Pastoralism was a risky and fluid business, in which substantial profits and drastic losses could be made. Shepherds whose flocks became too small might hire themselves out as herders, or settle into a sedentary existence. Those whose flocks grew to considerable size might invest in land and settle down to manage it, hiring others to take care of their animals. Many rulers, such as the Assyrian king Shamshi-Adad and the Mari royal family, had nomad ancestors and relatives who "lived in tents." Sedentism was also a response to climatic deterioration that reduced pasturage—as was raiding, especially in times of political instability. Frequently, however, farmers and pastoralists had a symbiotic relationship, exchanging grain for animals, wool, and other animal products.

Their mobility enabled pastoral groups to maintain large flocks of their own and to be employed as shepherds for those of temples, kings, and wealthy landowners, taking the animals to pastures distant from the settled land where grazing was limited. For example, administrative texts in the town of Nuzi name ninety hereditary herders as part of the community, although they spent most of the year elsewhere. Many surviving contracts set out the complex agreements between herder and animal owner. The shepherd was usually given food and clothing for himself and pay for an assistant, but took on considerable risks. One or two in every ten sheep would be accepted as a normal rate of annual loss; four in every five ewes were expected to produce a lamb, and every animal to yield around 2 minas (1 kilogram) of wool. The shepherd generally kept the milk and a proportion of the wool, fixed in advance. Any lambs over the agreed number were also his.

Large flocks were often dealt with by a herding contractor, who employed a group of shepherds, but the form of the contract was similar. The records of the great depot at Puzrish-Dagan, where animals paid in tribute were collected in Ur III times, give some idea of the huge numbers involved: Around 70,000 sheep and goats passed through it in the course of a year.

Sheep were kept almost entirely for their wool, the main material for making textiles. The spring sheep shearing (actually plucking) was a major landmark in the agricultural year. Bones excavated from temple complexes show that most sacrificial animals were young kids and lambs; their meat was consumed by temple personel and their hides processed for leather.

One important function of animals, particularly sheep and goats, was as a means of investment. Crop surpluses could be used to buy or feed additional animals. These would create "interest" in the form of lambs, kids, and wool, and could be "cashed in" for grain or other commodities when the need arose. A specialist practice was fattening animals for the table on barley, particularly fat-tailed sheep, the fatty tail being a delicacy appreciated in the Near East to this day.

Food

Ancient Mesopotamians usually ate two meals a day—in the morning and the evening. Most lived mainly on bread—a flat unleavened loaf of barley meal cooked on a hot stone or in an oven—served with barley beer and a few vegetables. A savory porridge or gruel flavored with spices and herbs provided a variation, and whole grains were also served with cooked dishes. Wheat was used to make the less common leavened bread, baked in molds. Pulses could be ground and made into bread, boiled whole, or cooked in soup. Sesame oil and pork fat were used in cooking, and vegetables were eaten raw or boiled. Grapes and other fruits were eaten both fresh and dried. Meat and fish were also dried or could be preserved by smoking, pickling, or salting.

Only the upper echelons of society ate meat frequently, particularly priests since animals were regularly sacrificed to the deities they served. For the ordinary person meat was a rare treat generally eaten only at public festivals or private celebrations like weddings and funerals. Fish and pork were eaten by country dwellers and the urban poor, whereas bureaucrats and the elite ate mutton, ducks, geese, pigeons, and partridges. Delicacies included gazelle, hare, mice, and gerbils. Cows' milk was drunk by town dwellers, although perhaps only as a medicine; pastoralists consumed the milk of their sheep and goats; and milk was also turned into yogurt, butter, and cheese.

More than fifty varieties of fish appear in Sumerian texts; during the third millennium, they were eaten, traded, or used to pay taxes. Fishing rights were often owned by the authorities and leased to individuals, but landowners were allowed to fish in the canals that they were responsible for maintaining. The eighteenth-century Mari archives record the deliberate stocking of artificial pools and ditches with fish, including eels, and letters from Mari and Karana mention dried and potted fish, including fish roe and shrimps from the distant seacoast. By the mid-second millennium B.C.E., however, fish had apparently declined in importance.

Other wild resources were also eaten—wild fowl and turtles, roots and tubers of rushes and sedge, and so on. Locusts were a delicacy and were cooked on skewers. Honey was sometimes gathered from wild bees; in the eighth century B.C.E. Shamash-resh-usur, the governor of Suhu and Mari, boasted of having introduced bee-keeping. A more common source of sweetness was a syrup made from dates. Although ordinary people probably ate simple fare, the wealthy had an elaborate cuisine, including cakes and pastries made of wheat flour, sweetened with honey, dates, and other fruit, and flavored with herbs and spices. Molds found in the royal kitchens at Mari may have been used for shaping these or other prepared dishes.

Beer was the customary drink throughout Mesopotamia, brewed from malted barley, spices, and honey or dates, probably made daily by private households and temple staff alike: It was nutritious and contributed significantly to the diet, but did not keep well. The daily ration issued to state employees was 1–4 liters. It was served warm, whereas wine, consumed by the elite, especially in the north, was chilled with ice. At Mari this was collected during the winter and stored in icehouses (*shuripum*). Wine was generally made from grapes, though date, pomegranate, and fig wines were also made, and grape wine was also imported as booty or tribute from the west. The storerooms of the Assyrian palace of Kalhu housed wine jars containing up to 2,000 liters. Some 6,000 employees here were listed in eighth-century records: They received a daily wine ration of 0.42 pints (2 deciliters). Drinks were often served in large communal jars, each person drinking from it using long straws made of reeds or metal.

When Ashurnasirpal inaugurated his new capital at Kalhu in 863 B.C.E., he celebrated by giving a ten-day banquet for 69,574 guests, some of them distinguished citizens of Kalhu or foreign visitors, but the majority workmen and women from throughout the empire. Their thirst was quenched with 10,000 jars of beer, 100 of fine mixed beer, and 10,000 skins of wine, and, to eat, they were served 14,000 sheep, 200 oxen, 1,000 deer, 1,500 ducks, 1,000 geese, 20,000 pigeons, 10,000 fish, 10,000 eggs, 10,000 gerbils, 10,000 loaves of bread, 10 donkey loads of shelled pistachios, as well as mustard, fresh grapes, dates, and figs.

THE MANAGEMENT AND REGULATION OF PRODUCTION

Estates and Offerings

In the earlier third-millennium cities, substantial estates were owned and administered by temple authorities and kings. Economic texts mainly record the official receipt, storage, and distribution of agricultural produce, the management of state-controlled craft production, particularly of textiles, and details of officially sponsored trade. Land was also privately owned, and as the millennium unwound, kings came increasingly to control land and the bureaucracy as "shepherds of the people," answerable to the tutelary god for the well-being of city and state. The most detailed and comprehensive administrative records come from the reign of the Ur III king Shulgi (2094–2047 B.C.E.), when the state had almost total control over the economy. In succeeding centuries, private enterprise grew in importance. Merchants' private archives give an insight into the organization of production and the flow of goods and materials.

Several mechanisms ensured the movement of goods and services between producer and state or employer: taxation or tribute; rent and the repayment of investments; and waged or compulsory employment. More haphazardly, booty from warfare also filled the state coffers and licensed looting the baggage of private soldiers and army officers.

The early city-states were regarded as the personal estate of the city's patron deity, whose temple was supported by offerings of agricultural produce and other commodities. A late fourth millennium alabaster jar (the "Warka Vase"; see p. 69) from Uruk vividly depicts a donative ceremony where people in procession bring baskets and jars of grain and fruit, animals and artifacts, which the priest presents to the deity. Making such gifts symbolized the individual's membership of and participation in the community. At a higher level, the Sumerian city-states recognized Nippur, seat of the chief deity Enlil, as their religious and symbolic center and all contributed to the upkeep of Enlil's temple, the Ekur, by making offerings on a rotating basis. A parallel institution may have united the city-states of the middle and upper Euphrates around the temple of Dagan at Tuttul, and Subartu (later Assyria) may also have had such a confederacy.

Despite later shifts in the balance of power toward kings, these offerings to local and national temples continued as a major source of state revenue. Under Shulgi, the provinces, which largely corresponded to the traditional city-states, took turns to contribute to the upkeep of Enlil's shrine, in proportion to their wealth. Enormous numbers of animals and quantities of grain and other produce were centrally accumulated and distributed as necessary to maintain the personnel of the temple, bureaucracy, and state industries—these offerings (taxes) were known as *bala*. Although other ideologies also operated later, this view of the population of the city and of larger political units (kingdoms and empires) as the community of a god continued throughout Mesopotamian history and had a major influence in structuring the economy.

Raising Revenue

This was not the only means by which the state exacted revenue. The Ur III Empire controlled not only the core region of city-states but also a periphery of conquered lands along its eastern and northern edge. From these revenue came in the form of rent (*gun mada* tax) paid by their military governors for the lands that they held, and from which they in turn extracted revenue in kind. A similar arrangement had operated under the earlier Akkadian Empire, where large areas of confiscated land were granted to Akkadian military colonists. In later times, defeated states were left under puppet native rulers or placed under Mesopotamian governors who paid tribute or taxes to the state, collecting these from their own subjects.

A variety of private activities could attract taxes. For example, the merchant houses that conducted trade between Assur and Anatolia in the nineteenth century B.C.E. (see pages 136–137) paid export taxes on their goods when they started out from Assur and import duties to the Anatolian authorities.

Considerable state and private revenue came from rents, investment, and landownership. Both temples and kings were major landowners, and in the case of conquered territory, the state might claim ownership of all the new land or confiscate large tracts from defeated leaders. These lands were granted to members of the royal household, powerful nobles, military or civil administrators, and temple dignitaries, and smaller holdings to lesser officials and state or temple employees in return for military or various forms of civil service. The lands could be farmed directly by these people and their households, managed for them by local officials or smaller landowners, or rented out to peasants. Areas of state land might also be rented by private entrepreneurs, particularly in later times. Land could also change hands privately—the price of a field in Sumerian times was equivalent to a year's anticipated yield, although typically its rent was between a quarter and half of the projected or actual yield, assessed annually. Similarly, contracts were negotiated between pastoralists and the owners of herds and flocks (see page 127). More complicated agreements were made where a return was not expected within a single year. For example, according to Hammurabi's law code, when land was rented to create an orchard, no rent was payable for five years, at the end of which the land, with its fruit trees, was divided, half going back to the landowner and half to the tenant, with the proviso that the latter include in his share any part of the plot that he had failed to plant with trees.

Both state and private investors participated in financing trading expeditions, putting up capital or making loans against interest from the eventual profits. Surplus goods, materials, or foodstuffs accumulated by the temple or palace from their taxes and tithes and from their lands and industrial activities could be sold to merchants, often as "futures" not yet received by the authorities, introducing legal complications if their tenant or employee failed to produce the goods to which title had been transferred.

Workers

Many people worked wholly or in part for the temple, the palace, or private establishments. Military service and corvée labor on major projects, such as constructing canals, temples, and palaces, were regularly required of the population. Large industrial establishments were maintained, in particular manufacturing textiles (where the employees were mainly women and children)—one at Lagash in the Ur III period employed 6,000 people. Palace and temple also ran smaller workshops, and their households included many specialist workers. The palace at Mari employed carpenters, leatherworkers, reed workers making baskets, mats, and fencing, millers, textile workers, gardeners, drawers of water, wood carriers, doorkeepers, barbers, potters, oil refiners and makers of perfumes, musicians, jugglers, and wrestlers, as well as male and female scribes, workshop managers, and other officials. Other employees included farmers, shepherds and herdsmen, fishermen, fowlers, and others whose duties took them far afield, including military personnel. Specific reference is made to the employment of blind people: At Mari they undertook a range of occupations, including gardening. The Creation story states that those blind from birth were destined to be musicians. Male prisoners of war were often blinded to discourage them from escaping (see photo p. 169) and were entrusted with monotonous tasks like raising water for irrigation.

Workers were paid largely in rations, particularly food and textiles, derived from temple offerings and tithes or state taxes. In Ur III texts the rate of pay for a male employee is given as 60 liters of barley per month, along with an annual allowance of 2 kilograms of wool. A worker hired on a daily basis generally earned a higher rate. Rations were usually dates, oil, and bread, along with beer in the south and wine in the north, and certain individuals received meat. In the first millennium, wages in silver often replaced rations: one to three shekels per month, sufficient to purchase 180 liters of grain or dates. The amount paid depended on status and responsibility.

Recipients of rations included full-time workers—such as slaves, deportees, household employees and dependents, tied workers in state factories, and farm laborers—as well as military conscripts, people undertaking corvée labor, and citizens, such as craftsmen, working freelance and hired on a daily basis or commissioned to produce particular items or render certain services. Conditions of service varied, but workers were generally entitled to some time off, particularly for the frequent religious festivals, for which they might also be issued extra rations of wool or textiles.

Measurement and Commerce

The smooth operation of the economy required the regulation of quantities and rates of exchange. It is therefore not surprising that both the Akkadian and the Ur III rulers standardized weights and measures, which previously had varied between cities and between commodities. The system established by the late third millennium was to endure for more than fifteen hundred years

A set of standardized Mesopotamian stone weights in the shape of ducks, dating from ca. eleventh–eighth century B.C.E. (Zev Radovan/Land of the Bible Picture Archive)

[*see* table 10.1, Weights and Measures]. Units of length were inscribed on graduated wooden, stone, or metal measuring bars, the earliest known from around 2200 B.C.E. at Nippur and Lagash. Stone or metal weights were often in the shape of ducks. Graduated vessels measured capacity. Standardization of the calendar also facilitated the control of production and labor.

Accounting and the buying, selling, and exchange of goods required some means of comparing value between different commodities. The Mesopotamians did not use coinage (invented in Asia Minor in the seventh century B.C.E.) but employed various commodities as media of exchange and measures of value: occasionally gold, copper, and tin, but most commonly silver and grain. The value of goods entrusted to merchants was reckoned in weights of silver or volumes of barley, as was that of the commodities that the merchants brought back from their expeditions. Silver rings, coils of silver wire that could easily be cut into pieces, and other small units (often of 5 shekels weight) were regularly used in transactions, the requisite quantity of silver being weighed out to make a purchase or pay for a service. Prices were often fixed by the authorities and are mentioned in law codes. Whether there were shops or regular markets is unclear, although there is little evidence for their existence: Purchases might have been made directly from the workshop or from traveling salesmen, and transactions may also have occurred in the open areas within cities or by their gateways *(rebitu)*.

TRADE

Iranian Caravans

From early times, desirable materials such as obsidian had circulated widely in the Near East and by the fifth millennium B.C.E., turquoise from Central Asia and lapis lazuli from Afghanistan were known in Mesopotamia, Susiana, and other lands thousands of miles from their sources.

During the Uruk period, the Sumerians became more proactive in their trade with their neighbors, establishing trading outposts to control the acquisition of resources, such as that located within the settlement of Hacinebi to obtain Anatolian copper. Sumer was closely involved with Susa and Khuzestan, through which it may have imported copper from Talmessi on the Iranian plateau. By 3000 B.C.E., copper was being alloyed with tin to produce bronze, making it harder and therefore more useful. Thereafter copper and bronze grew in importance, promoting trade.

The fourth millennium saw organized trade networks developing across the Iranian plateau, where more tenuous links had existed for millennia, with towns growing up at nodes in natural routes across the plateau and at places where desirable resources could be obtained. Shahr-i Sokhta in southeastern Iran acted as a break-of-bulk point on the route from the lapis lazuli source area at Badakhshan: Here raw lapis nodules containing impurities were chipped and cleaned into smaller pieces of pure lapis for more efficient transport. Tepe Yahya to its southwest was located close to a major source of chlorite. Many workshops here made chlorite artifacts, particularly decorated bowls, which were widely exported to various Elamite and Iranian towns, sites in the Gulf, Sumerian cities, and Mohenjo Daro in the Indus Valley—a fair illustration of the extent of contemporary trade networks.

A Sumerian literary composition, *Enmerkar and the Lord of Aratta*, probably set around 2700 B.C.E., recounts how Enmerkar, king of Uruk, wishing to build a temple to Inanna, employed various strategies to obtain lapis lazuli, silver, and gold from Aratta, a land beyond Anshan and seven mountains. Aratta also worshipped Inanna: Enmerkar at first attempted to bully the king of Aratta by claiming that the goddess preferred Uruk. Threats and demands were made on both sides, and at one stage Enmerkar dispatched donkey-loads of grain to Aratta, finally receiving the precious materials. Suggestions that Aratta may have been located in southeast Iran have been given a boost by the recent discovery of a civilized society on the Halil River in Kerman province, 200 kilometers north of the mouth of the Gulf. Named Jiroft after the local city, it came to international attention after looters ransacked a large cemetery. The cemetery and associated settlement are still in the early stages of investigation, but material believed to be from here appears to be contemporary with ED and Akkadian Mesopotamia and includes a large quantity of chlorite vessels.

In another tale *(Gilgamesh and Huwawa)* Enmerkar's grandson Gilgamesh and his bosom companion Enkidu undertake an expedition into the mountains where (by very underhanded means) they slay the demon Huwawa who is the guardian of the cedar forest and ship the trees back to Uruk. Although in later times cedar came from Cedar Mountain (Amanus range) in the Levant, it is possible that this poem refers to the importing of such valued timbers from the Zagros Mountains in the earlier third millennium.

Sailing through the Gulf

By 2500 B.C.E., major changes were occurring in the pattern of trade. Sumer ceased direct trading across the Iranian plateau, becoming instead a key player in the Gulf, where it had long-standing trade links. Here it interacted with three countries, Dilmun, Magan, and Meluhha.

Earlier, the name Dilmun had been applied to the Arabian coast around Tarut, but during the third millennium it came increasingly to mean Bahrein. The island is blessed with sheltered harbors and "sweet water." Three days' sail from Sumer, seagoing ships could put in here to take on water and fresh supplies, including the island's exceptionally fine dates. Agricultural land on the island is limited and probably became inadequate to support the burgeoning third-millennium population: In exchange for imported grain, Dilmunites could offer fish, mother-of-pearl, and "fish-eyes" (pearls). Increasingly Dilmun also served as an entrepôt, exchanging Mesopotamian goods for materials imported from farther south. Its role in international trade is underlined by the presence of weights on two different standards, that of Mesopotamia and that of Meluhha. Large warehouses and the island's distinctive "Persian Gulf seals"—round stamp seals bearing motifs such as two people drinking from a vessel through straws—attest the importance of trade to Bahrein, supported by the frequent mention of Dilmun in Sumerian texts as the source of many commodities that the island could not have produced.

These included copper, which in reality came from Magan, as did diorite. Like Dilmun, "Magan" probably shifted its geographical focus through time, including within its purview the Makran coast of Iran, but in the later third millennium it referred mainly to Oman. Substantial copper deposits on the Omani peninsula were mined by 2500 B.C.E. Maysar in the Wadi Samad has remains from various stages in processing copper ore. Pottery and other imported items found in burials and at Umm-an-Nar on the west coast attest to relations with traders from farther north, and on the east coast, the fishing village of Ras al-Junayz traded with people from the Indus Valley who sought their copper and bitumen and probably materials imported from farther west along the Arabian coast.

To the Sumerians, these Indians' homeland was known as Meluhha, source of many essential and luxury goods—fine timbers, ivory, gold, agate and carnelian, and other exotica such as "haia birds" (peacocks)—although they may never have visited it themselves. The Indus town of Lothal in Gujurat, through which some of the trade was channeled, has yielded abundant evidence of warehouses, tradeable goods and materials, and Indus seals—square steatite stamp seals bearing a motif and a short inscription, alas as yet undeciphered (and probably undecipherable)—as well as a Persian Gulf seal. If foreign traders came here at all, it seems they were from Dilmun.

The Meluhhans, however, certainly traveled to Dilmun and Sumer. Persian Gulf seals and cylinder seals have been found bearing Indus-style motifs and inscriptions in the Indus script but with unfamiliar sign sequences, suggesting non-Meluhhan words. A fine cylinder seal identified its bearer as a "Meluhha interpreter." In the Ur III period Lagash was said to have had a village of Meluhhans in its territory, presumably a trading colony. One of the Meluhhans' most valuable exports was lapis lazuli, the former mainstay of trade across the Iranian plateau. They did not prize this material themselves, preferring harder stones that could take a high polish, but they went to the lengths of establishing a colony at Shortugai in Afghanistan to monopolize the supply of lapis to West Asia. Shortugai may also have been used to control trade in other Afghan valuables, notably tin ore, which now reached Mesopotamia via the Gulf.

Sargon of Akkad boasted that ships of Meluhha docked at Agade; Ur's quays also saw trading ships arriving from the south. Numerous Akkadian and Ur III texts record goods issued to and received from merchants engaged in the Gulf trade. But in 2004 B.C.E., Ur was sacked and the highly bureaucratic Ur III Empire gave way to smaller political units centered on individual city-states. Gone was the capital and financial security needed to fund large-scale ventures. Merchants continued to trade, but their ships were smaller (40 gur maximum—a marked contrast to the vast 300-gur ships of former times) and their voyages more restricted, going no farther than Dilmun, whose role as middleman now increased significantly.

Further changes were soon to come. From around 1800 B.C.E., the Indus civilization experienced the decline and eventual collapse of city life. Rural communities, and in some areas towns, continued to flourish, but the era of international trading ventures was over. At much the same time, the political heart of Babylonia shifted northward to Babylon. Sumer ("Sealand") became a backwater, and for some centuries, Mesopotamia ceased to be involved in Gulf trade.

Kanesh

New sources had now to be sought for the copper upon which Mesopotamia had come to rely. One that opened up around 1750 B.C.E. was Alashiya (Cyprus): Copper from here was recorded in the archives at Mari. A more important source for Mesopotamia, probably already exploited, was eastern Anatolia. A later text, *King of Battle,* claims that Sargon of Akkad led a military expedition to the aid of merchants who were suffering persecution in the Anatolian city of Burushkhanda, although this story probably had little factual basis. However, an inscription of Sargon's grandson, Naram-Sin, at Pir-Hussein in southeast Anatolia confirms Akkadian activity in the general region. Excavations at Goltepe in the central Taurus have revealed substantial evidence of metal processing, possibly including tin, although this is unlikely.

The Taurus was rich in other metals, too—gold, silver, lead, and antimony—and had been known since the time of Sargon as the Silver Mountain. Lead isotope analysis of silver goods from Mesopotamian sites over a long period has demonstrated that all those tested came from the Taurus sources.

The Anatolian town of Kanesh (modern Kultepe) was favorably located at the intersection of several major routes north-south and east-west. Archives of clay tablets baked and thus preserved when Kanesh was destroyed by fire around 1820 (end of period II) and again around 1740 (end of period Ib) have yielded a fascinating picture of mercantile activities here. For some three generations in the period II, merchants from Assur operated a trading colony (*karum*) within the walls of Kanesh's lower town. A ground-floor room within their well-appointed houses was reserved for use as a sealed strongroom in which both valuables and their business archives were kept. Their houses and domestic objects were generally indistinguishable from those of local people, so we would have had no way of identifying them as foreigners were it not for their abandoned archives. Other merchants from cities in the Levant, including Ebla, also traded in the town.

The karum was established around 1880 B.C.E. to obtain Anatolian silver and, to a lesser extent, gold, in exchange for tin (*annakum*) and textiles brought from the merchants' home city of Assur. Some of the textiles were made by their wives and daughters, but most were the top-quality products of Babylonia (perhaps imported through the Assyrian colony in Sippar). The tin also came from farther afield: probably traded from Afghanistan across the Iranian plateau. Elam was the transit source of tin imported some years later by Mari and Sippar.

The heads of the trading houses resided in Assur, many of them local aristocrats who sat on the councils that advised the king. Here, too, dwelt the womenfolk of the merchant families, raising their children and making textiles, but often also dealing with the Assur end of the business for their husbands in Kanesh. The trade was strictly regulated by the authorities, who, for example, prohibited trade in Anatolian textiles and luxury goods. A tax of 1/120th of the value of the exports was payable to the palace when an expedition set out.

A council of senior family members oversaw the affairs of the karum at Kanesh, extracting a levy from incoming caravans to pay for its day-to-day running. The king of Kanesh received a tax of 2/65th of each shipment of tin and a fifth of the textiles, and could purchase 10 percent more at a favorable rate. Then there were the expenses of the caravans carrying the goods, including local taxes in the areas they passed through. Nevertheless, the value differentials between the regions (tin, for example, being valued at more than twice as much silver in Anatolia as it was in Assur) made the exercise highly lucrative and a profit of 100 percent was not unusual. Expeditions were financed partly out of profits from earlier trading and partly by investments. Individuals could add their own goods to a consignment. Partnerships of a number of merchants could put up capital (*naruqqam*), which was entrusted to a merchant for a long-term trading venture. Each investor bought shares costing 8 minas (4 kilograms) of silver each and was guaranteed a return of 100 percent at the end of the term (in one recorded case this was fixed at twelve years).

Kanesh was the head office of Assur's operations in Anatolia, with substantial branch karums or smaller offices (*wabartum*) in other towns, including Hattusas, the future Hittite capital, and Burushkhanda (Acem Hoyuk or Karahuyuk-Konya). Some facilitated the trade in silver, others dealt locally in less valuable trade goods such as copper or wool, the profits eventually being converted into silver. With care, using a "smuggler's path," merchants could also engage in tax evasion or illegal trade, for example in iron, still a rare and prestigious material whose acquisition was monopolized by the Assur authorities. After one of their merchants had been arrested for smuggling, an Assur house wrote to their karum representative advising him to leave their iron in a safe-house en route, pending further consultation.

The small donkey caravans from Assur were led by experienced carriers along several established routes. Each donkey carried two packs of around 65 minas (ca. 32.5 kilograms) of tin and a few textiles, making a total weight of around 180 minas (90 kilograms); sometimes the amounts varied or textiles alone made up the saleable part of a load. In addition, the donkeys carried around 10 minas of tin to pay the incidental expenses of the 1,200-kilometer (6–12-week-long) journey on foot. On arrival in Kanesh, the donkeys were probably sold since the far smaller bulk of silver could be borne home to Assur by the carriers themselves.

Around 1820 Kanesh was sacked, probably by the king of Hattusas, and the karum folded. It was revived, though as a much smaller and more circumscribed operation, when Shamshi-Adad ruled northern Mesopotamia, but it did not outlast his dynasty's collapse.

Later Operations

A glimpse of slightly later trade comes from the provincial town of Nuzi, on the eastern edge of Assyria, which yielded copious documents dated around 1500–1350 B.C.E. Its citizens imported horses and other commodities from the Zagros region to their east. They also obtained goods from Babylonia to their south and sent many of their imports on to their Mitanni overlords from whom they received manufactured objects. Seashells from the Mediterranaean, the Gulf, and the Indian Ocean attest the wide range of Nuzi's contacts.

Nomads, whose way of life involved travel over considerable distances, often acted as carriers and traders. They were probably responsible for collecting and trading salt crystals from saline lakes and marshes scattered across Babylonia. Aramaean and Arab nomads operated caravans along a number of routes in the first millennium.

Many commodities from the east, such as tin, reached Mesopotamia through intermediaries. These might be willing trade partners, for example Zagros pastoralists who had mutually beneficial arrangements with the villages of the adjacent lowlands—but huge quantities of Iranian materials and manufactured goods (as well as craftsmen and other people) were seized as booty when Babylonian or Assyrian armies invaded Elam or other eastern regions—a productive though unreliable means of obtaining foreign goods. Control of key re-sources could become an international issue—witness, for example, the war between Assyria and Urartu, vying for controlling influence in the western Iranian state of Mannai, the source of fine horses.

The Levant also suffered at Mesopotamian hands. Peaceful trade in its desir-able raw materials such as cedar and other timber (see photos pp. 141, 239) al-ternated with military expeditions, intimidation, or conquest to obtain booty, tribute, and eventually taxes. By the late second millennium Assyria was flex-ing its military muscles and in the earlier first millennium dominated most of the region, ruthlessly exploiting it. Much of the Levant had earlier been con-trolled by Egypt, but it still nurtured successful city-states engaged in overland and Mediterranean trade. Vivid evidence of sea trade comes from the world's earliest known shipwreck, a vessel probably originating from a Canaanite port, on a round trip calling at Cyprus, Crete, and Egypt, among other places, which sank around 1350 B.C.E. off the Anatolian coast at Uluburun (Kas). Its cargo included pottery, ingots of copper, tin and blue glass, amphorae contain-ing terebinth resin, and the world's earliest known book, a boxwood diptych from which the wax writing surface has long since decayed away.

By the later second millennium gold came to Mesopotamia mainly from Egypt, generally in the form of royal "gifts," closely monitored to ensure par-ity of value, as witness a letter of complaint from the Kassite king Burnaburiash over a gift of gold that fell short of the expected quantity. After 1000 B.C.E., camel transport opened up trade in incense and spices with south-western Arabia, and probably beyond it with East Africa, from which sporadic imports had arrived in earlier times. Prosperous towns grew up at oases in northwestern Arabia, including Taima, Dedan, and Duma, all nodes on the routes linking Arabia with Egypt, Babylonia and the Levant, Assyria, and Anatolia. It was probably to gain control of this lucrative trade that the Babylonian king Nabonidus established himself in Taima.

Gulf trade was revived under the Kassites, who directly controlled Dilmun, and its fortunes reflected the varying political situation in Sealand. In the early first millennium the Chaldaean tribes of this region were reputed to be ex-tremely wealthy, partly as a result of trade in the Gulf.

Ways and Means

Political, social, and economic considerations were significant in determining which routes were followed by trading expeditions—those through hostile or bandit-infested territories were avoided or used by well-armed caravans; vil-lages or towns were often visited to obtain food, other supplies, and some-times overnight accommodation, although caravans often camped. But the most critical factor was topography, and so the same routes have often been used for many millennia. Rivers and canals were the main highways wherever possible since water transport, particularly of bulk goods, was easier than that over land. In their upper reaches the Euphrates and Tigris were not easy to navigate, although canals and lesser rivers like the Khabur still provided wa-terborne routes through much of Assyria.

Maritime routes through the Gulf to India and around the southern coast of Arabia met others through the Red Sea. The Mediterranean was a major highway for the nations that bordered it, including the Phoenicians who were to provide maritime expertise and shipping for the landlocked Assyrians when the latter's expansion brought them into seagirt regions.

Land routes often followed rivers, allowing travelers to take advantage of settlements on their banks and providing a ready supply of drinking water, crucial in this hot land. Routes were often dictated by the location of oases, mountain passes, and river crossings, by bridge, ford, or ferry. Major landroutes followed the Euphrates in the west and the foothills of the Zagros in the east.

A fascinating Old Babylonian text documents a six-and-a-half-month roundtrip, for an unknown purpose, between Larsa in the east and Emar in the west. The travelers began their journey by water, traveling along the Euphrates and associated canals to the Tigris, which they abandoned at the point where its fast current made it no longer navigable. From here the boat returned home but the travelers pressed on overland, following the Tigris through Assur and Ekallatum. Three days farther north, they left the river and traveled to Shubat-Enlil, then across the steppe to Harran. Here they turned south, crossing the Euphrates near Tuttul and following it west to Emar, a total journey of around 1,000 kilometers. After a day there they began the return journey, following much the same route. At one place, Shuna, they were forced to delay their journey for nearly a month, perhaps because of local warfare.

Paved roads were rare outside the cities; the major highways and many minor ways were, nevertheless, genuine roads, created by leveling and compacting the ground, and regularly repaired after damage by rain and other natural hazards. Army engineers preceded military expeditions to identify the most appropriate line of march, check and clear or repair existing roads, and, where necessary, construct new ones. Their need for rapid troop movement and communications meant that the Neo-Assyrians went further, creating and maintaining an integrated network of "royal roads" with way stations (*bit marditi*) where travelers could rest and officials be accommodated. These also acted as collection points and relay stations with fresh horses for the "royal mail," the efficient network of couriers who carried messages between the king and his officials throughout the empire.

Horses provided the fastest mode of transport, but more usually kings and their officials, civil and military, traveled by chariot, drawn by horses from the early second millennium. Lesser individuals used donkeys or asses, and on occasion oxen, as everyone had had to do before the introduction of the horse. These animals also pulled the carts and wagons (and in earlier times sledges) used for short journeys. Where goods had to be transported longer distances overland, pack donkeys (and later also camels) were more practical. Ox teams were used to haul timbers from the mountains (such as Cedar Mountain in the west) to the rivers on which they could be floated down to their destination, either as single logs or lashed together into rafts for greater maneuverability.

Detail of a relief from Kalhu showing Assyrian soldiers crossing a river on inflated skins, the simplest form of water transport. (Getty Images)

A variety of watercraft were employed on the rivers and canals. The simplest, which could carry a person but not much else, was an inflated sheep- or goatskin. Larger rafts (modern *kelek*, Akkadian *kalakku*) were constructed by joining a number (sometimes hundreds) of these inflated skins and covering them with a wood and reed platform on which considerable loads could be carried. Steered by a poplar pole or pair of steering oars, they traveled in a leisurely fashion downriver to their destination where the wood from the platform could be sold and the skins deflated and carried back upriver on donkeys to repeat the process.

Almost as simple was the *quffa* (Akkadian *quppu*), a small vessel like a coracle made of hides stretched over a circular basketry framework. This was paddled and could carry up to four people. Another vessel with a very long history in the region is the reed boat, a shallow-bottomed craft constructed of bundles of reeds sewn or bound together with reed or palm fiber rope. More substantial vessels were built of wooden planks joined with dowels and mortices and probably rope; they are represented in clay models and on seals. Although boats sometimes used sails, they were more usually propelled with oars or paddles or steered with steering poles, while the current provided the motive power. To return upstream, boats could be towed, sailed, or rowed against the current, although this was a laborious process.

Wooden vessels varied considerably in capacity; those mentioned in texts range from 1 to 300 *gur*, a clear indication of the diverse roles that they played (including on occasion transporting troops), but whether these figures represented cargo space or the capacity of the whole vessel is unclear.

Textual references to maritime trade make it clear that ships from Dilmun, Magan, and Meluhha docked at Sumerian ports, and there is some indication that Sumer's merchants sailed to Dilmun and probably Magan. Very little in-

Three high-ended Phoenician cargo vessels loading and towing large logs. An Assyrian carving on alabaster now in the Musée du Louvre. (Library of Congress)

deed is known of the ships that plied these routes. The Sumerians probably employed their larger wooden vessels. Indus seals depict some ships, probably river craft similar to today's houseboats. A model from Lothal represents a sailing boat but gives little information on its form. Sturdy vessels with a considerable capacity for food stores and water would have been essential to travel the length of the hostile desert shores of Arabia or the equally hostile Makran shores, which nearly destroyed Alexander the Great's fleet many centuries later.

TEXT REFERENCES

Astour, Michael C. 2000. "Overland Trade Routes in Ancient Western Asia." Pp. 1401–1420 in *Civilizations of the Ancient Near East*. Edited by Jack M. Sasson. Peabody, MA: Hendrickson Publishers. (Reprint of 1995 edition. New York: Scribner.)

Bass, George F. 2000. "Sea and River Craft in the Ancient Near East." Pp. 1421–1431 in *Civilizations of the Ancient Near East*. Edited by Jack M. Sasson. Peabody, MA: Hendrickson Publishers. (Reprint of 1995 edition. New York: Scribner.)

Bienkowski, Piotr. 2000. "Beer," "Bread," "Economics," "Fishing," "Food," "Irrigation," "Weights and Measures," "Wine," and "Work." Pp. 47–48, 59, 100, 117–118, 120–121,

155–156, 318–319, and 323–324, respectively, in *Dictionary of the Ancient Near East.* Edited by Piotr Bienkowski and Alan Millard. London: British Museum Press.

Bienkowski, Piotr, and Alan Millard, eds. 2000. *Dictionary of the Ancient Near East.* London: British Museum Press.

Bottero, Jean. 2001c. "The Oldest Feast." Pp. 65–83 in *Everyday Life in Ancient Mesopotamia.* Edited by Jean Bottéro. Edinburgh: Edinburgh University Press.

Butzer, Karl W. 2000. "Environmental Change in the Near East and Human Impact on the Land." Pp. 123–151 in *Civilizations of the Ancient Near East.* Edited by Jack M. Sasson. Peabody, MA: Hendrickson Publishers. (Reprint of 1995 edition. New York: Scribner.)

Collins, Paul T. 2000. "Merchants" and "Shops and Markets." Pp. 270 and 194–195, respectively, in *Dictionary of the Ancient Near East.* Edited by Piotr Bienkowski and Alan Millard. London: British Museum Press.

Covington, Richard. "What Was Jiroft?" Saudi Aramco World 55:5. http://www. saudiaramcoworld.com/issue/200405/what.was.jiroft.htm (cited September/ October 2004).

Crawford, Harriet. 1998. *Dilmun and Its Gulf Neighbours.* Cambridge: Cambridge University Press.

Dalley, Stephanie. 1984. *Mari and Karana. Two Old Babylonian Cities.* London and New York: Longman.

———. 2000a. *Myths from Mesopotamia.* Revised edition. Oxford: Oxford University Press.

———. 2000b. "Banquets and Feasts." Pp. 46–47 in *Dictionary of the Ancient Near East.* Edited by Piotr Bienkowski and Alan Millard. London: British Museum Press.

Dilke, O. A. W. 1987. *Reading the Past. Mathematics and Measurement.* London: British Museum.

Electronic Text Corpus of Sumerian Literature. "The Debate between the Hoe and the Plough." http://www-etcsl.orient.ox.ac.uk/ (cited December 2, 2002).

———. "Enmerkar and the Lord of Aratta." http://www-etcsl.orient.ox.ac.uk/ (cited January 30, 2002).

———. "Gilgamesh and Huwawa." http://www-etcsl.orient.ox.ac.uk/ (cited January 30, 2002).

———. "The Farmer's Instructions." http://www-etcsl.orient.ox.ac.uk/ (cited December 2, 2002).

Eyre, Christopher J. 2000. "The Agricultural Cycle, Farming and Water Management in the Ancient Near East." Pp. 175–190 in *Civilizations of the Ancient Near East.* Edited by Jack M. Sasson. Peabody, MA: Hendrickson Publishers. (Reprint of 1995 edition. New York: Scribner.)

Fitzgerald, Michael A. 1997. "Uluburun." Pp. 430–432 in *Encyclopaedia of Underwater and Maritime Archaeology.* Edited by James P. Delgado. London: British Museum Press.

Grayson, A. Kirk. 2000. "Assyrian Rule of Conquered Terrritory in Ancient Western Asia." Pp. 959–968 in *Civilizations of the Ancient Near East.* Edited by Jack M. Sasson. Peabody, MA: Hendrickson Publishers. (Reprint of 1995 edition. New York: Scribner.)

Hawkins, J. D., ed. *Trade in the Ancient Near East. Papers Presented to the XXIII Rencontre Assyriologique Internationale.* London: British School of Archaeology in Iraq.

Hesse, Brian. 2000. "Animal Husbandry and Human Diet in the Ancient Near East." Pp. 203–222 in *Civilizations of the Ancient Near East*. Edited by Jack M. Sasson. Peabody, MA: Hendrickson Publishers. (Reprint of 1995 edition. New York: Scribner.)

Iranian Cultural Heritage News Agency. "Iranian Archeologists to Identify Jiroft Ancient Quarries." NetNative. http://www.payvand.com/news/04/jul/1134.html (cited August 9, 2004).

———. "Public Plunder of Jiroft Artifacts Resumes." http://www.chn.ir/english/eshownews.asp?no=2812 (cited August 9, 2004).

———. "Jiroft a Key Business Hub 5,000 Years Ago." NetNative. http://www.payvand.com/news/04/sep/1133.html (cited September 15, 2004).

Kohler-Rollefson, Ilse. 1996. "The One-Humped Camel in Asia: Origin, Utilization and Mechanisms of Dispersal." Pp. 282–294 in *The Origins and Spread of Agriculture and Pastoralism in Eurasia*. Edited by David R. Harris. Washington, DC: Smithsonian Institution Press.

Kramer, Samuel Noah. 1971. *The Sumerians. Their History, Culture, and Character*. Chicago: University of Chicago Press.

———. 1981. *History Begins at Sumer. Thirty-Nine Firsts in Recorded History*. Third revised edition. Philadelphia: University of Pennsylvania Press.

Kuhrt, Amelie. 1995. *The Ancient Near East. c. 3000–330 BCE*. 2 Volumes. London: Routledge.

Larsen, Mogen Trolle. "Partnerships in the Old Assyrian Trade." Pp. 119–146 in *Trade in the Ancient Near East. Papers Presented to the XXIII Rencontre Assyriologique Internationale*. Edited by J. D. Hawkins. London: British School of Archaeology in Iraq.

Leemans, W. F. 1977. "The Importance of Trade." Pp. 1–10 in *Trade in the Ancient Near East. Papers Presented to the XXIII Rencontre Assyriologique Internationale*. Edited by J. D. Hawkins. London: British School of Archaeology in Iraq.

Leick, Gwendolyn. 2001. *Mesopotamia. The Invention of the City*. London: Allen Lane, Penguin Press.

Lloyd, Seton. 1980. *Foundations in the Dust*. Revised edition. London: Thames and Hudson.

Macdonald, Michael. 2000. "Arabia," "Arabs," and "Camel." Pp. 24–26 and 64, respectively, in *Dictionary of the Ancient Near East*. Edited by Piotr Bienkowski and Alan Millard. London: British Museum Press.

McIntosh, Jane R. 2002. *A Peaceful Realm. The Rise and Fall of the Indus Civilization*. Boulder, CO: Westview.

Maidman, Maynard Paul. 2000. "Nuzi: Portrait of an Ancient Mesopotamian Provincial Town." Pp. 931–947 in *Civilizations of the Ancient Near East*. Edited by Jack M. Sasson. Peabody, MA: Hendrickson Publishers. (Reprint of 1995 edition. New York: Scribner.)

Mattingly, Gerald L. 2000. "Animal Husbandry," "Roads," "Transport and Travel," "Trees," and "Water." Pp. 19–20, 244–245, 299–302, and 317, respectively, in *Dictionary of the Ancient Near East*. Edited by Piotr Bienkowski and Alan Millard. London: British Museum Press.

Millard, Alan. 2000. "Money" and "Taxation." Pp. 201 and 284, respectively, in *Dictionary of the Ancient Near East.* Edited by Piotr Bienkowski and Alan Millard. London: British Museum Press.

Muhly, James D. 2000. "Mining and Metalwork in Ancient Western Asia." Pp. 1501–1519 in *Civilizations of the Ancient Near East.* Edited by Jack M. Sasson. Peabody, MA: Hendrickson Publishers. (Reprint of 1995 edition. New York: Scribner.)

Nissen, Hans J. 1988. *The Early History of the Ancient Near East.* Chicago: University of Chicago Press. (Paperback edition 1990.)

Oates, Joan. 1986. *Babylon.* Revised edition. London: Thames and Hudson.

Oates, Joan, and David Oates. 2001. *Nimrud. An Assyrian Imperial City Revealed.* London: British School of Archaeology in Iraq.

Oppenheim, A. Leo, and Erica Reiner. 1977. *Ancient Mesopotamia. Portrait of a Dead Civilization.* Revised edition. Chicago: University of Chicago Press.

Parpola, Asko. 1994. *Deciphering the Indus Script.* Cambridge: Cambridge University Press.

Philip, Graham. 2000. "Silver." P. 272 in *Dictionary of the Ancient Near East.* Edited by Piotr Bienkowski and Alan Millard. London: British Museum Press.

Pollack, Susan. 1999. *Ancient Mesopotamia. The Eden that Never Was.* Cambridge: Cambridge University Press.

Postgate, J. Nicholas. 1994. *Early Mesopotamia.* London: Routledge.

———. 2000. "Royal Ideology and State Administration in Sumer and Akkad." Pp. 395–411 in *Civilizations of the Ancient Near East.* Edited by Jack M. Sasson. Peabody, MA: Hendrickson Publishers. (Reprint of 1995 edition. New York: Scribner.)

Potts, D. T. 1997. *Mesopotamian Civilization. The Material Foundations.* London: The Athlone Press.

———. 2000. "Distant Shores: Ancient Near Eastern Trade with South Asia and Northeastern Africa." Pp. 1451–1463 in *Civilizations of the Ancient Near East.* Edited by Jack M. Sasson. Peabody, MA: Hendrickson Publishers. (Reprint of 1995 edition. New York: Scribner.)

Potts, Timothy. 1994. *Mesopotamia and the East. An Archaeological and Historical Study of Foreign Relations ca. 3400–2000 BC.* Oxford University Committee for Archaeology Monograph 37. Oxford: Oxford University Committee for Archaeology.

Powell, Marvin A. 1977. "Sumerian Merchants and the Problem of Profit." Pp. 23–30 in *Trade in the Ancient Near East. Papers Presented to the XXIII Rencontre Assyriologique Internationale.* Edited by J. D. Hawkins. London: British School of Archaeology in Iraq.

———. 2000. "Metrology and Mathematics in Ancient Mesopotamia." Pp. 1941–1957 in *Civilizations of the Ancient Near East.* Edited by Jack M. Sasson. Peabody, MA: Hendrickson Publishers. (Reprint of 1995 edition. New York: Scribner.)

Ratnagar, Shereen. 1981. *Encounters. The Westerly Trade of the Harappa Civilization.* Delhi: Oxford University Press.

Renfrew, Jane Margaret. 2000. "Vegetables in the Ancient Near Eastern Diet." Pp. 191–202 in *Civilizations of the Ancient Near East.* Edited by Jack M. Sasson. Peabody, MA: Hendrickson Publishers. (Reprint of 1995 edition. New York: Scribner.)

Roaf, Michael. 1990. *Cultural Atlas of Mesopotamia.* New York: Facts on File.

Sasson, Jack M., ed. 2000. *Civilizations of the Ancient Near East.* 4 Volumes. Peabody, MA: Hendrickson Publishers. (Reprint of 1995 edition. New York: Scribner.)

Schwartz, Glenn M. 2000. "Pastoral Nomadism in Ancient Western Asia." Pp. 249–258 in *Civilizations of the Ancient Near East.* Edited by Jack M. Sasson. Peabody, MA: Hendrickson Publishers. (Reprint of 1995 edition. New York: Scribner.)

Skinner, F. G. 1954. "Measures and Weights." Pp. 774–784 in *A History of Technology.* Edited by Charles Singer, E. J. Holmyard, A. R. Hall, and Trevor I. Williams. Oxford: Oxford University Press.

Snell, Daniel C. 2000. "Methods of Exchange and Coinage in Ancient Western Asia." Pp. 1487–1497 in *Civilizations of the Ancient Near East.* Edited by Jack M. Sasson. Peabody, MA: Hendrickson Publishers. (Reprint of 1995 edition. New York: Scribner.)

Stein, Gil J. 2001. "Indigenous Social Complexity at Hacinebi (Turkey) and the Organization of Uruk Colonial Contact." Pp. 265–305 in *Uruk, Mesopotamia and Its Neighbours. Cross-Cultural Interactions in the Era of State Formation.* Edited by Mitchell S. Rothman. Santa Fe, NM: School of American Research Press.

Summers, Geoffrey D. 2000. "Kanesh." Pp. 163–164 in *Dictionary of the Ancient Near East.* Edited by Piotr Bienkowski and Alan Millard. London: British Museum Press.

Van de Mieroop, Marc. 1997. *The Ancient Mesopotamian City.* Oxford: Oxford University Press.

Veenhof, Klaas R. 1977. "Some Social Effects of Old Assyrian Trade." Pp. 109–118 in *Trade in the Ancient Near East. Papers Presented to the XXIII Rencontre Assyriologique Internationale.* Edited by J. D. Hawkins. London: British School of Archaeology in Iraq.

———. 2000. "Kanesh: An Assyrian Colony in Anatolia." Pp. 859–872 in *Civilizations of the Ancient Near East.* Edited by Jack M. Sasson. Peabody, MA: Hendrickson Publishers. (Reprint of 1995 edition. New York: Scribner.)

Yoffee, Norman. 2000. "The Economy of Ancient Western Asia." Pp. 1387–1399 in *Civilizations of the Ancient Near East.* Edited by Jack M. Sasson. Peabody, MA: Hendrickson Publishers. (Reprint of 1995 edition. New York: Scribner.)

Zohary, Daniel, and Maria Hopf. 2000. *Domestication of Plants in the Old World. The Origin and Spread of Cultivated Plants in West Asia, Europe and the Nile Valley.* 3d edition. Oxford: Oxford University Press.

VI

CHAPTER 6

Social Organization and Social Structure

SETTLEMENT PATTERNS

Introduction

Settlement studies provide an important tool for understanding past societies and their organization. The raw materials for such studies are mainly the distribution and nature of artifacts collected from both excavations and surface surveys; recently this evidence has been supplemented by studies of the environment and of the micromorphology of sites. The Gulf War of 1991 and the decade of sanctions isolated Iraq from the many recent advances in settlement archaeology and cut short several projects focused on the study of entire urban layouts. The fall of Saddam Hussein now offers Iraqi archaeologists the opportunity to become familiar with new techniques, but the utter devastation in the aftermath of the war of liberation could well mean that little survives for them to investigate.

Earlier regional surveys shed considerable light on prehistoric land use and settlement hierarchy but far less on those of the historical period, although for this there is also some documentary evidence such as land-sale and inheritance documents, and *kudurrus* and other records of land grants. The settlement terms used in Mesopotamian texts are often ambiguous: Both the Sumerian word *uru* and its Akkadian equivalent, *alum,* denote a settlement regardless of size, from farmstead to city, giving a valuable insight into the Mesopotamian worldview, but providing no information on settlement hierarchy, for which it is necessary to turn to archaeological evidence regarding the size, layout, facilities, and relative positions of the settlements within an area. However, erosion has removed traces of some settlements, dunes and alluvium have buried others, and deep tells mask earlier occupation in long-lived settlements, making it impossible for the picture of settlement patterns through time to be complete.

Spatial analysis within settlements can be a potent tool for understanding social organization, but the vast scale of tells means that only in relatively short-lived sites, such as Abu Salabikh, can whole settlements be studied. The spectacular remains of palaces and temples have attracted most archaeological attention, and domestic architecture has been investigated in only a handful of sites, such as Old Babylonian Nippur. The documentary record is also patchy and not always straightforward. These factors can produce a skewed picture of settlement patterns.

Settlement Surveys and Settlement Patterns

Mesopotamia was an urban land par excellence. Its literature firmly contrasts the ordered and civilized existence of the fortunate denizens of town or city with the lot of their uncouth pastoral neighbors who "dwell in tents" or the turmoil of the soldier's life in camp and on the battlefield. Southern Mesopotamia especially was heavily urbanized, with cities and towns so close together that they were intervisible. The classic study of the landscape around Uruk by Adams and Nissen (1972) provides the most detailed picture of the changing pattern in the distribution and nature of settlements through time. Environmental reconstructions indicate that southern Mesopotamia during the fifth to early third millennia B.C.E. developed from a landscape dissected by small watercourses to one with a few much larger rivers, branches of the Euphrates and to a lesser extent the Tigris. Thereafter the branches of the Euphrates shifted their course on occasion, but the pattern otherwise changed less drastically.

Small early settlements were scattered through the landscape, taking advantage of favorable situations along streams and on marsh edges. By the late fourth millennium, larger settlements were emerging in various locations in Babylonia, Uruk being the first to attain the size and complexity that qualify it to be called a city. At this time the area surveyed by Adams and Nissen contained the city of Uruk, around 120–200 hectares in extent, and 107 villages. In the population explosion of the subsequent Jemdet Nasr and Early Dynastic I periods, Uruk grew to ca. 400 hectares; four sizable towns of more than 50 hectares appeared, along with some twenty-four small towns and around 140 villages. The increasing population brought competition between settlements, particularly for water, which was the critical resource in Babylonia, and during the later ED period the greater part of the population in the Uruk survey area moved into towns and cities, which were now defended with walls. In the ED II–III periods Nissen and Adams identified only seventeen villages and six small towns, while Umma developed into a city and there were now eight large and three medium-sized towns.

The Babylonian political, economic, and social landscape now consisted of city-states set along the river branches, with a network of irrigation channels the extent and sophistication of which was dependent on the power of the state to organize their construction and maintenance and to mobilize the necessary workforce. The uncultivated steppe outside their territories was home to pastoralists whose nomadic lifestyle and "barbaric" ways were seen as strongly contrasted to the civilized life of the city dweller or rural inhabitant of the city-state. The villages of the latter remained few in number, the majority of the population living in the city or its unwalled suburbs. The city-states vied with each other to control larger areas but maintained their identity even during periods when they were incorporated into larger empires.

With the fall of the Ur III Empire, the Uruk survey area saw a decline in the number of settlements and in the size of those that remained. After the reign of the Old Babylonian king Samsu-iluna, the economic and environmental decline that had been sweeping over the region finally brought the virtual abandonment of the south, and northern Babylonia, to which the focus of settlement had shifted in the early second millennium, became and remained the heartland of the region. In the later second millennium the south saw some local revival under the Kassites who founded new settlements and resettled earlier ones, but the scale of occupation was and remained far below that of the region's third-millennium heyday, and a greater proportion of the population lived in rural settlements. From the ninth century Assyrian kings forcibly resettled prisoners of war in depopulated areas, although only in the final century under the Neo-Babylonian Empire did the region see real urban regeneration. Investment in irrigation canals improved local productivity, and the area around Uruk itself was extensively developed as state-run date plantations; the surrounding marshy region provided rich pasturage as well as fish, waterfowl, reeds, and other resources, but favored dispersed settlement.

The Uruk region was precocious in its early development; surveys in the region around Ur and Eridu show substantial urbanization considerably later, in the mid-third millenium, whereas in the Diyala region, although some towns and cities developed, the bulk of the population continued to live in villages. Elsewhere in Sumer and in Akkad the pattern of early development was equally varied, but from the later third millennium most of the south underwent a similar pattern of growth and decline to that experienced by Uruk.

In Assyria, where arable land was more widespread but less intensively productive, settlement was more dispersed and population growth slower. Urbanism came later here and was never as well developed as in Babylonia. Although there were a number of towns and cities, some in the Neo-Assyrian Empire being on a huge scale, the bulk of the population was rural and the landscape was not carved up between city-states. Nevertheless in Assyria, as in Babylonia, the notion of the city as the focus of civilized existence was central to the Mesopotamian view of the world, reflecting a country that was much more heavily urbanized than any other early states, such as those of the Greeks.

The ebb and flow of population and settlement were dependent on both environmental and political conditions, particularly in regions on the margins such as the foothills of the Zagros. The drastic contraction and abandonment of settlement in southern Babylonia and its subsequent reoccupation at a lower density is only the most extreme example of the dramas played out in many parts of Mesopotamia over the centuries. Natural fluctuations in the availability of water from river or rainfall and changes in temperature and vegetation affected the viability and density of settlement generally; in the areas where conditions were more marginal and settlement more precarious, these effects were more strongly felt. In addition, these areas were more vulnerable to the depredations of similarly affected nomads living on their doorstep. Strong central government could to some extent counteract these effects, constructing networks of irrigation channels and long feeder canals linking cities and their hinterland with distant sources of water. Kings boasted of such endeavors, which brought civilization and prosperity to hitherto unsettled land, for example Sargon II who created canals and orchards for his new capital of Dur-Sharrukin (Khorsabad). Governments and major landowners could take financial risks not open to the small private entrepreneur, bringing marginal land into cultivation, often for specialized crops such as timber; the government could also provide military protection for new settlements and their fields against raiders. Conversely, the collapse of central authority would result in the reversion to smaller-scale economic units—rural settlements with little infrastructure, greatly at the mercy of environmental and climatic fluctuations and marauders. While major state and private landowners could weather some setbacks and tenants were able to move to other, more productive land, the small landowner was the first to suffer since all his investment of labor and resources was in his own land, and he stood and fell with it.

The City

Palaces and temples were the heart of the Mesopotamian city. In first-millennium Assyria these were generally close together on a citadel surrounded by a wall, situated in one corner of the city. In contrast, in Babylonian and earlier Assyrian cities, the palace and the temples were often located in different parts of the city: The temple precincts, which might be surrounded by their own separate walls, were at the city's heart, and palaces were constructed where an adequately sized piece of ground could be found, often on the outskirts of the city. Housing occupied much of the remaining area enclosed within the city wall, although cities and towns in the north seem to have been less densely settled than those in the south.

Walls had been built around the first cities, not merely for defense but also as a potent symbol of the city's power and prestige, and they remained a vital element of a city's design, while their destruction by enemies symbolized the city's loss of autonomy and vitality. They also divided city from countryside, although suburbs set among gardens and fields often grew up outside the walls. A biblical reference (Jonah 3:3) claimed that the Assyrian city of Nineveh was "three days' journey in breadth," indicating extensive suburbs. Villages within the city's territory might also have been regarded as part of the city. The later third-millennium Hurrian town of Tell Taya in the north, one of the few sites investigated as a whole, had an inner town of ca. 5 hectares enclosed within the city wall, with a further 2 hectares' extension. Dense suburbs covered a further 65 hectares, and more dispersed settlement in the surrounding 90 hectares was also part of the town.

Within the city itself there were often rivers or canals, sometimes with quays, parks, private gardens, and even fields, as well as areas of waste ground, particularly in periods when the city's population fell and only parts of the intramural city were occupied. At other times, however, the population rose and housing was at a premium, dwellings crammed close together (see photo p. 72), houses sharing party walls and sometimes subdivided. Estimating the population of the towns and cities is not easy. The extent of suburban occupation is hard to determine, as is the density of settlement inside

The remains of a substantial structure in the center of Uruk which can claim to be the world's first city. Most early Mesopotamian architecture was of mud brick, a practical, cheap, and durable material but one that produced buildings that are not visually as impressive as the stone monuments of other regions. (Nik Wheeler/Corbis)

the walls. Even an accurate assessment of the extent of this occupation, however, only provides a starting point for population estimates, since the number of occupants in a house could vary and the houses themselves might or might not have more than one story. Census and tax records, which could be very helpful in answering such questions, are lacking, and only a few settlements have yielded some details of household composition. Different scholars, consequently, often produce widely different figures for a settlement's population at any given period. Nevertheless crude estimates of area give some impression of the huge scale of Mesopotamian urbanization. At its height, for example, Babylon covered around 1,000 hectares and Kalhu 325—compared with 225 hectares for Athens at the peak of its power. Uruk at the beginning of the ED period had an extent of 400 hectares.

Residential areas have been investigated in only a few towns and cities. The streets were generally unpaved and winding, although they could be uniform in width. Raised thresholds prevented the rubbish dumped in the streets from being washed into the houses by rain. These were built up repeatedly as the street level rose.

Town houses generally followed a plan that was widely adopted in the ancient Near East and is still usual in the region today. Architects' plans of some survive, from the later third millennium onward. The entrance passage led into a central courtyard, often offset or turning a corner so that the interior of the building was shielded from view and from the dust of the street outside. In the Mesopotamian climate, stiflingly hot for much of the year, the courtyard provided a welcome combination of fresh air, shade, and light, allowing much of life to be lived out of doors but in privacy. In Ur's houses, the courtyard floor sloped inward to a central drain, allowing rain to run off. Water jars, filled from the public wells, stood in one corner.

Houses could vary greatly in size. In the smallest, one room would be used for storage and the other for all the functions of normal domestic life, including cooking, washing, and sleeping. Larger houses had substantial blocks of rooms opening from three or four sides of the courtyard and might even have more than one courtyard; these were the homes either of wealthier families or of extended families. Guests were entertained in a public room facing the entrance to the courtyard. Mats were provided for them to sit on, with cushions and, at night, mattresses. Other rooms opening from the courtyard would include the kitchen, furnished with a quern for grinding grain, a hearth for cooking, and a bread oven; storerooms; sometimes a bathroom and perhaps a toilet—some were found in Ur; and in some houses, there were also stalls for animals. The private family rooms might also lead off the courtyard, or the house might have a second story on which these rooms were located, accessible from a stair and opening from a balcony supported on pillars around the edge of the courtyard. In the far south, the scarcity of wood for construction would have made it difficult to build houses with an upper story, and it is not established for certain that they existed here, although in Sippar farther to the north, legal documents referring to their lease makes it clear that upper stories were built. In the fifth century, after the fall of the Babylonian Empire, Herodotus speaks of houses in Babylon with three or four stories: These may well have existed here in earlier centuries, too.

Stairs, or alternatively a ladder, led also to the flat roof—a place to sleep in the heat of summer, to dry clothes or food for storage, and to carry out many other domestic activities. Some houses, particularly in second-millennium Ur, also included a private domestic shrine, with an altar and sometimes figurines of deities. It was not uncommon also to bury family members beneath the house floor.

The houses were generally constructed of mudbrick, although the foundations and lowest courses were often of the more durable baked brick in Babylonia or stone in Assyria. Floors were generally of beaten earth, but many were plastered, as were the walls. The few surviving traces of windows indicate that they had wooden frames and shutters made of reeds. Wooden beams supported the roof (see photo p. 60) and formed the intermediate floor in two-story buildings; in southern Mesopotamia wood was so valuable that doors and roofbeams appear as inheritance in wills. Wood was also used for the simple furniture of the houses, usually no more than a table, some chairs or stools, and one or two chests in which to store clothing and other household items. Cupboards and shelves might be built into the thickness of the walls. Cushions and rugs enlivened the house's appearance and contributed to its comfort, and on occasion there were pots of flowers.

Some houses seem to have included rooms that functioned as workshops. In Neo-Babylonian times at least, references to such places as "the city of metal-workers" shows that parts of the city might be given over to the practitioners of particular crafts. Evidence from the short-lived city of Mashkan Shapir indicates that particular craft activities could be both concentrated in individual locations and scattered throughout the settlement. Woolley claimed to have also identified shops; many scholars now think this unlikely. However the literature does record taverns; these were often also brothels, decorated therefore with erotic pictures and suggestive prayers to the goddess of love.

Although shops may not have existed, there may have been markets and other commercial activity in the open area immediately inside the city gates. These were probably also used for meetings of the ward assembly, and it was here that the garrison was stationed. Cities were divided into administrative wards (*babtum*), apparently corresponding to the city gates.

Housing continued in suburbs outside the city walls. Here also lay the *karum,* a term originally meaning "quay," the heart of trading activity, where merchants and other travelers from other cities and regions were accommodated. Other strangers included the nomads who often worked for or with the city dwellers while often retaining a separate identity. They dwelt in tents, in encampments outside the city walls that sometimes became permanent settlements, as for instance, around the city of Sippar, probably a port of trade.

Our knowledge of rural housing is far more limited, but some village dwellings have been excavated. Early Dynastic rural settlements had rectangular or sometimes round houses set within large compounds enclosed by a wall: These were probably the homes of extended families, structures being erected within the compound for each nuclear family as required. By the second millennium B.C.E., however, the evidence from two excavated rural sites, Haradum and Shaduppum (Tell Harmal), suggests that many villages had adopted the urban arrangement of contiguous courtyard houses.

The Palace

The palace (Sumerian *e.gal,* Akkadian *ekallum*) was the residence of the royal family in city-states and imperial capitals, such as Mari and Nineveh, and of governors in provincial cities and towns, such as Eshnunna. It was also an administrative, industrial, and economic center. A few buildings of the Uruk period, notably in the Eanna complex at Uruk itself, may have been the residences of the ruler or chief priest, but their function is uncertain. In the ED period a possible palace was situated beside the temples at Kish (palace A) and a much larger complex (Plano-convex Building) at some distance in another part of the city, and a possible palace was also found at Eridu. Most later cities probably contained a palace although very few have been excavated.

Palaces followed domestic architecture in being arranged around court-yards. At Eshnunna, the "Governor's Palace," dated around 2000 B.C.E., lies between the temple of Shusin and a similar but smaller private chapel, both of which could be entered either from the street or from inside the palace. An entrance near the temple led into a narrow set of guard rooms running the width of the palace, and from the far end the visitor entered a courtyard surrounded on two sides by rooms. On the right an entrance led into the throne room, which ran the length of the palace and from which a second courtyard was accessed. This became the standard layout of palaces: a suite of public rooms off an outer courtyard (*babanu*), an inner courtyard giving access to residential and service areas (*bitanu*), and a throne room used by the ruler as an audience chamber and the focus of propagandist decoration as early as ED times.

The palace at Mari followed the same division of areas but was much larger; built and added to over a period of three centuries, in its final form under Zimri-Lim it had around 260 ground-floor rooms and an extensive upper story. The archive here and the well-preserved structures that survive to a height of up to 5 meters make it the best-known example of early palace architecture. The entrance gate led through a series of rooms into the main courtyard, which gave access to the shrine of Ishtar and the great sanctuary in the southeast quarter of the palace and from which opened the gateway into the official quarters in the northwest. A corridor led from here into a large courtyard with an artificial palm tree of wood clad in bronze and silver at its center and a number of real palm trees. On the walls around the court were painted scenes including a sacrificial procession and, on the far wall under a colonnade, the investiture of the king. Beyond lay an antechamber with a statue of the goddess of the flowing vase and then the throne room. These constituted the public areas of the palace, where visitors would be received. The royal apartments occupied two parts of the rest of the palace: the chambers of the king and his staff and the separate apartments of the royal women. Elsewhere in the complex were kitchens, workshops in which a variety of crafts were practiced, including textile manufacture, administrative offices and archives, and a large number of storerooms, as well as mausoleums.

Other second-millennium palaces included those of King Sinkasid at Uruk, Shamshi-Adad at Shubat-Enlil, and the Kassite kings at Dur-Kurigalzu, and the governor's palace at Nuzi, which had more than a hundred rooms, including bathrooms and toilets. Wall paintings, mosaics, marble paving, stone sculptures, wall hangings, and other sumptuous fittings often adorned the palaces. Most magnificent were the first-millennium palaces of the Neo-Assyrian kings at Kalhu, Dur Sharrukin, and Nineveh, and the Neo-Babylonian kings in Babylon. The Assyrian palaces were situated in a separately walled citadel, alongside the major temples, with an adjoining complex of administrative buildings and housing for the elite. Kings often built themselves a new palace, competing in magnificence with those of their predecessors: The citadel at Kalhu housed palaces built by Ashurnasirpal (North-West Palace), Shalmaneser III, Adad-Nirari III, Tiglath-Pileser III (Central Palace), and

Esarhaddon (South-West Palace). Shalmaneser also built a separate Review Palace, or arsenal ("Fort Shalmaneser"), in a different part of the city. At Dur-Sharrukin, Sargon II built a monumental pillared entrance portico (*bit hilani*) to his palace, following the fashion of the lands to the west: It had cedar pillars supported on the backs of bronze lions. Like earlier palaces, those of the Assyrian kings had outer courtyards and rooms for public functions, including reception rooms, storerooms, administrative offices, and the residential quarters of officials. These courtyards led through doorways flanked by gigantic stone statues of winged bulls and lions, originally painted, into the throne room, dominated by the throne on its monolithic stone slab. The largest and most magnificent room of the palace, the throne room was decorated with reliefs depicting the king victorious in war and successful on the hunting field, monumental enterprises such as the creation and transport of the huge statues, and processions of tribute bearers and religious scenes, while the floors may have been covered with fine carpets. Reliefs, glazed wall tiles, and wall paintings might also ornament other major and private rooms within the palace.

Beyond the public apartments lay the *bitanu*, which included the harem. Domestic suites with well-appointed living room, cupboards, and bathroom make up the *bitanu* of Ashurnasirpal's palace at Kalhu, perhaps the most completely preserved example. Vaulted underground chambers beneath the private apartments here seem to have been the treasuries of the royal ladies, and elsewhere in the palace were small stone-paved strongrooms, which were only accessible through other rooms and which could be barred. A number of princesses' burials were found beneath the domestic quarters of the Kalhu palace. Other rooms within the *bitanu* included kitchens.

At Babylon, the main palace complex lay beside the Ishtar Gate. To the south of the city wall was the "Southern Citadel," five courtyards with attached reception rooms and the throne room opening from the middle courtyard, perhaps the scene of the biblical Belshazzar's Feast. The facade of the throne room was decorated with a magnificent frieze of glazed bricks, depicting lions at the bottom, stylized palm trees above, and crenellations at the top, with geometric floral patterns filling in the rest of the space. Blue enameled bricks adorned the upper walls of the palace; the doors were of cedar and other luxury timbers, such as sissoo and ebony; and gold, silver, lapis lazuli, and ivory were also used in the construction of the palace. Numerous administrative and residential rooms, storerooms, and workshops made up the rest of the substantial complex. The Western Outwork, a massive mudbrick construction, protected the palace against erosion by the river flowing by its side. Immediately to the north, outside the wall, was the "Northern Palace," of which two courtyards survive. Its eastern wall ran along the Processional Way and was decorated outside with glazed brick friezes of lions. Among the remains in the Northern Palace was found Nebuchadrezzar's museum, a collection of earlier antiquities made by Nebuchadrezzar and his successors (see photo p. 24). Finally in the angle of the outer city wall at the extreme north of the city was the Summer Palace, of which the main surviving element is the system of ventilation shafts that enabled the palace to be kept cool in summer.

Literary and pictorial evidence shows that private gardens were incorporated into or attached to palaces: These contained pavilions and a great variety of fruit trees, as well as plants and trees imported from conquered or more distant lands, including such exotica as incense bushes and cotton plants, and might also have housed some small animals such as deer.

THE PEOPLE OF MESOPOTAMIAN SOCIETY

Law codes and other documents divided free individuals into two classes. Many people were referred to as *awilum* ("man"), a term that denoted citizens who owned property, particularly land but often also houses and livestock. They included powerful officials, high-ranking soldiers, successful merchants, senior clergy, and wealthy landowners, but also more modest individuals, small farmers, self-employed craftsmen, and the like.

Less certain is the significance of the second-rank designation *mushkennum*. The mushkennum did not own land or livestock, and by Old Babylonian times, the term denoted a pauper. People referred to as mushkennum were dependents of the temple or palace, reliant on the institution for work for which they received rations of food and clothing. Often they lived on royal estates, paying a part of their agricultural produce to the king and being liable for military service. Many were employed as artisans, men for instance as gardeners, carpenters, or metalworkers, women particularly in the huge textile industry. References to mushkennum in law codes and other public documents show that their welfare was considered an important royal responsibility. Their political rights were probably relatively restricted although they could speak in the citizens' assembly (*puhrum*).

Both men and women could work as scribes, of whom the bureaucracy required large numbers, particularly in Ur III times. Surprisingly, literacy was not necessarily associated with high status: The majority of female scribes in the palace at Mari were probably slaves, and slave girls trained as scribes were sometimes included in a dowry.

Slaves (*wardum*) occupied the lowest social status specified in the law codes. Distinctions were made between the three tiers of society, for example in the amount payable in compensation for injury, which was highest for awilum and lowest for slaves. Slaves included both prisoners of war and local people who had descended into slavery through debt. Society also included a number of manumitted slaves (*hupshu*).

Foreigners, such as traders or pastoralists, were distinguished by their ethnic identity, reflected in their outlandish names, and aspects of their behavior (for example, the Amorite who "eats his food raw"). Those who settled in Mesopotamia were quickly assimilated, as the Amorites illustrate. Originally pastoralists living in the desert region west of Mesopotamia, a few appeared in Babylonia from around 2400 B.C.E., and by 2100 they were a major nuisance, making frequent raids and settling in some regions. In the early second millennium many cities came under the rule of Amorite chieftains. Settled Amorites, like the royal family at Mari, maintained family ties with their still-nomadic tribal cousins but were largely indistinguishable from the native population; and by 1700 B.C.E. Amorites were no longer referred to.

Down the centuries, Mesopotamia, and particularly the cosmopolitan city of Babylon, continued to attract settlers from adjacent regions and tribes: Hurrians and Kassites in the second millennium, Chaldaeans, Aramaeans, and Arabs in the first, as well as small numbers of Egyptians, Elamites, Phoenicians, and others; the ranks of foreigners were swelled, in the first millennium in particular, by large numbers of deportees from the Levant, Elam, and other conquered regions. The absence of racism and religious intolerance facilitated the integration of people of all creeds and ethnic affiliations. For instance, although the Bible paints the Babylonian Exile as a universally abhorred episode, in fact when Cyrus offered to repatriate the Jewish exiles some fifty years later, many chose to stay in Babylon, where a highly respected Jewish community and center of Jewish scholarship flourished for many centuries.

SOCIETY AND THE LAW

Our knowledge of Mesopotamian law comes piecemeal from law codes and court records. The "law codes" were collections of legal provisions set down by the king, often after he had conquered new territory where laws might be different. The earliest attested example was that of Uru-inim-gina of Lagash; others were compiled by the Ur III king Shulgi, Lipit-Ishtar of Isin, Hammurabi, and later monarchs. They include statements about a selection of cases and situations, along with the appropriate action to be taken. These often followed customary law but also included reforms made by the king. Hammurabi's Code (see photo p. 246) includes the harsh "lex talionis" (punishment by reciprocal injury: "an eye for an eye, a tooth for a tooth") that is often thought to have reflected the traditions of the nomadic Amorites. In contrast earlier codes tended to prescribe more humane punishments involving compensation.

These codes are by no means comprehensive and many recorded court judgments follow other systems, reflecting custom and tradition and the experience of the judiciary. As society changed, traditional law was modified to reflect contemporary practice and attitudes. Many of the recorded cases deal with civil matters such as inheritance, adoption, and the sale of property. Others relate to crimes: injury, manslaughter and murder, adultery and rape, theft and criminal damage. The penalty might depend on the wishes of the victim. In the case of murder, for example, the victim's family could choose whether the murderer was to be executed or should pay them compensation.

Often courts had to deal with conflicting claims such as disputed ownership. In such cases the parties involved might be required to swear an oath on a sacred object, such as a divine emblem, fear of commiting sacrilege constraining them from perjuring themselves. In the most serious cases, one or both litigants might be required to undergo the river ordeal to demonstrate their guilt or innocence. The selected party(s) had to plunge into a given part of the river: If they sank their guilt was established.

The judiciary operated at three levels. Local councils of elders representing a village or an urban ward dealt with everyday matters such as divorce applications, disputed paternity, and conflicts over inheritance. The members of the council took decisions based on their experience of and familiarity with the litigants, and could call upon local witnesses with inside knowledge to testify under oath. Where oral testimony was unavailable, documentary evidence could also be produced, such as records of former transactions or agreements, or of the outcome of pertinent earlier legal proceedings.

If the council felt unable to deal with a case or one of the parties at law was dissatisfied with its outcome, the matter could be referred to a higher authority, a judge appointed by the king, or to the king himself, the highest authority. Some serious offenses, such as murder, known as *din napishtim* ("case of life"), were referred directly to the king as a matter of course—but he could send cases back to the council whose detailed local knowledge could be important in establishing or disproving guilt.

The role of the judiciary was not only to resolve disputes and punish criminal behavior but also to administer and enforce government decrees and to witness and record legally binding agreements between individuals. Most contracts were agreed upon orally, often before witnesses, and took their force from the power invested in the words of the legal formulae used, which were often backed up by performing symbolic gestures. The use of such formulae and actions in creating a legal marriage bond is familiar in modern society across the globe; in ancient Mesopotamia they were used also to legalize many other contracts, such as that between a landowner and his tenant. Written records of these transactions did not increase their legality, which was made binding by the oral pronouncements, but served as a record in case of future disputes. In the third millennium, these documents were authenticated by an official seal; later the seals of the parties involved and of witnesses were generally required.

MESOPOTAMIAN LIFE

The Household

In the early Near East, the basic social unit was probably the extended family: a man and his wife, his grown-up children (or at least his sons) and their partners and children, and his own unmarried children. Houses like the fifth-millennium example at Tell Madhhur (see chapter 4) seem designed to accommodate such a family, of perhaps twenty people, each nuclear unit having its own room, and the whole extended family sharing a large living room, storerooms, and kitchen. Alternatively, the family home might be adequate only for the patriarch, his wife, and unmarried children, their other children each building an adjacent house within the family compound when they married.

Residence in extended families may have continued down the millennia in rural Mesopotamia, where space for building was relatively unrestricted, and it was still the norm in Early Dynastic towns. By the early second millennium, however, the density of settlement within towns and cities made it difficult for extended families to live together and favored residence in smaller houses accommodating only nuclear families, often not located close together. Documents from Kish show that most households there consisted of a man, his wife, and their unmarried children, sometimes along with one or two other family members such as a widowed mother, an unmarried sister, or an underage brother. A slave girl could also be part of the family circle, in the role of surrogate mother (see section entitled "Marriage"); and within the household there might be a few other slaves, male or female.

The social significance of the urban move to residence in nuclear families is uncertain. Some scholars argue that it reflects a change in the makeup of society, the bonds of the extended family having given way to other ties, such as those to professional associations or to institutions that offered employment, the temple and the palace. Others cite the (limited) evidence from legal documents that indicates the continuing importance of the extended family in the inheritance and sale of land.

A Mesopotamian clay tablet depicting a woman with a child, third or second millennium B.C.E. (Zev Radovan/Land of the Bible Picture Archive)

Children

Early Years. The Mesopotamian infant was protected in the womb against the baleful she-demon Lamashtu by magical amulets and incantations (in which the child was visualized as a ship on a dark sea carrying an unknown cargo). Abortion was illegal, although a recipe for an abortion-inducing potion shows that it was illicitly practiced. Children, however, particularly sons, were earnestly desired, for who else would care for a couple in their old age and make offerings to ensure the well-being of their spirits after their death? Where children were more abundant than resources, the baby might be adopted by a childless couple.

The baby was delivered with the mother in a crouching position, sometimes supported by two stones. A midwife assisted her, massaging her stomach, giving her the bark of certain trees to chew as a drug, and, if the birth was difficult, singing incantations. Soon after birth, the baby was given a name, often incorporating the name of the family god or the family's city of residence.

Babies were fed by their mother or by a paid wet-nurse for their first two or three years. During this time they were still threatened by Lamashtu, who was held responsible for infant mortality: The average family was lucky if more than two or three of their children survived into adulthood. Thereafter, life expectancy was good, seventy being considered a good age and 120 stated as the greatest age that the gods would allow; timely death was not feared but welcomed. Fifty was considered too young to die; early death through disease, accidents, or warfare was regarded as a sign that the gods, particularly the family deity, had turned their back on the individual concerned, often because of some consciously or unconsciously impious act.

Schooldays. Children generally learned their trade and other skills from their parents, although they might be appenticed, as young slaves often were. For the children of the well-to-do, many of whom would become scribes, there were formal schools. Schoolrooms—known as "tablet houses"(*e-dub.ba*, Akkadian *bit tuppi*)—have been uncovered in Ur, Nippur, Sippar, and the Mari palace, and Sumerian texts describe the curriculum and other aspects of schooling. School was run by a master scribe, the "school father," paid out of the students' fees and assisted by an advanced scholar known as "big brother" and sometimes by masters in particular subjects such as drawing and Sumerian. Pupils were kept hard at work, with only six days a month off, and they were beaten for various offenses, including lateness, speaking or standing up without permission, and poor-quality work. An Old Babylonian text ("Schooldays") vividly conjures up the student's day and his sufferings: rising in haste, he urges his mother to hurry with his packed lunch—two breadrolls—but arrives late and is punished, not for the last time that day. In the evening his father listens sympathetically to his son's complaints and invites the teacher over, plying him with food, drink, and gifts, while his son strives to display his deference and desire to do well. The teacher is mollified and flattered; eventually he praises the boy's application and assures him of success.

This little story was a popular text that students copied to practice their writing skills. In late-third-millennium and Old Babylonian times, there was a set curriculum pursued in schools; earlier and later the course of study varied but the basic elements were the same. The beginner, seated on a cloth in the courtyard, was taught to form cuneiform symbols in the sand. He progressed to learning how to prepare a clay tablet and reed stylus for writing and began his studies, copying on one face of the tablet the signs that his teacher had written on the other. Schooling since the earliest days around 3000 B.C.E. had been in Sumerian, but by the early second millennium this was a dead language that the pupil had also to learn. Many of the surviving "textbooks" are Akkadian-Sumerian dictionaries. The student copied lists that introduced him to the written forms of many categories of words—plants, animals, professions, places, minerals, and many others. As he became more proficient he began copying more complex texts, including literature, model letters, and law codes, acquiring a knowledge both of grammar and vocabulary and of broader skills and information that would stand him in good stead in his adult career. Surveying and mathematical exercises also loomed large, concerned with such practical matters as the rations required to feed enough workmen to dig a canal of a given length or the time needed to build a siege ramp.

Life was not all work. Little model animals set on boards must have been pull-along toys for small children, and their older brothers and sisters played knucklebones, dice, and board games, or skipped and danced to the music of a flute. Board games had a more serious side, too, being used in divination. Boys might accompany their fathers hunting or practice shooting at a target. Literary skills could be honed in debating contests. On occasion there would be professional entertainers to watch: jugglers, wrestlers, clowns, and acrobats, instrumental musicians and singers, snake charmers, and performing bears.

The teacher was expected to help his students obtain suitable posts in the civil or temple service. Literacy was a valuable asset, even to those not destined to work as scribes. Several kings boasted of their scholarship. Many royal and private family letters survive in archives like those from Kanesh and Mari: They range from exchanges on purely business matters to chatty information on domestic dramas and complaints about parental neglect and filial bad behavior.

Marriage

By her teens, a girl was ready for marriage, although her brothers would not marry for another decade. Marriages were arranged by fathers between their families, often for economic or political reasons; if the girl's father was dead, her mother or brothers would shoulder the responsibility. A verbal contract (*riksatum*) was agreed on, and in some communities was marked by a party. The groom's family then had to pay "bridewealth" (*terhatum*), often a lump sum in silver, paid either in full or in installments. The girl might move into her future in-laws' house immediately or might remain under her parents' roof until the wedding, visited by her fiancé. During this period the engagement was sometimes broken off, the groom's family often forfeiting the portion of the terhatum already paid.

The marriage was finalized by a feast (*kirrum*) provided by the groom's family, which could last for several days and might be accompanied by valuable gifts. The terhatum was balanced or exceeded by the dowry (*sheriktum* or *nudunnum*) paid by the girl's family, mainly items that would enable the young couple to set up house—domestic utensils, furniture, and textiles, as well as jewelry—and in the case of wealthier families, houses, fields, and slaves. The dowry was administered by the husband, but remained the property of the bride, returned to her if the marriage was dissolved (unless she had committed adultery), used by her after her husband's death, and inherited by her children, or, if she died childless, by her brothers. In some communities, the terhatum was added to the dowry and treated in the same way.

Monogamy was the norm in mainstream Mesopotamian society, although peripheral communities might have different practices. A letter from Mari comments on the three wives who accompanied a Hurrian coppersmith. It was thought proper to allow two or three years before despairing of offspring, but the wife might then select a slave girl to act as surrogate mother for children that would officially be hers. Alternatively the husband might contract a second marriage with the bride's real or adopted sister, a favored option when the first marriage could not be consummated, due to the wife's ill health or because she was a priestess vowed to celibacy. A husband could not discard his sick or injured wife, but childlessness was one of the main grounds for divorce.

A man and a woman in a loving pose, clay tablet from Mesopotamia, third or second millennium B.C.E. (Zev Radovan/Land of the Bible Picture Archive)

A dim view was taken of divorce after the wife had borne sons, and the husband might incur a substantial penalty, such as the forfeiture of his house and property. Men could initiate divorce, but the laws governing women varied. Many marriage contracts in the Old Babylonian period expressly forbade the wife to seek divorce; at other times she might enjoy rights of divorce equal to those of her husband, a fine in silver being payable when this took place. Often her conduct and morals were investigated before divorce was granted, to ensure she was not motivated by an adulterous passion. A divorced wife usually retained her dowry and could remarry if she chose.

Although marriages were arranged, love and desire were both regarded as a natural part of married life. Sumerian poems reflect both, describing the pastoral idyll of the goddess Inanna's courtship of her husband Dumuzi, or dwelling in graphic detail on her enthusiastic sexual activities. Others describe Inanna as a girl, awaiting Dumuzi's visit with anxious anticipation or sneaking out with him for a night of stolen kisses. Later snippets of love poetry also survive. When problems arose there were amulets and incantations to treat impotence, attract new partners, or reawaken a husband's faltering desire. Sexual promiscuity among the unmarried was not discouraged: In the poem "Inanna's Descent into the Underworld," its abandonment is viewed as an unnatural state of affairs:

"No young man impregnated a girl in the street,
The young man slept in his private room,
The girl slept in the company of her friends." (Dalley 2000a: 158)

Homosexuality was permitted as long as the older man was the senior partner, but it was regarded with disfavor as a relationship that did not produce children. Prostitution was an accepted activity, practiced by the city wall or in the harbor area, and in taverns, the walls of which were decorated with explicit scenes of sexual activity alongside prayers to Ishtar. A career as a prostitute was no bar to eventual marriage, although wisdom texts warned that ex-prostitutes made inconveniently independent-minded wives!

Frequenting prostitutes was tolerated if it did not endanger a man's marriage. Male adultery, however, was an affront to the injured wife's relatives and to the gods, and in some areas or periods it was severely punished. Adulterous married women were universally condemned and were liable to suffer death or other severe penalties. Where suspicion had arisen, it was up to the accused wife to prove her innocence, which she might demonstrate by undergoing the river ordeal; however, a deliberately slanderous accusation would bring an equivalent penalty upon the slanderer, so there was some slight protection against injustice.

Women

On marriage a girl became part of her husband's household, her fate intimately tied up with his fortunes. If things went badly, she and her children could be hired out to work, and in extreme financial trouble they could be pledged as slaves against unpaid debts. A wife's dowry property was managed by her husband, and in some periods and regions, she was confined to the house. Royal Assyrian ladies, from the Middle Assyrian period onward, were segregated in a harem, guarded by eunuchs, seeing only their husbands, children, and female attendants. In this hothouse environment, rivalry and quarrels were common. Some relief from the monotony came when the court traveled, as they accompanied the king. Apart from nomads, however, and itinerant entertainers, such as jugglers and acrobats, Mesopotamian women rarely traveled.

On the other hand, women often enjoyed considerable responsibility, running large establishments, deputizing for their absent husbands, and owning property in their own right. They could bring court cases and be called as witnesses. The Mari letters include a number from queen Shibtu to her husband Zimri-Lim about the palace administration—managing and acquiring stores, running the workshops, deploying new slaves, observing religious rites—as well as discussing personal matters. Her contemporary Iltani, queen of Karana, had to deal in addition with legal cases and petitioners on behalf of her husband. Even the Assyrian royal ladies in their harem could wield considerable political power as advisor to the king—their husband or son. On occasion their authority was overtly acknowledged—for example, the ninth-century queen Sammuramat was named in inscriptions alongside her son Adad-Nirari III.

The wives of the Assur merchants who lived in Kanesh also shouldered business responsibilities, often running the Assur end of operations—supervizing the textile workshops staffed by slave girls, dispatching consignments of textiles, keeping their husbands informed about the situation in Assur, handling financial matters, and, when necessary, selling off their jewelry—gold earrings, silver bracelets, and rings—to raise capital.

As brides were generally younger than their husbands, many women were widowed while their children were still young. Women in this situation often enjoyed the same business rights as men, managing the family's property on behalf of their sons. The Nuzi archives show the successful and sometimes aggressive business dealings of several such women, who managed and acquired land and engaged in trade.

An exceptional group were the well-born girls dedicated to the service of Shamash in Sippar, and other gods elsewhere, as *naditum* priestesses. One of the girls' main tasks was to ensure through prayers that the deity was kept aware of their families' interests. Perhaps equally important, however, was the disposal of property, for the dowry that the girl brought to the temple "cloister" (*gagum*) generally reverted to the family on her death. In return, the naditum could expect to be supported by her father or brothers. She exercised full control over her dowry lands and their revenue during her lifetime, often using the income to buy and sell goods and land, acting as a shrewd and vigorous businesswoman.

The sexual status of naditum women varied. Those in Nippur were vowed to celibacy, but the Sippar ladies could, it seems, take lovers, raising children who were adopted by their brothers, again ensuring that the dowry lands stayed within the family. In Babylon, in contrast, Marduk's naditum ladies were allowed to marry but had to remain celibate, often introducing a real or fictional younger sister as a subordinate wife to furnish the marital bed.

At the opposite end of the social scale were women whose families owned no property and who worked for a living, many of them in the woollen textile industry, especially in Babylonia, where great cities like Ur had enormous factories employing hundreds or even several thousand women and children. Although their main occupation was weaving, they might be required to undertake a variety of other tasks, including agricultural work. Large palace or temple kitchens also employed many female staff, grinding grain, making bread, cakes, and beer, and preparing and cooking various dishes.

Central to the existence of every married woman, however, was the bearing and raising of children. Pregnancy was a dangerous time, when a woman's health was monitored and treated both medically, using herbal drugs, and ritually, with spells, prayers, and divination. The outcome was always uncertain, with the possibility of miscarriage and stillbirth, or of dying in labor. One heartrending letter records the despair of a young wife who has lost her baby in late pregnancy while her husband is far away.

Men

Warfare, trade, diplomacy, or business took many men far from home, and from war at least some were never to return. Communications were slow: The journey between Assur and Kanesh, for example, took between six and twelve weeks, and travelers to more distant lands could be absent for a year or more. Wives might therefore remain for long periods ignorant of whether they were wife or widow; when the latter seemed likely, a wife could contract a second marriage, with the proviso that she must return to her original spouse if he eventually reappeared, leaving the children of her second marriage with their father.

In Mesopotamian society the man was head of the household. Sons remained subordinate to their fathers even after marriage, and family property was controlled by the father until his death. The patriarch's brothers also enjoyed domestic authority and could exercise it in the father's absence.

The Mesopotamian Creation myth (see page 214) recounts how humanity had been created to take on the burden of work that had been too demanding for the gods. It was therefore the duty of every citizen to toil in one field of endeavor or another—from the lowly peasant dredging canals to the king bowed down by the weight of responsibility for the smooth running of society. The majority of the population, rural dwellers and townsfolk alike, were concerned in some way with the land and its produce, whether as corvée laborers, tenant farmers, pastoralists, or landowners, and agriculture was the mainstay of the economy. Although many city dwellers were involved in other occupations, such as craft production or trade, landownership remained important to them.

A man needed to provide himself with children to inherit his property and to care for him in his old age and for his spirit after death. When Enkidu describes the underworld, the spirits of those who died childless are the most pitiful, whereas those with many sons prosper. Nevertheless, by Ur III times, eunuchs are recorded, at that time the castrated male children of working women. Their numbers increased in the second and especially the first millennia when they could enjoy positions of power and responsibility at court, serving not only as attendants in the harem but also as officials and army officers. By this time even high-ranking families might castrate a son to improve his career prospects. Eunuchs were present throughout society, from senior court officials to members of private households and slaves. Most were castrated in infancy; adult castration was a legal punishment, usually reserved for serious offenses like adultery.

The Family in Law

Many of the surviving legal documents are concerned with inheritance and the transfer of property, a major preoccupation. Inheritance arrangements were often detailed and complicated. In general, when a man died, the family's property would be divided among his sons, after providing a dowry for any of his daughters still unwed, and likewise a brideprice for any unmarried son. Although most communities gave the sons equal shares, some allocated a double or larger share to the eldest son, who also frequently inherited the family home. Also passed on were the rights to certain religious or civil offices, along with public duties and outstanding debts.

Dividing land could result in landholdings too small and inconvenient for practicable cultivation. The division was therefore frequently in name only, and the land continued to be cultivated as a single unit under joint ownership. Transferring ownership of such land was naturally a complicated undertaking, and there is some indication that land sales were not permitted, at least in some areas and in some periods. The Nuzi records reveal a legal fiction designed to circumvent this: A debtor could adopt his creditor, enabling the latter to "inherit" the land in discharge of the debt.

Inheritance issues were a frequent source of litigation. To prevent disputes and ensure the desired transfer of goods and estates, a man in his prime could draw up a will, witnessed by his brothers. He generally could not alter the usual inheritance rules for real estate, but he could specify the disposal of his moveable property, making bequests to and provision for individual members of the household; this might include the manumission of household slaves. Chief among the beneficiaries would be his widow, to whom he could bequeath a "gift in contemplation of death" to provide for her through the rest of her lifetime, along with her dowry. Only in exceptional circumstances could a man disinherit his children, and this extreme step had to be approved by the courts.

Given the importance of children, adoption was another major source of legal contracts. A man could adopt the children borne to him by his slave girl, who then shared in the paternal inheritance; if he did not do so these children and their mother would at least gain their freedom after his death. Outsiders could also be adopted by men or women as a way of providing security in their old age, and this contract was regarded as a very serious commitment on both sides. An adopted son could be disinherited but, like legitimate offspring, only with the approval of the courts. If a man repudiated his adopted father, he lost his inheritance and could in extremis be punished by being sold into slavery.

Slaves

Methods of Enslavement. Slaves—*wardum* in Hammurabi's law code—occupied the lowest rank in society. Textual clues suggest slavery already existed by the later fourth millennium B.C.E. Initially all or most slaves were war captives and generally female. Male prisoners were often slaughtered, although they might be restrained in a neck stock until cowed enough to be used as slaves, or blinded to make them easier to manage. Enslavement was not inevitable, and some prisoners became *mushkenum*. By Old Babylonian times prisoners of war of either sex were becoming economically more important and were therefore valuable booty. Several letters from Mari and Karana's royal ladies refer to promises of new slaves after a successful military campaign, and most or all of the slaves in the Mari palace workshops were prisoners of war. These captives were initially state property, sent to work in the temples or palaces, but in late Assyrian and Neo-Babylonian times, even private soldiers could acquire prisoners as their private booty, often selling them to wealthier individuals or hiring them out as prostitutes.

By the second millennium there was a flourishing trade in slaves, fed by slave-taking raids in addition to the flow from regular warfare. In Old Babylonian times, tribesmen and women from the eastern mountains were popular as slaves, but the mountains to the north and the desert to the west also supplied tribal captives. Slaves did not come cheap—from 20 to as much as 90 shekels of silver at Old Babylonian rates, compared with around 10 shekels a year to hire a laborer; but in addition to work they could give a return on investment by producing children. Many of the slaves in Mesopotamian households and institutions were the offspring of slaves or of slave women and free men.

Not all slaves were war captives or their descendants. Enslavement was a punishment for certain crimes in Hammurabi's code. A substantial proportion of slaves in most periods were local people whom misfortune had forced into slavery. In times of extreme hardship, for example during a long siege, it was a recognized practice for a man to sell himself or members of his family to the temple or palace to keep them from starvation. In Neo-Babylonian times children could be dedicated to the temple as oblates for the same reason: They were free to practice a craft or other occupation but had to pay the temple part of their earnings.

Debt drove many into slavery. High rates of interest on loans (one-fifth) and on loaned grain and other perishable goods (one-third) meant that it was easy for individuals who suffered a succession of bad harvests or a run of ill luck to spiral into debt. A man could bind himself or a member of his family to serve his creditor for a period of time—fixed at three years in Hammurabi's law code—or sell them to pay off the debt. Unlike foreign captives who were generally slaves for life unless manumitted, debt slaves could redeem themselves

A detail from the bronze panels decorating the great doors erected by Shalmaneser III (858–824 B.C.E.) at Balawat showing prisoners being taken from one of the conquered cities to be enslaved. (Zev Radovan/Land of the Bible Picture Archive)

by paying off the debt. Periodically an enlightened ruler (such as Lipit-Ishtar of Isin or Ammisaduqa of Babylon) would annul such debts, releasing those trapped in debt slavery.

The Late Assyrian kings deported vast numbers of conquered people; unlike war captives, these initially retained their freedom and many settled peacefully into their new homes, enjoying rights equal to those of the native population. But from the reign of Sennacherib onward, their status changed. They now became royal slaves and were distributed by the king alongside other booty, some becoming the property of temples, nobles, and private citizens, and others being conscripted into the army or serving the palace by cultivating its fields and gardens or tending its flocks and herds.

Slaves, Work, and the Law.   Kings offered many of their prisoners of war to the temple, and it was not uncommon for private individuals to dedicate slaves as offerings. Slaves might also be transferred from private to state ownership to pay taxes. In the third millennium most temple workers were free employees and temple and crown estates were cultivated by free tenants, and public works were undertaken largely by citizens as corvée labor. Increasingly as time went on, however, slaves worked alongside, or instead of, free individuals on public works, in state factories, and on large royal, temple, or private estates.

Most domestic slaves undertook household activities, but if they had a particular skill they might work as craftsmen or -women in the home or be hired

Three Assyrian prisoners from Phoenicia or Palestine playing lyres; they may have been blinded to prevent them escaping. A detail from the reliefs decorating Sennacherib's palace at Nineveh. (Zev Radovan/Land of the Bible Picture Archive)

out to make a profit for their owner. In later times, slaves could be apprenticed to learn a useful trade or skill, such as baking, cobbling, brewing, or weaving. In some cities or in some periods, slaves were allowed to operate in many ways like free individuals, earning an income by working, owning and renting out houses, land, animals, and even their own slaves, and becoming involved in business ventures—but they had to make their owner a regular payment (*mandattu*), and they could not buy their freedom but could still be sold by their owner, their earning power and accumulated savings increasing the price they fetched. Temple slaves could attain senior administrative positions but likewise remained slaves.

Careful records were kept of the origins and personal details of state-owned slaves, who were housed in barracks. Slaves were rarely physically restrained but were identified by their hairdo or *abbuttum* (*apputtum*), probably a style of forehead hair since *clearing the forehead* was the term for manumission. It was a grave offense, attracting severe punishment, for a barber to shave this off or for anyone to coerce him into doing so or to aid a slave in escaping. On the other hand, at least at Mari, slaves themselves were not punished for attempting to escape, although habitual "bolters" might be chained. A more permanent mark, branded on the forehead or hand, was initially rare but had become usual by the first millennium B.C.E. One text recorded an escaped domestic slave's attempt to turn her ownership mark into a temple brand to improve her lot. Temple slaves received the same rations as free employees—basic food, with extras on feast days, and an allowance of clothing or wool. The conditions of domestic slaves varied, but they enjoyed no legal protection against harsh treatment, and their families could be split up and sold separately.

On the other hand, slaves were often valued and well-treated members of the household, and usually few in number. Letters found at Mari and Karana show that it was thought bad form to get rid of a long-serving slave; one records a combined protest by the other household slaves against such an action, and another was directed by a slave to King Zimri-Lim himself, begging him not to sell her mother. A slave girl who had borne a son to her master could not be sold, and she and her children became free on their master's death, whereas other slaves were inherited by the next of kin. Other slaves might be granted their freedom on the death of their owner; the children of a freed slave automatically became free, too.

TEXT REFERENCES

Adams, Robert McCormack, and Hans J. Nissen. 1972. *The Uruk Countryside. The Natural Setting of Urban Societies.* Chicago: The University of Chicago Press.

Bienkowski, Piotr. 2000. "Childbirth," "Crime and Punishment," "Education," "Eunuchs," and "Houses." Pp. 71–72, 82–83, 101, 110, and 148, respectively, in *Dictionary of the Ancient Near East.* Edited by Piotr Bienkowski and Alan Millard. London: British Museum Press.

Bienkowski, Piotr, and Alan Millard, eds. 2000. *Dictionary of the Ancient Near East.* London: British Museum Press.

Black, Jeremy, and Anthony Green. 1992. *Gods, Demons and Symbols of Ancient Mesopotamia. An Illustrated Dictionary.* London: British Museum Press.

Bottero, Jean, ed. 2001. *Everyday Life in Ancient Mesopotamia.* Translated by A. Nevill. Edinburgh: Edinburgh University Press.

Buccellati, Giorgio. 1997. "Amorites." Pp. 107–111 in *The Oxford Encyclopedia of Archaeology in the Near East.* Vol. 1. Edited by Eric M. Meyers. Oxford: Oxford University Press.

Charpin, Dominique. 2000. "The History of Ancient Mesopotamia: An Overview." Pp. 807–830 in *Civilizations of the Ancient Near East.* Edited by Jack M. Sasson. Peabody, MA: Hendrickson Publishers. (Reprint of 1995 edition. New York: Scribner.)

Dalley, Stephanie. 1984. *Mari and Karana. Two Old Babylonian Cities.* London: Longman.

———. 2000a. *Myths from Mesopotamia.* Revised edition. Oxford: Oxford University Press.

———. 2000b. "Gardens." P. 124 in *Dictionary of the Ancient Near East.* Edited by Piotr Bienkowski and Alan Millard. London: British Museum Press.

Frame, Grant. 1997. "Chaldeans." Pp. 482–484 in *The Oxford Encyclopedia of Archaeology in the Near East*. Vol. 1. Edited by Eric M. Meyers. Oxford: Oxford University Press.

Frankfort, Henri. 1996. *The Art and Architecture of the Ancient Orient*. 5th edition. New Haven, CT: Yale University Press.

George, Andrew. 1999. *The Epic of Gilgamesh. A New Translation*. London: Allen Lane, Penguin Press.

Grayson, A. Kirk. 1997. "Assyrians." Pp. 228–233 in *The Oxford Encyclopedia of Archaeology in the Near East*. Vol. 1. Edited by Eric M. Meyers. Oxford: Oxford University Press.

Greengus, Samuel. 2000. "Legal and Social Institutions of Ancient Mesopotamia." Pp. 469–484 in *Civilizations of the Ancient Near East*. Edited by Jack M. Sasson. Peabody, MA: Hendrickson Publishers. (Reprint of 1995 edition. New York: Scribner.)

Harris, Roberta L. 1995. *The World of the Bible*. London: Thames and Hudson.

Kramer, Samuel Noah. 1981. *History Begins at Sumer. Thirty-Nine Firsts in Recorded History*. 3rd revised edition. Philadelphia: University of Pennsylvania Press.

Kuhrt, Amelie. 1995. *The Ancient Near East. ca. 3000–330 BCE*. 2 Volumes. London: Routledge.

Leick, Gwendolyn. 2001. *Mesopotamia. The Invention of the City*. London: Allen Lane, Penguin Press.

Maidman, Maynard Paul. 2000. "Nuzi: Portrait of an Ancient Mesopotamian Provincial Town." Pp. 931–947 in *Civilizations of the Ancient Near East*. Edited by Jack M. Sasson. Peabody, MA: Hendrickson Publishers. (Reprint of 1995 edition. New York: Scribner.)

Margueron, Jean-Claude. 2000. "Mari: A Portrait in Art of a Mesopotamian City-State." Pp. 885–900 in *Civilizations of the Ancient Near East*. Edited by Jack M. Sasson. Peabody, MA: Hendrickson Publishers. (Reprint of 1995 edition. New York: Scribner.)

Meyers, Eric M., ed. 1997. *The Oxford Encyclopedia of Archaeology in the Near East*. 5 Volumes. Oxford: Oxford University Press.

Millard, Alan. 2000. "Kudurru." Pp. 171–172 in *Dictionary of the Ancient Near East*. Edited by Piotr Bienkowski and Alan Millard. London: British Museum Press.

Nissen, Hans J. 1988. *The Early History of the Ancient Near East*. Chicago: University of Chicago Press. (Paperback edition 1990.)

Oates, Joan. 1986. *Babylon*. Revised edition. London: Thames and Hudson.

Oates, Joan, and David Oates. 2001. *Nimrud. An Assyrian Imperial City Revealed*. London: British School of Archaeology in Iraq.

Oppenheim, A. Leo, and Erica Reiner. 1977. *Ancient Mesopotamia. Portrait of a Dead Civilization*. Revised edition. Chicago: University of Chicago Press.

Pearce, Laurie E. 2000. "The Scribes and Scholars of Ancient Mesopotamia." Pp. 2265–2278 in *Civilizations of the Ancient Near East*. Edited by Jack M. Sasson. Peabody, MA: Hendrickson Publishers. (Reprint of 1995 edition. New York: Scribner.)

Postgate, J. Nicholas. 1994. *Early Mesopotamia*. London: Routledge.

———. 1997. "Abu Salabikh." Pp. 9–10 in *The Oxford Encyclopedia of Archaeology in the Near East*. Vol. 1. Edited by Eric M. Meyers. Oxford: Oxford University Press.

Reade, Julian. 1997. "Taya, Tell." Pp. 158–160 in *The Oxford Encyclopedia of Archaeology in the Near East*. Vol. 5. Edited by Eric M. Meyers. Oxford: Oxford University Press.

Roaf, Michael. 1990. *Cultural Atlas of Mesopotamia*. New York: Facts on File.

———. 2000. "Palaces and Temples in Ancient Mesopotamia." Pp. 423–441 in *Civilizations of the Ancient Near East*. Edited by Jack M. Sasson. Peabody, MA: Hendrickson Publishers. (Reprint of 1995 edition. New York: Scribner.)

Russell, John Malcolm. 1991. *Sennacherib's Palace without a Rival at Nineveh*. Chicago: The University of Chicago Press.

———. 1996. "Nineveh." Pp. 153–170 in *Royal Cities of the Biblical World*. Edited by Joan Goodnick Westenholz. Jerusalem: Bible Lands Museum.

Saggs, H. W. F. 1995. *Peoples of the Past. Babylonians*. London: British Museum Press.

Sasson, Jack M., ed. 2000. *Civilizations of the Ancient Near East*. 4 Volumes. Peabody, MA: Hendrickson Publishers. (Reprint of 1995 edition. New York: Scribner.)

Stol, Marten. 2000. "Private Life in Ancient Mesopotamia." Pp. 485–499 in *Civilizations of the Ancient Near East*. Edited by Jack M. Sasson. Peabody, MA: Hendrickson Publishers. (Reprint of 1995 edition. New York: Scribner.)

Stone, Elizabeth. 1997. "Mesopotamian Houses." Pp. 90–94 in *The Oxford Encyclopedia of Archaeology in the Near East*. Vol. 3. Edited by Eric M. Meyers. Oxford: Oxford University Press.

———. 2000. "The Development of Cities in Ancient Mesopotamia." Pp. 235–248 in *Civilizations of the Ancient Near East*. Edited by Jack M. Sasson. Peabody, MA: Hendrickson Publishers. (Reprint of 1995 edition. New York: Scribner.)

Thuesen, Ingolf. 1997. "Diyala." Pp. 163–166 in *The Oxford Encyclopedia of Archaeology in the Near East*. Vol. 1. Edited by Eric M. Meyers. Oxford: Oxford University Press.

Van de Mieroop, Marc. 1997. *The Ancient Mesopotamian City*. Oxford: Oxford University Press.

Veenhof, Klaas R. 1977. "Some Social Effects of Old Assyrian Trade." Pp. 109–118 in *Trade in the Ancient Near East. Papers Presented to the XXIII Rencontre Assyriologique Internationale*. Edited by J. D. Hawkins. London: British School of Archaeology in Iraq.

Westenholz, Joan Goodnick. 1996. "Babylon." Pp. 197–220 in *Royal Cities of the Biblical World*. Edited by Joan Goodnick Westenholz. Jerusalem: Bible Lands Museum.

Wiseman, D. J. 1991. *Nebuchadrezzar and Babylon. The Schweich Lectures of the British Academy 1983*. Oxford: Oxford University Press.

Woolley, Leonard. 1982. *Ur "of the Chaldees."* The final account, *Excavations at Ur*, revised and updated by P. Roger and S. Moorey. London: Book Club Associates / Herbert Press.

Yoffee, Norman. 2000. "The Economy of Ancient Western Asia." Pp. 1387–1399 in *Civilizations of the Ancient Near East*. Edited by Jack M. Sasson. Peabody, MA: Hendrickson Publishers. (Reprint of 1995 edition. New York: Scribner.)

VII
CHAPTER 7
Politics

POLITICAL ORGANIZATION

Early Dynastic Period

With the emergence of cities and a greatly increasing population, the organization and administration of society in Sumer became increasingly complex toward the end of the fourth millennium. The written records from this time, albeit limited, reflect the accumulation of produce by the authorities and its deployment to support the personnel employed by the state.

Heavy reliance on one substantial temple archive from Lagash state initially suggested that in the third millennium the temple authorities ran the administration, controlling most of the land and employing most members of society, whether as agricultural laborers, soldiers, traders, or artisans, and that only at the end of the ED (Early Dynastic) period did secular authorities come to dominate the administration.

Evidence from archaeology and other ED texts had overturned this view by the 1970s, indicating that secular and sacred authority developed together in the ED period. It has become clear that, although temples were major landowners and exerted a powerful influence on society, the secular royal establishment (the "Palace") controlled as much or more land in the ED city-states. Growing interstate conflict enabled kings to increase and consolidate their power. Competition between the palace and the temple developed, and gradually the palace came to wield greater power, the king, as the gods' representative, controlling many of the temple lands and personnel. Nevertheless, throughout Mesopotamian history, both palace and temple remained powerful, and the tensions between them continued.

A number of scholars see the third millennium as a time of change when a kinship-based society of largely self-sufficient households, supporting the temple and king through the payment of tribute, gave way to an *oikos* (household)-structured society, in which kings and temple authorities controlled agriculture, industry, and other activities by maintaining vast households of dependents who produced goods and performed services. Temples existed for the direct benefit of the gods, requiring substantial resources to feed, clothe, and house the statue of the deity and support his or her attendants. They had therefore to own substantial estates and command the services of large numbers of people. Many people, such as widows, orphans, or prisoners of war, became temple dependents through misfortune or poverty. Distressed individuals might borrow from the substantial temple resources, but repayment could be difficult and many debtors had to sell themselves or their families into dependency. Free citizens might also become temple dependents as sharecroppers, cultivating temple or palace lands in return for a portion of the resultant produce. Similar processes, particularly indebtedness, turned many citizens into dependent members of the royal household.

Nevertheless, the idea that the state completely controlled land and industry in the third millennium is now also questioned. Despite the paucity of documentary evidence, many scholars argue that a private sector existed at this time, rather than developing in the early second millennium when many texts attest its importance. Legal documents and other evidence show that kinship ties were important at least into the late ED period, and it is clear that kinship groups often owned land. Some texts attest to the buying of land by the palace and the transformation of individuals and families into crown dependents.

A key text, the Standard Professions List, provides clues to the ordering of society from around 3000 B.C.E., when it is first known. Although this early version is broken and its signs cannot be perfectly read, its format is so closely followed in later versions that most of its contents can confidently be ascertained. The list reflects the hierarchical nature of the society that developed in the late Uruk and ED periods. Grouped by occupation, the list gives the titles of personnel engaged in particular activities, headed in each case by a supervisory official. Variations reflect changes taking place in the organization of society through time. For example, the lists from the substantial ED IIIa archives at Shuruppak for the first time include the profession of tax collector. Other administrative texts also provide information on political organization.

At Shuruppak the bureaucracy was organized into units with up to a hundred employees, supervised by officials answerable to heads of departments controlled by the head of state. At Shuruppak the latter was called the *ensi*, a secular title used in most ED cities, although the direct ideological relationship between the city and its temple meant that the head of state also had a sacred role. Kingship was generally vested in dynasties, although the citizens may have played some part in selecting a king's successor from among his sons or brothers. The essential approval of the gods was probably obtained by divination. Misfortunes reflected divine disapprobation, and an unsuccessful monarch could be overthrown. One entry in the Sumerian King List indicates the diverse nature of ED kings: "Kug-Bau, the woman tavern-keeper, who made firm the foundations of Kish," reigning for one hundred years. (Electronic Text Corpus of Sumerian Literature "Sumerian King List," lines 224–231).

The two highest offices in the early version of the Standard Professions List are *sanga* and *en*—probably respectively sacred and secular titles, although by ED IIIa (or earlier) *en* had become a title with sacred connotations, signifying the spouse of the deity. This was the title borne by the leader in Uruk. *Sanga* was the title of the chief temple administrator in a number of city-states and of the rulers of Umma and Isin. Another title was *lugal*, used particularly to denote the office of King of Kish, who apparently exercised a higher authority over the rulers of Sumer's city-states. For example around 2550 B.C.E. the warring *ensi* of Lagash and *sanga* of Umma accepted arbitration by Mesalim, *lugal* of Kish.

During the early ED period, city-states were emerging throughout Sumer and much of Akkad, and some, such as Assur, Ebla, and Mari, in the north and the west. Texts attest to conflict between adjacent or competing states, of which the running border dispute between Umma and Lagash is best documented. There were also elements of cooperation between states. The secular authority of the *lugal* of Kish (not necessarily, it seems, the incumbent king of that city but often the king of another city invested with the title) was frequently acknowledged; and by ED III, if not earlier, the priests of Enlil (who had emerged by or during this period as the chief of the gods) in Nippur could endorse a king's actions and authority by giving them the god's sanction. A number of texts suggest the existence of a cooperative league of the six cities of Adab, Lagash, Umma, Uruk, Shuruppak, and Nippur during ED I and ED II; such alliances could obviate harmful interstate conflict over land and water resources. The sack of Shuruppak in early ED IIIa may signal a breakdown in the operation of such alliances—and it is in the years that followed that the bitter conflict between Umma and Lagash developed.

The Emergence of Empire

After 2500 B.C.E. there was a gradual shift in political perceptions. Individual kings of powerful states, particularly Lagash and Uruk, began to harbor territorial ambitions, culminating in Sargon's creation of the first empire, of Sumer and Akkad, an integrated state in which authority was centralized in his hands. His capital, Agade, was main beneficiary of the agricultural, industrial, and traded produce of the empire. In place of the old Sumerian kings Sargon and his successors appointed Akkadian governors to administer the individual city-states. Estates were settled on loyal supporters, and a substantial army played a large part in maintaining royal authority. In the northern parts of the empire, where political life had not previously been highly developed, this seems to have been successful, but frequent rebellions show how bitterly the loss of independence was resented by the traditional city-states of the south.

Nevertheless, when the Akkadian Empire collapsed the political situation did not return completely to the ED mosaic of small states, and larger political entities came and went. The imperial experiment was successfully repeated by the Ur III dynasty a century later and from then onward, sizeable territorial states were to be the norm, their extent and power depending on the strength and competence of individual rulers and dynasties. When a state's leaders lost their grip, there were usually other up-and-coming leaders ready to carve out a new state, often with a new center. The earlier second millennium saw the rise of competing states centered on Isin, Larsa, Babylon, and others, as well as lesser players like Eshnunna and Mari. With the emergence of Hammurabi's Babylonian Empire and the stability given later by the long-lived empire of the Kassites, Babylonia became an enduring political entity, although the environmentally and economically degraded south (Sealand) was at times either politically separate or disaffected. Northern Mesopotamia took longer to develop a political identity. Culturally linked to and following Babylonia from the start, Assyria enjoyed an uneasy schizophrenic relationship with its southern neighbor during the first millennium, culturally and spiritually its disciple, while politically often its master.

The Administration of Empire

The Akkadian and Ur III Empires. The organizational requirements of empire demanded a more complex bureaucracy than the ED *oikos* system. Sargon and his successors, particularly Naram-Sin, imposed a cadre of Akkadian provincial governors, known by the traditional title of *ensi*, to administrate the former city-states. Answering to the crown, the *ensis'* authority was backed by military garrisons. These governors visited Agade regularly to confer with the king, who also periodically visited the *ensis* in their provinces. Although temples continued to enjoy considerable power as the seat of the gods from whom monarchs derived their legitimacy, the Akkadian kings took steps to bring them more firmly under their own authority, creating or filling existing temple posts with their own appointees, often members of the royal family. Although the Akkadian kings built and embellished temples, they also seized opportunities to reduce temple estates and the independence of the temples. Nevertheless, there was not a complete break with tradition, the Akkadian kings maintaining the traditional roles and titles derived from control of Kish and Nippur.

Trade, taxation, tribute, and offerings provided substantial resources, but these were swelled by the booty derived from war. Defeated cities yielded not only material booty but also prisoners, who could be employed in public works, and land confiscated from defeated cities and their authorities, which was granted to loyal servants of the crown. *Ensis* were given estates to support them, located in provinces other than the one they governed in order to prevent the buildup of localized power. Military colonists were settled on expropriated land and contributed to the maintenance of Akkadian authority.

The Ur III kings elaborated the administrative legacy of their Akkadian precursors. Ur-Nammu and Shulgi created a bureaucracy of stifling efficiency, with a huge civil service obsessively recording the minutiae of taxes, tribute, and yields from state lands. In principle they upheld traditional Sumerian political organization, dividing Sumer and Akkad into twenty provinces that coincided largely with the main city-states and which were governed by *ensis* who belonged to the local elite. These *ensis* also controlled the local temples and their households, a major source of state revenue in agricultural produce and the products of industry. On the other hand, the Ur III kings imitated the Akkadians by appointing a military governor (*shagina*) alongside each *ensi*, drawn from the royal family or from nonlocal sources loyal to the crown. The names are known of more than a hundred princes and princesses, many holding civil or temple posts. The *shaginas* had responsibility not only for the armed forces stationed in the provinces but also for state dependents settled on crown land, and were independent of the *ensi*. From the time of Shulgi onward, the Ur III state maintained a standing army.

Although the Sumerian city-states resented their loss of independence, the Ur III kings created an ideology that helped win them support throughout Babylonia, claiming descent from Uruk's king Gilgamesh. They made much of their piety and role as divinely appointed protectors of the people and promoters of their well-being. They also followed tradition in adopting the system through which temples, and in particular, the temple of Enlil in Nippur, were supported by offerings (*bala*) paid on a rotating basis by the individual provinces: Although in principle destined to support the temple, these amounted to taxes. Huge state-run industrial complexes, particularly for making textiles, also contributed to the empire's economic prosperity.

Beyond the core of Sumer and Akkad there was no need for the Ur III kings to subscribe to traditional ideology; these regions, to the east and north, were ruled by military governors who were granted crown lands. They were liable for service and paid a tax (*gun mada*) from their produce—settlers on crown land had paid the same tax under the Akkadians.

Despite the Ur III state's economic efficiency and centralized bureaucratic control and the reverence felt for its kings, it eventually fell apart. No later Mesopotamian state attained its degree of control over its dominions.

Old Babylonian States.   In the centuries that followed, the temples gained in power and authority, private entrepreneurship flourished, and many smaller states vied for power, many falling to Amorite sheikhs. In the Sumerian city-states the loyalties of the people and their rulers had long been to their city and its god. Among the nomadic peoples of the west, however, including the Amorites, tribal loyalties took priority over those of place. This for the first time produced states whose basis was ethnic instead of or as well as territorial. Ethnic ties also became a factor in international relations—between the families of Shamshi-Adad and Hammurabi, for example, who offered each other succor and support.

Shamshi-Adad consolidated his authority by ensuring that he was seen as the appointee of the local god in each of the city-states he conquered or controlled. He made his two sons viceroys for the major cities of Mari and Ekallatum, the capitals respectively of provinces on the Euphrates and the Tigris, and progressively extended the areas under their rule, retaining control of the region around his capital, Shubat-Enlil. The princes directly ruled the district surrounding their capitals, while a number of lesser officials administered outlying districts. Some districts were left in the hands of local rulers who had submitted to Shamshi-Adad, and peripheral regions exposed to hostile neighbors were run by military governors. Officials rose through the ranks of the bureaucracy and were regularly moved to prevent them establishing a local power base. The princes were responsible for the civil administration of their territories, although Shamshi-Adad retained supreme authority in political and military matters.

Private entrepreneurship, which had flourished in the more open political climate that succeeded the Ur III Empire, was progressively curbed by the authorities in the rising states, notably of Rim-Sin and Hammurabi. Formerly free agents often became bureaucrats in the new centralized regimes. Under Hammurabi, Babylon become the focus for the flow of wealth and the center of administration for the south, a position it held for more than a millennium. A tangible expression of this was the transfer of supreme divine authority from Enlil with his shrine at Nippur, to Babylon's god Marduk, henceforth the chief god of the Babylonian realm. Thus spiritual as well as secular authority now passed to Babylon. Hammurabi established a substantial royal bureaucracy to run his large and centralized realm. One of the mainstays of the state economy was the *ilkum* system, in which crown land was granted to individuals in return for military service. Archives at Sippar show that the king ruled here through an official who was not a native of the city and who had royal troops at his disposal. An army of officials assessed and collected taxes in grain and animals, or in silver from professionals like scribes and tavern keepers. Hammurabi kept a tight personal grip on the bureaucracy and the minutiae of government throughout his realm: He appointed temple officials and controlled royal workshops where textiles were made, and surviving texts include notes he sent to officials on matters such as tax arrears and the payment of ransoms. His successors were less able and the empire gradually disintegrated.

Kassites and Mitanni.   After a hiatus following the sack of Babylon in 1595, a state centered on Babylon was reestablished by the Kassites, under whose stable rule a lasting empire was finally created. Unlike the dense pattern of city-states of the third millennium, Babylonia in the later second and first millennia (like Assyria) had few large urban centers, of which Babylon was by far the most important, surrounded by countryside with villages. Kassite Babylonia was divided into provinces run by a hierarchical bureaucracy that undertook public works, collected taxes, and issued rations to state dependents such as temple staff, guards, and craftsmen. The stelae known as *kudurru* (see photos pp. 94, 213) documenting land grants give details of rural taxes, which included agricultural produce and animals but also vehicles and donkeys for transport. Corvée labor was used to build and maintain bridges, roads, walls, and irrigation systems. Rural communities had also to provide pasture for the cattle of provincial bureaucrats, fodder for military animals, and billets for military personnel. The crown granted parcels of land to a wide variety of individuals, as a reward for military bravery or for other exceptional service. This introduced a new element that has been likened to feudalism, but such grants were ad hoc and exceptional, and often concerned land in sparsely occupied areas such as Sealand, where they served the purpose of colonizing and developing territory. Unlike a feudal system, moreover, the grant of land did not give the recipient control over the people living there.

In earlier periods, parts of the geographically far less united north were at times incorporated into adjacent states, such as the Ur III Empire, but only briefly, under Shamshi-Adad, was most of it unified into a larger polity. Some time after the latter disintegrated, however, the whole north saw the development of the huge Mitanni state. Its political organization was a pyramidal hierarchy: All land belonged to the king, now the supreme secular authority with no ideology of responsibility to the gods. He awarded authority over it to vassals, who in return provided troops and served the state in other ways; these vassals in turn controlled lesser rulers. At the empire's height Mitanni's vassals included Alalakh in the northern Levant, Kizzuwatna in the northwest (which later transferred its allegiance to the Hittites), Assyria, and Arrapha in the east. The extensive archives from the provincial town of Nuzi, subject to Arrapha, shed light on local government under Mitanni rule (see section entitled "Local Government"). The vassal states were clearly required to act subordinately: When the Assyrian king sent an independent embassy to Egypt, the Mitanni king sacked Assur.

The Neo-Assyrians and Neo-Babylonians. The Assyrians gained their revenge when Mitanni crumbled in the mid-fourteenth century. From then until 612 B.C.E., Assyria became the dominant force in northern Mesopotamia, owing largely to their army, a professional and effective force that was also in the forefront of technological progress. Successive strong kings pushed the frontiers of the state ever outward, although it often shrank again under weaker rulers. Within Assyria proper—*mat asshur*, "the Land of Ashur," which stretched as far west as the Euphrates valley—the crown made grants of land to dependents in return for a proportion of their produce, corvée labor, and military service as irregulars, continuing the ancient *ilkum* system. Militarism underlay the whole state, most officials holding both civil and military posts and every man being obliged to serve in the army if required, and the king was also the commander in chief. The Assyrian state enjoyed a simpler structure than the Mitanni hierarchy, all landowners being responsible directly to the king, who, as in former times, was answerable to the gods, especially Ashur. Through time, power was transferred away from the traditional landowning elite; as the crown gained control of an increasing proportion of the land, it granted estates to bureaucrats and generals. The ancient *bala* system was employed to provision temples, and especially that of Ashur: Offerings were made in turn by regions throughout the empire.

In the conquered lands beyond, vassal kingdoms were ruled by governors (*shaknu*) drawn from local dynasties or prominent local families. They paid tribute (often enormous quantities) to their Assyrian overlords and acted in concert with them. Much of the wealth from provincial tribute was used to create and embellish new Assyrian capitals. Kalhu, built by Ashurnasirpal, was established with a population of 16,000. Its construction involved not only huge resources but also the labor of 7,000 people for three years. Later capitals, Dur Sharrukin and Nineveh, also tied up vast material and human resources. The royal court and central administration were also supported largely out of tribute.

In the ninth century the Assyrians began to establish military outposts in conquered territory, supported by local taxes. These became administrative centers, developing into regional capitals. It was not until the eighth century under Tiglath-Pileser III that the Assyrians actually began to take the administration of the greater empire into their own hands, dividing the conquered ter-

Detail of a relief in Sennacherib's palace in Nineveh, depicting the siege of the Judaean city of Lachish in the year 701 B.C.E. Rebellion against the Assyrian state was savagely punished. (Zev Radovan/Land of the Bible Picture Archive)

ritories into provinces under Assyrian governors instead of local rulers. The changeover occurred gradually, vassal states passing into direct rule when they rebelled.

Military force backed bureaucratic authority, and Assyrian actions were seen as the will of Ashur. The highest officials were the majordomo (*rab sha muhhi ekalli*), who had direct access to the king, the vice-chancellor (*ummanu*), who acted as the king's scribe, and two field marshalls (*turtannu*), who could deputize for the king on the battlefield. Other high-ranking courtiers, who also held senior military offices, included the cupbearer (*rab shaqe*), the steward (*abarakku*), and the palace herald (*nagir ekalli*).

High court officials held the governorships of provinces, and lesser provinces were ruled by less senior officials. A provincial governor maintained his own court and was backed by a standing army. The province was regarded as his private estate, and the office often passed from father to son: a temptation to extortion or the exercise of independent rule. Nevertheless, provincial governors were generally honest, loyal, and conscientious. Bureaucrats were frequently illiterate, but there were many scribes attached to the administration, who wielded considerable power. Important bureaucrats were often eunuchs, enjoying particular trust because they could not entertain dynastic ambitions. Although most officials were Assyrians, foreigners in principle could also become part of the bureaucracy.

Under Neo-Assyrian and Neo-Babylonian kings, the temple became an integrated part of the political structure. Endowed by the king with substantial lands confiscated from rebellious individuals, the temples were given a considerable measure of responsibility for their local community, temple officials acting as local judges and presiding over district assemblies. They collected tithes from the citizens of their districts and paid a proportion of these to the crown. They also had to provide labor and resources as the palace required, for example pasturing royal herds and provisioning royal officials. Temple accounts and activities were open to scrutiny by royal officials.

The Assyrians increased agricultural productivity, founding new settlements and estates in both the Assyrian heartland and the provinces, under Assyrian generals and senior bureaucrats, and using deportees as labor. Conquered peoples also made up an increasingly large proportion of the armed forces, a circumstance that by weakening loyalty to the regime contributed to its eventual downfall. Another factor was the imbalance between the center and the provinces: The latter were drained of manpower and resources to aggrandize the former, causing economic depression.

Among the Assyrian provinces, Babylonia was a special case. Assyria needed peace along its southern frontier, and periodic hostility had to be dealt with. For several long periods, Babylonia was under Assyrian control, but the respect felt by the Assyrians for the elder state meant that it was not treated as a conquered land and not administered as an ordinary province. Instead the two realms were united, and Babylonia came directly under royal control, although the actual administration could be delegated to a royal chief minister. When Babylonia attempted to throw off Assyrian rule, it was not subjected to the brutal treatment usually meted out to insubordinate regions. Sennacherib's aberrant behavior in sacking Babylon was widely viewed as hubristic. He swiftly paid the price of his impiety, and his son Esarhaddon lost little time before attempting to restore the city. When Assyria fell in the reign of Esarhaddon's grandson, Babylonia was swift to seize control of the whole empire.

Local Government.   In general, a king's influence on the life of the individual depended on the strength of the monarch and his authority: Strong kings could make demands upon their subjects' resources and labors, through taxation, military service, the appropriation of land, and the resettlement of people, whereas weak kings might make little impact on life.

Although political, economic, and military matters were controlled by the king and his officials, many aspects of civil life were governed by local bodies. In the countryside and particularly in the less urbanized north, villages governed themselves through village councils, under a local headman. Towns were governed by assemblies (Sumerian *unken,* Akkadian *puhrum)* probably composed of all free adult males, although some legal documents suggest that women might also have been included at times. Some matters were dealt with by an inner council of leading citizens or elders (*shibutum*). Cities, being larger, were divided into wards (*babtum*), each with their own assembly or council. These could issue warnings and convene hearings on local matters such as the unsatifactory condition of buildings or the unacceptable behavior of domestic animals; they monitored the movement of strangers in the neighborhood, checked local morals, and made good losses sustained through robbery if the thief was not apprehended. They also dealt with cases in civil law, such as divorce and inheritance disputes (see chapter 6).

Professional associations also administered their own affairs. Many cities had a separate trading quarter (*karum*) where merchants could set up their offices, often outside the city walls and usually legally and administratively independent although sanctioned by the state government. The archives at Kanesh in Anatolia provide a picture of the running of a major Assyrian trading station. Karum Kanesh was the organizational center to which merchants in other Assyrian trading stations were answerable. The "lords and fathers" here passed on orders from head office in Assur, collected the taxes and duties payable to the local ruler, arbitrated in disputes, and took other decisions; when appropriate they could convene an assembly of the whole karum, where decisions were taken by majority vote. Back home in Assur, although the city-state was under the ultimate authority of the ruler (*waklum*—"overseer"—a post held by a member of one leading family), many decisions were taken by the council of city elders or the larger city assembly.

Within the tribal society of the nomad groups, the organization was kin-based, each tribe (known as *Bitu*—"house") having a hierarchy under the authority of its tribal sheikh. When tribal groups such as the Amorites, Aramaeans, and Chaldaeans gained control of substantial areas, these were divided into tribal territories where this organization held sway—such as Bit Yakin from which came the dynasty of Chaldaean kings of Babylon. Village communities also had stronger kinship ties than city dwellers.

Considerable information on local government comes from the archives at Nuzi, a town in the province of Arrapha, whose king was a vassal of Mitanni. One of his queens resided in Nuzi as his representative, and the town maintained her household out of local taxation. Local government in the town and its hinterland was run by the mayor (*hazannu*) who, along with other officials, resided in the government house (*ekallu)*. The center of local administration, this contained archives, storerooms, and offices as well as public reception rooms. The mayor was responsible for ensuring the military security of the town and its surrounding area: The Assyrians eventually sacked the town, and the administrative texts record the mustering, equipping, and provisioning of troops in the town's final days. The bureaucratic records also detail the taxes collected by the town to support the infrastructure and personnel of local government, including the army and the town's temples, and for payment to the king in Arrapha: These included finished goods and agricultural produce as well as labor and military service.

Some centuries earlier, in the northern Babylonian city of Sippar, documents refer to *hazannu* as the official representing a ward of the city, whereas the mayor was known as *rabianum,* an office particularly concerned with legal matters and held for a relatively short period, perhaps a year. The state administration was involved in public works such as the maintenance of irrigation facilities, but the responsibility was shared by the city authorities—the assembly (known as "the city") led by its chairman (*gal.ukken.nal*), the *rabianum, hazannu* and other officials. Local affairs, such as leasing local property and maintaining law and order, the courts, and sanitation, were also in the purview of the local authorities.

Royal Propaganda

The universally recognized role of the king was to ensure the welfare of his subjects, defending them against external threats; promoting prosperity through appropriate construction projects (particularly of irrigation systems), good management of land and resources, and the encouragement and sponsorship of trade and industry; supporting justice; and caring for the most vulnerable members of society such as orphans and widows. To this end some kings issued an edict (*misharum*) cancelling outstanding debts. Many kings also fixed wages and prices and standardized weights and measures. Kings also had important ritual duties, representing the community in making offerings, and in some cities, notably Uruk, taking part in a sacred marriage with the goddess.

In their inscriptions, kings informed the gods of their pious, appropriate, and successful activities following divine wishes; they also addressed future monarchs, offering themselves as models of righteous behavior, and the public at various levels. Royal inscriptions began in ED times with simple dedications of objects or structures by a named monarch to a deity, but by late ED times had developed into considerable narrative descriptions. Royal propaganda grew progressively more detailed, eulogizing the military and civil achievements of the king. By early Neo-Assyrian times, substantial records were created as texts and inscriptions, giving full details of campaigns and other achievements. The great reliefs on the walls of the Assyrian palaces provided a particularly vivid visual message: reassuring citizens of the power and piety of their ruler and the effectiveness of their army, and striking terror into the hearts of visiting foreigners. Those without direct access to the message—for example villagers—eventually became party to it through hearsay and gossip. Thus the ordinary citizen gained confidence in the divinely supported actions of the monarch. Like all propaganda, however, what the kings claimed was not always true.

Success was in itself indicative of legitimacy and divine approval. Nevertheless, royal inscriptions might offer an apologia for unorthodox actions: for example, usurpation justified by emphasizing the misdeeds of the deposed ruler and the need to restore the status quo. Often stories from history were reworked to give the sanction of tradition to a king's present actions.

International Relations

Foreign lands were often a source of desirable materials, which could be obtained either by diplomacy and trading, or by aggression. Both strategies were variously employed by Mesopotamian states, depending on the nature of the players with whom they had to deal. Other lands could also be the source of aggression, whether raids by tribal groups or full-blown invasions by hostile states, or they might become allies against the aggression of third parties.

Traders and ambassadors played a key role in articulating international relations. The economic and political importance of their activities made it expedient for rulers to protect messengers and merchants traveling through their domains; where the local leader, whether settled king or tribal sheikh, could not maintain law and order, travelers were at risk from highwaymen or hostile natives. A messenger might therefore be a military man, furnished with a fast horse by the first millennium, and accompanied by an armed escort. The Neo-Assyrian kings built royal highways with way stations to expedite the movement of couriers throughout their lands. Rulers often issued their messengers with a passport valid for a particular mission: This prevented local red tape impeding his journey, although it did not guarantee safe passage beyond the messenger's own state. However, a reciprocal arrangement developed between states that wished to engage in diplomatic activity, the envoy being furnished with an escort by the state to whom he was sent; failure to supply such an escort was a strongly hostile sign.

Particular events might encourage an exchange of messengers, for instance expressing good wishes for a monarch's recovery from ill health or congratulations on a victory. Envoys (*mar shipri*) bore written messages, although they were often illiterate themselves. A senior envoy, a relative or close confidante of the king, might also be empowered to conduct oral negotiations. Although envoys were often treated well and generously entertained, they were at the mercy of the ruler to whom they were sent and could be visited with the displeasure or hostility he felt toward their masters or held as hostages.

Good relations were promoted and maintained by the exchange of gifts and by treaties negotiated orally or by letter and ratified by solemn oaths, whose breaking would call down devastating divine retribution. Their terms might include a commitment not to aid each other's enemies, agreements to repatriate runaways, and arrangements to support and protect merchants. Despite superficially good relations underwritten by treaties, there were often undercurrents of suspicion or friction between states, and diplomats were expected to keep their eyes and ears open as spies for their own ruler. Although treaties were often sealed by royal marriages, hostages might also be taken to encourage the honoring of commitments. Fugitive princes from overthrown regimes might also be kept as political pawns, to be used as a threat to keep the current monarch in line or installed as a puppet ruler. Failure to return such rival claimants to the throne, on the other hand, was a hostile gesture and could be a source of prolonged friction.

WARFARE

Early Warfare

"If my city becomes a ruin mound, then I will be a potsherd of it, but I will never submit to the lord of Uruk" (Electronic Text Corpus of Sumerian Literature "Enmerkar and En-sughir-ana," lines 132–134).

Some scholars trace violent conflict back to the dawn of humankind. Others argue that warfare arose well after the advent of farming, through competition for land and resources and the need to defend them. Some early farming settlements were fortified, notably Jericho around 7000 B.C.E.—but its walls and towers were not necessarily for defense. They may alternatively have protected people and livestock against wild animals, demarcated the settlement, and been designed to impress other communities by concretely demonstrating power and prosperity. The early walls of Mesopotamian towns and cities such as Uruk and Abu Salabikh may have served similar purposes; defense against floods is another possibility.

Unequivocal evidence of armed conflict comes in the late fourth millennium B.C.E., with artwork on seals depicting fights between men armed with spears and bows, and bound prisoners. During the earlier third millennium (ED period) cities, often housing the bulk of their state's population, began erecting walls for defense as well as for territorial demarcation and prestige. Excavation has confirmed the slightly later literary descriptions of Uruk's city walls: A circuit 9.5 kilometers long and 4–5 meters thick built of typical ED plano-convex bricks enclosed an area of 550 hectares. At least two city gates with rectangular towers have been traced, and the wall may have had as many as 900 semicircular towers. Similar towers have been found in the strong walls around Tell Agrab on the Diyala.

The epic tale of conflict between Gilgamesh, king of Uruk, and his one-time benefactor and overlord, Agga, king of Kish, climaxes when Agga's forces besiege Uruk and Gilgamesh defeats and captures Agga, possibly after a pitched battle. Sieges in the ED period were often decided by force of arms in attacks and sallies rather than by attrition during long investments. However, attempts might be made to break into a fortified settlement using scaling ladders, and defenses began to be enhanced with a glacis.

The walls of captured cities were broken down, partly to humiliate their citizens. Booty and prisoners were taken, and much of the city might be sacked. Some of the spoils of war went by custom to the king and some to the god of the victorious city in his temple. Stone bowls found in the Ekur temple in Nippur bear inscriptions showing they were booty from Rimush's Elamite wars. Such inscriptions were an important part of the offering, demonstrating to both the god and the people that the king had fulfilled the god's intention in prosecuting war and benefitting his people. Inscriptions quickly grew in length and substance from their terse early-third-millennium beginnings, and by the first millennium, royal inscriptions gave a long and detailed, although often exaggerated and inaccurate, account of the campaign, serving both as

The victory stele of Naram-Sin, king of Akkad, 2254–2218 B.C.E. The king, wearing a horned helmet, stands above his soldiers who are trampling the enemy. (Zev Radovan/Land of the Bible Picture Archive)

justification to the god and propaganda to the people. The form, style, phraseology, and content of inscriptions were dictated by tradition.

In conflicts between Sumerian city-states the victor usually respected the integrity of a defeated city's temples: Outrage at Lugalzagesi's failure to do so is forcefully expressed in the inscriptions of his enemy, Uru-inim-gina of Lagash. In contrast, attacks by outsiders—nomads of the Syrian Desert and Zagros Mountains, such as the Amorites and Guti, and foreign states, particularly Elam—were ruthless and spared nothing and no one. Sumerian distress at the devastation wreaked by their attacks—the noble buildings destroyed or infested by the enemy, the fields laid waste, the people slain or taken into captivity—is poured out in a series of Lamentations describing the sack of great cities like Agade, Ur, and Nippur (see chapter 10).

ED art vividly captures the citizen armies of the period. "The Standard of Ur" and "The Stele of Vultures" (see p. 75) depict foot soldiers armed with spears or pole-mounted axes, their heads protected by leather or felt helmets. A force of heavy infantry carrying large rectangular shields marches in a solid and impenetrable phalanx bristling with couched spears, behind a king armed with a dagger. Maces and throwing sticks were also used as weapons at this time. The leaders ride in ponderous war-carts with four solid wheels, drawn by donkeys or mules. These were used mainly for transport to the battlefield and in pursuit of retreating enemy

Adad, god of storms, was also a patron of warfare. He is shown standing on a bull and holding in his hands prongs representing lightning. (Zev Radovan/Land of the Bible Picture Archive)

forces, and as a vantage point from which the leader could see and be seen, to direct his forces and impress friend and foe. The dead of the opposing army lie beneath the wheels of the carts or are heaped up in a communal burial mound, while the living are marched off into slavery, their hands tied behind them, or are held in a net by the god whose approval of the victors' just cause had precipitated the conflict and ensured its successful outcome. Later wars by larger states enjoyed the support of the war goddess Ishtar (Inanna), Nergal (Erra), god of strife, and the storm god Adad (Ishkur). Defeat, and even more terribly, the loss of the king in battle, betokened the withdrawal of divine favor.

Troops also included archers and soldiers armed with slings and ovoid stones, probably mainly recruited among the hunters and fishermen of the south. An inscribed object from ED Mari shows a bowman shooting from behind a wicker screen held by a spearman: This combination of archer and shield-bearer continued down the ages in Mesopotamian armies. The later-third-millennium development of the composite bow revolutionized warfare. Constructed as a sandwich of three contrasting materials, wood glued between a horn inner layer (to resist compression) and a sinew outer layer (for elasticity), it had a far greater penetration and range (around 175 meters) than the conventional bow. The composite bow benefited both attackers and defenders, enabling a wider area to be covered from the walls and troops on the ground to shoot defenders with more success.

In the ED period armed conflict arose generally from competition between settled states for land and water or nomad raids. Expeditions abroad to obtain commodities not available locally might also need armed protection or aggressive "sales tactics"—hence, for example, the fortifications around the Uruk-period settlement at Habuba Kabira and the military threats uttered by Enmerkar of Uruk against the distant state of Aratta (see chapter 4).

By about 2350 B.C.E., however, some states and their kings were also interested in territorial expansion, and the military unification of the south was eventually achieved by Sargon of Akkad. He probably employed the first standing army who made up some at least of the 5,400 men who "ate daily" in the king's presence. The Ur III king Shulgi created a standing army in years twenty to twenty-three of his reign: Many of the soldiers were holders of state land in return for various state duties, particularly military service, a system referred to later as *ilkum*. The landholder was liable to serve but in practice (though not in principle) could pay someone to take his place.

Warfare in the Second Millennium B.C.E.

Attacks by the nomadic Amorites led the later Ur III kings to construct a massive wall between the Euphrates and the Diyala, a vast undertaking, reflecting the empire's ability to call upon huge labor reserves. Settled farmers and urban dwellers were immobilized by their possessions and were tied to the agricultural year, which allowed warfare only in slack seasons; in contrast, pastoral nomads could rapidly move themselves and their possessions out of danger, deploy lightly armed forces swiftly and easily over long distances, and fight at any time of year. History worldwide has many instances of pastoralists raiding, defeating, and conquering settled communities, often settling in the aftermath and adopting the civilized ways of their new subjects. Many of the states that arose after the fall of Ur III came under the rule of Amorite sheikhs who often maintained ties with their nomadic kin, in some cases raising bodies of troops from among them. The kingdom of Mari was one such. Many of the militarily successful kings, like Shamshi-Adad, Hammurabi, and Rim-Sin, had nomadic forebears.

Earlier armies had been numbered in hundreds or the low thousands, but warfare in the Old Babylonian (OB) period was conducted on a larger scale. The king of Mari, a modest sized kingdom, regularly deployed armies of between 1,000 and 10,000 men; and when Shamshi-Adad besieged Nurragum he

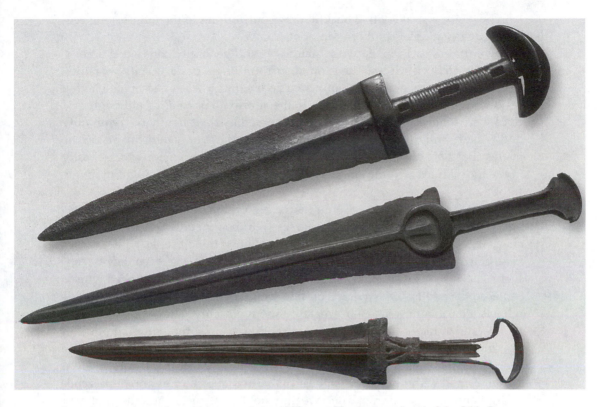

Swords and a dagger from Mesopotamia, ca. 1500 B.C.E. (Zev Radovan/Land of the Bible Picture Archive)

apparently commanded a force of some 60,000. Innovations in weapon technology were matched by increasing elaboration of defenses. The city of Assur was strongly defended on two sides by cliffs above the Tigris and on the other two by a massive wall probably built by Shamshi-Adad, to which at least eight impressive gates were added, along with a moat 20 meters wide, in the thirteenth century B.C.E. Moats were becoming a common feature of city defenses, along with improved glacis surfaced with clay or lime and increasingly elaborate gates with guard chambers. Attackers, however, now employed siege towers, raising them above or level with the defenders on the city walls. Their troops below operated battering rams: wheeled vehicles with a projecting beam, protected by shields or a wood and leather framework, which were rolled back and forth to chip or lever out bricks, creating a breach. Sappers might also undermine the walls with tunnels. To focus the effect of battering rams on the weaker upper part of the walls, besiegers built ramps of earth and rubble, often surfaced with planks or mortar, up which the ram could be dragged—the arduous and dangerous task of their construction was often inflicted on prisoners of war. Substantial siege engines could be brought in by water when the city lay by a river, as was often the case. Hammurabi and his successors several times also took the drastic step of diverting a river to bring ruin on a city, a strategy that backfired by contributing to the long-lasting economic devastation of southern Mesopotamia.

Nevertheless, warfare between states was still generally conducted according to civilized principles. The ground surrounding a besieged city was often cleared to give the attackers unimpeded access, but it was unacceptable to fell productive trees or to destroy crops. In the aftermath of conflict, although captives were often enslaved, some were ransomed by their family or community and treated well in the interim. Treaties contained not only agreements on the issues that had brought about the conflict but also provisions for sending home individuals or communities who had accidentally been caught up in the fighting.

The introduction of horses set in train a revolution on the battlefield. Faster and more powerful than donkeys, horses were better suited for drawing war chariots, particularly later in the millennium when the bit replaced the earlier nose-ring, improving their control and traction power. The seventeenth century B.C.E. also saw structural improvements to chariots. Light spoked wheels replaced the earlier heavy wheels of solid wood; fitted with two instead of four wheels, chariots now had far greater maneuverability. They were still used mainly for transport, carrying officers rapidly around the battlefield and in pursuit of fleeing enemies. Later in the millennium, however, chariots became mobile fighting platforms, carrying a charioteer to control the horses and a fighter armed with a bow. The expense of maintaining chariots and horses confined their use to royal troops and wealthy nobles. Armies would be deployed with chariots flanking the central body of infantry.

Chariots also provided a fast mode of travel for royal messengers. For more rapid communication, for example warning of an armed raid, beacons could be used. Spies were employed to provide information on potentially hostile foreign regimes, and diplomats might also engage in some spying. Information about the lay of the land and routes through it was of vital importance for planning troop movements and attacks.

As warfare gained in importance during the later second millennium, kings increasingly employed professional soldiers, who fought during the campaigning season and undertook other military activities for the rest of the year. Army personnel also included specialist noncombatants, such as carpenters and metalworkers. Records found at Nuzi show that the Mitanni accorded a high priority to their military organization and to supplying and maintaining the army over substantial distances. It was during this period that swords first began to appear among international armaments; but they were rare in Mesopotamia. It was not until iron came into widespread use in the early first millennium that swords in particular and iron weapons in general began to replace the more expensive bronze spears, arrowheads, axes, and daggers of earlier times. Protection against weapons was still generally made of leather or thick felt, although the later second millennium saw growing use among those who could afford it of body armor made of overlapping copper or bronze platelets sewn onto leather. It became more common in the first millennium, now made with iron rather than bronze scales.

First Millennium: The Assyrians and Their Enemies

Military professionalism and warfare reached their peak in the first millennium. In the forefront were the Assyrians, fighting initially to defend their borders and trade routes but later creating a vast empire. Their enlarging international borders brought the Assyrians into conflict with other major states, and revolts in discontented subject regions kept the Assyrian armies active. The size of the army vividly illustrates the escalating scale of military involvement: Sources refer to forces numbering 44,000 under Shalmaneser III in the ninth century, 73,000 under Tiglath-Pileser III in the eighth century, and 208,000 under Sennacherib forty years later.

Tiglath-Pileser III instituted a number of military reforms, building roads and bridges to facilitate communications and troop movements, establishing an efficient courier service, and creating a professional army with elite chariot and cavalry forces led by the chief eunuch (*rab sha reshe*) and infantry mercenaries, especially Aramaeans. Specialist individuals and corps included engineers and allied troops, at times including Phoenician ships and naval forces. When the army had to cross rivers on campaign, they might construct pontoons, use rafts, or float across individually on inflated skins (see photo p. 140).

The scale of Assyrian and Babylonian military activity was matched by the vast quantities of treasure they acquired in loot and tribute. Exquisite ivories that had decorated furniture (see chapter 9) were among the booty stored in the Review Palace (*ekal masharti*) at Kalhu. Now known as "Fort Shalmaneser," the Review Palace was built by Shalmaneser III and used by his successors down to Ashurbanipal. As well as the treasury and other storerooms, the complex included a royal palace, residential rooms for officials and perhaps barracks for the royal troops, official records, an arsenal, military workshops, and a huge parade ground where the king mustered and inspected his troops.

Nineveh also had a Review Palace, built by Sennacherib on what is now the Nebi Yunus mound. The Assyrian capitals—Kalhu, Dur Sharrukin, and Nineveh—constructed and embellished by the warlike kings from Ashurnasirpal II to Ashurbanipal were modeled on a military camp, round or rectangular in shape, with moats, regularly placed gates in their massive walls, and a citadel in one corner surrounded by its own impressive wall. Here successive kings built palaces and temples. Sennacherib strengthened the fortifications of the earlier city of Assur, adding an outer wall. Sargon II's capital Dur-Sharrukin, being built on flat ground, required exceptional fortifications: a wall of mudbrick 28 meters thick with 150 towers and seven or eight gates, surrounding a square city of 300 hectares. Its citadel had a separate wall with thirty-six towers and two gates.

The Babylonian capital, Babylon, was the most impressive of all, the area within its fortifications totalling 850 hectares. The Euphrates ran through it, dividing the city into two unequal parts. A moat and three walls, 8 kilometers long, surrounded the whole vast eastern part, with space between the walls wide enough to turn a four-horse chariot. The inner wall, 7 meters wide, was of sun-dried brick; the two outer ones, 7 and 3 meters wide respectively, were

Lachish—the ramp leading to the first city gate. (Zev Radovan/Land of the Bible Picture Archive)

of baked bricks. Two further walls and a moat surrounded the eastern inner city, with the famous Ishtar Gate in the center of the northern wall, at the head of the Processional Way. The Etemenanki, the precinct containing the "Tower of Babel," was also fortified, and the palace complex in the northwest corner was defended by a massive wall 25 meters thick.

Reliefs in the Assyrian palaces at Kalhu and Nineveh show the marked contrast between the Assyrians and some of their opponents, such as Elamites armed only with bows and without armor. The soldiers of the Levant, particularly Israel and Judah, who were frequently engaged in internecine warfare, were better equipped, often adopting technological advances made by the Assyrians in weapons, siege craft, and defensive architecture. They also devised their own, for example projecting balconies that made it hard for attackers to scale city walls, but which increased the area of the ground below that could be covered by fire from the defenders stationed on them.

Assyrian reliefs bear vivid witness to the wars in the Levant. Sennacherib's siege of the Judaean city of Lachish in 701 provides a particularly fine example (see photo p. 180). The Assyrians constructed a ramp to bring battering rams and siege towers against the walls and gate in the southwest. This has been excavated: It contained 25,000 tons of stones. The design of battering rams had

The city walls of Lachish, besieged by the Assyrians in 701 B.C.E. (Zev Radovan/Land of the Bible Picture Archive)

been improved in the ninth century, the beam now being suspended on chains or ropes; some rams had two beams. The ram often formed part of a combined siege engine, with a siege tower above manned by archers to pick off the defenders. The wood and leather framework that protected the men swinging the ram also sheltered archers. Soldiers armed with spears and axes assaulted the walls and particularly the gate, protected by heavy shields. Sappers dug tunnels, inserting wooden supports that were then set alight to bring about the wall's collapse. In response the people of Lachish built a huge sloping rampart of loose stones and earth against the wall's inner face to close any breach that might be achieved, and those on the ramparts threw burning torches at the flammable siege engines and lowered chains to catch and pull up the beam of the battering rams. The Assyrians countered by continually pouring water over the siege engines to prevent them igniting and by wielding hooks to pull down the chains or hold down the beam.

Despite the defenders' valor and determination, Lachish fell. The city was fired; its leaders were brutally tortured and executed; and its common people were marched off into exile in Assyria (see photo p. 169). Although some cities fell to a direct assault, others were reduced by a long siege—for example, the three-year investment of Samaria, or the siege of Nippur during which many

An aerial view of Lachish, a royal city in the kingdom of Judah until its destruction by King Sennacherib of Assyria in 701 B.C.E. (Zev Radovan/Land of the Bible Picture Archive)

inhabitants sold their children to the temple to prevent them from starving. More horrifyingly, cannibalism was said to have occurred in some long sieges, such as that of Babylon in 648.

Success also attended the Assyrians on the battlefield. Their soldiers were well equipped, with metal helmets and iron-scale body armor and a range of weapons. Shock troops were stationed in the first two ranks: Armed with long spears and well defended with shields, they could effectively resist a chariot charge. They were backed up by ranks of archers and behind them slingers, who kept up a constant and devastating fire, bringing down the enemy at long range. Already previously a formidable weapon, by the eighth century chariots, now pulled by larger horses imported from Egypt and Nubia, were able to carry a team of four: a charioteer, two archers, and a shield-bearer. Nevertheless chariots were gradually superseded by the faster and more maneuverable cavalry.

For riding, the smaller horses from Urartu and Mannai were preferred. Horse riding had initially been an awkward business, with the rider perched on the horse's rump as donkeys were ridden. An eighteenth-century B.C.E. letter from a nobleman advised Zimri-Lim of Mari that his horse-riding activities were beneath his dignity and that he should travel in the conventional manner in a chariot drawn by mules. Moving to the middle of the horse improved matters, but the simple harness made it difficult to control a horse while fighting. Cavalrymen in the early first millennium therefore rode in pairs, one man to fight and the other to hold the reins controlling both horses; otherwise horsemen were used for other tasks such as carrying messages and reconnaissance. The invention of better bridles improved the rider's control, allowing cavalry soldiers to act singly, and by the seventh century, cavalry were replacing chariotry on the battlefield, chariots being reserved for carrying kings and commanders and for nonmilitary activities such as hunting and processions.

Success in war was not left to chance and to good planning and equipment: The will of the gods was seen as the paramount consideration. This was ascertained by taking omens before military activities were initiated, so diviners were an important element in the Mesopotamian army. The most common method was to study the liver of a sacrificial animal (see chapter 8).

The Assyrians have acquired a reputation for merciless brutality and savagery; although it was not undeserved, because they regarded ruthless reprisals as a deterrent to rebellion, this view of them is based on the hostile propaganda of their inveterate opponents, the Israelites and Judaeans, and it is unlikely that the Assyrians were any crueler than their contemporaries. Evidence shows that they were staunch, supportive, and generous to their loyal subjects and allies. Despite the excellence of their military machine, they regarded war as the last resort after diplomacy and threats had failed to achieve the desired results.

The Assyrian war machine was not inviolable, and the Assyrians finally succumbed to the combined might of the Babylonians and the Medes. Discoveries at Kalhu (Nimrud) and the Assyrian capital, Nineveh, bear witness to their fall in 612 B.C.E. The gateways of the Review Palace at Kalhu, damaged in the assault of two years before, were still being repaired when the final attack came in 612. Many parts of the city were destroyed by fire. A well in the looted North-West Palace contained abandoned booty and the remains of more than 180 manacled men of military age, presumably Assyrian soldiers who had been taken prisoner and murdered. At Nineveh, archaeologists have uncovered the skeletons of forty of the defenders, including the mangled remains of nine in one of the gateways, pierced by arrows and mingled with their weapons and the debris from the burning gate that had collapsed over them. The sack of the city was thorough and complete. The attackers selectively mutilated the wall reliefs, defacing Sennacherib, who had sacked Babylon, Ashurbanipal, who had defeated the Elamite king Te-Umman, and the soldier who had cut off the latter's head. They smashed records of Elamite submission, ritually destroying the power of the Assyrian kings. Then, setting fire to the palaces and flooding the city, "They carried off the vast booty of the city and the temple and turned the city into a ruin heap." ("The Fall of Nineveh Chronicle": Lendering, quoting Grayson 1975).

TEXT REFERENCES

Anglim, Simon, Phyllis G. Jestice, Rob S. Rice, Scott M. Rusch, and John Serrati. 2002. *Fighting Techniques of the Ancient World. 3000 BC–AD 500. Equipment, Combat Skills and Tactics.* London: Greenhill Books.

Bienkowski, Piotr. 2000. "Provincial Administration." Pp. 220–221 in *Dictionary of the Ancient Near East.* Edited by Piotr Bienkowski and Alan Millard. London: British Museum Press.

Chapman, Rupert. 1997. "Weapons and Warfare." Pp. 334–339 in *The Oxford Encyclopedia of Archaeology in the Near East.* Vol. 5. Edited by Eric M. Meyers. Oxford: Oxford University Press.

Charpin, Dominique. 2000. "The History of Ancient Mesopotamia: An Overview." Pp. 807–830 in *Civilizations of the Ancient Near East.* 4 Volumes. Edited by Jack M. Sasson. Peabody, MA: Hendrickson Publishers. (Reprint of 1995 edition. New York: Scribner.)

Dalley, Stephanie. 1984. *Mari and Karana. Two Old Babylonian Cities.* London: Longman.

———. 2000. "Ancient Mesopotamian Military Organization." Pp. 413–422 in *Civilizations of the Ancient Near East.* 4 Volumes. Edited by Jack M. Sasson. Peabody, MA: Hendrickson Publishers. (Reprint of 1995 edition. New York: Scribner.)

Electronic Text Corpus of Sumerian Literature. "Enmerkar and En-sughir-ana." http://www-etcsl.orient.ox.ac.uk/ (cited January 30, 2002).

Electronic Text Corpus of Sumerian Literature. "The Sumerian King List." http://www-etcsl.orient.ox.ac.uk/ (cited January 30, 2002).

Forde, Daryll. 1954. "Foraging, Hunting and Fishing." Pp. 154–186 in *A History of Technology.* Edited by Charles Singer, E. J. Holmyard, and A. R. Hall. Oxford: Oxford University Press.

Franke, Sabina. 2000. "Kings of Akkad: Sargon and Naram-Sin." Pp. 831–841 in *Civilizations of the Ancient Near East.* 4 Volumes. Edited by Jack M. Sasson. Peabody, MA: Hendrickson Publishers. (Reprint of 1995 edition. New York: Scribner.)

Grayson, A. Kirk. 1975. *Assyrian and Babylonian Chronicles.* New York: J. J. Augustin.

———. 2000. "Assyrian Rule of Conquered Terrritory in Ancient Western Asia." Pp. 959–968 in *Civilizations of the Ancient Near East.* 4 Volumes. Edited by Jack M. Sasson. Peabody, MA: Hendrickson Publishers. (Reprint of 1995 edition. New York: Scribner.)

Greengus, Samuel. 2000. "Legal and Social Institutions of Ancient Mesopotamia." Pp. 469–484 in *Civilizations of the Ancient Near East.* 4 Volumes. Edited by Jack M. Sasson. Peabody, MA: Hendrickson Publishers. (Reprint of 1995 edition. New York: Scribner.)

Harris, David R. 1996. *The Origins and Spread of Agriculture and Pastoralism in Eurasia.* Washington, DC: Smithsonian Institution Press.

Hodges, Henry. 1971. *Technology in the Ancient World.* Harmondsworth: Penguin.

Klein, Jacob. 2000. "Shulgi of Ur: King of a Neo-Sumerian Empire." Pp. 842–857 in *Civilizations of the Ancient Near East.* 4 Volumes. Edited by Jack M. Sasson. Peabody, MA: Hendrickson Publishers. (Reprint of 1995 edition. New York: Scribner.)

Kramer, Samuel Noah. 1981. *History Begins at Sumer. Thirty-Nine Firsts in Recorded History.* 3rd revised edition. Philadelphia: University of Pennsylvania Press.

Leick, Gwendolyn. 2001. *Mesopotamia. The Invention of the City.* London: Allen Lane, Penguin Press.

Lendering, Jona. "The Fall of Nineveh." http://www.livius.org/ne-nn/nineveh/nineveh01.html (cited October 28, 2004).

Liverani, Mario. 2000. "The Deeds of Ancient Mesopotamian Kings." Pp. 2353–2366 in *Civilizations of the Ancient Near East.* 4 Volumes. Edited by Jack M. Sasson. Peabody, MA: Hendrickson Publishers. (Reprint of 1995 edition. New York: Scribner.)

Maidman, Maynard Paul. 2000. "Nuzi: Portrait of an Ancient Mesopotamian Provincial Town." Pp. 931–947 in *Civilizations of the Ancient Near East.* 4 Volumes. Edited by Jack M. Sasson. Peabody, MA: Hendrickson Publishers. (Reprint of 1995 edition. New York: Scribner.)

Mazar, Amihai. 2000. "The Fortification of Cities in the Ancient Near East." Pp. 1523–1537 in *Civilizations of the Ancient Near East.* 4 Volumes. Edited by Jack M. Sasson. Peabody, MA: Hendrickson Publishers. (Reprint of 1995 edition. New York: Scribner.)

Meyers, Eric M., ed. 1997. *The Oxford Encyclopedia of Archaeology in the Near East.* 5 Volumes. Oxford: Oxford University Press.

Nissen, Hans J. 1972. "The City Wall of Uruk." Pp. 793–798 in *Man, Settlement and Urbanism.* Edited by Peter Ucko, Ruth Tringham, and Geoffrey W. Dimbleby. London: Duckworth.

———. 1988. *The Early History of the Ancient Near East.* Chicago: University of Chicago Press. (Paperback edition 1990.)

Oates, Joan, and David Oates. 2001. *Nimrud. An Assyrian Imperial City Revealed.* London: British School of Archaeology in Iraq.

Oller, Gary H. 2000. "Messengers and Ambassadors in Ancient Western Asia." Pp. 1465–1473 in *Civilizations of the Ancient Near East.* 4 Volumes. Edited by Jack M. Sasson. Peabody, MA: Hendrickson Publishers. (Reprint of 1995 edition. New York: Scribner.)

Oppenheim, A. Leo, and Erica Reiner. 1977. *Ancient Mesopotamia. Portrait of a Dead Civilization.* Revised edition. Chicago: University of Chicago Press.

Pollack, Susan. 1999. *Ancient Mesopotamia. The Eden that Never Was.* Cambridge: Cambridge University Press.

Postgate, J. Nicholas. 1994. *Early Mesopotamia.* London: Routledge.

———. 2000. "Royal Ideology and State Administration in Sumer and Akkad." Pp. 395–411 in *Civilizations of the Ancient Near East.* 4 Volumes. Edited by Jack M. Sasson. Peabody, MA: Hendrickson Publishers. (Reprint of 1995 edition. New York: Scribner.)

Potts, D. T. 1999. *The Archaeology of Elam. Formation and Transformation of an Ancient Iranian State.* Cambridge: Cambridge University Press.

Reade, Julian. 1983. *Assyrian Sculpture.* London: British Museum Publications.

Roaf, Michael. 1990. *Cultural Atlas of Mesopotamia.* New York: Facts on File.

Robertson, John. 2000. "The Social and Economic Organization of Ancient Mesopotamian Temples." Pp. 443–454 in *Civilizations of the Ancient Near East.*

4 Volumes. Edited by Jack M. Sasson. Peabody, MA: Hendrickson Publishers. (Reprint of 1995 edition. New York: Scribner.)

Saggs, H. W. F. 1995. *Peoples of the Past. Babylonians*. London: British Museum Press.

Sasson, Jack M. 2000. "King Hammurabi of Babylon." Pp. 901–916 in *Civilizations of the Ancient Near East*. 4 Volumes. Edited by Jack M. Sasson. Peabody, MA: Hendrickson Publishers. (Reprint of 1995 edition. New York: Scribner.)

Sasson, Jack M., ed. 2000. *Civilizations of the Ancient Near East*. 4 Volumes. Peabody, MA: Hendrickson Publishers. (Reprint of 1995 edition. New York: Scribner.)

Schwartz, Glenn M. 2000. "Pastoral Nomadism in Ancient Western Asia." Pp. 249–258 in *Civilizations of the Ancient Near East*. 4 Volumes. Edited by Jack M. Sasson. Peabody, MA: Hendrickson Publishers. (Reprint of 1995 edition. New York: Scribner.)

Smith, Donald. "Armed Skeletons Confirm Fall of Nineveh." National Geographic News Service. http://www.bibleprobe.com/ninevehskel.htm (cited October 28th, 2004).

Sommerfeld, Walter. 2000. "The Kassites of Ancient Mesopotamia: Origins, Politics and Culture." Pp. 917–930 in *Civilizations of the Ancient Near East*. 4 Volumes. Edited by Jack M. Sasson. Peabody, MA: Hendrickson Publishers. (Reprint of 1995 edition. New York: Scribner.)

Van de Mieroop, Marc. 1997. *The Ancient Mesopotamian City*. Oxford: Oxford University Press.

———. 1999. *Cuneiform Texts and the Writing of History*. London: Routledge.

———. 2004. *A History of the Ancient Near East. ca. 3000–323 BC*. Oxford: Blackwell.

Veenhof, Klaas R. 2000. "Kanesh: An Assyrian Colony in Anatolia." Pp. 859–872 in *Civilizations of the Ancient Near East*. 4 Volumes. Edited by Jack M. Sasson. Peabody, MA: Hendrickson Publishers. (Reprint of 1995 edition. New York: Scribner.)

Villard, Pierre. 2000. "Shamshi-Adad and Sons: The Rise and Fall of an Upper Mesopotamian Empire." Pp. 873–884 in *Civilizations of the Ancient Near East*. 4 Volumes. Edited by Jack M. Sasson. Peabody, MA: Hendrickson Publishers. (Reprint of 1995 edition. New York: Scribner.)

Yoffee, Norman. 2000. "The Economy of Ancient Western Asia." Pp. 1387–1399 in *Civilizations of the Ancient Near East*. 4 Volumes. Edited by Jack M. Sasson. Peabody, MA: Hendrickson Publishers. (Reprint of 1995 edition. New York: Scribner.)

VIII CHAPTER 8
Religion and Ideology

RELIGION AND SOCIETY

Introduction

The distinguished Mesopotamian scholar Leo Oppenheim (1977) famously claimed that it was impossible to write an account of Mesopotamian religion: This impossibility is not unique to Mesopotamia. It is difficult to enter the minds of the practitioners of any religion and understand their beliefs, sentiments, and worldview, even when material for this study is plentiful, and far more difficult to penetrate the belief systems and practices of people long gone. Although excavated buildings and other material traces allow some aspects of Mesopotamian ritual practices to be reconstructed, they do not yield information on the beliefs with which they were associated, while the fragmentary surviving texts shed only a partial light on beliefs and rituals. But although we can never enter fully the hearts and minds of the ancient Mesopotamians, and many aspects of religious practices and beliefs will forever elude us, nevertheless the surviving evidence does allow many aspects of religious life to be studied.

Early Mesopotamian Shrines and Religion

The information is most elusive before the beginning of writing around 3000 B.C.E. A few Ubaid and Uruk buildings have been excavated, the location and contents of which suggest a ritual function. In some sites, for example Eridu and Uruk, structures dating from the fifth or fourth millennia onward were periodically reconstructed, enlarged, and embellished, reaching by the third millennium a form that became standard for Mesopotamian shrines. Uruk period temples were often strikingly decorated with mosaic patterns created from clay cones with painted heads embedded in the wall plaster, or in one case, using cones of white alabaster and red and black limestone. The interior walls of a temple at Uqair bore paintings of people, leopards, and other animals.

The earliest shrine at Eridu was a single room, raised on a platform, with an altar set in a niche opposite the entrance and an offering table before it. The shrine was periodically leveled and reconstructed, becoming increasingly elaborate, with a tripartite plan of central nave and side chambers and with the later addition of further rooms, buttresses, niches, and an increasingly substantial platform with access ramp. In historical times Eridu belonged to Enki, god of the waters; numerous fish bones found on the floor of the shrine—offerings or the remains of ritual meals—suggest it was dedicated to him from the outset. A similar association is assumed between other prehistoric shrines and the deities historically associated with their city, notably the shrines in the Kullaba and Eanna districts of Uruk with An and Inanna.

Thorkild Jacobsen, in his seminal work *The Treasures of Darkness*, argues that the deities revered during the fourth millennium and earlier were the *élan vital* of natural features, such as earth, sky, river, sea, tree, cereal, sheep, and cattle, worshipped to ensure fertility and the continuity of life and the seasons. As Mesopotamia developed from small agricultural communities into complex city-states, vying for control of land, water, and other resources, however, the gods became visualized in human form, their lives mirroring human society, engaged in conflict and concerned with ordering the world. Whether or not Jacobsen's thesis is accepted in detail, it strikes a salutary warning note that the practices and beliefs associated with a shrine may have evolved even though the architecture implies continuity of worship.

Temples and Ziggurats

The tripartite temple plan continued in the ED period as a large hall flanked by side chambers, with a cella (sanctum) at the far end and its entrance in one of the long sides. Although this "bent axis" approach did continue later, most temples from late ED onward had their entrance in the short front wall, often through a monumental gateway with towers. Instead of a hall, a courtyard flanked by rooms often lay between gate and cella, which might be raised, with steps giving access to its interior. This basic temple unit could be multiplied to form a much larger temple complex: For example, the Ishtar-Kititum temple at Nerebtum (Ishchali) contained three temples of different sizes, fitted together to form a rectangle with a massive buttressed outer wall.

Temples were usually built of baked brick, their external walls elaborated with buttresses and niches. The desire for valuable materials to embellish the temple was a major incentive to international trade, as an inscription of Gudea, *ensi* of Girsu, exemplifies. To build a temple to Ningirsu he obtained timber from Meluhha and Magan and copper, gold, silver, and "red stones"(carnelian) from Meluhha. He had trees felled in Cedar Mountain and Pine Mountain and floated downriver and brought stone from new quarries.

The temple lay within a precinct, often walled, generally in the center of the city. This was the hub of the huge organization that was the temple establishment: It included granaries and storerooms for the products of the temple's lands and industry; offices and archives of records for the administration of the temple and its dependents; the residences of at least some of the full-time temple staff, including the chief priest of the god to whom the precinct was dedicated, and in some cities the *gagum* ("cloister"), a substantial walled enclosure that housed women dedicated to the god's service; sometimes workshops, particularly for the manufacture of textiles; kitchens for the preparation of the god's food; and rooms for the performance of ritual activities, such as ablution to purify officiating priests. In Ur the precinct contained the *giparu*, the palace of the high priestess *(en / entum)* of the city's patron god Nanna, which included the temple of Nanna's spouse, Ningal, storerooms,

Ruins at Ur, the capital of the Sumerian Ur III empire. The ziggurat built by Ur-Nammu is visible in the background. (Nik Wheeler/Corbis)

public rooms, and private quarters, as well as a crypt where priestesses were buried. Other cities may have had similar establishments within their precincts. As well as the shrine of the principal deity, the precinct generally included smaller temples dedicated to his or her spouse and offspring, with associated buildings.

Although the normal "low" temple was the home of the deity, some ("high") temples were raised on platforms, and it is suggested these were portals through which the deity might descend to earth. The practice of building temple platforms, whose height increased with each rebuilding, dates back to Ubaid times. It reached its climax in the construction from Ur III times of ziggurats—sacred pyramids that dominated the precinct of many cities (see photo p. 82). Ziggurats were constructed of solid layers of sun-dried brick, separated at every seven courses by a layer of reed matting as protection against rising damp. Weep-holes set at intervals and internal drainage shafts also kept the structure dry. A thick facing of baked bricks protected the exterior. The Ur III ziggurats, epitomized by the well-preserved example at Ur itself, consisted of three staged tiers, sloping inward, with a platform at each stage, accessed by a triple stair on one side; later examples, such as that at Dur

Sharrukin, might alternatively be approached via a spiral ramp. The platform on the summit bore a building, probably a shrine. The best-known later example, Etemenanki, the ziggurat at Babylon (famously known as the "Tower of Babel"), was repeatedly rebuilt and embellished, eventually reaching seven tiers. A small lake outlines its base today: Its bricks were completely plundered after the excavators left in 1917. A block of solid brick masonry, wind-scoured but still monumental, remains from the Kassite ziggurat in Dur-Kurigalzu (Aqar Quf), and in neighboring Elam, the short-lived city of Al-Untash-Napirisha (Choga Zanbil) was centered on the largest surviving ziggurat, still substantially preserved. Ziggurats were apparently painted; the traditional colors for seven-tiered examples like those at Babylon and Dur-Sharrukin were, from the bottom up, white, black, red, blue, orange, silver, and gold.

Though the precinct was its central focus, the temple institution also owned substantial lands and buildings outside. These included urban houses for temple personnel and workshops, such as the weaving establishment ("North Palace") at Eshnunna. Others lay in the countryside, where the temple might have large industrial complexes, such as the workshop at Guabba outside Lagash staffed by 6,000 workers, and storage facilities, such as those maintained in various villages by the Sin temple at Khafajeh, to store grain grown on temple lands.

Although most is known about the major precincts, some smaller neighborhood shrines have also been excavated. These included the Small Temple at Khafajeh and the Single Shrine at Eshnunna. Not all rituals took place in temples; for example, there were rural festivals to which the statue of the god was brought.

The God at Home

The temple, known simply as E / Bitu ("house"), was both the home and, in some transcendental sense, the embodiment of the deity. Within the temple the god was more precisely located within his or her image. Many commentators make heavy weather of the concept of a god being manifest as a man-made statue and simultaneously in many places; but similar mysteries are at the heart of most religions: for instance, the Christian tenet that "God sees all." It is in the very nature of deities that they can be present at one and the same time in many (or all) places and can inhabit or give life to objects created by their human servants or natural objects that they themselves created.

Written descriptions show that divine images were made from the most precious materials, including gold covering a wooden core, and clothed in the finest raiment and the choicest jewels. A larger-than-lifesize golden ear from the Shamash temple at Mari probably came from such a statue. The manufacture and installation of a divine image was a major event, undertaken as a pious duty by kings and giving its name to the year in which it took place. Other years were designated by the addition of paraphernalia to the statue, such as a fine robe or a model of the god's emblem. Solemn and secret rituals attended the transforming moment when the image changed from a mere human creation into the god himself: These included ceremonies for opening its eyes and mouth.

The temple was the god's house, staffed by his or her servants, in which he or she lived a life similar to that of a king. The image was bathed, anointed, and dressed in fine garments, and served food and drink. Sweet-smelling incense from Mediterranean forests was burned in braziers during meals, served in the morning and afternoon. Drinks of beer, water, or wine were served in a cup or poured into channels in the altar, and the food, including bread, cakes, fish and meat dishes, and fruit, was set on a table (*pashshurum*) before the deity. Often a curtain was then drawn to allow the god to eat in privacy. After a decent interval, the remains of the god's repast were removed, to be sent to the king or consumed by the temple staff. On occasion the god might entertain a visiting deity, his servants laying on a special feast.

Records show that huge quantities of food (including bread, flour, beer, and fruit) were brought into the temple as regular offerings (tithes or, as Postgate suggests, "membership subscriptions" to the temple community): Some was prepared for the deity, and the rest fed the temple staff. The famous Warka vase (late fourth millennium B.C.E.) shows a procession bearing fruit, grain, and other food (see photo p. 69), which is offered by a priest to the goddess standing on a dais. Offerings were made not only to the chief deity but also to his or her emblems and household and even to parts of the temple, such as locks and drainpipes. To keep the gods pleased with their devotees and happy to reside in their city, hymns were sung in their praise and dramas enacted that glorified their achievements. The earliest literary compositions of known authorship are hymns to Inanna written by Sargon's daughter Enheduanna, *entum* priestess of Nanna. Music played on drums, lyres, tambourines, and pipes, and sung or chanted, played a major part in many rituals.

Since the divine image was the presence of the god in his shrine and city, its absence meant the absence of the deity too. When a city was conquered, the pillage of the gods' statues was the ultimate catastrophe, signifying the withdrawal of divine patronage. In times of danger, therefore, the images might be removed to a place of safety. When Marduk-apla-iddina II fled to the marshes, he took with him both the divine statues and the bones of his ancestors to keep them from Sennacherib.

Rituals

Lamentations from the third and early second millennia chronicled the god's wrath against his city and its consequent fall to the enemy, graphically described. A joyful finale saw the god relenting and the city's good fortune restored. Such poems were probably sung by the lamentation priest, accompanied by harps and pipes, at a ceremony inaugurating the rebuilding of the temple, to avert any sacrilege attached to clearing the surviving remains. Lamentations not tied to specific historical events became part of the liturgy, performed during festivals or ceremonies on days of cultic significance, accompanied by tambourines in the second millennium and harps in the first.

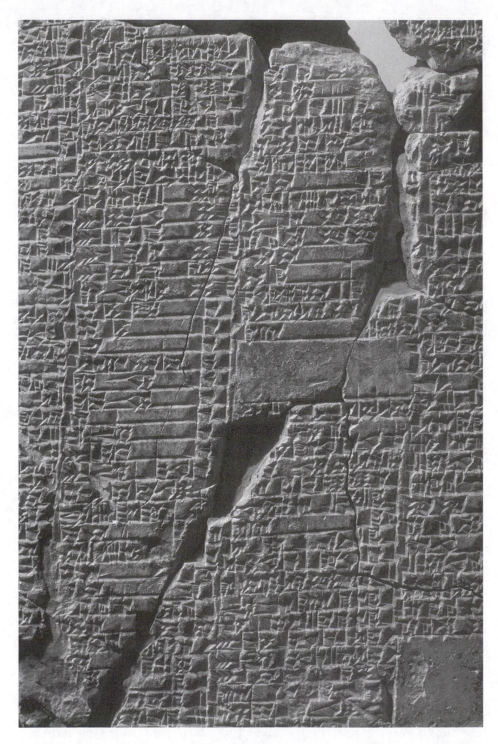

A cuneiform baked clay tablet, ca. 1820 B.C.E, from Larsa in Babylonia. This tablet documents in detail the worship of the sun god, Utu/Shamash, the patron god of the city of Larsa, Ninisina, goddess of healing and patroness of the city of Isin, and the other gods of the Babylonian pantheon. (Zev Radovan/Land of the Bible Picture Archive)

Children destined for the clergy studied versification, singing, and instrumental music in addition to a normal scribal education, probably in a school attached to the temple. Temples had an orchestra of harps and lyres, wind instruments and drums, and a chorus of singers directed by a lamentation priest (*gala / kalum*) or singer (*nar / naru*). The making of instruments for the temple was important enough to be recorded in date formulae.

Major public enterprises such as temple construction were attended by rituals at every stage, beginning with the king molding the first brick or carrying the first basket of soil, a theme frequently appearing in dedicatory art. Public rituals were performed to protect the king or the state, for example, to safeguard the army when it went to war. The investiture of a new king was a solemn religious occasion during which his symbols of office—crown, scepter, and throne (actually hat, rod, and stool)—were presented to him in the temple and sacrifices were made.

The king played the chief role in his realm's religious life. He was directly responsible to the gods for his kingdom's well-being and had to make decisions and take action on the basis of divine communications delivered either through divination or directly to him in dreams. His good management ensured that the state prospered and could provide offerings to the gods in abundance, and the state's prosperity and well-being were proof of the gods' approval of his regime. The king commissioned the construction, embellishment, and renovation of temples and divine images, and played the leading role in major ceremonies such as the New Year festival and the Sacred Marriage, as well as in lesser rituals. In the early Sumerian city-states he could officiate in person in all the required ceremonies, but as states grew in size, deputies (often members of the royal family) fulfilled many of his obligations across the realm.

Although the king had access to the god on appropriate occasions (see photo p. 35), it is not clear whether ordinary people could enter the cella of the city temple. However, smaller neighborhood shrines probably served their needs, and they could participate in processions and festivals. They addressed and made offerings to their own personal god in their domestic shrine and through him might also approach the city deity, a scene shown on numerous seals. When people were in particular need of divine favor, for instance when someone was ill, they sought the help of a priest such as a diviner (*baru*) or exorcist (*ashipu*) to perform the appropriate rites and incantations.

Prayers enabled the individual to communicate with the gods. Figurines probably representing an individual or his or her personal god could be set up in the temple. They show the reverent pose adopted by the worshipper, hands clasped against the chest (see photo p. 71) or holding a cup or animal, presumably representing offerings. An extreme form of these perpetual worshippers was the *naditum:* a girl dedicated to the god by her family to keep him mindful of their needs, as Erishti-Aya, daughter of Zimri-Lim of Mari, emphasized in a letter complaining of her family's neglect: "Am I not the praying emblem who says regular prayers for your life?" (Dalley 1984: 120).

The Organization of the Temple

The temple combined ritual activities with the practical business of running the god's household and estate. The more important or specialist cultic officials ("priests," although there was no blanket Mesopotamian term with this meaning), administrative staff, scribes, and artisans would have been permanent employees of the temple, as were a number of other essential personnel, such as barbers to shave the priests' heads and cooks to prepare the gods' daily meals.

At their head was the *sanga / shangum* (chief priest), whose role was as much administrative as religious. Others had a more exclusively ritual role, headed by the *en* priest or *en / entum* priestess, who was the spouse of the city deity: This post lapsed after the OB period, although it was revived by the Neo-Babylonian king Nebuchadrezzar II. Other cultic personnel included snake charmers, acrobats, musicians, and singers, and more senior staff included diviners, exorcists, and lamentation priests; the latter may have been homosexuals, transvestites, or eunuchs.

The administrative staff included managers, overseers, surveyors, foremen, scribes and archivists, servants and slaves. Many posts that did not require specialist skills were filled by members of the community who performed regular but limited duties and received rations, wages, or the use of temple land in return. These "prebends" (as these posts are conventionally known) became the closely guarded privilege of individuals; they were heritable and could be bought and sold. Over the years they frequently became subdivided, and by OB times an individual might be called upon to perform his task as rarely as once a year. Prebendary duties included sweeping the temple courtyard, acting as water carriers or doorkeepers, and baking bread or brewing beer for the temple. Some ritual duties were performed by prebendary priests known as *gudu / pashishum.*

The temples commanded enormous manpower, in dependents and corvée labor: in ED Girsu around a third of the city's population of ca. 100,000 worked for the temples. Sharecroppers who worked temple lands could be required to undertake corvée labor, receiving daily rations. The temple also maintained many people whom adverse circumstances had made its dependents or slaves: widows, orphans, physically disabled people, and other unfortunates; those who had sold themselves or been sold by their family in payment of debts; children offered as neophytes when their parents could no longer feed them, through destitution or during famine or sieges; and war captives donated to the temple by kings or citizens. Their labor was entirely at the disposal of the temple, which supported them with daily food rations and periodic issues of other necessities or perquisites. These people cultivated temple fields and orchards, tended temple herds and flocks, and worked in temple industries, manufacturing textiles and objects of wood, stone, metal, clay, and leather.

Temples often owned substantial estates—for example, around 10 percent of the lands of Girsu in the ED period belonged to the temples. From these, the temple drew enormous revenues in grain and other produce including wool, which was then converted by temple workers into textiles for local use or export by merchants employed or commissioned by the temple. Usury also brought in revenue: The temple made loans at the relatively low rate of 20 percent (the norm being 33.3 percent) to fund private enterprise or buy back prisoners of war or debt slaves, and sometimes waived the interest altogether. The temple also entered into business partnerships.

Food and other offerings came both from the community as obligations and from the king and individuals as gifts *(arua)* when divine help was sought or as thank-offerings. *Arua* included land and slaves as well as precious materials and fine objects, often inscribed with the donor's name, and the humbler gifts of private citizens. Many of the everyday objects and materials were issued to the temple staff: For instance, textiles and wool were among the recorded rations. Gifts of fine clothing, jewelry, and other valuables, however, accumulated in far larger quantities than the god could wear or use. The surplus was stored in what became substantial temple treasuries. A magnet for plunderers when cities were sacked, such treasures have not survived but are known to have existed from detailed inventories kept in temple archives, which list large numbers of metal vessels, fine robes, seals, precious jewelry, drapes for the god's throne, and many other valuable items. Owned by the temple, these nevertheless represented the wealth of the community as a whole, and their loss in war would have had devastating economic consequences.

GODS AND PEOPLE

Introduction

Although the pantheon when first recorded around 2600 B.C.E. lists around five hundred deities with Sumerian names, only thirty or so Akkadian deities are known, suggesting that the communities' original attitudes to religion were fundamentally different, although by ED times Sumerian and Akkadian speakers were probably well integrated. Jacobsen (1976) argues that during the fourth millennium and probably earlier, the Sumerians conceived of divinity as a numinous presence within natural phenomena: an intransitive power that made these phenomena what they were but did not act beyond them. During the third millennium, however, he argues that a new conception of the gods developed, giving them a far wider role as the active and conscious agents of the creation and maintenance of the world. By the second millennium the pantheon took the form of around thirty major deities, referred to by name, and a great many others, known collectively as the Anunnaki and Igigi, each said to number three hundred.

During the third millennium, the gods came to be seen as members of a family, their society mirroring that of Sumer and perhaps Akkad, with Enlil at their head. Individual city-states were the domain of particular deities: Uruk of Inanna, Ur of Nanna, Lagash of Ningirsu, Nippur of Enlil, and so on. Here were located their principal temples, although they also had shrines in many other cities: Inanna in Kish, Nippur, and eventually Agade, for example, as

A serpentine cylinder seal of the Akkadian period depicting the legendary King Etana of Kish ascending to heaven on the back of an eagle, while people and animals look up in amazement. (Zev Radovan/Land of the Bible Picture Archive)

well as elsewhere. By the end of the ED period, if not before, Nippur had acquired spiritual authority over Sumer, enjoying the right to endorse or reject kings who gained temporal authority beyond their own city, and Enlil's temple in Nippur, the Ekur, was supplied with offerings from all Sumer's cities. Nippur was the place of assembly of the gods, as it may have been of Sumer's leaders. Postgate (1994) suggests that the Semitic deity Dagan, and his city Tuttul, enjoyed a similar preeminent position in Akkad and the middle Euphrates region. Major political changes were explained and sanctified by changes in the political order on high, with Marduk, god of Babylon, gaining a preeminent role in the divine hierarchy during the second millennium and Babylon superseding Nippur as the spiritual as well as political center of Babylonia.

As the regions of the Near East became more familiar with each other, considerable syncretization took place. The gods of the Sumerian pantheon became assimilated with their Akkadian equivalents—Sumerian Nanna with Akkadian Sin, the god of the moon, for example—or the Akkadians accepted deities from the much larger Sumerian pantheon, often changing or modifying their names—An becoming Anu, for instance. Deities with similar attributes from different cities came to be regarded as a single deity with several names, such as the thunder god called Ninurta in Nippur and Ningirsu in Lagash. Those from further afield were also syncretized or recognized as equivalent, and their attributes merged: Thus Inanna, the Sumerian goddess of love, the morning and evening star, rain, thunder, and war, became synonymous with Akkadian Ishtar and the Levantine goddess Astarte. The incorporation of new deities into the pantheon also mirrored and explained new developments. For instance, when the Amorite nomads began to settle in Babylonia, a new no-madic shepherd deity, Martu (Amurru), was admitted into the pantheon. Uncouth and alien, he was nevertheless accepted as the husband of the daughter of Numushda (possibly a storm god), patron deity of Kazallu in northwest Babylonia.

The syncretization of originally different deities and the changing human political scene led to some anomalies in the arrangement of the pantheon, with particular deities being regarded as the offspring or spouses of different gods at different times or in different places. The Mesopotamians tended to accept and accumulate rather than to change or displace, and they seem to have had no problem accommodating these anomalies. Bottero (2001) has argued that by the first millennium, if not earlier, there was a clear trend toward henotheism, where the qualities and powers of all the different deities were attributed to or channeled through the deity to whom the worshipper addressed himself.

From the late fourth millennium B.C.E. gods began to be represented in art in human form, crowned with a horned headdress, although this was rare before Akkadian times. Gods also had their own symbols or emblems, often depicted in place of the deity, for example on kudurrus. Emblems included the tools of the god's role, such as Ninurta's plough, and natural phenomena identified with the god, such as the sun to represent Utu / Shamash or the lightning bolt wielded by storm gods such as Ishkur / Adad (see photo p. 94). Images of these emblems could be carried into battle as standards representing the god's presence or used when the god was required to witness an oath, preside over an ordeal, or participate in other solemn proceedings. Often animals were associated with individual deities, such as the Imdugud bird, a supernatural creature defeated by Ninurta and thereafter associated with him.

Demons and monsters were often portrayed as animals, real, imaginary, or a composite of different creatures. Protective spirits were similarly portrayed: for instance the man-headed winged bulls that guarded the entrance to Neo-Assyrian palaces. Cylinder seals often bore images with a religious content: the owner being introduced by his personal god to a senior deity; scenes of demons being defeated; or episodes from legends. While some portray well-known stories such as the tale of Etana, others remain impenetrable, illustrating tales of which there is no surviving literary account. The durable nature of much artwork and the vagaries of survival of literary material also mean that many myths are known in written versions that reflect only a particular time and do not necessarily match the visual iconography of the same myths over the course of history.

Major Deities

An and the Creation of the Gods. The ancient Mesopotamians visualized the primeval cosmos as water. In some versions of their creation myth this was a single salty body, Nammu, from which freshwater, the Abzu, was separated in the beginning, whereas in others both the ocean, Tiamat, and the Abzu originally existed together, their coupling at the point where their waters met producing silt from which the Earth was formed. From these bodies of water deities emerged or were born, the first inchoate and monstrous be-ings, later ones gradually assuming a more perfect form. From the latest, Anshar "All there is of Heaven" and Kishar "All there is of Earth," was born the first true god, An, god of the sky. An had a number of partners who bore him sons and daughters, notably Enlil and Enki. Although acknowledged as the most powerful of the gods, An was remote in his heavenly domain and did not play a major part in Mesopotamia's religious life by the time of recorded history.

Enlil.   Though An was the king of the gods, by the mid-third millennium the active ruler was his son Enlil. An and Enlil formed a triad of principal deities with Ninhursaga, the embodiment of motherhood. Enki sometimes combined with them to make a tetrad, although in later texts he often displaced Ninhursaga, whose creative function he usurped. The rise of Enlil paralleled the mid-third millennium political situation, in which Enlil's city Nippur gained spiritual preeminence.

Enlil married Ninlil, a mother goddess and goddess of grain, who bore him the moon god Nanna and several underworld gods. In one account, Enlil raped her when she was a maiden "too young for kissing" (Leick 2001: 153) and was banished, although Ninlil followed him and they later regularized their relationship. In another version, he came as a stranger to her home in Nippur and courted her in the proper manner, perhaps a reflection of the adoption of a foreign god into the local pantheon, because, although it was previously thought that Enlil was a Sumerian name meaning "Lord Air," re-cent studies suggest that he was originally an Akkadian deity (Ellil, from the Semitic *il*, "god"). His association with mountains (for example, in the name of his temple, Ekur, meaning "Mountain House") supports this, because *kur*, "mountain," also meant "foreign lands." In one myth, he lay with the goddess of the mountain foothills, who bore the gods of winter and summer. Enlil's identity as the god of wind, and more particularly, the winds bringing the life-giving spring rains, links him more with the north, where spring rainfall was vital, than with the south. Here, indeed, his association with storms and de-structive floods made him more feared than welcomed, and he is depicted in mythology as irascible, impatient, and violent as well as all-powerful. On the other hand, Enlil also introduced the hoe, making him the deity most closely associated with agriculture. In one myth, he separated Heaven and Earth to enable the seeds to grow and with his hoe broke the soil's hard surface, not only allowing plants to spring up but also uncovering the heads of men. Ninhursaga then completed the creation of humanity by causing them to come forth.

Ninhursaga.   Ninhursaga was the principal mother goddess, known by many names, including Ninmah and Belit-ili (Akkadian: "Lady of the Gods"). Originally she was probably seen as the numinous power of the lands border-ing the alluvial plains, the foothills of the Zagros and the western desert; as such she was mother to the animals and especially herd animals. Many of the gods were her children, and she played a key role in the creation of humanity, often in collaboration with Enki. In one version, people were shaped from the clay of Enki's realm, the Abzu, and borne by Nammu; at the celebratory feast afterward, Ninmah (Ninhursaga) and Enki had a drunken competition in which Ninmah created people crippled by disabilities and Enki had to find them a niche in society. He succeeded, for example allotting blind people the role of musicians and barren women that of priestesses. When the contest was reversed, Enki won, stumping Ninmah by creating a totally helpless creature: the first baby, which he advised her to nurse. As Nintur, "Lady Birth-hut," Ninhursaga was the divine midwife; having nurtured the fetus in the womb, she loosed it when it reached maturity and watched over the birth.

Enki.   Although Enki (Akkadian Ea) did not enjoy supreme authority, he was one of the most venerated gods, and his original shrine at Eridu was revered long after the city it served had been abandoned. Enki was the most intelligent of the gods and well disposed toward humanity, often finding ways to protect or aid them against the violent wrath of Enlil. As the god controlling the freshwater, Abzu, that lay beneath the Earth, the source of rivers, springs, marshes, and rain, he was the essence of the water upon which Mesopotamia depended for life and was portrayed with the Tigris and Euphrates flowing from his shoulders, full of fish. In the Abzu dwelt a great number of creatures that served him, including giants and great fishes.

The fertility brought to the land is echoed in Enki's association with semen and amniotic fluid, and he played a leading role in creation myths, shaping humanity out of clay, filling the empty world when the cosmos was formed, and impregnating not only Ninhursaga but also her daughter, granddaughter, and great-granddaughter. With his wife Damgalnuna (another name for Ninhursaga) he was the father of Marduk. Although Marduk became supreme deity, in texts concerning magic, Enki's special province, he is always shown consulting his father on the appropriate course of action.

In one legend, the Tablet of Destinies, a symbol of supreme divine authority, was stolen from Enki by Imdugud (Anzu), a vast lion-headed bird that raised sandstorms, whirlwinds, and other violent weather with the beating of its wings. After a devastating battle, Imdugud was slain by Ningirsu (Ninurta), whose symbol it became, and the Tablet of Destinies and its powers were restored to Enki. In the Akkadian verion of this story it was from Enlil that the Tablet of Destinies was stolen but Ea (Enki) who worked out how Anzu could be defeated.

Principal among the divine powers held by Enki were the *ME* (Akkadian *parsu*), which embraced everything related to civilized existence. *ME* were infinitely precious and sacred and the concept was fundamental to how the Mesopotamians viewed their own world. In one story, the goddess Inanna traveled to Eridu where Enki was keeping the *ME* to himself and was lavishly entertained by him. When Enki became inebriated, Inanna succeeded in stealing the *ME* and taking them to her own city of Uruk, bringing civilization to it and to the world in general.

Inanna.   Variously portrayed as the daughter of An, Enlil, Enki, or Nanna, Inanna was a complex deity with many attributes. When Enki brought order to the world, he entrusted a diversity of tasks to her. A mass of contradictions, she appears to embody the archetypal male perception of unmarried womanhood. Goddess of carnal love, she was the patron of prostitutes, a spoiled girl delighting in her courtship by the handsome youth Dumuzi, and the bride in the sacred marriage that ensured the Land's fertility. At the same time she was the goddess of battle ("the Dance of Inanna"), a storm goddess bringing tempest as well as life-giving rain, and implacable in avenging insults. In addition she was the goddess of the morning and evening star (Venus), waking people and signaling the end of their working day.

Inanna / Ishtar was a widely popular deity, patron of a number of cities in addition to her traditional home in Uruk. According to the great poem, "The Curse of Agade," when the Akkadian capital Agade was founded she was installed amid great rejoicing as its goddess, only to be withdrawn by Enlil at a later date when Naram-Sin offended him; her departure presaged the city's ruin.

Other Major Deities.   In some myths Inanna was the daughter of the moon god Nanna (also called Suen: Akkadian Sin), who was also the father of Utu (Shamash). Nanna's principal shrine was at Ur where the precinct included his temple, Ekishnugal, and a magnificent ziggurat built by the Ur III king Ur-Nammu. Nanna was linked not only to the moon and its light but also to the calendar and to fertility, particularly of cattle. A story in which Nanna traveled by boat from Ur to Nippur to visit Enlil may reflect a real annual journey of the god's statue in the boat carrying the first fruits. In later times Sin had a major shrine at Harran and was the favored deity of Nabonidus, a native of that city.

Utu, Nanna's son, was the god of the sun, shedding radiant light upon all the world, banishing darkness and dark deeds, and upholding justice and righteousness. Myths show him giving aid to individual humans and indulging his sister Inanna. In stark contrast, Inanna's relationship with her sister Ereshkigal, Queen of the Netherworld, was one largely of hostility; in one myth Inanna unsuccessfully attempted to usurp her sister's throne. After a stormy courtship, Ereshkigal wedded the god Nergal, sharing with him authority in her grim realm.

The Mesopotamian pantheon included several storm gods: Ishkur (Adad) may have been another son of Nanna, and Ninurta was a son of An or Enlil and Ninhursaga (Ninmah). Both were revered as gods of rain and spring floods, and therefore fertility, Adad being particularly linked to pastoralism and the increase of herds, while Ninurta introduced the plough and was associated with cultivation. They also represented the more terrible side of storms, with hail, tempest, and uncontrolled flooding, and were associated with war. In the Sumerian poem "Lugale," Ninurta (or, in another version, Adad) took on the demon Asag and his army of stones, defeating them in a great battle. From the stones he then built a mountain barrier to prevent the Tigris and eastern rivers from flowing uselessly away into the mountains and marshes, instead making them available for irrigation; the mountain

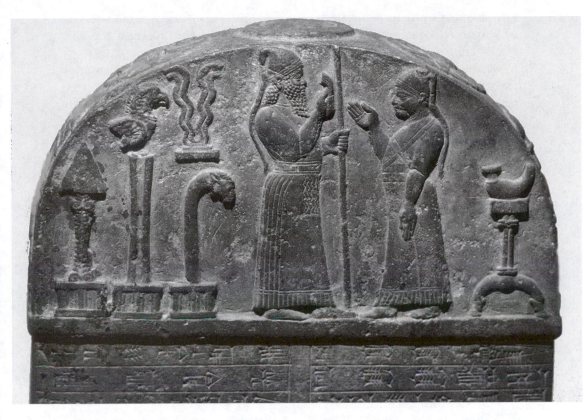

A Babylonian kudurru (land grant stele) from Uruk, dated around 850 B.C.E. On the left are the emblems of the Babylonian deities whose protection of the land grant is invoked. These include the spade of Marduk, the Babylonian national god, a bird on a perch representing the war god Ninurta, and the lion-headed staff of Nergal, god of the underworld. (Zev Radovan/Land of the Bible Picture Archive)

(*hursaga*) he endowed with vegetation, animals, and minerals and gave it as a gift to his mother, Ninmah, who then took the name "Lady of the Foothills" (Ninhursaga).

The Creation—Enuma Elish

Marduk rose to prominence in the second millennium as his city, Babylon, gained political preeminence. The magnificent poem known as the *Babylonian Epic of Creation, Enuma elish* ("When On High," its opening words), recounts his divine advancement. Composed probably during the later second millennium it survives only in first-millennium copies.

In the beginning the primordial waters of Tiamat and Abzu produced many monstrous but quiescent deities, but their later progeny, Anu and his descendants, were more active and troubled their repose. Abzu proposed to destroy these later gods, but Ea (Enki) magically put Abzu into a permanent sleep and established his own dwelling above him. Here his son Marduk was born. Marduk's fond grandfather Anu created the winds as his playthings. This intolerable further disturbance drove Tiamat to muster an army of monsters. Ea was unable to deal with this threat, but Marduk offered to act if the gods granted him supreme authority.

Marduk slew Tiamat in single combat and defeated and captured her army. He split Tiamat in two "like a fish for drying" (Dalley 2000: *Epic of Creation,* tablet IV, line 135), creating from the two halves Heaven and Earth, with the Ocean contained between and Abzu and the netherworld below; he created mountains from her head and breasts, and made the Tigris and Euphrates flow from her eyes. Marduk set constellations in the sky and organized the sun and moon and the calendar of their movements.

Next he freed and pardoned Tiamat's defeated army, setting them to work to create Babylon, where the gods made their home. Their leader, Qingu, however, was executed, and from his blood Ea created humanity to relieve the gods from future toil. Marduk was now king of the gods and Babylon the seat of both earthly and heavenly authority.

When the Assyrian king Sennacherib seized power in Babylonia, this myth was usurped, the god Ashur being substituted for Marduk. Ashur is a somewhat shadowy deity, originally the god just of Assur city with no place in the Babylonian pantheon. As the destinies of north and south became more closely interwoven, Ashur was identified with Enlil and his consort Mullissu with Enlil's wife, Ninlil. Under Sargon II Ashur became syncretized with Anshar, father of An, while Sennacherib strengthened his position by identifying Ashur with Marduk and performing the chief role in the New Year festival himself.

Atrahasis: The Origins of Humanity and the Flood

An earlier mythological poem, "Atrahasis," explains the creation of people, touched on in *Enuma elish.* The earliest surviving text of this was written down in Akkadian by Ipiq-Aya around 1700 B.C.E., but it probably existed earlier in Sumerian versions.

In the beginning, the gods cast lots for the three parts of the universe, Anu gaining On High (heaven), Enlil the Earth, and Enki the Abzu. In addition to the principal gods there was a host of lesser deities known collectively at this period as the Igigi. To these fell all the labor of maintaining the earth, while the higher gods took their ease. At last, worn out with digging and cleaning canals, creating rivers, and building mountains, the Igigi went on strike, setting fire to their tools and surrounding the house of their ruler Enlil in a menacing mob. The senior gods took counsel, and Enki spoke up for the Igigi: Instead of exhausting them, he suggested that people should be created to bear the burden.

The Mother goddess, variously called Belet-ili, Mami, and Nintu in the poem, agreed to join Enki in creating humanity. One of the gods, possibly the ringleader of the revolt, was slain and his flesh and blood mixed with clay from the Abzu, which Belet-ili formed into fourteen pieces. These were given to fourteen womb goddesses, who after ten months gave birth to seven men and seven women.

The Igigi were now relieved of their toils as mankind labored in their stead, but problems arose. Though people did their work well they lived for an immense time and bred enthusiastically. Eventually there were so many that their noise prevented Enlil from sleeping. Angrily he ordered Plague to be sent upon them.

Atrahasis, king of Shuruppak, consulted Enki, who advised him to make offerings to Namtar, the god of plague, in order to lift the curse. Humanity was saved, but after another interval of six hundred years the problem arose again. This time angry Enlil sent Drought by ordering Adad the storm god to hold back the rain, and again Enki advised Atrahasis to make offerings.

The third time, Enlil in his anger withdrew both rain and the annual inundation, depriving the land of plants and covering it with salt. For six years there was no food, and eventually the starving people resorted to cannibalism. Again Enki came to their rescue, probably sending a flood of fishes (this portion of the story is lost). Enlil was beside himself, accusing Enki of betrayal; he determined to destroy humanity without fail by sending a great flood.

He forbade Enki to help humanity again, but crafty Enki got around this by speaking his advice to the wall of Atrahasis's house. Following this advice, Atrahasis built a boat, filling it with his family and all the beasts of the land and birds of the air. (In a later version, Ut-napishtim (Atrahasis) also took representatives of every craft and skill on board his ship.)

When the weather began to menace, Atrahasis sealed the ark. Storm and flood ensued, all the gods doing their worst for seven days and nights, and humanity turned to clay, according to the later account. Nintu (Belit-ili, the mother goddess) was overwhelmed with grief by the destruction of the people she had created, and her horror spread to the other gods, who were also becoming parched and famished without their offerings. But as the flood subsided, they smelled the fragrant scent of offerings made by Atrahasis in gratitude when his boat came to land. Nintu berated the gods for the destruction they had wrought; most were contrite though Enlil was unappeased. The gods conferred and decided to maintain humanity for the their own benefit. To control human numbers, however, Enki and Nintu ordained that some people should be barren, others celibate, and that some babies should be stillborn or die in infancy. Furthermore, a crucial broken line seems to indicate that a reasonable natural limit was now set for the span of human life.

Interacting with the Gods

The wise and benevolent Enki and the irascible Enlil epitomized the Mesopotamians' perceptions of their gods. Omnipotent and magnificent, the gods were generally just and beneficent but could be unpredictable and terrible. People felt respect, awe, fear, and reverence for their gods, rather than love, and regarded them as inaccessible but at the same time immanent within their image and their shrine. The relationship of Mesopotamians to their gods was usually that of servant to master: It was their place to perform to the best of their ability the tasks for which humanity had been created. In return the gods, their masters, were expected to protect them, be responsible for them, look after their interests, and treat them justly, but might act in ways that caused individuals to suffer, for their own impenetrable reasons or as punishment for conscious or unwitting misdeeds.

Gods were described as having *melammu* (from the Sumerian *ME + lam* = incandescent), aura or luminous power, and were associated with the most powerful and awe-inspiring aspects of the natural and man-made world, such as mountains, floods, fire, generative power, lions, and weapons. The heavenly bodies were all seen as supernatural beings, some like the sun (Utu / Shamash), moon (Nanna / Sin), and Venus (Inanna / Ishtar) associated with major deities, others divine but of lesser status and power.

The personal relationship of love and devotion characteristic of the later revealed religions had no place in ancient Mesopotamia. Nevertheless, individuals could enjoy a closer relationship with a personal deity who acted like a parent and ensured their well-being. The personal god conferred good fortune, as the language made clear: "to get a personal god" meant "to be lucky." Children were often given names reflecting their association with the family deity, and individuals who had seals often named themselves as this god's servant. Families frequently had a private shrine where they worshipped their deity and might also have made offerings to the dead (*kispum*). Excavated examples of probable domestic shrines comprise a solid pedestal set in one corner of a special room, with a niched surround imitating the architecture of temples, often associated with a hearth or chimney. No texts, however, offer information on the practices of domestic religion.

Suffering and Security

In early times, misfortune was seen as the hostile action of lesser supernatural beings, the embodiment of harmful and dangerous forces, greater in power than people but inferior to the gods. These are commonly referred to as "demons," although the Mesopotamians themselves had no such term. Acting without provocation, these malevolent spirits were deemed responsible for illness, untimely death, and other disasters and ill fortune. Unquiet spirits of the dead were also blamed for some calamities, for example, mental illness. The spirits of children who had died unmarried (*lilu* and *lilitu*) were particularly dangerous, as they could cause the death of another child to become their partner in the netherworld. Particular common catastrophes were attributable to specific demons: For instance, miscarriage, stillbirth, and infant death were seen as the work of the demoness Lamashtu. Amulets and spells or incantations were used against such known dangers, and representations or symbols of benign spirits were placed above or beside the openings into houses—doors, windows, and even pipes—to prevent evil spirits from entering. Unforeseen ills were dealt with by exorcism or magic, a sorcerer driving away the demon responsible, using spoken formulae and ritual gestures and procedures, and attempts were made to avoid them by using divination. Although most sorcerers practiced magic to help people, certain evil magicians were believed to perform secret malevolent rites and spells to harm them.

A change of attitude gradually developed from the mid-third millennium onward. Although demons were still the perpetrators of misfortune, they came to be regarded as the agents of the gods, sent to punish people for their sins or their failure to perform the gods' commands. Although it was ultimately up to the gods to remove the demons of suffering, with the gods' approval rituals, magic, and incantations could be used to avert or drive them away. Treatment of illness involved such practices alongside straightforward medical remedies. An exorcist *(lu.mash.mash / ashipu)* would perform a ritual *(Namburbu*—"Undoing"), at an auspicious time in an appropriate place, such as a riverbank or the invalid's home, suitably purified. This could involve diagnosis of the cause of the illness or misfortune, the destruction or burning of an object to which the sin was transferred, such as a piece of wool or an onion, and formulaic prayers expressing general contrition for the victim's unwitting transgressions, praise for the god, and a prayer to lift the divine sanctions, with promises of future praise. Known as *Er.sha.hun.gar* ("lament for appeasing the heart of the angry deity"), many examples of these prayers survive in Mesopotamian literature: In them people often contrasted their sufferings and good conduct with the good fortune enjoyed by others whose behavior was less satisfactory, and sought to discover in what way they had unknowingly offended the gods. One great poem of the later second millennium, "Ludlul" (the "Poem of the Righteous Sufferer"), elevates such laments into a philosophy of resignation and trust in the ultimate goodness of the gods, however mysterious and seemingly harsh their actions.

The *ashipu* could be a court official or a private practitioner, but he was inevitably a member of the cultic staff of a temple; his remit was quite wide. His was the task of ritually cleansing the temple before ceremonies took place and of enacting purification rituals for the king or state; he ascertained the causes of illness and affliction, decided on and undertook the appropriate treatment and rituals; he performed the prophylactic rituals during the construction of temples and the making and installation of divine images; he recited spells and performed rites that provided magical protection for people, from humble citizens to the national army before battle; and in Neo-Assyrian times, an ashipu could act as adviser to the king. He often possessed a library of relevant books, including pharmacopia, compendia of omens and symptoms (such as *Enuma ana bit marsi ashipu illiku),* collections of prayers and incantations, and *shurpu,* volumes of spells and the detail of rituals. As well as warding off or dispelling evil, misfortune, and disease, spells and incantations were used for a wide range of purposes, even including soothing a fractious baby. Many were to deal with marital problems such as infidelity, impotence, and loss of desire, such as the incantations addressed to Ishtar by women whose husbands had "turned away." While an ashipu added medicines to his incantations and rituals, a doctor *(asu)* would increase the efficacy of his drugs by adding ritual formulae: Their roles in treating the sick overlapped.

Omens and Divination

An ashipu might be assisted in his rituals by other specialists, chanters *(gala / kalu)* and singers *(naru).* Another important ritual practitioner, the *baru,* or diviner, was attached to a temple, or to the palace or another branch of state organization, particularly the army. He might be called in by the ashipu or asu to divine the cause of an illness, but his main function was to take omens for the future.

Everything that took place in the world was planned by the gods, who communicated their intentions in ways that could be interpreted by those with the relevant knowledge. Seers were collecting and recording divine portents by the third millennium B.C.E., along with the events that followed these, and by the second there was an extensive scientific literature on the subject, comprising handbooks that practitioners consulted when foretelling the future. These texts were respected and assiduously copied in many neighboring lands, eventually reaching Europe.

Predicting the future from portents was a common practice across the Near East. People uttering prophecies are recorded, but only in areas of Mesopotamia bordering the western Near East, where this was more common. When unusual and aberrant things occurred, such as the birth of an abnormally formed animal, a seer could be consulted to determine the significance for the individual concerned. Such phenomena were also reported to higher authorities, since the portents could have wider significance. Not all signs were warnings: Their meaning might be favorable, indicating future good fortune. The seer would consult his compendia of portents and work out what these signs might presage. A collection of birth omens, *Shumma izbu*, widely used not only in Mesopotamia but also elsewhere in the Near East, ran to twenty-four tablets. A more extensive (but poorly preserved) omen collection, *Shumma alu*, dealt with a range of portentous occurrences. Omen-bearing patterns could be read in the behavior of birds, a practice that enjoyed some popularity in Assyria, and occasionally in the behavior of other creatures, especially at critical moments, for instance when a war was initiated or during a festival. Kings might experience dreams containing divine commands or warnings, and various types of portentous dreams are listed in omen collections. Specialist interpreters of dreams *(sha'iltu, sha'ilu)* were frequently women. Such unsolicited omens were, however, less common in Mesopotamia than those actively sought by divination.

Divination worked on the premise that the gods would respond to questions by "writing" the answers in the medium used by the diviner. The most usual method of divination involved the examination of the entrails of sacrificial animals (extispicy), and in particular the liver (hepatoscopy). The diviner would pray to the oracle gods Shamash or Adad, framing the question (frequently to require a yes / no answer) and inviting the god to write his answer in the entrails or on the liver of an animal, generally a lamb. He would then sacrifice the animal and closely examine the relevant organs, comparing details of their condition, formation, and appearance with information learned from the omen collections. Several model livers have been found, the earliest surviving examples coming from early-second-millennium Mari: These record the state of a liver and its interpretation. More complicated examples mark the features that a *baru* would examine and their significance: From these a trainee diviner could learn to recognize the details necessary to interpreting the god's message.

The payment for providing a divination was probably the sacrificial animal itself. This made it an expensive business, probably beyond the means of many ordinary citizens. Alternative, cheaper methods of divination used the patterns obtained by pouring oil on water or those made by smoke rising from a censer. At the opposite end of the spectrum, where matters of national importance were at stake, omens could be obtained by studying the heavens. This was a specialist branch of divination, undertaken by expert astrologers generally in the employ of the king and stationed at appropriate places throughout the land. Their knowledge of the science of astronomy was detailed, accurate, and precise. This discipline was particularly fostered in Babylonia, where it was becoming important during the Old Babylonian period and reached a pinnacle in the mid-first millennium when Chaldaean (Babylonian) astrologers were famous and respected throughout the Near East and beyond. The astrologers observed and mathematically calculated the movement of heavenly bodies, particularly the phases of the moon in relation to the sun, eclipses, and the movement of the planets, especially Venus, among the fixed stars. They also observed storms, rain, and other weather conditions and natural phenomena such as earthquakes, and might also report on other things such as the state of the harvest or local civil unrest. They interpreted the significance of the celestial signs, using omen texts, particularly a collection known as *Enuma Anu Enlil*. When signs portended disaster, the ill effects might be averted by performing the appropriate apotropaic ritual (listed for each omen in some omen texts) to encourage the god to change his plans. Such rituals were often elaborate, going on for a number of days.

Omens were generally taken to find out if a projected action, often on a suggested day, had the approval of the gods and would have a successful outcome. If the omen was unfavorable, the action could be abandoned or postponed, pending a more favorable omen. Private individuals might consult a diviner on a few personal occasions—for example, about the likely success of a new business venture or marriage to a particular individual. The king, however, in whose hands the well-being of the state resided, had a far closer relationship with the gods and would receive or seek omens on a regular basis; this was particularly so in the first millennium, a period when religion became prone to superstition, the gods were more frequently seen as violent and unpredictable, and magic and other ritual defenses were much used.

The Story of Erra

The violence and brutality to which many ordinary people fell prey in the first millennium and their exposure to the arbitrary decisions of absolute monarchs, which promoted this feeling of religious insecurity and apprehension, had their roots in the international disintegration that occurred around the end of the second millennium. The people's sufferings at this time are reflected in the "Epic of Erra," composed by Kabti-ilani-Marduk (probably *fl.* ninth / eighth century B.C.E.), who claimed it had been revealed to him in a dream.

The poem opens with Erra (Sumerian Nergal), god of plague and strife, taking his ease in inactivity. The warrior gods who serve him criticize his neglect of the pleasures of war, saying that people despise him. Erra, roused, approaches Marduk, urging him to go and have his now-shabby divine statue refurbished. Marduk has been unable to leave his post for fear of things going wrong, but Erra persuasively offers to stand guard in Marduk's absence. Erra is spoiling for a fight, but no one attacks, so he works himself up into a battle fury and creates universal chaos, inciting wars, rebellion, and savage reprisals, killing people and animals, destroying cities, and promoting sacrilege. The other gods abandon their cities, sick with disgust at the wanton destruction and anarchy. Erra exults in the universal devastation, but Ishum, his level-headed captain, channels the violence in a more useful direction, attacking the mountain lands of the enemy Sutaeans. He flatters Erra by pointing out his supreme power and ability to strike terror, and at last Erra allows Babylonia to restore itself, promising prosperity to those who recite the poem to keep his "valor" known and appreciated.

FESTIVALS

Dumuzi, Inanna, and Sacred Marriage

To the early period before the development of cities and of a hierarchical and orderly pantheon belongs the story of Dumuzi's wooing of Inanna, the subject of many poems. Dumuzi is the spirit of new life in the date palm; seen as a farmer, he is the power causing the crops to grow; and he is most especially the shepherd bringing about the increase of his flocks. Pictured as a young man at the height of his powers, handsome and vigorous, he is the essence of the desirable lover but also the suitable bridegroom who can amply support his bride. Inanna is depicted as a teenager, spoiled, capricious, and flirtatious.

In one poem Inanna makes the first move, confiding her love for Dumuzi to his sister Geshtinanna, knowing the information will be passed on. In another, Dumuzi follows the accepted rules, making a formal offer of marriage to Inanna's brother and guardian, the sun god Utu, and having to demonstrate that he can keep her in the manner to which she is accustomed—which includes exemption from household chores. Dumuzi and Inanna slip away together to exchange kisses, or Inanna teases Dumuzi by playing inaccessible: The scope of the genre was endless.

The courtship reaches its destined conclusion, the marriage ceremony, which is dealt with in detail. Dumuzi and his three best men come bearing gifts. Inanna is bathed and anointed and dressed in her finery. After a show of reluctance, she opens her door, a symbolic gesture that leads to the consummation of the marriage. The story symbolizes the harnessing of nature's fertility to provide for the community.

This is echoed in the sacred marriage, a major festival about which tantalizingly little is known. Probably originating in Uruk, Inanna's city, and celebrated by the Ur III kings and Isin-Larsa-period kings of Isin, it may have been more widespread, possibly elsewhere involving a marriage between the king and a different deity. The entum priestess at Ur was regarded as the bride of Nanna, and there are indications that a sacred marriage formed part of the New Year festival here, presumably with the king enacting the part of Nanna and the entum representing his wife, Ningal. A bedroom in the shrine in her residence, the *giparu*, was probably intended for this celebration. An Isin text describes in detail the preparation of the bedchamber, then the goddess bathing and anointing herself, before the king Iddin-Dagan "went to the pure loins with head high" (Postgate 1994: 265, after Romer 1965, lines 167–168). Nevertheless, accounts of the ceremony make it impossible to say whether the ritual was purely symbolic, the king spending a night in the goddess's chamber in her spiritual presence, or entailed the actual physical union between the king, representing Dumuzi, and Inanna, personified by a priestess. Nor is it known whether this took place annually as part of the New Year festival, or more infrequently, for example, at the first New Year after the king's accession.

Although the union between Dumuzi and Inanna brought fertility to the land, Inanna did not become a mother. All too soon, the marriage was cut short by tragedy: The reflection of the end of vernal lushness and abundance as the summer's drought took hold. Dumuzi was attacked, pursued, and eventually killed, as in mythologies the world over (cf. "John Barleycorn"), dying to provide food and drink, cut down in the harvest and the slaughter of the year's new lambs and calves.

Distraught, Dumuzi's womenfolk sought him. Inanna yielded to lamentation but Geshtinanna, his sister, and sometimes Ninsun, his mother, continued the quest, eventually locating him in the underworld. Lamentations for the death of Dumuzi formed an integral part of a major summer festival, widely celebrated in early times and perhaps later, which also involved processions and paeans for Dumuzi.

The Babylonian New Year Festival

The Akitu festival, the most important of the Babylonian year, was the celebrated in Babylon at the New Year, from the first to twelfth days of the first month, Nisannu (March/April). Only the second to fifth days are well known, from surviving fragments of a detailed Neo-Babylonian text.

The main purpose of the festival was to inaugurate the New Year when the gods not only began the annual cycle anew but also recreated the world. For this reason, a complete reading of *Enuma elish* had become an integral part of the ceremonies in Babylon by the first millennium. The New Year also coincided with the time of the barley harvest in Babylonia, the high point of the agricultural year. Marduk, as chief of the gods in later Babylonia, creator of the universe according to *Enuma elish*, and city deity of Babylon, played the central role in the festival.

It opened with purification ceremonies, and rituals began in earnest on the second day. One priest known as *sheshgallu* rose early each morning, washing in river water and offering prayers before the statue of Marduk before opening the doors of the shrine to admit other priests, who performed a number of rituals. On the fourth day the curtains were drawn back from the images of Marduk and his wife, and the Esagila was blessed. Later in the day the sheshgallu recited the whole of *Enuma elish*.

On the fifth day an exorcist purified Marduk's shrine by sprinkling it with water. The shrine of Marduk's son Nabu, patron of the nearby city of Borsippa, was also purified, ready for his arrival in the person of his statue. The shrine was wiped ritually clean with the body of a sacrificed sheep, which was then thrown in the river, carrying away any evil.

In Marduk's temple prayers were said, and he and his wife were served a meal. Now came one of the high points of the festival, when the king answered to Marduk for his year's care of Babylonia. Everyone left the cella except the sheshgallu and the king. The priest removed the king's regalia—scepter, circle, and sword—which he placed before Marduk. He then slapped the king's face and dragged him by the ear before Marduk, forcing him to bow. The king assured the god of his righteousness in avoiding sin and fulfilling his duties throughout the year; he "took Bel (i.e., Marduk) by the hand" and the priest restored the regalia to him. He then slapped the king again hard: If tears came to the king's eyes, this signified that Marduk was pleased and well disposed.

At sunset of the fifth day, a trench was dug in the courtyard outside Marduk's sanctum. Into it were poured oil, honey, and cream, along with reeds. The king set this alight and sacrificed a white bull, reciting prayers along with a priest.

The rest of the festival is only scrappily known. One of the ceremonies involved breaking and burning two divine images made earlier in the festival from valuable wood covered by sheets of precious metal. Statues of Marduk and his divine court were brought together to discuss the fate of the king and the Babylonians, with Nabu recording their decisions. The climax was a great procession that carried these statues in palanquins along the magnificent Processional Way, paved with limestone slabs, its walls and the magnificent Ishtar Gate (see photo p. 34) decorated with glazed bricks, blue for the background contrasting with orange low-relief figures of the dragon of Marduk (*mushhusshu*) and the bull of Adad on the gate and lions on the wall. This road led from Esagila through the Ishtar Gate to the Akitu temple outside the inner city wall. The procession, which may have taken more than a day to complete, had seven stages, including each god crossing the Euphrates in his own boat. At the Akitu temple, Marduk was installed in the central shrine and it is likely that a ceremony took place commemorating and perhaps reenacting Marduk's great victory over Tiamat.

This supremely important festival could not be celebrated in the dark years when Marduk's statue was absent, stolen by the city's conquerors. Nor could it take place without the king, as for example during Nabonidus's decade in

Taima. The accepted performance of the festival by certain Assyrian kings was an affirmation of their authority over and responsibility for Babylonia.

Other Festivals

A New Year festival was performed from early times in many cities, with different deities at its center (in Ur, for example, the festival centered around Nanna), but little is known about their form outside first-millennium B.C.E. Babylon. The "Offerings to Ishtar" festival at Mari may have taken place at the New Year: Held in the king's garden, it involved feasting and probably the reinvestiture of the king by the goddess, a ceremony shown in a painting on the palace wall. In Assyria the festival also involved the renewal of oaths of allegiance to the king by his principal followers.

Like Babylon, Assur and Uruk both had a processional way leading to an extramural *akitu* temple (*bit akitu*). Although *akitu* in Babylon was the New Year festival, the term was widely used in earlier times for a variety of rural festivals, not necessarily associated with the New Year. Though little is known of festivals other than the Babylonian akitu, they probably generally included processions, music and dancing, feasting, and other communal activities. People probably traveled from a wide area to attend festivals. Individual deities had their own special festival days, and smaller-scale celebrations were widely held for the phases of the moon, on the first, seventh, and fifteenth days of each month.

A Neo-Babylonian seal of the eighth or seventh century B.C.E., showing two figures engaged in the worship of the moon god Sin (Nanna). (Zev Radovan/Land of the Bible Picture Archive)

Mesopotamian gods paid each other formal visits in the person of their statues, often traveling by water in a sacred boat. In third-millennium Sumer and Akkad, city gods visited their mentor Enki in Eridu and their leader Enlil in Nippur, as well as more local visits between deities of similar status. The occasion of these visits might be a festival in which the deity wished to participate, like Nabu attending the New Year festival, or an important event such as the consecration of a major temple. In addition, a god's statue, or more commonly his emblem, often traveled locally to support situations where an oath was to be taken or divine authority required, for example in a lawsuit or for official validation of the size of a harvest.

DEATH AND THE AFTERLIFE

Adapa

Human mortality was explained and justified in the story of Adapa, a sage (*apkallu*) living in Eridu before the time of the Flood. Eridu's god Ea (Enki) entrusted Adapa with divine knowledge and wisdom in order to oversee the smooth running of the city and especially Ea's temple. One day a sudden gust from the South Wind capsized Adapa's boat, and in anger he cursed it. After seven days without its wind the disastrous effects were being felt even in Heaven. Anu, strongly displeased, sent for Adapa, who was advised by Ea not to eat the food and drink offered him in Heaven, which would be the bread and water of death.

The intercession of the heavenly doorkeepers, whom Adapa had flattered, placated Anu when he questioned Adapa. Although disquieted by the amount of knowledge that Ea had given humanity, An offered Adapa the bread and water of Heaven, which would confer immortality. Obeying Ea's instructions, however, Adapa refused, to Anu's considerable amusement.

Adapa was sent back to Earth, unharmed but deprived of the chance of immortal life. Ea's intentions are ambiguous: Did he deliberately mislead Adapa in telling him to refuse food and drink, or was the "smart" god outsmarted by Anu?

Rites for the Dead

Written sources show that, ideally, a Mesopotamian should spend his or her last hours on a special funerary bed, surrounded by family and friends. After breath had left the body, rituals were spoken to enable the soul also to leave, seating itself on a chair beside the bed. The body was prepared for burial: washed, anointed, and dressed in a red robe. During the wake (*taklimtu*) the deceased was laid out surrounded by the objects that were to accompany him or her to the grave. These included personal possessions, food, drink, and sandals for the journey to the netherworld, and gifts for the deities who ruled there to ensure the deceased's welcome. Incense was burned and torches carried around the bed.

The funeral entailed considerable expense. Burial officials received the funerary bed and chair, along with the clothes in which the person had died and a quantity of grain, bread, and beer. Even in ED times, this was seen as an opportunity for extortion, for Uru-inim-gina of Lagash included a reduction in funerary payments to such officials among his reforms.

The dead were always buried, since the body was needed to enable the deceased to enjoy offerings of food and drink; the grave acted as the "house" of the dead where communication between them and the living could take place. Carrying off the bones of a deceased enemy prevented his family from making the necessary periodic offerings to his spirit: This extreme measure was adopted, for example, by Ashurbanipal against the rulers of Susa. However, if the body was not properly buried the ghost could roam free, tormenting the living: Victors in battle would raise a mound over the enemy dead to prevent this happening.

The deceased could be placed either in a family vault or in a cemetery, depending on various factors such as status and local customs. One well-established practice, attested throughout Mesopotamian history and perhaps confined to kings, was burial in tombs in the "abode of Enki," particular locations in the marshes of the south. Some houses had a vaulted burial chamber; other families simply dug a pit beneath the house in which to place the body. Similarly, cemeteries contained both simple burials in pits and more substantial shaft graves or brick tombs, often vaulted, in which the dead were placed. The lavishly furnished graves in the Royal Cemetery at Ur consisted of a shaft leading down into a substantial pit containing a vaulted brick and stone chamber in which the principal burial was laid.

The body might be simply wrapped in a cloth or a reed mat, but more affluent families would place the body in a reed or wooden coffin or stone or terracotta sarcophagus. Children were often placed within a pottery vessel, and adults could be buried within two, laid on their sides, or one particularly large pot. Some burials throughout Mesopotamian history had the body laid between two layers of potsherds. Graves generally contained single burials; in some early graves the presence of another body suggests that a slave had been included among the grave goods: One appeared in an ED list of grave goods from Lagash. The spectacular burials in the Royal Cemetery at Ur contained up to seventy-four bodies accompanying the main burial, although whether these were human sacrifices is debated (see chapter 11).

With the body were placed the offerings displayed during the wake. Curiously in ED times, after a decent interval of perhaps fifty years, the grave was frequently reopened and valuable offerings removed and presumably put back into circulation. Poor people generally had only a few pots and personal ornaments as well as food and drink; at the opposite extreme, royal burials were lavishly furnished. The most striking examples are the rich burials in the Royal Cemetery at Ur. Dating to the Early Dynastic period, and most to period IIIa, these burial pits contained exquisite gold jewelry, lyres decorated with gold and lapis lazuli, gaming boards, gilded furniture, silver vessels, richly decorated sculptures, and in one grave a beautiful helmet of gold. Few royal graves have been discovered; one exception is a series of vaulted chambers beneath the women's quarters in the North-West Palace at Kalhu where several queens and other members of the Assyrian royal household were buried, including Yaba, wife of Tiglath-Pileser III, and Atalia, wife of Sargon II, along with many fine vessels of alabaster, gold, and silver, jewelry of gold and precious stones, a gold mirror with an ivory handle, and other treasures.

A period of mourning was important among the funerary rites. Public mourning ceremonies for the death of a king went on for seven days. In a private burial, the mourners included not only family and friends, dressed in sackcloth or torn garments, unwashed and unkempt, anointed with ash, but also professional mourners, who might include prostitutes. Women might tear their hair and scratch their faces, and the men bewail loudly, and both would fast. There was wailing and drums might be beaten. Lamentations in which the deceased was praised and his or her passing bitterly regretted were sung or spoken, sometimes accompanied by music. Failure to mourn properly indicated profound and culpable disrespect: Appropriate mourning for an adoptive parent was specified as a duty; and when Inanna visited the netherworld and was given up for dead, her husband Dumuzi's shocking disregard of proper mourning earned his own banishment to the netherworld.

After Death

Death at seventy or more was accepted and even welcomed, but the prospect of death was not appealing. The spirit (*etemmu*) left the body and walked west across demon-infested steppe; those buried with a chariot could ride instead. Reaching the infernal river Khubur, the spirit was ferried across and entered the underworld, which lay beneath the Abzu and the Ocean. Here the deceased was welcomed by Ereshkigal, Nergal, and their court of Anunnaki, and Geshtinanna checked off his or her name against a master list of humanity. The dead endured a gray and empty existence, their happiness directly related to the quantity and quality of the offerings of food and drink made by their children and grandchildren. Later generations forgot them, and they became part of the general undifferentiated mass of the dead, although there is some suggestion that they were then recycled as spirits for new babies. The grim and dreary realm was somewhat enlivened by the nightly visit of Shamash, who came here when the sun left the sky to judge cases involving the living and the dead. Local underworld problems went before a court presided over by Gilgamesh.

Strong walls surrounded the underworld, and the dead could not generally escape. Some ghosts, however, returned to haunt the living: These unquiet spirits were usually dangerous and often malevolent. These ghosts (*etemmu*) included people whose bodies had not been buried; those who had died by violence (although not those who had fallen heroically in battle); and individuals who had died young or tragically. Stillborn children, however, played happily in the underworld "at a table of gold and silver, laden with honey and ghee" (Electronic Text Corpus of Sumerian Literature "Gilgamesh and the Netherworld"). Ghosts could trouble the living by entering their bodies via their ears, or by appearing in their dreams. They generally acted on their own initiative but could also be called up and used by an evil sorcerer. The living made offerings to ward off ghosts: second-rate food and drink, less appealing than that which they offered to their own personal dead. They could also protect themselves with amulets and potions. The ghost of someone unburied might be laid by interring a figurine as a substitute.

The dead were allowed to return for the annual ceremonies (*kisega / kispum*), where offerings were made by their relatives—this was particularly the responsibility of the eldest son who therefore inherited the family home (beneath which the family dead might lie) and often an extra share of his parents' estate. If there were no sons, a daughter could perform the rites instead, as was also the duty of a person adopted by a childless individual. Offerings were made at the end of every month and during three-day festivals at the end of the months of Du'uzu (June / July) (the feast of Dumuzi) and Abu (July / August). The visiting dead could "smell incense," and food such as bread, honey, grain, and sometimes meat was placed by the grave for them, while water, beer, wine, and other liquids were poured onto the grave or down a pipe into it. Jewelry and clothing might also be placed on a statue of the deceased. The dead were invoked by name, to prevent unconnected ghosts receiving the benefit of the offerings. These occasions were the chance for the living to communicate with the dead, asking favors or advice of them or begging them to desist from ill-intentioned haunting. The actual conversation was carried on through an intermediary, the ghost raiser, who smeared a special ointment on his forehead to enable him to see and hear the ghosts. At the end of the visit, the spirits of the dead set sail in boats to return to the underworld.

Inanna's Journey to Hell

Several Mesopotamian poems give detailed descriptions of the underworld. One, which exists in two rather different versions, Sumerian and Akkadian, recounts Inanna's visit to the underworld, it seems with the intention of wresting its control from her sister Ereshkigal. She arrayed herself in all her glory but before leaving told her trusty attendant Ninshubur what to do if she did not return. Then she walked down to the gates of the underworld where she demanded entry from the doorkeeper, Neti, mendaciously claiming she had come to share Ereshkigal's mourning for her deceased husband, Gugalanna. Neti reported to Ereshkigal, who reluctantly instructed him to admit Inanna, following the usual procedures. Neti led Inanna through the seven gates in the seven walls of the underworld, and at each he stripped her of an item of her attire: her crown, her staff, her jewelry, and finally her garment, so that she came before Ereshkigal naked and bereft of power. Ereshkigal completed the process by transforming her into a rotting side of meat or an empty water flask.

When after three days she had not returned, Ninshubur donned mourning rags, scratched her eyes and mouth, wailed, and beat a drum; she went to Enlil and then Nanna, seeking their help in rescuing Inanna. Both declined, saying Inanna had brought the situation on herself. Ninshubur then tried Enki who was more sympathetic and resourceful. From the dirt under his nails, in the Sumerian version, he created two mourners whom he sent to the underworld. On his instructions they sympathized with Ereshkigal's sufferings and were rewarded with Inanna's corpse, which they reanimated using the grass and water of life. In the Akkadian version, Enki created a glorious youth, Asushunamir, who beguiled Ereshkigal and obtained the water skin, which Ereshkigal was forced to restore to its true form as Inanna, cursing him for his duplicity.

Although restored to life, Inanna could not be released unless a substitute took her place in the netherworld. Accompanied by demons impatient to carry off the substitute, she returned to Earth. First she met the faithful Ninshubur, then the gods Shara and Lulal (Latarak), all sincerely mourning her, and protected them from the demons. But finally she came upon her husband,

Dumuzi, who had taken the opportunity of her absence to dress in finery and sit on her throne. With no compunction she delivered him to the demons, and he was hauled off to the underworld. But his sister Geshtinanna took his place for half of the year, allowing him to return every year to the land of the living.

Gilgamesh and the Netherworld

In one tale Gilgamesh, legendary king of Uruk, lost a favorite plaything into a hole whence it rolled down to the underworld. Gilgamesh's fearless friend Enkidu went to recover it but foolishly ignored advice on appropriate behavior, wearing good clothes rather than mourning rags and generally drawing attention to himself; in consequence he was detained there. Gilgamesh petitioned the gods to intercede on Enkidu's behalf, but (as usual) only Enki was helpful, persuading Utu (Shamash) to bring Enkidu back with him after his nightly sojourn in the netherworld.

Enkidu was much shaken by the awful sights of the underworld and recounted them to Gilgamesh with mounting horror. First he spoke of men who had had sons, their fate becoming increasingly comfortable as the number of sons rose, from the man with one son, lamenting bitterly, to the man with seven, enjoying a position of comfort and responsibility among the lesser gods of the underworld. But then he described those less fortunate: the man with no sons, eating "a bread-loaf like a kiln-fired brick"(George 1999: 188), the woman who had never borne children, cast aside "like a defective pot" (George 1999: 188), the miserable shades of those who suffered disfiguring afflictions or mutilating injuries in life and were still suffering, the man whose parents had cursed him and who wandered as an unquiet ghost, and, ultimate horror, the man who had burned to death, who wasn't there at all but had turned to smoke.

Seeking Immortality

Gilgamesh later offended Inanna by insultingly rejecting her sexual advances, and he and Enkidu compounded his crime by destroying the Bull of Heaven, which Inanna had loosed to punish him. This sacrilege caused the gods to decree the death of Enkidu, who fell sick and after twelve days miserably died in his bed.

Gilgamesh plunged into unrestrained grief and lamentation, praising Enkidu and calling upon Uruk's citizens to share his mourning. He organized magnificent grave goods: huge quantities of gold, gems, and ivory from his treasury; a sacrifice of many animals; and gifts for each of the gods and staff of the netherworld, right down to the cleaners. But he refused to accept the fact of death and give up his friend's body for burial until on the seventh night a maggot fell from Enkidu's nose.

Now for the first time Gilgamesh, fearless hero of many dangerous adventures, became afraid of death. Half crazed, he left Uruk and wandered through strange lands, searching for the immortal hero of the Flood, Ut-napishtim, who knew the secret of eternal life. Finally he reached the land beyond the Waters of Death where Ut-napishtim dwelt with his wife. In a bracing speech, Ut-napishtim told him that death is unavoidable and its timing unpredictable, and upbraided him with wasting his allotted span in this futile and degrading quest instead of shouldering his responsibilities as king.

> You exhaust yourself with ceaseless toil,
> you fill your sinews with sorrow,
> bringing forward the end of your days.
> (*The Epic of Gilgamesh* X 298–300, trans. George 1999: 86)

As a preliminary to seeking immortality, he challenged Gilgamesh to go without sleep for seven nights. Gilgamesh was boastful and confident, but instantly fell asleep. Ut-napishtim's wife baked a loaf and placed it beside him each day, and on the seventh Ut-napishtim touched Gilgamesh, who woke, protesting that he hadn't slept more than a moment. Ut-napishtim pointed out the loaves, in various stages of decay, and Gilgamesh had to admit that he had failed to conquer even sleep, let alone death. In despair he made ready to leave. As a parting gift, however, Ut-napishtim instructed him how to obtain from the ocean floor the Plant of Life, which would restore his youthful vigor.

Feeling more optimistic Gilgamesh began his return journey. When he stopped to bathe, however, the Plant of Life was stolen by a snake, which instantly sloughed its skin, demonstrating the plant's efficacy. Knowing he could never find the plant again, Gilgamesh returned to Uruk with a heavy heart. Here, however, he was uplifted by the sight of the city wall he had built: This was his immortality.

Thus the great epic exemplifies the Mesopotamian philosophy of life: Enjoy the pleasures of the world, for they are transient and their duration unknowable, and seek immortality in well-performed duties and lasting achievements.

TEXT REFERENCES

Biggs, Robert D. 2000. "Medicine, Surgery, and Public Health in Ancient Mesopotamia." Pp. 1911–1924 in *Civilizations of the Ancient Near East*. Edited by Jack M. Sasson. Peabody, MA: Hendrickson Publishers. (Reprint of 1995 edition. New York: Scribner.)

Black, Jeremy, and Anthony Green. 1992. *Gods, Demons and Symbols of Ancient Mesopotamia. An Illustrated Dictionary*. London: British Museum Press.

Bottero, Jean. 2001. *Religion in Ancient Mesopotamia*. Chicago: University of Chicago Press.

Charpin, Dominique. 2000. "The History of Ancient Mesopotamia: An Overview." Pp. 807–830 in *Civilizations of the Ancient Near East*. Edited by Jack M. Sasson. Peabody, MA: Hendrickson Publishers. (Reprint of 1995 edition. New York: Scribner.)

Dalley, Stephanie. 1984. *Mari and Karana. Two Old Babylonian Cities*. London: Longman.

———. 2000. *Myths from Mesopotamia*. Revised edition. Oxford: Oxford University Press.

Electronic Text Corpus of Sumerian Literature. "Gilgamesh and the Netherworld." http://www-etcsl.orient.ox.ac.uk/ (cited January 30, 2002).

Farber, Walter. 2000. "Witchcraft, Magic, and Divination in Ancient Mesopotamia." Pp. 1895–1910 in *Civilizations of the Ancient Near East.* Edited by Jack M. Sasson. Peabody, MA: Hendrickson Publishers. (Reprint of 1995 edition. New York: Scribner.)

Foster, Benjamin R. 1995. *From Distant Days. Myths, Tales and Poetry of Ancient Mesopotamia.* Bethesda, MD: CDL Press.

George, A. 1999. *The Epic of Gilgamesh. A New Translation.* London: Allen Lane, Penguin Press.

Green, Anthony. 2000. "Ancient Mesopotamian Religious Iconography." Pp. 1837–1856 in *Civilizations of the Ancient Near East.* Edited by Jack M. Sasson. Peabody, MA: Hendrickson Publishers. (Reprint of 1995 edition. New York: Scribner.)

Greengus, Samuel. 2000. "Legal and Social Institutions of Ancient Mesopotamia." Pp. 469–484 in *Civilizations of the Ancient Near East.* Edited by Jack M. Sasson. Peabody, MA: Hendrickson Publishers. (Reprint of 1995 edition. New York: Scribner.)

Hallo, William W. 2000. "Lamentations and Prayers in Sumer and Akkad." Pp. 1871–1882 in *Civilizations of the Ancient Near East.* Edited by Jack M. Sasson. Peabody, MA: Hendrickson Publishers. (Reprint of 1995 edition. New York: Scribner.)

Jacobsen, Thorkild. 1976. *The Treasures of Darkness. A History of Mesopotamian Religion.* New Haven, CT: Yale University Press.

Kilmer, Anne Draffkorn. 2000. "Music and Dance in Ancient Western Asia." Pp. 2601–2613 in *Civilizations of the Ancient Near East.* Edited by Jack M. Sasson. Peabody, MA: Hendrickson Publishers. (Reprint of 1995 edition. New York: Scribner.)

Kramer, Samuel Noah. 1981. *History Begins at Sumer. Thirty-Nine Firsts in Recorded History.* 3rd revised edition. Philadelphia: University of Pennsylvania Press.

Kuhrt, Amelie. 1995. *The Ancient Near East. c. 3000–330 BCE.* 2 Volumes. London: Routledge.

Leick, Gwendolyn. 1991. *A Dictionary of Ancient Near Eastern Mythology.* London: Routledge.

———. 2001. *Mesopotamia. The Invention of the City.* London: Allen Lane, Penguin Press.

Lloyd, Seton. 1980. *Foundations in the Dust.* Revised edition. London: Thames and Hudson.

McCall, Henrietta. 1990. *The Legendary Past. Mesopotamian Myths.* London: British Museum Press.

Matthews, Roger. 2000. "Uqair (Tell)." Pp. 308–309 in *Dictionary of the Ancient Near East.* Edited by Piotr Bienkowski and Alan Millard. London: British Museum Press.

Oates, Joan. 1986. *Babylon.* Revised edition. London: Thames and Hudson.

Oates, Joan, and David Oates. 2001. *Nimrud. An Assyrian Imperial City Revealed.* London: British School of Archaeology in Iraq.

Oppenheim, A. Leo, and Erica Reiner. 1977. *Ancient Mesopotamia. Portrait of a Dead Civilization.* Revised edition. Chicago: University of Chicago Press.

Pearce, Laurie E. 2000. "The Scribes and Scholars of Ancient Mesopotamia." Pp. 2265–2278 in *Civilizations of the Ancient Near East.* Edited by Jack M. Sasson. Peabody, MA: Hendrickson Publishers. (Reprint of 1995 edition. New York: Scribner.)

Pollack, Susan. 1999. *Ancient Mesopotamia. The Eden that Never Was.* Cambridge: Cambridge University Press.

Postgate, J. Nicholas. 1994. *Early Mesopotamia.* London: Routledge.

———. 2000. "Royal Ideology and State Administration in Sumer and Akkad." Pp. 395–411 in *Civilizations of the Ancient Near East.* Edited by Jack M. Sasson. Peabody, MA: Hendrickson Publishers. (Reprint of 1995 edition. New York: Scribner.)

Potts, D. T. 1997. *Mesopotamian Civilization. The Material Foundations.* London: The Athlone Press.

Roaf, Michael. 1990. *Cultural Atlas of Mesopotamia.* New York: Facts on File.

———. 2000. "Palaces and Temples in Ancient Mesopotamia." Pp. 423–441 in *Civilizations of the Ancient Near East.* Edited by Jack M. Sasson. Peabody, MA: Hendrickson Publishers. (Reprint of 1995 edition. New York: Scribner.)

Robertson, John. 2000. "The Social and Economic Organization of Ancient Mesopotamian Temples." Pp. 443–454 in *Civilizations of the Ancient Near East.* Edited by Jack M. Sasson. Peabody, MA: Hendrickson Publishers. (Reprint of 1995 edition. New York: Scribner.)

Romer, W. H. P. 1965. *Sumerische Konigshymnen der Isin-Zeit.* Leiden.

Sandars, Nancy K. 1971. *Poems of Heaven and Hell from Ancient Mesopotamia.* Harmondsworth: Penguin.

Sasson, Jack M., ed. 2000. *Civilizations of the Ancient Near East.* 4 Volumes. Peabody, MA: Hendrickson Publishers. (Reprint of 1995 edition. New York: Scribner.)

Scurlock, JoAnn. 2000. "Death and the Afterlife in Ancient Mesopotamian Thought." Pp. 1883–1894 in *Civilizations of the Ancient Near East.* Edited by Jack M. Sasson. Peabody, MA: Hendrickson Publishers. (Reprint of 1995 edition. New York: Scribner.)

Stol, Marten. 2000. "Private Life in Ancient Mesopotamia." Pp. 485–499 in *Civilizations of the Ancient Near East.* Edited by Jack M. Sasson. Peabody, MA: Hendrickson Publishers. (Reprint of 1995 edition. New York: Scribner.)

Wiggermann, F. A. M. 2000. "Theologies, Priests, and Worship in Ancient Mesopotamia." Pp. 1857–1870 in *Civilizations of the Ancient Near East.* Edited by Jack M. Sasson. Peabody, MA: Hendrickson Publishers. (Reprint of 1995 edition. New York: Scribner.)

Woolley, Leonard. 1982. *Ur "of the Chaldees."* The final account, *Excavations at Ur,* revised and updated by P. Roger and S. Moorey. London: Book Club Associates / Herbert Press.

Yoffee, Norman. 2000. "The Economy of Ancient Western Asia." Pp. 1387–1399 in *Civilizations of the Ancient Near East.* Edited by Jack M. Sasson. Peabody, MA: Hendrickson Publishers. (Reprint of 1995 edition. New York: Scribner.)

IX
CHAPTER 9
Material Culture

ARTISTS AND ARTISANS

Production and Producers

In early times most artifacts were made within the household, but by the late sixth millennium some were the specialist products of artisans who worked part or full time in a craft: Of these pottery has survived best, but there were probably others. The beginning of metallurgy also required some degree of specialization, at least by those who obtained and smelted copper ore, although smithing may have been practiced within the community. Specialization was well advanced by historical times, with some products being mass-produced in workshops where individuals had responsibilities for different parts of the production process: In pottery workshops, for example, the various tasks of preparing the clay, throwing the pots, and decorating them were probably undertaken by different people, managed by a supervisor. Texts reflect the range of occupations. Early examples of the Standard Professions List refer to jewelers, potters, smiths, and bakers, as well as various grades of official. In the town of Nuzi under the Mitanni, artisans included potters, glassmakers, leatherworkers, carpenters, stonemasons, and bronze and coppersmiths manufacturing tools, weapons, armor, and fittings for wheeled vehicles. Not all artifacts were made by specialists; households would probably make their own reed baskets, their own wooden tools, and perhaps their own workaday pottery; wool might also be spun and textiles woven at home.

The status of artisans varied with time, region, and craft. In Alalakh, for instance, lapidaries, masons, and carpet makers enjoyed a higher status than weavers or potters. In the first millennium young slaves were sometimes apprenticed to learn a craft. Artisans might also use slaves to undertake the menial tasks involved in their work, such as preparing clay or stoking furnaces and kilns. Although most artisans were not slaves, they were often employed as servants for life by a temple or king and were at the disposal of their patron, obliged to work wherever he required. They might be sent to places within a kingdom to undertake particular commissions or be lent or given to foreign rulers. It was expected that they would be well treated, but many became homesick or unhappy with their conditions and occasionally they fled; conversely, artisans who had been lent to a ruler might be induced to stay with their new patron instead of returning home, to the dissatisfaction of their original master. Some of the acrimonious correspondence between Shamshi-Adad and his son Yasmah-Addu, viceroy of Mari, concerned skilled people who had fled to the easygoing conditions of Yasmah-Addu's court and had not been sent back.

There are some representations of artisans making textiles and working stone or wood, and occasionally the artifacts in burials suggest the occupation of the person buried there. A few workshops have been confidently identified, such as one at Eshnunna that belonged to a sculptor: They are recognized from clues such as half-finished objects, pieces that went wrong (such as the kiln full of abandoned ill-fired pottery at fifth-millennium Tell Ziyadeh), equipment such as tools, workbenches, and kilns, working debris such as flint chips and glass or metal slag, and materials for recycling. Pots filled with salvaged materials such as scrap metal, broken stone objects, and old seals whose surface would be ground down for reworking have been found in a number of sites. Since many materials were imported, little was wasted. Workshops might be scattered throughout a settlement or concentrated in one part of the town or in an area outside it, such as the OB terra-cotta plaque production site in the Diqdiqqeh area northeast of Ur, situated on a canal (supplying both transport and the water needed for mixing clay). While some craft activities were undertaken in large establishments, such as the temple textile "factories," others might be performed by individuals on their own small premises: An Uruk text, for example, refers to an amount of gold issued to a goldsmith, the finished object to be returned in five days' time. Workshops that produced noxious by-products, such as potting and metalworking, were often located on the outskirts of settlements, but the maintainance of external workshops outside the city, and sometimes deep in the countryside, required stable political conditions.

Art and Technology

The modern distinction between artisans and artists was not one made by the people of ancient Mesopotamia. Objects were valued mainly for their materials and their significance, though skill was appreciated and an object's quality contributed to its fitness for the purpose for which it was created. Materials such as precious metals, glass or glazed brick, and alabaster and other lustrous stones enhanced buildings and objects by imparting light, radiance, and brilliance to them, qualities that reflected the divine. That there were skill and artistry can be seen in many media: the exquisite craftsmanship of the jewelry from the royal tombs of third-millennium Ur and eighth-century Nimrud, the miniature perfection of some of the engraved seals, the drama and sensitivity of the lion-hunt reliefs from Nineveh (see photo p. 106), the power and realism of the bronze head of an Akkadian king, or the quality of the ivory depiction of a woman at a window that has earned it the nickname "Mona Lisa." Expertise was appreciated, but there was no linguistic distinction made between artists, artisans, and those with other skills such as cooks and physicians. Nevertheless, the quality of workmanship could increase the worth of an object beyond the value of its materials by as much as a third. Much of the credit for the creation of fine objects went to the designer rather than the artisan who executed the design. Those who commissioned the work, such as kings or priests, were often closely involved in the design themselves, and the god himself might be consulted on proposed details of a divine image via an oracle. Workers were often defined by the material they worked rather than the type of artifacts they produced. For instance a jeweler would make not only beads and ornaments but also vessels and figures of precious metals, as well as decorating furniture with sheet gold. Workshops might be used by a variety of workers with a shared interest in particular equipment, such as a furnace for heating glass and metal. On the other hand, artifacts that were made of different materials were often submitted to a series of workshops for the individual elements to be incorporated: Chariots, for example, were constructed by carpenters, wheelwrights, leatherworkers or basket weavers, and bronze smiths.

Many technological innovations, including advances in metallurgy and pottery manufacture, were invented by the people of Mesopotamia. Others, such as developments in glassworking around 700 B.C.E., also took place on Mesopotamian soil but were likely to have been the work of foreign craftsmen taken captive in the Assyrian wars.

The secrets of the artisan were closely guarded. Surviving technological texts contain an admonition to the initiate reader not to allow the noninitiate access to the information that "belongs to the tabooed things of the great gods" (Lamberg-Karlovsky 1993 quoting Saggs 1962). To this end recipes for the manufacture of glass and glazes, for example, abound in jargon that is difficult to penetrate. Often trade secrets and skills were handed down through families, with children being trained by their parents to pursue the same craft; long-established families of carpenters, metalworkers, and goldsmiths are known, and it has been suggested that myopia, which is associated with exceptionally good near vision, was a inherited disability that benefitted sealcutters, given the tiny scale at which they worked.

CONSTRUCTION

Houses were generally built of locally available materials, but for palaces and temples, city walls, and other public buildings the materials, which often included such things as as cedar beams, decorative stones, and precious metals, were drawn from a wide area and the work of their construction would be undertaken by large sectors of the community, including both laborers and specialists such as architects, builders, stonemasons, carpenters, painters, and those skilled in creating inlays. Some of the reliefs in the Neo-Assyrian palaces depict the work of quarrying stone and creating and transporting the huge statues of winged bulls that guarded the palace entrances; texts often detail the materials used and the effort expended in obtaining them, and the records indicate the size of the labor force. The quantities of bricks required for public buildings could be vast. For example, the archaeologist Max Mallowan calculated that the city wall at Kalhu required in the region of 70 million bricks, which, at the rate of brick-laying recorded in Assyrian times, would have taken 700,000 man-days to lay.

The symbolic beginning of the construction of a temple was performed by the king, who carried the first basket of soil (see photo p. 20) or made the first brick, as is stated in royal inscriptions and vividly shown in carved reliefs or stone or metal pegs incorporated into the buildings. Inscribed clay cylinders,

Reed huts of the Marsh Arabs, Chebayish, southern Iraq. The inhabitants of the region in ancient times dwelt in similar structures. (Corel Corp.)

cones or tablets, and votive deposits of beads or protective figurines might be placed within the foundations. In Ashurnasirpal's palace at Kalhu the excavators found a gazelle beneath the paving of a passage and miniature pots and sheep bones beneath the floor of one of the rooms in the domestic wing.

Building Materials

The nomads who traveled through regions of Mesopotamia dwelt in tents, probably constructed of skins or cloth over wooden poles or branches, but the majority of Mesopotamians lived in houses.

Reeds. In southern Mesopotamia and particularly in the marshy region around the head of the Gulf, buildings could be constructed of reeds, bound together in bundles and covered with reed mats. Some fourth-millennium seals depict houses or farm buildings of reed bundles, and the rarity of early settlements detected in the region could reflect the widespread use of such structures. The tall bundles that flanked the entrance to these buildings were the symbol of the goddess Inanna, probably originally the numen of the storehouse. Reed structures built by the Marsh Arabs of modern times demonstrate the material's versatility, allowing the construction of substantial and beautiful halls *(mudhifs)*.

Mud. The most widely available material for construction was mud, which was mixed with straw, dung, or another temper such as sand. This could be simply used as *tauf* (pisé—packed mud) to build house walls but was generally made into bricks (see photo p. 72). The latter were shaped by hand or formed in molds and dried in the sun. Early bricks were rectangular but in the ED period plano-convex bricks were made. Shaped like a low loaf of bread, they had the advantage of allowing unskilled laborers rapidly to construct walls by laying them in herringbone courses of alternating bricks on their sides, held in place by liberal applications of mud mortar. Later bricks were generally square.

Bricks could also be fired in a kiln or brick stack. Baked bricks were used for the lowest courses of walls, for drains, where bitumen was employed to make them watertight, and for paved courtyards and other exposed architecture such as the facades of buildings; important buildings, such as the ziggurat at Ur (see photo p. 201), might be encased in baked bricks as a protection against the elements. The use of bitumen as a mortar, particularly in the construction of large structures such as city walls, also provided an effective protection against damp. Courses of reed matting and layers of bitumen were interspersed between those of brick in the construction of ziggurats to counteract rising damp from the foundations, and weepholes also assisted drainage and prevented damp decay. Bitumen was also employed as a waterproofing material for bathrooms and constructional timbers such as doors. Brick walls were often plastered to protect them against rain. Mud could be used as the plaster but a stronger and more attractive plaster was made of gypsum or lime, made by burning limestone. Floors could also be plastered but were often just of beaten earth.

By the later second millennium bricks were occasionally molded into more ambitious shapes. An early example of this is in the Kassite temple of Innin (Inanna) at Uruk, where walls were decorated with statues of water and mountain deities built up of courses of specially molded bricks, each bearing a section of the design. The glazed low-relief images of dragons, bulls, and lions that adorn the Ishtar Gate (see photo p. 34) and the walls of the Processional Way and the bricks that decorate the throne room entrance at Babylon are the culmination of the technique. Flat glazed ornamental bricks were also found in Assyrian cities, including Kalhu, and in Fort Shalmaneser they depicted a magnificent gateway in which stood two figures of King Shalmaneser beneath the winged disc of Ashur.

Early brick-built temples were strengthened with buttresses. Making a virtue of necessity these soon became a decorative feature too, relieving the monotony of the brick walls and creating patterns of light and shade. These were echoed in the interior by recesses. The constraints of roofing using brick also led to the early development of arches, used above doors in houses and tombs, and brick-built barrel or corbelled vaults, seen, for example, in ED tombs at Ur where they were also executed in limestone.

Stone.   In northern Mesopotamia where stone was more easily acquired, the foundations and lower courses of houses and walls were often made of stone. Stone came into more common use in first-millennium Assyria when the brick walls of palaces were clad in stone slabs decorated with low-relief carvings. In the south, where most stone had to be imported, it was less commonly used, but construction in stone did occur. An early and probably experimental example was the Limestone Temple in the Eanna precinct of fourth-millennium Uruk. Another early temple here was built of limestone in conjunction with a mixture of crushed baked brick and gypsum, which formed a sort of concrete. Some of the tombs in the Ur Royal Cemetery were built of stone. Diorite and other types of stone were used for some architectural elements, such as the sockets in which the door pole turned. Sometimes the bottom of the pole was fitted with a copper or bronze shoe. Limestone slabs were used for paving, for instance in Fort Shalmaneser at Kalhu.

Wood.   Although some buildings had brick vaults, the roofs of most were constructed of timber beams over which reed mats or palm fronds were laid then covered with mud plaster. The beams needed to roof houses could be made of trees that grew in Mesopotamia, such as date palm, pine, and poplar, but for larger buildings such as temples, more massive beams were required. These came from imported trees, particularly cedar from the Amanus Mountains. Timber was also used to make doors, window frames, and other fittings. Cedar, being aromatic, was also favored for constructing palace and temple doors, which would give off a delightful scent as they were opened or closed, but for most people and buildings lesser timbers such as pine and box-wood sufficed. Wooden pillars might support a first-floor balcony in houses, and timber centering could be used to give support to brick and stone vaults.

Decoration.   Uruk-period temples were often decorated with cone mosaics: geometric designs constructed from clay cones whose flat surface was painted, usually red, black, and white, and which were embedded into the wall plaster so that only the painted surface was visible. In one example from Eanna in Uruk, the clay cones were replaced with cones of colored stone. As well as being decorative, cone mosaics reinforced the surface of these structures, which at Uruk included semi-engaged pillars. Using a similar technique, large clay nails with glazed heads were used to decorate the temple of Nabu in the Assyrian city of Dur-Sharrukin.

   The plaster walls of buildings could be brightened up by being painted, although traces of these paintings have rarely survived. One exception is the Uruk-period temple at Uqair, where the inside walls were painted with geometric designs and animals including leopards. Another is the early-second-millennium palace at Mari. Here many of the public rooms had painted decoration: murals showing offerings to the god Sin and the goddess Ishtar in the latter's shrine; the investiture scene in the Court of Palms; and the hunting scenes and other royal activities on the walls of the king's apartments. Many paintings survive on the walls of the eighth-century provincial palace of Til

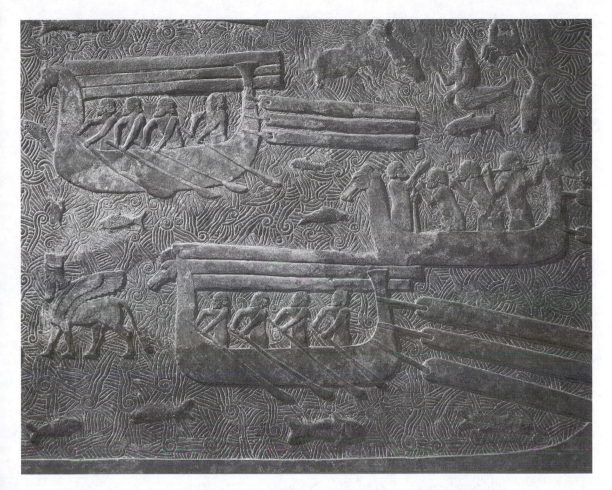

A relief from the palace of Sargon II (721–705 B.C.E.) at Dur Sharrukin showing Phoenicians transporting timber by boat from the Levant to Assyria. (Gianni Dagli Orti/Corbis)

Barsip, where the king is shown in audience and on the hunting field. Paintings are also known from other palaces, such as the floral and geometric murals at Kar-Tukulti-Ninurta, the figures of courtiers on the walls of Dur-Kurigalzu, the magnificent royal scene from Dur Sharrukin, and the painted decoration at Fort Shalmaneser in Kalhu, including a procession of eunuchs in the queen's apartments. The latter has been analyzed, revealing that it was executed on a plaster base composed of clay, chalk, and fine sand, covered by a finer light brown plaster. On this the designs were painted using iron-based pigments for red and brown, carbon for black, Egyptian blue (an artificial copper carbon silicate), and a mixture of limestone and gypsum for white. In other paintings lapis lazuli and copper oxide were also used for blue, bitumen for black, and malachite for green. Paint was probably applied to many of the stone reliefs and statues of Assyrian palaces and to the tiers of ziggurats: These traditionally were colored (from bottom to top) white, black, red, blue, orange, silver, and gold.

Panels of aromatic wood might also decorate the walls of major buildings, or they might be hung with carpets or textiles. Carpets may also have been laid on the floors: In Nineveh stone imitations of such carpets, beautifully patterned and with tasseled edges, were carved on some of the floors. From the later second millennium external walls were sometimes decorated with glazed bricks, of brilliant blue, orange, green, yellow, red, and white. In the Assyrian palaces of the first millennium, the walls were often faced with carved stone relief scenes depicting military victories, lion hunts, and other royal achievements: powerful propaganda reinforcing the divinely accepted authority of the regime. Stone statues of imposing size depicting winged bulls and lions guarded the gateways of these palaces (see photos pp. 28, 104, 106, 169, 180).

ART AND ARTIFACTS

Wood

Wood was commonly used for a wide range of purposes, known from textual references, artistic representations, and the few charred fragments of wooden artifacts that have survived. Wooden objects, vehicles, and furniture, now vanished, have also been reconstructed from their surviving metal fittings and inlaid decoration of colored stone, ivory, shell, and other materials, and from the discolorations left by them in the soil: The Royal Cemetery at Ur and the sacked palaces of Nimrud have been particularly fertile sources of such remains. Texts provide some information on what types of wood were used for various purposes, although the Sumerian or Akkadian names cannot always be identified with known woods; the rare wooden artifacts can sometimes, although not always, be identified to genus (see tables 9.1 and 9.2).

Although Babylonia was unforested, it grew both date palms and a range of scrubby trees and bushes such as poplar and tamarisk, which answered many of the needs of the region's inhabitants for fuel, construction, tools, and furniture. Trees were planted and managed, and by the time of Hammurabi severe penalties awaited those who felled timber without authorization. Trees were more abundant in the north, with forests in some parts such as the Jazireh, and massive timbers for building temples and palaces could be obtained from neighboring regions such as the Zagros and the mountains of Lebanon and the Taurus. "Cedar Mountain" (the Amanus Mountains) was the chief source of cedar as well as yielding other valuable timbers such as pine, cypress, fir, and juniper, and control of this region was of great concern to Mesopotamian leaders from early times. Many texts describe the felling of trees here and their transport to and down the rivers, and a relief in the palace of Sargon II at Dur-Sharrukin shows the cedar trunks being transported on boats or towed behind them. Timber such as sissoo, ebony, bamboo, and teak were also imported from more distant suppliers—Magan, the Indus region, and Africa. The high value placed on timber can be seen in wills where roof beams, doors, and door frames were specifically mentioned among the deceased's bequests.

TABLE 9.1

Sources of Wood Used by the Mesopotamians

Timbers	Sumerian name (gis. plus name)	Akkadian name	Assyria	Baby-lonia	Cedar Moun-tains/ Lebanon/ Anatolia	Elam/ Anshan	Magan	Meluhha
oak			x		(x)	x		
oak?	mes.ha.lu.ub	tatitu, haluppu					x	
pine	u-suh	asuhum	x	x	x	(x)		
terebinth			x	x	(x)			
date palm	gishimmar	tilmununu, asnu, makkanu, gishim-marum		x			x (also Dilmun)	
tamarisk	shinig	binum		x		(x)		
acacia				x	(x)	(x)		
poplar	asal	sarbatum +		x		(x)		
mulberry		sarbatum +						
willow	manu or shakal	e'rum or shakkullum		x		(x)		
apple	hashur		x	x	(x)	(x)		
boxwood	taskarin	taskarinnum?		x?	x	(x)		
liquorice				x				
Christ's thorn					(x)			
jujube (zizyphus)								
fig	pesh	tittum			(x)	(x)		
walnut					(x)	(x)		
pistachio					(x)	(x)		
juniper		dapranu	x		x	x		
cane		qanu						
cedar	eren	erenu			x	(x)		
sissoo	mes ma.kan.na / me.luh.ha	musukannu, mesu					x	x
teak								x
seawood*	a.ab.ba	kusabku meluhhie						x
deodar								x
cypress	shu.ur.man	shurminum			x	(x)		
fir		ashuru			x			
plane				x	x			
ebony?***	MES.me.luh.ha	sulum meluhhi						x
ebony?	esi	eshu, ushu						x
sandalwood								
Magan reed**							x	
?	gi gid			x				
?	gul-bu			x				
?	isu sa eleppi							
?	gurushu							
?	husabu							
?	she-du			x				
?	elammakum				x			

* identified as either mangrove or, more probably, teak
** probably bamboo
*** ebony also from Africa
+ sabutum identified as poplar by Potts, mulberry by Ratnagar

TABLE 9.2

Uses of Wood

Types of Wood	Buildings	Doors, Windows, Roofs, Planks		Vehicles		Tools, Handles, Weapons		Fuel		Aromatic		Other Uses
		Large Beams		Boats		Furniture		Bowls, Spoons, etc.		Boxes		
oak? (haluppu)	x	x			x	x						
pine	x	x		x		x						resin to seal inside of wine jars
pine? u-suh			x	x			x					
terebinth			x	x	x	x	x	x				resin; perfumed oil; culinary preservative;
date palm			x	x	x	x	x	x				fronds for roofing; fibres; basketry; fruit; cords
tamarisk	x		x	x	x	x	x	x				
acacia	x		x	x	x	x	x	x	x			
poplar	x	x	x	x	x	x	x	x	x			
willow	x		x	x	x	x	x	x	x			
apple				x								fruit
boxwood			x	x		x	x					(Kas writing boards)
fig												fruit
walnut						x	x					nuts; writing boards
pistachio							x	x		x		nuts
juniper	x	x	x			x						berries, (inlays)
mulberry				x	x							pulley wheels
cane				x								
cedar	x	x	x	x		x				x		resin
sissoo				x	x	x		x				
teak	x			x								
seawood*	x			x		x						
cypress	x	x	x									
fir	x	x		x								
ebony? (eshu)	x	x			x	x						inlays
Magan reed**						x	x			x		
gi gid	x			x		x	x		x			
gul-bu					x	x	x		x			
she-du					x	x						
isu sa eleppi				x								
gurushu				x								
husabu				x								
elammakum		x				x						

* identified as either mangrove or, more probably, teak
** probably bamboo

Sources: Dalley 1984; Gilbert 2000; Mattingly 2000; Oates 2001; Potts 1997; Ratnagar 1981; Roaf 1990, 2000; Simpson 2000

Wood was used for handles and many tools and weapons such as spears and hoes, with or without a stone or metal head. Texts from Mari refer to food served in bowls of sissoo wood and eaten with small wooden bowls and spoons. Wooden trays were used for carrying food from the kitchen; these might have an integral stand of vertical or diagonal struts. Stools represented on the "Standard of Ur" (see photo p. 73), around 2600 B.C.E., had legs and feet shaped like bulls' legs and hooves. Chairs with backs first appeared in art in the ED period; references in later-third-millennium texts show that many types of wood were used for the frame, while the seats might be upholstered with leather. Stools, chairs, and tables might have a framework of wood, supported by struts, or be woven of withies or reeds. Beds were probably uncommon until the later third millennium: Their frames were of wood, sometimes decorated, supporting a bed surface of interwoven rope.

Wooden objects from the Royal Cemetery at Ur included a storage chest, gaming boards, and lyres, inlaid with mosaic designs in shell, lapis lazuli, and red stone. The lyres' sounding boxes were adorned with bovine heads in gold and lapis lazuli, and the uprights of one from the "Great Death Pit" were clad in alternating bands of mosaic and gold. A sledge from Puabi's tomb in the cemetery was decorated with mosaic inlay and lions' heads in gold with manes of lapis lazuli and shell. Sledges, warcarts, and wagons are known from fourth- and third-millennium art, and the remains of one such wagon were uncovered in an ED grave at Kish: It had a wooden platform surrounded by rails and four solid wooden wheels. These were made of three pieces clamped together, with copper nails set in the rim to make them more durable. Terra-cotta models of wheels show that such protection was common, although in neighboring Elam and in early-second-millennium Assyria tires made from strips of metal were used. Spoked wheels came into use in the early second millennium, and an improved version with a metal nave into which the spokes fitted was devised in Assyria in the early first millennium for use on chariots.

References in the Amarna Letters show that luxury furniture was given as gifts between kings, such as the ebony beds, tables, and chairs overlaid with gold sent by the pharaoh to Mesopotamian monarchs. Fine furniture was also a desirable commodity plundered by Assyrian armies from the areas they invaded, such as the Levant and Urartu. The finds from Nimrud (Kalhu) provide examples of the stools, chairs, and tables shown in first-millennium Assyrian reliefs. The finest pieces were often partially sheathed in bronze or gold and had decorations of shell, ivory, metal, and other materials. Some tables had elegant legs with lions' feet, and in some cases the legs were entirely of ivory.

Kings and queens took their ease on stools and thrones once decorated with ivory panels, their feet supported by footstools. Bronze hinges from Nimrud may support the idea that the cross-legged tables and stools shown in many reliefs of military camps and hunting expeditions were portable folding furniture. The wells at Nimrud yielded a number of wooden objects, including pulley wheels of mulberry wood, several derricks, and a number of hinged writing tablets of walnut.

Stone

Stone, used to make tools from the earliest times, served many purposes in Mesopotamia, although in the south, where stone was rare, tools were often made of wood or clay instead. Assyria had sandstone and limestone, and an outcrop of limestone at Ummayyad to the west of the lower Euphrates was probably exploited by the people of Babylonia. Assyria also had local supplies of alabaster in the upper Khabur region and flint along the Balikh and upper Euphrates. The Zagros foothills yielded lava, quartzite occurred in large amounts in the Hamrin, and gypsum was available in the Jebel Bishri. Some stone reached Babylonia as rocks carried down by the rivers: The quartzite, and perhaps the flint, used for tools at Tell 'Oueili may have been transported in this way. Obsidian could be obtained from Anatolia, and basalt, diorite, granite, haematite, serpentine, and jasper were also imported from neighboring areas. Other decorative stones such as carnelian, steatite, agate, and lapis lazuli came from more distant Iranian, Afghan, or Indian sources.

Cutting tools such as sickle blades, arrowheads, chisels, and hoe heads were originally made of chipped flint, chert, or quartzite, and these materials were still in use in the first millennium as a cheaper substitute for metal; other utilitarian objects like netsinkers, slingshots, and griddles for cooking were also made of stone. Grindstones and pestles could be made of lava, basalt, or coarse limestone. Open molds for casting metal tools and weapons such as axes and spearheads were cut into blocks of sandstone: Often several faces of the block would each have a mold for a different object. Stone was also cut and polished to make weights, often in the shape of ducks (see photo p. 132), and was among the materials used for making calibrated measuring bars and coffins. Obsidian was prized in early times for making sharp blades and a variety of attractive objects, including mirrors, but in historical times it was made into jewelry, vessels, and seals. It was so highly valued that some obsidian vessels were ornamented with gold and given as gifts between royalty.

Attractive stones were used in making jewelry, worn by people and divine images and an important form of wealth, given in dowries, listed in wills, and exchanged as gifts between rulers. Beads and other ornaments, such as pendants, bracelets, and rings, as well as amulets, were made from a variety of stones, such as rock crystal, chalcedony, haematite, agate, and lapis lazuli; some of these were manufactured locally; others, such as the long barrel beads and "etched" beads of Meluhhan carnelian were imported ready-made. Beads were strung as necklaces, armlets, headdresses, and anklets, and were also sewn onto clothing. Fine stone was also set into ornaments made of metal such as bracelets and pendants: For example the gold ribbon from one of the royal Assyrian tombs at Nimrud was set with tigereye agate discs. Inlays of stone such as obsidian and lapis lazuli were added to statues, using bitumen to hold them in place. Pieces of attractive stone were also employed as architectural decoration: The walls of many temples were embellished with eight-petaled rosettes made of colored stone.

Stone was quarried and shaped using pounders and grinders of very hard stone such as dolerite, and in the first millennium, iron saws, although the softer stones such as limestone and sandstone could be extracted with picks of copper, bronze, or iron. Hammers and chisels were used to carve the stone into the required shape and execute details such as relief carving, while the finer details and inscriptions were drilled using an abrasive such as sand and bow drills with bits of hard stone: These were also used to perforate beads. Objects were then polished with sandstone or quartzite rubbers and sand. Stones padded with bitumen acted as a vice to hold objects being worked on. A stoneworking workshop was uncovered at Nimrud in the Review Palace: Among the equipment found here was a doubled-handled iron frame-saw, 1.73 meters long, used for cutting stone. At the time the palace was sacked, a broken alabaster statue was being repaired here with dowels.

Sculpture and Art in Stone.   Alabaster, obsidian, sandstone, gypsum, and chlorite were among the stones used for making bowls and jars, which were often dedicated as royal votive offerings. From the city of Uruk in the Uruk period come several fine vessels decorated with relief carving, including the Warka vase, an alabaster vessel around a meter high (see photo p. 69), and a gypsum trough carved with a relief design of sheep and a reed hut. Other vessels were more elaborately decorated, with plastic designs, including a sandstone ewer with a solid figure of a lion pacing alongside the spout as well as a lion attacking a bull around the body of the vessel, their heads standing out from it. Sculptures of animals in the round are also known from this period: Some seem to have supported offering stands, but there is also a powerful sculptured limestone figure of a creature that is part man, part lion.

Probably the finest piece from this period is the female mask found at Uruk, perhaps a depiction of Inanna herself. The head is of marble and must originally have had eyes of shell with lapis lazuli pupils and eyebrows and gold-inlaid hair. While this figure is naturalistic, the period has also produced a huge number of extremely schematic "eye-idols," stone or clay votive plaques with a flat body, sometimes engraved with a zigzag to represent arms, and a short neck surmounted by a pair of large eyes.

Votive figurines became one of the main genres of sculpture (see photo p. 71). An early collection of rather stylized figures was found in an ED II temple at Eshnunna. Ten are worshippers; the other two, which are considerably larger, represent the god and his wife. Carved of gypsum, their eyes are inlaid with shell and lapis or black limestone, and bitumen colors their beards and hair. A charming statue of a woman was found in a soldier's grave of the ED III period at Ur. Carved of limestone, her eyes and hairline are inlaid with bitumen. She wears a layered woolen dress that leaves her shoulders bare, and her hands are clasped on her chest in an attitude of reverence. Later sculptures are often naturalistic, including both human figures and animals. Some of the finest were the seated or standing votive diorite figures of King Gudea of Lagash (2141–2122 B.C.E.): portraits showing a man of reflective serenity but also strength (see photo p. 80). In contrast the gypsum statues dedicated in small domestic and urban

Stele, known as the Law Code, of Hammurabi, king of Babylon, in the eighteenth century, B.C.E. The stele is of black diorite and was carved with the figure of Hammurabi standing before the seated sun god, Shamash, god of justice. (Zev Radovan/Land of the Bible Picture Archive)

shrines were generally simple and might be quite crudely modeled, although they might also have a certain charm, like the statue of a man and woman holding hands that was found beneath the Inanna shrine at Nippur.

By the second millennium, human figures were being depicted with every detail of their clothing, hair, and other features painstakingly carved. This attention to detail was still to be seen in the stiff, stylized statues of Assyrian kings and in the gigantic figures (lamassu) guarding the first-millennium palaces of Assyria—lions, bulls, and benevolent genies, and winged human-headed bulls shown with five legs so that they looked balanced from both the front and the side (see photo p. 28). These figures are carved partially in the round, but they are engaged, still a part of the architectural block to which they belong, recalling the figures of more than two millennia earlier that were shown in relief with heads in the round.

Narrative relief carvings began in the Uruk period with a basalt boulder on which a king is shown hunting lions with spear and bow. ED-period limestone plaques depict royal warfare and the victory feast, or pious construction, such as the plaque of Ur-Nanshe of Lagash (ca. 2494–2465), where he is shown in the presence of his family, carrying the first basket of soil. These plaques were presumably attached to walls. The later stele of Naram-Sin (2254–2218) (see photo p. 186) is a unified composition, concentrating on a single dramatic moment of military victory rather than being split into narrative scenes. A stele of the Ur III monarch Ur-Nammu (2112–2095) emphasizes the religious role of the king, and the relief carved on the top of Hammurabi's law-code stele is in a similar vein, depicting the king before the divine judge Shamash, affirming the god's favor and his own commitment to justice. Kings feature as donors on the later kudurrus (land-grant records), particularly numerous in the Kassite period; the gods are represented by their symbols. The contemporary Assyrian kings appear on altars and inscribed obelisks, but also in scenes of warfare, a theme elaborated in the beautifully carved and detailed reliefs that adorn the walls of the palaces of later Assyrian kings. The aftermath of war is also vividly depicted, with processions of the defeated wending their weary way into exile, subject envoys bringing tribute, and Assyrian kings taking their ease. A few show other remarkable achievements, including the quarrying and transporting of the enormous statues that guarded the palaces. The scenes of Ashurbanipal hunting lions from his palace at Nineveh are a masterpiece, full of drama, vigor, and movement, the lions

A second-millennium cylinder seal and its modern impression. The seal bore a text naming its owner, Taribum, the son of Etel-pi-Ishtar, the servant of Shamash the sun god, and a design, in this case probably a depiction of Taribum's personal deity. (Zev Radovan/Land of the Bible Picture Archive)

closely observed and feelingly depicted. In one scene a lioness, paralyzed by an arrow, roars her dying defiance, while a lion hurls himself upon the king's chariot. In another, the king is tackling a wounded lion on foot: As the lion rears on its hind legs, face-to-face with the king, he catches it by the throat and delivers the coup de grâce with his sword (see photo p. 106).

Seals.   Seal cutting was a specialist craft, distinct from other forms of stoneworking. Designs were usually carved into the surface of seals, so they made an impression on clay in which the design was raised and the background depressed, but occasionally seals have the background cut away leaving the design in relief. The flat surface of stamp seals was relatively easy to carve, but the curved surface of cylinder seals required considerable skill both in layout and in execution. A text of the Achaemenid period stated that a seal cutter served an apprenticeship of four or more years, and a similar period must have been required to attain the level of craftsmanship shown by Mesopotamian seal cutters. The details of the designs and particularly of the inscriptions are so small that they seem to demand that seal cutters employed magnifying glasses, and indeed a polished rock crystal disc with one flat and one convex face found at Nimrud might have been a magnifying lens. Attractive and colorful materials were favored for seals: They varied through time, with steatite, serpentine, and limestone used in the earlier third millennium, lapis employed in some quantity from the mid-third millennium, and jasper, banded agate, and rock crystal coming into fashion from Akkadian times. Haematite was the preferred medium in the earlier second millennium. Carnelian and chalcedony were also used in later times, as was glass.

The art on seals ranges wide in its themes. Among Uruk-period examples are seals depicting a king surveying bound prisoners, people bearing offerings to the temple, contests between bulls and lions, and real and mythical beasts. The skill in the design lay in filling the surface but creating a design that would be equally satisfactory if only a portion of the design was rolled out or if the design was rolled out to a considerable length so that it began to repeat. The "Brocade style" of the ED period fulfilled this by cramming the cylinder surface with small repeated motifs, such as a line of goats surrounded by stars, fishes, rosettes, or geometric figures. Contests between animals or between man and beast similarly filled the space and continued smoothly throughout the seal impression. The modeling on the seals improved, producing figures that were more three-dimensional. Akkadian seals became less cluttered and increasingly emphasized narrative themes, with the gods frequently shown. Thereafter seal design declined until revived in the later second millennium by the Assyrians, who produced a wealth of vivacious naturalistic and narrative scenes, often featuring animals.

Decorative Materials

Shell.   The shells worked by Mesopotamian craftsmen came from all the seas to which they had access and included cockles from the Mediterranean, cowries and mother-of-pearl from Dilmun, chank and *Lambis* from the Indian Ocean, and *Tridacna* (giant clam) from the Indian Ocean or the Red Sea. For example, under the Mitanni the provincial town of Nuzi, near the Zagros foothills in northeastern Mesopotamia, used shells from the Mediterranean, the Gulf, and the Indian Ocean. Tortoiseshell and ostrich eggshell were also used. Flint microborers and bladelets for working mother-of-pearl were found in a workshop at Mari. Shell and mother-of-pearl were used for decorative inlays and for small objects, including unmodified cockleshells used as containers for cosmetics. Simple cowrie-shell beads were made by slicing off the back to make them flat and perforating them longitudinally. Small figurines and flat shapes were cut from shell. For instance bovids decorated with circle and dot motifs were popular in the central Euphrates region in the later third millennium. Some of the shell and mother-of-pearl plaques and figures were intended as inlays for architecture or furniture, including an ED military scene of shell figures decorating the wall of the Ishtar temple at Mari and many of the inlays on objects from the Royal Cemetery at Ur; others were artifacts in their own right, perhaps with some religious significance. A set of eighteen decorated discs of *Lambis* shell attached to bronze pins found at Nimrud may have decorated a horse harness. Larger shells were made into vessels: Often they were cut open to make lamps. A beautiful cup from the Royal Cemetery at Ur was made of an ostrich eggshell to which had been added a pedestal, neck and mouth of bitumen inlaid with patterns in mother-of-pearl. Giant clamshells were made into containers, perhaps for cosmetics; examples from Nimrud were elaborately decorated, the hinge carved into a head and wings engraved over the back.

Ivory. Until the early first millennium B.C.E., when it was hunted to extinction, a small species known as the Syrian elephant roamed the northern Levant and provided ivory as well as sport for the elite of the Near East. Ivory was also imported during the third millennium from the Indus civilization and later reached Mesopotamia from Africa, via Egypt, and India. The canines and lower incisors of Egyptian, Syrian, and southern Palestinian hippopotamuses also yielded ivory.

Ivory was used for a variety of small objects like combs, jewelry, plaques, and figurines, as well as decoration on furniture and divine statues. Small ivories, probably mostly imports from the Levant, are more commonly known from first-millennium cities: these included small boxes for storing cosmetics or jewelry. Royal gifts, tribute from subject lands, and booty from defeated states brought enormous quantities of ivories into the hands of the conquering Assyrians. Such treasures were stored at Nimrud (Kalhu), the seat of the Assyrian kings from 863 to 707 B.C.E. Thousands of ivory artifacts have been recovered from the Review Palace known as Fort Shalmaneser and from wells and elsewhere in the main palace complex. These were abandoned by looters during the sack of the city in 612 B.C.E. after they had stripped off the gold leaf with which most, if not all, of them had been covered. Some resemble the stone relief carvings of Assyrian palaces in style and subject matter; many were Phoenician, often showing strong Egyptian influences and making frequent use of glass and stone inlays, and others were in a north-Syrian style, or a style combining Syrian and Phoenician features, and a few were from Urartu, perhaps those taken when Sargon II sacked the city of Musasir in 714 B.C.E. Phoenician craftsmen were particularly skilled in working ivory, and many probably worked for Assyrian kings as prisoners of war.

Many of the Nimrud ivories are panels and plaques that had decorated furniture or the palace walls, depicting small scenes or figures, among which sphinxes and griffins were popular. Ivory was also made into table legs, chair and couch backs, mirror handles, elaborately decorated boxes and flasks, cheek pieces for horse harnesses, and hinged writing boards. The latter were recovered as innumerable tiny pieces of burned ivory and had to be pieced together; they had originally been covered with a writing surface of beeswax, mixed with orpiment to soften it. One stopper for a container was carved in the form of a shallow bowl over which loomed the heads of a pair of lions acting as spouts. The containers were often covered with busy interwoven decoration, showing animals, griffins, lions, and bulls attacking people or other an-

Levantine craftsmen were skilled in the production of ivories of many kinds. This sphinx from the palace of King Ahab of Israel was part of a furniture decoration. Very similar pieces were found among the ivories at Nimrud (Kalhu). (Zev Radovan/Land of the Bible Picture Archive)

imals, birds, and other motifs. A number of small ivory pots, generally with geometric decoration, were probably used for kohl: Cosmetic pencils found with them matched holes in their lids.

Some ivory plaques had inlays of glass or fine stone. One superb example showed a boy being mauled by a lion, against a background of lotus and papyrus flowers, their heads inlaid with tiny red and blue pieces of carnelian and lapis lazuli, while their stalks and the boy's loincloth were overlaid with gold leaf. His hair was represented by blackened ivory pegs with gilded tops. A number of ivories took the form of human figures or heads, including an elegant flask partly formed by the head and torso of a woman in an Egyptian-style wig, a series of small statues of young men carrying and leading animals, and the female mask nicknamed the "Mona Lisa"; there were also several fine figurines of bulls. A fragment from a larger object consisted of ivory birds and lapis lazuli fruit attached to bronze-wire branches.

Many of the ivories from Nimrud were blackened by fire. Although in many cases this happened when the city was sacked, some pieces were probably deliberately heated to produce a uniform and attractive black surface, which was enhanced by polishing. In other cases ivory was colored by staining or painting. Ivory was carved with tools and drills of stone or metal; compasses were sometimes used in creating the designs. Tusks were divided into sections; from the hollow pulp cavity boxes were made, and the solid sections were cut horizontally into slices for the manufacture of plaques. Mortice and tenon joints were employed to join pieces together, and Aramaic letters inscribed on the back allowed them to be correctly assembled. Inlays were set into champlevé or cloisonné cells and fixed with adhesives, which were also used to join ivory pieces. Frequently objects were gilded or covered in gold foil, applied before inlays were added.

Bitumen. Substantial quantities of bitumen (natural asphalt) were obtained from the stretch between Hit and Ramadi on the middle Euphrates, where it welled up and could be collected either as a viscous liquid or as lumps; it was also available in other areas including Jebel Bishri, the Zagros foothills east of the Tigris, the banks of the Karun River in Elam, and the area around Ur. The wide range of uses to which it was put included construction (discussed previously), caulking boats, strengthening and waterproofing leather, lining baskets to make them watertight, sealing jars, and burning as a fuel. It was employed as a decorative inlay in stone and faience and also as an adhesive holding inlays of other materials in place. Figurines were sometimes carved from dry lumps of bitumen. Its "magical" properties were employed in rituals and medicine where it was an ingredient of ointments. It was a versatile material that was easily recycled: old bitumen was removed from boats with a hammer and chisel and when required for reuse was heated to a liquid.

Pottery

The clays that were the raw material for making pottery were readily available as river sediments throughout the area watered by the Tigris and Euphrates. These might be used with little working to make coarse wares such as storage vessels and cooking pots, but finer textured pottery, such as that made on the tournette or the potter's wheel, had to be worked well to remove mineral inclusions. The clay was brought to the required degree of plasticity by adding fillers (tempers) such as chaff, dung, sand, or ash.

Early Mesopotamian pottery was handmade, using a variety of techniques (see photos pp. 54, 57, 59). The simplest method was to press a hollow into a ball of clay and smooth and thin its walls between thumb and fingers. Slabs of clay could be pressed together and used to build pots. Most commonly handmade pots were built up of coils or rings of clay. From the mid-fifth millennium, pottery throughout Mesopotamia began to be made on the tournette ("slow-wheel" or turntable), a flat disc balanced on a pivot or spindle set into the ground, which could be turned by hand, speeding up the shaping and decorating of pots. In the fourth millennium, the potter's wheel appeared in southern Mesopotamia: This device had a lower flywheel set in motion with a stick or propelled with the foot, attached to an upper wheel, disc, or working head, on which the clay was thrown. A disc 75 centimeters wide found in the Uruk-period levels at Ur may have been such a flywheel: A small hole on its rim would have taken the stick used to set it spinning. Although some vessels were entirely wheel thrown, others had their base finished by hand. Alongside the finely shaped wheel-thrown pots of the Uruk period, crude "beveled-rim bowls" were also produced in large numbers: These were made by pressing coarse clay into a mold.

Wheel-made pottery was initially confined to Babylonia but was later made throughout Mesopotamia. Some of the wares produced were extremely fine. For example, a ware with eggshell-thin walls made at Nuzi in the fourteenth century B.C.E. was so delicate that it could not be lifted from the wheel without distortion, so it was strengthened and decorated by impressing dimples into the sides. Similar dimpled cups remained a popular prestige ware in the first millennium, including the late-seventh-century Palace Ware found at Nimrud. A variety of different shapes were regularly made for different purposes: Types mentioned in texts included beer jars with an upward-pointing spout; pointed-based jars for milk and tripods to support them; jars for storing and transporting oil; vats for serving wine and probably beer; and honey containers. Cups, bowls, dishes, goblets, pedestaled vessels, fenestrated stands, jars, and vases are among the shapes known from excavated sites; sealed jars were used for storing archives of tablets. Clay was also used to make human and animal figurines, spindle whorls, beads, architectural materials, including cones for decorating walls, and slingshot, as well as substituting for stone as the material for sickles, hammers, pestles, and other tools. Molds for casting metal objects were often made of clay, and the kitchens in the eighteenth-century palace at Mari had terra-cotta molds for shaping or decorating food: These included shallow discs and trays with relief designs of people, animals, or geometric patterns and deeper molds in the shape of a fish, complete with details of its scales.

Newly formed vessels might be decorated by incising, impressing, or excising designs into the surface, such as the patterns of lines, slashes, and dots that decorate some of the "Ninevite 5" pottery of early-third-millennium northern Mesopotamia; stamps might also be used to impress designs: Some Assyrian pottery was stamped with small rosettes. Other types of decoration were applied after the pottery had been allowed to dry to leather-hard. At this point the vessel might be covered with a slip (a clay wash), which could then be burnished, making the vessel relatively watertight. This was a common treatment throughout Mesopotamian prehistory and history. Early pottery was also decorated by painting: By the Halaf period, elaborate geometric designs were being painted in three colors. Ubaid-period pottery was decorated in bands on the tournette by holding a paint-laden brush against the vessel. Brushes with a number of tufts were used to create multiple patterns. However, the beginning of wheel-made pottery saw the decline of decoration, pottery thereafter being mass-produced wares that were of good quality but often dull and generally plain. Exceptions include the pottery made by the Mitanni, painted with geometric and figurative designs, including spirals, birds, and floral motifs. An unusual cup found at Tell Brak in northern Mesopotamia had a molded nose, surrounded by the painted features of an unshaven man.

From the later second millennium, some ceramics began to be glazed. Initially the technology was applied to small objects such as figurines and wall plaques and the glaze was a pale blue green, but by the early first millennium glazed bottles for holding precious liquids such as perfumes were being manufactured in considerable quantities and were decorated with geometric designs in a variety of colors—white, yellow, brown, blue, turquoise, and green. Glazed ceramic tiles and bricks were also made and used architecturally to great effect, for example on the Ishtar Gate at Babylon and along the associated Processional Way.

Pottery could be fired in clamps (bonfire kilns), a technique still in use, but by about 6000 B.C.E. updraft kilns were also used: The fuel was placed in a pit with a stokehole at the side through which more fuel could be added during the firing. Above this was a perforated floor on which the pots were stacked. A cylindrical chamber of baked clay surrounded the pottery and was roofed with large sherds, which were removed after the firing was completed. The difficulty of controlling the firing temperature is illustrated by pottery of the Ubaid period, which ranges from a soft friable ware with a poorly fired pink body and pink or red painted decoration, through medium-fired yellow or white on which the paint had turned brown, to overfired vessels of a grayish green hue with the decoration turned black. Later wares show greater mastery of firing conditions.

A few sites have yielded evidence of pottery making, and texts also provide information. In the Old Babylonian settlement of Mashkan Shapir, pottery workshops seem to have been distributed throughout the settlement, with each neighborhood being served by their own potter. Kilns and workshops have been found in or on the outskirts of a number of cities, such as Lagash and Ur, where Woolley found an extensive Uruk-period pottery production area with kilns, misfired wasters, and other kiln debris. Texts from the Ur III period refer to workshops of fewer than a dozen people with a supervisor, whose output might be confined to vessels intended for particular purposes or serving the needs of the establishment to which they were attached, and larger potteries producing a wider range of pots, such as those at Umma, which made forty-six different types of vessel. There were also villages and small towns of potters: One, situated at Umm al-Hafriyat near Nippur, had around five hundred kilns. In the highly regulated environment of the Ur III Empire, texts record the amount of time that needed to be spent on producing vessels of particular types and volumes.

Terra-Cottas.   Pottery figurines were hand-modeled, and some were not fired but merely dried in the sun. Clay plaques with high-relief decoration were used as divine images in small shrines, as were crudely carved gypsum figurines. Copies of the divine image were made into small clay plaques with relief decoration or small clay figurines for use in domestic shrines and might be acquired by pilgrims visiting the shrine. These were mass-produced by pressing the clay into molds. Simple figurines of worshippers were also made as offerings to place in shrines. Plaques also depicted a range of other themes (see photos pp. 32, 159, 162), such as people at their work or scenes from mythology. The Kassite dynasty made more extensive use of the medium: Objects included a sensitive portrait head of an individual, with details picked out in paint, and a beautiful closely observed image of a lioness.

Faience and Glass

Faience.   The production of vitreous materials began in Mesopotamia in the Ubaid period with the appearance of small objects of glazed siliceous stone and of faience with a crushed quartz core and a vitreous surface. A number of faience beads, seals, and amulets in the form of animals come from fourth-millennium levels at Tell Brak. In the third millennium the number and range of faience objects increased, including small vessels, figurines, seals, and votive weapons such as mace heads. Faience tiles and wall inlays were used in some architecture, such as the mausoleum of the Ur III king Shulgi, and statues of gods sometimes had a beard of faience. Small faience vessels were embellished with incised designs or sculpted decoration. Faience paste was modeled by hand or pressed into a mold to form the shapes required, and when dry, these pieces were fired.

   In the later second millennium faience production grew in scale, with palace workshops in Mesopotamia and the Levant mass-producing jewelry, cylinder seals, and vessels. Nuzi and Tell al-Rimah have yielded many faience objects, and Kassite-period Babylon had a series of kilns for firing faience. Among the most impressive objects of this period were rhytons in the shape of women's or animal heads, made in the Levant and widely distributed. Pendants in the form of women's faces, inlaid with bitumen or pieces of colored faience set in bitumen, and cups with floral decoration in contrasting colors were also popular throughout Mesopotamia. The range of colors produced included black from ferrous manganese, blue, green, and blue-green from copper, and yellow from antimony. Other faience objects included ornaments such as discs to sew onto clothing and tassels for horse harnesses, inlays for furniture, knobs for decorating architecture, wall tiles, small flasks for perfumes and ointments, and votive figurines. Faience objects such as beads and cylinder seals continued to be produced into Neo-Assyrian times although they declined in popularity with the development of polychrome pottery and glass.

Glass.   Some beads of true glass were made in the third millennium, probably accidentally when faience was overheated, but raw glass found at Eridu, Eshnunna, and Tell Brak in the late third millennium suggests that glass was already being produced deliberately. Glass has a similar composition to faience but is heated until the mixture of silica, alkali, lime, and metal-oxide pigments melts to a viscous liquid. It was not until around 1600 B.C.E. that glass began to be made in some quantity and its properties fully exploited: Mitanni could well have been the center of these developments. Glass vessels (usually blue) were formed by wrapping a trail of molten glass around a core of clay and dung, which was dug out when the glass had cooled; alternatively the core could be dipped into molten glass. The soft vessel was then marvered (rolled on a smooth stone slab) to smooth the surface and even up the shape. Blobs and lines in contrasting colors, generally yellow and white, were often added as decoration. Beads were similarly made by wrapping a molten thread of glass around a metal rod. Molten glass was also drawn out into rods of various thicknesses, which were used to decorate or manufacture mosaic or marbled-glass beakers and bottles: Many of these are known from Nuzi and Tell al-Rimah, and from Tell Brak where blue glass ingots were also found. Glass objects produced in northern Mesopotamia at this time included spacer beads and plaques depicting nude women. Around the same time the technical problems of bonding glass with the surface of ceramics were solved, and the manufacture of glazed pottery began, followed later by that of glazed figurines, tiles, bricks, and architectural knobs. Pottery vessels with polychrome designs began to be made in Assyria around the turn of the millennium, the colors being kept separate by thin ribs between them, and Babylonia followed its lead. Around the eighth century objects such as pendants and inlay pieces for jewelry and furniture began to be made by casting in an open mold or in a closed mold, using a method similar to the cire-perdue (lost-wax) casting of metals. Cast-glass vessels were finished by grinding and polishing and might be decorated with cut designs. One of the earliest and finest examples of this was a vase from the North-West Palace at Nimrud inscribed with the name of Sargon II and the figure of a lion. To this period also belongs the beginning of production of clear glass resembling crystal. It is uncertain how this was made: Glassblowing is generally thought to have been invented in the Levant only in the first century B.C.E., but the fineness of this glass suggests that the technology may already have been in use in Assyria in the early first millennium. Another first for this region was painted glass, known from two tiny plaques of clear glass painted with sphinxes found in Fort Shalmaneser at Nimrud.

Glass was an expensive commodity, used for producing luxury items owned by royalty and the elite and for decorating important buildings; faience was probably a cheaper alternative, as was glazed pottery. Both faience and glass originally imitated precious stones and were used in similar ways, and the clear glass made from around 700 B.C.E. onward simulated rock crystal. Texts from the second millennium onward give recipes for producing glass and glazes, including mixtures that would reproduce the colors of valued stones like lapis lazuli, carnelian, and sapphire.

Metalworking

Copper and Bronze.   Copper and lead were being smelted in the Near East by the late seventh millennium B.C.E., and by the fourth millennium copper metallurgy was a well-established industry in southern Mesopotamia. Copper with a high arsenic content, probably imported from Talmessi in western Iran, was used, producing an alloy that was harder than pure copper and easier to cast. Although most objects from this period and later were produced in simple open molds, the discovery of a few small Uruk-period figurines made by cire-perdue (lost-wax) casting demonstrates that more advanced techniques were already known.

Around 3000 B.C.E., the first bronzes began to appear in various parts of the Near East, including Tepe Gawra and ED I Kish, but bronze was for a long time a prestige material reserved for the finest objects. This is well illustrated by artifacts in the Royal Cemetery at Ur: Here the highly prized sheet-metal vessels were made of bronze, whereas more ordinary objects were cast in ar-senical copper, despite the fact that copper is easier to hammer into sheet metal and bronze is easier to cast. Bronze objects did not become common until the early second millennium B.C.E., and third-millennium metal tools, weapons, statues, and architectural ornaments were generally of copper. Exceptional ex-amples of the latter survive from the temple of Ninhursaga at al-Ubaid, where three friezes depict standing bulls, kneeling calves, and the Imdugud bird flanked by deer; some parts were hammered up from sheet copper, but the heads of the cattle and the deer and bird figures were made of cast copper. The large portrait head of an Akkadian king, probably Naram-Sin (see photo p. 77), was also still made of copper rather than bronze. This was an exceptionally fine piece, depicting the king realistically, with meticulous attention to the de-tail of the elaborate hair arrangement and beard, but also conveying an im-pression of majesty and power.

By the end of the fourth millennium, copper from Magan (Oman), at first imported via Dilmun (Bahrein), began to be used in southern Mesopotamia and by 2100, if not earlier, gold, copper, and tin were among the imports from Meluhha (the Indus civilization) as well. Tin was used not only for alloying with copper but also as a solder and occasionally to make artifacts. Its source is controversial. It is now known to be among the metal ores present in the Taurus, although this source was probably not exploited in antiquity; Neo-Assyrian texts do refer to tin from Anatolia, but this could have been alluvial tin. Earlier tin most probably came from various sources in Central Asia, from where it was traded both overland to enter Mesopotamia via Elam, and, in the later third millennnium, overland to the Indus and thence by sea to Mesopotamia; tin from the Arawalli hills, a source of Meluhhan copper, might also have been mined and traded. In the early second millennium the Gulf trade was abandoned and copper came from sources in the west, particularly Anatolia and Alashiya (Cyprus); other sources could have included Arabia.

Gold, Silver, and Lead. The Taurus range ("Silver Mountain") was the proba-ble main source of silver and lead from the third millennium onward, al-though these may also have been obtained from parts of Iran, including Elam and Aratta. Lead was used for occasional objects from the sixth millennium onward and was popular in the Jemdet Nasr period for making vessels, al-though these declined in number thereafter and few were made after the end of the ED period. Jewelry such as pendants and beads, statue bases, and weights might also be made from lead. By 3500 B.C.E. there is evidence at Habuba Kabira of cupellation to extract the silver from the lead. Lead was on occasion alloyed with copper to produce a soft but ductile metal; silver was also alloyed with copper in the late Uruk period, probably experimentally. Silver was made into small prestige objects, and a few vessels such as the magnificent mid-third-millennium vase of Enmetena from Girsu. It was frequently made into wire from which rings and coils were formed: These were used as a medium of exchange, commodities being valued with reference to weights of silver. In the Kassite period, gold was similarly used, as was tin at Nuzi in the Middle Assyrian period, but silver was for most of antiquity the main exchange medium and value standard employed throughout the Near East.

Anatolia also produced electrum, a natural alloy of gold and silver that is similar in color to gold. Much of the "gold" used in the ancient Near East was actually electrum. However, one Ur III text lists salt as a commodity present in a goldsmith's workshop at Ur, suggesting that the gold was sometimes extracted from electrum by cementation, a process in which electrum and salt were heated together so that the silver was given off as silver chloride. Most gold probably came from alluvial deposits and was obtained by panning. Sources are hard to pin down, but textual evidence shows that gold was obtained from a number of places, including eastern Iran and Anatolia, Meluhha in the third millennium, and Egypt in the second. Gold was little used before the mid-third millennium, but the large number of gold objects from the Royal Cemetery at Ur (ca. 2600 B.C.E.) already display mastery of a range of advanced techniques, including gilding, cloisonné inlaying, and the manufacture of gold wire. The wig-shaped helmet of Meskalamdug, created of sheet gold by repoussé work and chasing, faithfully reproducing every lock of hair, is probably the finest piece, but it is closely rivaled by the gold and lapis lazuli dagger decorated with gold studs, in a sheath decorated by granulation and filigree, and the fine bulls' and cows' heads of sheet gold with hair and beards of lapis lazuli that ornamented the sound boxes of lyres. Fine leaves of beaten gold formed part of the headdresses of the women buried in the tombs. Later objects included solid-gold jewelry, figures, vessels, and decorative weapons, and gold foil was used to cover the statues of deities. The gold and electrum objects found in the eighth-century Assyrian royal tombs at Nimrud show that the high standards of craftsmanship were maintained and extended: They included a crown of flowers and vines worked in granulation, an extraordinary ribbon inlaid with agate, elaborate earrings covered with tiny granulated designs, substantial armlets with cloisonné inlays of gemstone and glass, and plates with fine figurative decoration.

Metalworking.   Texts referring to metalworking are known from the early third millennium onward. Some give the recipe for bronze, usually around one part tin to eight to ten parts copper, although in practice many artifacts had a far lower tin content. This might have come about through the reuse of scrap metal, bronze being mixed with copper, reducing the proportion of tin present.

A small forge from Eshnunna, equipped with a hearth and an anvil stone, may have been used by a smith who made simple objects from scrap metal and mended tools for local residents. Although some smiths and metalworkers were independent artisans, most probably worked for the palace or temple.

Bureaucratic texts refer to the process of manufacture and in particular to the amounts of metal lost at various stages. Only a tiny fraction of gold was expected to be lost during manufacture, reflecting the pure nature of alluvial gold. Copper, however, was often impure. Smelting generally took place near the area where the ore was mined, using wood, charcoal, or reeds for fuel. An extensive ore reduction site has been discovered at Goltepe in the Taurus, and a number in Magan. Copper sulphide ore is difficult to purify, and the records show that copper was imported as ingots of two grades, "good," or refined, ore, which could be used directly, and unrefined ore, which had to be "washed" before use, in other words, refined. The loss in the process is recorded as being up to one-third of the weight of the ingots used. Also lost in manufacture was a substance, *su-gan*, which has not been identified but which was probably a flux, perhaps borax, used in the smelting process: This was more expensive than copper, but only small amounts were used. The texts refer to a number of different specialist workers: smiths who smelted and cast metal (*simug / nappahum*), metalworkers who produced objects by other methods (*tibira / gurgurrum*), jewelers (Sum. *zadim*), and goldsmiths (*kudim / kutimmum*).

Records refer to workshops, and the artifacts themselves demonstrate that metal was worked, but there is little direct evidence of metal production until the second millennium when a number of metallurgical workshops have been found in Mesopotamia and in the Assyrian trading outpost of Kanesh in Anatolia. At the Isin-Larsa period workshop site of Tell edh-Dhiba'i, metalworking equipment included pot bellows of baked clay and a tuyere nozzle, used in maintaining the temperature in the smelting or melting furnace, crucibles and molds of baked clay, as well as a model of an axehead in clay. Finds of metal slag throughout the city of Mashkan Shapir show that the processing of metal ores or unrefined copper was not confined to a special part of the city.

Iron and Bronze. Bronze was in widespread use for making weapons, jewelry, and statuary by the second millennium and was also used for tools, although poorer individuals probably used stone tools into the first millennium, when iron began to circulate. A very few objects of iron are known from as early as the fourth millennium: Some were probably made of meteoritic iron; others could have been hammered out of slag produced in the smelting of iron-rich copper ores or copper ores to which iron oxide had been added as a flux. The technology of ironworking was quite different from that used to work other metals: The conditions necessary to produce cast iron were never achieved in antiquity in the Western world (in contrast to China), and wrought iron, made by hammering the bloom produced when iron was smelted to knock out the impurities, was inferior to bronze in toughness. The few iron objects produced in the third and second millennia were highly valued prestige items, and the circulation of iron was strictly controlled (see chapter 5) and operated at the highest level, discussed by kings. Around 1200 B.C.E., however, things changed dramatically. The discovery of the techniques of carburization (by which iron is alloyed with carbon to produce steel), quenching, and tempering transformed iron into a hard, strong metal that could be used effectively for tools and weapons. The abundance of iron ores and the relatively simple though laborious technology required to smelt and smith iron, compared with the intricacies of casting copper and bronze, made iron a revolutionary material for making tools within the reach of ordinary people, once the transition from elite monopoly to free availability had been made. It is possible this was linked to the economic and political disruptions that affected much of the Near East in the twelfth century B.C.E. In the first millennium, therefore, iron was widely used for utilitarian objects, including tools such as saws, axes, and chisels, military equipment such as arrowheads, sword blades, and scale armor, and materials for construction such as nails, whereas bronze was made into ornamental and prestige objects, including not only jewelry, mirrors, figurines, vessels, and sheathing for furniture but also larger pieces, such as Assyrian bathtub coffins (more usually made in clay) and sheet-metal cladding for doors and gates. The best-preserved example of this is the ninth-century series of bronze panels, engraved and embossed with relief decoration, that had covered the wooden gates of the palace at Imgur-Enlil (Balawat) (see photos pp. 31, 168): The gates measured 6.8 meters high by 2.3 meters wide and had bronze-capped posts and bronze cladding on the gate edges in addition to the eight panels that depicted Shalmaneser III's campaigns, subject peoples bringing tribute, and Shalmaneser's discovery of the source of the Tigris. Other kings also set up such gates at Balawat and other Assyrian cities.

Composite Creations

Some of the finest works of Mesopotamian craftsmanship were created from a mixture of materials: Objects of wood, glass, metal, terra-cotta, or stone were inlaid with colored stones, shell, glass, and bitumen, or encased in gold, silver, or bronze, while others were skillfully constructed of several different materials, best illustrated by objects from the Royal Cemetery at Ur. The "Standard of Ur" may have been the sounding box from a lyre: One of the most impressive creations of the First Dynasty of Ur, it consisted of a wooden box with inward-sloping sides, entirely covered with designs built up of shapes cut out of shell and red stone against a background of pieces of lapis lazuli set in bitumen. The panels in the trapezoidal ends had designs taken from mythology; the sides were divided into three registers and showed scenes from life. On one side, dubbed "War," the bottom register shows victorious spearmen and charioteers riding in warcarts over the bodies of the slain enemies, the middle register shows the infantry marching, their front ranks engaging the enemy, and the top shows the king inspecting war captives, attendants ranged behind him along with his warcart. The other side, "Peace" (see photo p. 73), represents the victory celebrations: The king and his courtiers are seated in the top register, drinking and listening to a musician playing a lyre, while below a procession of people bring animals and fish and porters carry heavy packs, the spoils of war. Similar in construction were the gaming boards, carved of wood and inlaid with bone squares edged with lapis lazuli and decorated with shell, lapis lazuli, and red limestone. Panels on the lyres also have scenes built from shell cutouts. One shows preparations for a banquet staffed by animals: A wolf carries in food on a stand, followed by a lion bearing a jar and bowl, and a gazelle brings cups, while a bear steadies a harp played by a donkey, accompanied on a rattle and drum by a smaller creature.

Also from the Royal Cemetery at Ur came a pair of statues of goats, standing on their hind legs and eating the leaves from a plant. They were built over a wooden framework. A baseboard inlaid with mosaic lozenges held a post to which branches were attached, completely covered in gold sheet with gold leaves and flowers attached. The roughly shaped wooden goat, made in pieces, was given its final shape by adding plaster of Paris, where necessary, and was then coated in bitumen. This acted as an adhesive holding in place the rich materials with which the outer form of the goat was created: the legs and face of gold and the belly of silver sheet, the horns, the eyes, and the locks of hair on its shoulders of lapis lazuli, and the rest of its fleece of shell, carved as individual locks of hair.

Later pieces, such as the furniture from Nimrud, show that the skills in working with a combination of materials continued throughout Mesopotamian civilization.

Textiles

Textiles were of key importance in the Mesopotamian economy and trade, but little physical evidence of Mesopotamian textiles has survived. This is compensated to some extent by the wealth of written and artistic sources of information, and deductions can also be drawn from physical remains in adjacent regions and from impressions of textiles on pottery and seals or in corrosion products on metal objects.

Early Near Eastern textiles were made of leather, goat's hair, or flax, but from the fourth millennium wool was used and became the main basis of the Mesopotamian textile industry. Linen, which was expensive to produce, became a luxury fabric, worn by kings, priests, and the statues of gods. Archaic texts from Uruk referred to a number of flocks of woolly sheep, and by the late third millennium there were four different varieties, producing various grades of wool, and one kind of sheep bred for its hair. The earliest reference to cotton was by Sennacherib who had "trees bearing wool" in his botanical garden in the seventh century B.C.E.

The wool was gathered from the sheep by plucking or combing, the latter method apparently yielding better wool. After cleaning and combing, the wool was spun on a spindle and woven on a horizontal loom, both generally women's work. The cloth was then cleaned and treated by fullers, a long and demanding process. By the late third millennium the Babylonians may also have practiced tablet weaving to produce narrow bands of cloth with complex patterns. Syria, a region of pastoralists, was also a center of textile innovation, and from here Mesopotamia probably adopted the two-beam vertical loom in the second millennium, along with the technique of tapestry weaving for which it was designed. A late-thirteenth-century document refers both to a maker of tapestry and a "knotter," presumably a maker of pile carpets. Assyrian reliefs show that carpets were elaborately patterned, and textual references suggest that they were being made on the western fringes of Mesopotamia by early in the second millennium, although they were probably invented in the Caspian region. The colors used in woven and knotted textiles can be reconstructed from an Assyrian chemist's treatise, which gives recipes for making a number of them, and from other sources, including traces of red cloth in the Royal Cemetery at Ur (which disintegrated when excavated). Various sources of red dye were known, including the kermes beetle, madder, and lichen fixed with an alum mordant. There was also the expensive and prestigious "sea-purple," the dye extracted as a monopoly by Ugarit and other cities of the Levant from various marine molluscs: This could yield a range of colors from red to brown and purple to blue. Blue also came from indigo or woad. Yellow was made from turmeric fixed with soda as a mordant, saffron, and pomegranate rind. Alum, another important mordant, also used in treating leather, was imported from Egypt where it was mined. The natural colors of wool were also exploited. The Sumerians placed a high value on fleeces of a reddish brown color; other shades ranged from white through yellow to brown, and black, which was the least esteemed.

Reeds and palm leaves were used for making baskets and mats as well as for construction, and palm fibers were used for rope making. Rope and baskets coated in bitumen to make them watertight were among the remains recovered from the wells in the palaces of Nimrud. Textiles of various qualities were made into soft furnishings such as rugs, covers, and cushions, horse cloths, tents, and sails, the latter perhaps of hemp. Felt for covering seats and tables and for lining objects was made from wool or goat's hair. Fine textiles were traded and used as diplomatic gifts. Babylonia had an international reputation for the manufacture of woolen textiles.

Clothing.   Much of the cloth was produced for clothing: Workers were given regular issues of woven cloth or wool from which to make their own. In the third millennium men wore a rectangle of cloth or a sheepskin with the fleece outward wrapped round their waist as a short or calf-length kilt or as a long robe wrapped round the upper body and over the left arm with the right arm free, and often a cap; women similarly wore a long robe, draped over one or both shoulders; and the arrangement of the robe changed through time. In addition people might wear a leather or sheepskin cloak and various types of footwear, including shoes with turned-up toes and sandals. By the Old Babylonian period tailored, short-sleeved dresses for women had appeared and sometime later robes began to be made of longer lengths of cloth draped diagonally round the body a number of times. In the first millennium ceremonial robes preserved this spiral arrangement of cloth but were now sewn to an undergarment. Men generally wore a short-sleeved tunic or tunic and skirt of various lengths with a belt or cummerbund, whereas women wore a long tunic with a shawl. Kings and officials also wore an elaborate shawl.

Fringes, sometimes with tassels and often elaborate, decorated the edges of wrapped and stitched garments, and the neck and the ends of the sleeves of tunics might be embroidered. Royalty might wear garments embroidered all over. Some cloth was decorated with appliques of leather or other materials: A linen textile from eighteenth-century B.C.E. Anatolia (when the Assyrians were trading textiles to the region) had tiny faience beads stitched on with gold thread; elaborate gold appliques from clothing were found in the princesses' tombs in Nimrud, and such decorations are shown on royal robes in relief carvings.

TEXT REFERENCES

Akkermans, Peter M. M. G., and Glenn M. Schwartz. 2003. *The Archaeology of Syria. From Complex Hunter-Gatherers to Early Urban Societies (ca. 16,000–300 BC).* Cambridge: Cambridge University Press.

Armstrong, James A. 1997. "Mesopotamian Ceramics of the Neolithic through Neo-Babylonian Periods." Pp. 453–459 in *The Oxford Encyclopedia of Archaeology in the Near East.* Vol. 1. Edited by Eric M. Meyers. Oxford: Oxford University Press.

Bahrani, Zainab. 2000. "Jewellery and Personal Arts in Ancient Western Asia." Pp. 1635–1645 in *Civilizations of the Ancient Near East.* Edited by Jack M. Sasson. Peabody, MA: Hendrickson Publishers. (Reprint of 1995 edition. New York: Scribner.)

Barber, Elizabeth J. W. 1991. *Prehistoric Textiles.* Princeton, NJ: Princeton University Press.

———. 1997. "Textiles of the Neolithic through Iron Ages." Pp. 190–195 in *The Oxford Encyclopedia of Archaeology in the Near East.* Vol. 5. Edited by Eric M. Meyers. Oxford: Oxford University Press.

Bienkowski, Piotr. 2000. "Art, Artists," "Craftsmen," "Sculpture," and "Wall Painting." Pp. 32–33, 80–81, 256–257, and 314–315, respectively, in *Dictionary of the Ancient Near East.* Edited by Piotr Bienkowski and Alan Millard. London: British Museum Press.

Bienkowski, Piotr, and Alan Millard, eds. 2000. *Dictionary of the Ancient Near East.* London: British Museum Press.

Black, Jeremy, and Anthony Green. 2000. "Figurines." Pp. 116–117 in *Dictionary of the Ancient Near East.* Edited by Piotr Bienkowski and Alan Millard. London: British Museum Press.

Caubert, Annie. 2000. "Art and Architecture in Canaan and Ancient Israel." Pp. 2671–2691 in *Civilizations of the Ancient Near East.* Edited by Jack M. Sasson. Peabody, MA: Hendrickson Publishers. (Reprint of 1995 edition. New York: Scribner.)

Collon, Dominique. 2000. "Clothing and Grooming in Ancient Western Asia." Pp. 503–515 in *Civilizations of the Ancient Near East.* Edited by Jack M. Sasson. Peabody, MA: Hendrickson Publishers. (Reprint of 1995 edition. New York: Scribner.)

Crawford, Harriet. 1991. *Sumer and the Sumerians.* Cambridge: Cambridge University Press.

Crouwel, J. H., and Mary Aiken Littauer. 1997. "Wheel." Pp. 343–344 in *The Oxford Encyclopedia of Archaeology in the Near East.* Vol. 5. Edited by Eric M. Meyers. Oxford: Oxford University Press.

Dalley, Stephanie. 1984. *Mari and Karana. Two Old Babylonian Cities.* London: Longman.

Frankfort, Henri. 1996. *The Art and Architecture of the Ancient Orient.* 5th edition. New Haven, CT: Yale University Press.

Freestone, Ian C. 1997. "Vitreous Materials. Typology and Technology." Pp. 306–309 in *The Oxford Encyclopedia of Archaeology in the Near East.* Vol. 5. Edited by Eric M. Meyers. Oxford: Oxford University Press.

Gilbert, Allan S. 2000. "The Flora and Fauna of the Ancient Near East." Pp. 153–174 in *Civilizations of the Ancient Near East.* Edited by Jack M. Sasson. Peabody, MA: Hendrickson Publishers. (Reprint of 1995 edition. New York: Scribner.)

Green, Anthony. 2000. "Clothing" and "Foundation Deposits." Pp. 75–77 and 121–122, respectively, in *Dictionary of the Ancient Near East.* Edited by Piotr Bienkowski and Alan Millard. London: British Museum Press.

Gunter, Ann C. 2000. "Material, Technology and Techniques in Artistic Production." Pp. 1539–1551 in *Civilizations of the Ancient Near East.* Edited by Jack M. Sasson. Peabody, MA: Hendrickson Publishers. (Reprint of 1995 edition. New York: Scribner.)

Harden, D. B. 1956. "Glass and Glazes." Pp. 310–346 in *A History of Technology. Vol. II. The Mediterranean Civilizations and the Middle Ages.* Edited by Charles Singer et al. Oxford: Oxford University Press.

Hodges, Henry. 1971. *Technology in the Ancient World.* Harmondsworth: Penguin.

———. 1988. *Artifacts. An Introduction to Early Materials and Technology.* Kingston: Ronald P. Frye and Co.

Lamberg-Karlovsky, C. C. 1993. "Introduction." Pp. ix–xii in *The Discovery of Glass. Experiments in the Smelting of Rich, Dry Silver Ores, and the Reproduction of Bronze Age-Type Cobalt Blue Glass as a Slag.* Edited by John Dayton. Cambridge, MA: Harvard University Press.

London, Gloria Anne. 1997. "Ceramics: Typology and Technology." Pp. 450–453 in *The Oxford Encyclopedia of Archaeology in the Near East.* Vol. 1. Edited by Eric M. Meyers. Oxford: Oxford University Press.

Maidman, Maynard Paul. 2000. "Nuzi: Portrait of an Ancient Mesopotamian Provincial Town." Pp. 931–947 in *Civilizations of the Ancient Near East.* Edited by Jack M. Sasson. Peabody, MA: Hendrickson Publishers. (Reprint of 1995 edition. New York: Scribner.)

Matson, Frederick R. 2000. "Potters and Pottery in the Ancient Near East." Pp. 1553–1565 in *Civilizations of the Ancient Near East.* Edited by Jack M. Sasson. Peabody, MA: Hendrickson Publishers. (Reprint of 1995 edition. New York: Scribner.)

Matthews, Donald. 2000. "Artisans and Artists in Ancient Western Asia." Pp. 455–468 in *Civilizations of the Ancient Near East.* Edited by Jack M. Sasson. Peabody, MA: Hendrickson Publishers. (Reprint of 1995 edition. New York: Scribner.)

Mattingly, Gerald L. 2000. "Furniture," "Textiles," "Trees," and "Wood." Pp. 122–123, 288–289, 301–302, and 321–322, respectively, in *Dictionary of the Ancient Near East.* Edited by Piotr Bienkowski and Alan Millard. London: British Museum Press.

Meyers, Eric M., ed. 1997. *The Oxford Encyclopedia of Archaeology in the Near East.* 5 Volumes. Oxford: Oxford University Press.

Muhly, James D. 2000. "Mining and Metalwork in Ancient Western Asia." Pp. 1501–1519 in *Civilizations of the Ancient Near East.* Edited by Jack M. Sasson. Peabody, MA: Hendrickson Publishers. (Reprint of 1995 edition. New York: Scribner.)

Oates, Joan, and David Oates. 2001. *Nimrud. An Assyrian Imperial City Revealed.* London: British School of Archaeology in Iraq.

Peltenberg, Edgar. 1997. "Vitreous Materials. Artifacts of the Bronze and Iron Ages." Pp. 309–314 in *The Oxford Encyclopedia of Archaeology in the Near East.* Vol. 5. Edited by Eric M. Meyers. Oxford: Oxford University Press.

Philip, Graham. 2000. "Tools and Weapons." P. 294 in *Dictionary of the Ancient Near East.* Edited by Piotr Bienkowski and Alan Millard. London: British Museum Press.

Pittman, Holly. 2000. "Cylinder Seals and Scarabs in the Ancient Near East." Pp. 1589–1605 in *Civilizations of the Ancient Near East.* Edited by Jack M. Sasson. Peabody, MA: Hendrickson Publishers. (Reprint of 1995 edition. New York: Scribner.)

Pollack, Susan. 1999. *Ancient Mesopotamia. The Eden that Never Was.* Cambridge: Cambridge University Press.

Postgate, J. Nicholas. 1994. *Early Mesopotamia.* London: Routledge.

Potts, D. T. 1997. *Mesopotamian Civilization. The Material Foundations.* London: The Athlone Press.

Ratnagar, Shereen. 1981. *Encounters. The Westerly Trade of the Harappa Civilization.* Delhi: Oxford University Press.

Reade, Julian. 1982. "Nimrud." Pp. 99–112 in *Fifty Years of Mesopotamian Discovery.* Edited by John Curtis. London: British School of Archaeology in Iraq.

Roaf, Michael. 1990. *Cultural Atlas of Mesopotamia.* New York: Facts on File.

———. 2000. "Palaces and Temples in Ancient Mesopotamia." Pp. 423–441 in *Civilizations of the Ancient Near East.* Edited by Jack M. Sasson. Peabody, MA: Hendrickson Publishers. (Reprint of 1995 edition. New York: Scribner.)

Saggs, H. W. F. 1988. *The Greatness that Was Babylon.* New York: Hawthorn Books.

Sasson, Jack M., ed. 2000. *Civilizations of the Ancient Near East.* 4 Volumes. Peabody, MA: Hendrickson Publishers. (Reprint of 1995 edition. New York: Scribner.)

Simpson, Elizabeth. 2000. "Furniture in Ancient Western Asia." Pp. 1647–1671 in *Civilizations of the Ancient Near East.* Edited by Jack M. Sasson. Peabody, MA: Hendrickson Publishers. (Reprint of 1995 edition. New York: Scribner.)

Spycket, Agnes. 2000. "Reliefs, Statuary, and Monumental Paintings in Ancient Mesopotamia." Pp. 2583–2600 in *Civilizations of the Ancient Near East.* Edited by Jack M. Sasson. Peabody, MA: Hendrickson Publishers. (Reprint of 1995 edition. New York: Scribner.)

Van de Mieroop, Marc. 2004. *A History of the Ancient Near East. ca. 3000–323 BC.* Oxford: Blackwell.

Winter, Irene J. 2000. "Aesthetics in Ancient Mesopotamian Art." Pp. 2569–2582 in *Civilizations of the Ancient Near East.* Edited by Jack M. Sasson. Peabody, MA: Hendrickson Publishers. (Reprint of 1995 edition. New York: Scribner.)

Woolley, Leonard. 1982. *Ur "of the Chaldees."* The final account, *Excavations at Ur,* revised and updated by P. Roger and S. Moorey. London: Book Club Associates/Herbert Press.

X CHAPTER 10
Intellectual Accomplishments

Writing was invented in Mesopotamia by the end of the fourth millennium, initially for accounting, and was used almost from its inception to produce lists that show the Sumerian fascination with the organization of the world. By the later third millennium there was a huge variety of written materials ranging from practical materials such as accounts and architect's plans, through inscriptions recording royal deeds and pious dedications, to works of literature such as hymns, stories of the gods, and epics of heroic achievement. Many of the surviving texts come from the Old Babylonian period; the mid-first millennium also produced a wealth of written materials, including both the library of King Ashurbanipal in which every available text was collected and the private reference collections of professionals such as doctors, exorcists, and astronomers. Despite the huge volume of material available, however, not all aspects of Mesopotamian intellectual life are covered—of the sciences, only astronomy, medicine, and mathematics are included.

NUMBERS, TIME, AND SPACE

The Mesopotamians were accomplished mathematicians and students of the heavens. Many of the systems that they developed underlie those used throughout the world today: positional notation, the divisions of time and space (seconds, minutes, degrees in a circle), the mapping of the firmament. Even writing began with Mesopotamian accounting devices.

Mathematics

The Sumerians used mathematics initially for accounting and later developed it to solve other practical problems. Fourth-millennium clay tablets bear witness to the emergence of numerical written records. By the third millennium more complex accounts were being kept, mathematics was being employed in civil engineering, construction, and the organization of labor, and theoretical problems in arithmetic and geometry were also being considered. Figuring became a key part of education and by the OB period, from which most of the surviving texts come, complex mathematics were being used.

The Number System. The Mesopotamians used a base-sixty counting system. Evidence indicates that in early times there were separate numbering systems for counting different things: sheep, measures of grain, jars of oil, and so on. With early writing, however, abstract counting came into use. Instead of the sign for a commodity being written the appropriate number of times (tallied), numbers and commodities were represented separately, so that a number of sheep, for example, was written as a number sign and the sign for sheep. Until the late third millennium, however, different systems were used for counting discrete objects, discrete rations, and measures of grain. By the Ur III period a single sexagesimal positional system was used for writing numbers when performing calculations, although the different commodities were still written at the beginning and end of the sum with their own units.

Abstract numbers were counted in powers of sixty: 1, 60, 3,600, 216,000, and even 12,960,000. These were broken down into decimal units—six lots of ten, six lots of six hundred, and so on. Although initially there were separate signs for each of these, by the Ur III period the signs had become greatly simplified, using vertical wedges for units and powers of sixty, and diagonal wedges for tens and tens of powers of sixty, and relying on position rather than shape to indicate the number in question. A vertical wedge stood for a unit and numbers up to nine were written as an arrangement of these wedges in two rows. Ten was written as a slanting wedge and numbers up to fifty-nine were written as a combination of tens and units, the tens arranged to the left of the units. Sixties were again written vertically, to the left of the tens, and six hundreds diagonally to the left of the sixties, and so on, up to the fourth power of sixty. Fractions were similarly written, in the manner of decimals, to the right of units, although there were also separate symbols for the most common fractions: one-half, one-third, two-thirds, and five-sixths. One problem with positional notation is the need to indicate the absence of a value in a particular position, for example to distinguish the Babylonian number 1, 0, 1 (3,601) from 1, 1 (61). When writing figures the Babylonians sometimes left a gap as a placeholder, and from around 700 B.C.E. onward they occasionally made a mark instead. In most cases, however, they relied on the context to make the appropriate value clear.

Weights and Measures.   Mesopotamian units of weight, length, area, and volume used various factors and multiples of 60, particularly 3, 6, 10, 60, and 180 (see table 10.1 and photo p. 132). This is clearest in the units of weight; length also introduced a multiple of 2, and in measures of capacity 5 was also a multiple.

These measures were standardized by the Akkadian king Naram-Sin, including the gur, which he fixed at 300 silas = 5 barigas (about 300 liters). This standardization produced a neat interrelationship among the units of length, area, and volume.

Geometry, Arithmetic, and Others Mathematics.   Many mathematical exercises survive in texts, mainly from the Old Babylonian period, although some go back to the Ur III period and even to ED IIIa. These exercises were probably mainly didactic aids used in school, demonstrated by the teacher and copied and learned by his pupils. The problems often dealt with practical matters: for example, calculating the size of siege ramp that could be built with a given volume of soil and the time required to build it; the volume of water required to irrigate a

TABLE 10.1

Weights and Measures

	Unit	Unit	Unit	Unit	Unit	Unit
Weight	homer/ donkey-load	talent	mina	shekel	little shekel	barleycorn, grain
Sumerian	*anshe*	*gu(n)*	*mana*	*gin*		*she*
Akkadian	*imeru* (donkey)	*biltu* (load)	*manu*	*shiklu*		*uttetu*
Value	180 minas	60 minas	60 shekels	180 barley-corn	3 barley-corn	
Metric Equivalent	90 kg	30 kg	c. 500 g	c. 8 g	0.12–0.15 g	0.04–0.05 g

	Unit	Unit	Unit	Unit	Unit	Unit
Capacity	bushel	measuring basket			shekel	barleycorn
Sumerian	*gur lugal* (king's gur)	*bariga* (*nigida*)	*ban*	*sila*	*gin*	*she*
Akkadian			*sutu*	*qu(m)*	*shiqlu*	
Value	5 *bariga**	6 *ban*	10 *sila*	60 *gin*	180 *she*	
Metric Equivalent	300 liters	60 liters	10 liters	1 liter	1/60th liter	

	Unit		Unit	Unit	Unit	Unit	Unit	Unit
Length	stage, league		line	measuring rod	reed	cubit	finger	barley-corn
Sumerian	*danna*	*USH*	*eshe*	*gardu*	*gi*	*kush*	*shusi*	*she*
Akkadian	*beru*		*ashlu*	*nindan*	*qanu*	*ammatu*		
Value	30 *USH* / 1800 *nindan*	6 *eshe*	10 *nindan*	12 cubits	6 cubits	30 fingers	6 *she*	
Metric Equivalent	10.8 km	360 m	60 m	6 m	3 m	0.5 m	1.66 cm	1/360 m

	Unit	Unit	Unit	Unit	Unit	Unit
Area			field		garden plot	little shekel
Sumerian	*bur*	*eshe*	*iku*	*ubu*	*sar*	*gin*
Akkadian						
Value	3 *eshe* =18 *iku*	6 *iku*	100 *sar*	50 *sar*	1 square *nindan* = 60 *gin*	36 square *shusi*
Metric Equivalent	6.48 ha	2.16 ha	0.36 ha		36 square m	1 square m

*an earlier (pre-Akkadian, i.e., before Naram-Sin's standardization ca. 2250 B.C.E.) *gur* = 4 *bariga* = 240 liters in some cities

Sources: Dilke 1987; Kramer 1971; Postgate 1994; Potts 1997; Powell 2000

certain area of land; the number of laborers needed to construct or clean out a canal and the quantity of food rations they would require; the amount of grain needed to sow a field of a given area and the yield to be expected from it; or prices of commodities and interest rates on loans. Other problems, however, were theoretical and might involve quadratic equations or arithmetic progressions. Some texts give problems and worked solutions, step-by-step, while others just give long lists of related problems. Although early texts were in Sumerian, from the OB period onward Akkadian was generally used.

A large number of tables were available to aid in solving these problems and in undertaking calculations in the real world, such as surveying land (particularly for dealing with sales and inheritance), calculating the prices of commodities, or computing simple or compound interest. These included straightforward multiplication, division, and metrological tables, but also more advanced mathematical information such as squares, square and cube roots, reciprocals, coefficients, and lists of key numbers. A good approximation to root two was calculated, 1.414212963 (the correct value, to ten significant figures, is 1.414213562), but for *pi* the Babylonians generally used 3, although lists of reciprocals show that they were aware that 3.125 was a closer approximation (the value used today, to four significant figures, is 3.142).

Their calculations required a good grasp of plane and solid geometry, including knowledge of "Pythagoras's Theorem" (some 1,300 years before Pythagoras), and skill with dealing with triangles, circles, trapezoids, and regular polygons as well as squares and rectangles; and prisms, cylinders, and truncated pyramids as well as cubes and cuboids; but they did not use cones, pyramids or spheres, nor did they work with angles. Some calculations were expressed as algebraic problems with one or several unknown values, and much of the methodology of problem solving was algebraic, although the Babylonians did not use symbolic notation.

Calendrics

Divisions of Time. The Babylonians used a calendar based on cycles of both the moon and the sun. Time was divided into solar days, lunar months, and luni-solar years. Days ran from sunset to sunset and were divided into four parts or into twelve "double-hours." Astronomical texts such as *Enuma Anu Enlil* provided information on how to calculate the length of daylight at different times in the year.

A cycle of the moon lasts a fraction over twenty-nine days. Mesopotamian months were reckoned as the time from the first sighting of the new moon on the western horizon to its first appearance in the following month: They were therefore either twenty-nine or thirty days long. The first, seventh, and fifteenth days of the month were marked by special religious observances. These provided a measure of the passing of time within the month: There was no division of the month into weeks (an innovation of the Roman period).

The year had twelve lunar months, making it only 354 days long. This is shorter than the solar year of 365 1/4 days, and if left uncorrected, the lunar-based calendar would rapidly get out of step with the solar calendar. An inter-

TABLE 10.2

The Calendar

	Sumerian Month	Babylonian Month
March–April	bara-zag-gar-ra	Nisannu
April–May	gu-si-sa	Ayau *or* Ayyaru
May–June	sig-ga	Simanu
June–July	shu-numun	Du'uzu
July–August	ne-ne-gar-ra	Abu
August–September	kin-inanna	Ululu *or* Elulu
(Intercalary Month	diri-kin-inanna	Atra sha Ululu)
September–October	du-ku	Tashritu
October–November	apin-du-a	Arahsamma
November–December	gan-gan-e	Kislimu
December–January	ab-e	Tabetu
January–February	ziz-a	Shabatu
February–March	she-gur-ku	Addaru
(Intercalary Month	diri-she-gur-ku	Artu sha Addaru)

Sources: Bienkowski and Millard 2000: 63; Rochberg 2000; Bottero 1998

calary month was therefore inserted periodically to correct this discrepancy, usually after the sixth month or at the end of the year; the introduction of this month was made known by royal decree. Although this practice is attested to in Babylonia from the third millennium onward, in Assyria it was not certainly adopted until the twelfth century B.C.E. (see table 10.2).

The Babylonian year began with the month Nisannu in the spring (March/April), whereas Assyria originally started the year in the autumn, although by the first millennium this had been brought in line with the Babylonian year. The Babylonian New Year (*resh shatti*), which fell around the spring equinox, was celebrated in Babylon with a major festival that lasted for twelve days.

The Passing of Time. By the time of the Akkadian Empire, records were dated by reference to the reigning king and an important event within that year, a method that continued in use in Babylonia until around 1500 B.C.E. Official lists of these year names were kept from Ur III times onward. A year might

A cuneiform tablet bearing a copy of the Assyrian King List. (Library of Congress)

be named for the founding of a temple, the appointment of a particular individual as chief priest of the city deity, the installation of a divine image, or even the furnishing of the god's statue with a new garment. Other year names marked significant military achievements. Rim-Sin I of Larsa was so satisfied with his defeat of Isin in 1794 that he dated all the remaining years of his reign as so many years after this victory. Public works might also be celebrated, such as the construction of a canal or a city wall. Sometimes more than one event was recorded in the year name.

From the Kassite period onward, dates in Babylonia were reckoned by the king's regnal years. In addition, Babylonian priests kept a daily record of omens and observations of the heavens and the world around them, for the sake of divination, often including references to important contemporary political events and other interesting occurrences; these were compiled into lists that allowed particular years to be identified and the lapse of time recorded. When Ashurbanipal sacked Susa and recovered the statue of Inanna stolen from Uruk, he was able to claim that 1,635 years had elapsed since the Elamites had carried it off.

Other historical records included king lists, which named the kings and gave the lengths of their reigns. The Sumerian King List, known from OB texts but probably first compiled in the Ur III period, began before the Flood and ended when Hammurabi conquered Isin. It included only some of the Sumerian city-states: Lagash, for example, was omitted. The Babylonian King List began with the First Dynasty of Babylon, and the Assyrian King List started with a number of kings "who lived in tents," the tribal ancestors of Shamshi-Adad. The Synchronistic King List gave details of Assyrian kings, their contemporary Babylonian monarchs, and their viziers.

In some periods chronicles were compiled giving a year-by-year list of events. The earliest surviving example, the *Eponym Chronicle,* comes from eighteenth-century Mari. Royal annals, recorded by Assyrian kings from the thirteenth century onward, gave details of campaigns, dated by the regnal years of each king. In addition, from the nineteenth century B.C.E. the Assyrians used a system of naming each year after an important official *(limmu).* These names, often accompanied by details of a significant event during the year, were preserved in eponym lists, which provided the main dating framework for Assyrian timekeeping: the relevant eponym year was noted when writing legal, administrative, and business documents. Many fragments of the eponym lists have survived, allowing parts of the list to be reconstructed, but only for the period 910 to 649 B.C.E. is an unbroken sequence known.

The inclusion of material in the Assyrian annals was very selective, only victories being recorded. In contrast, the *Babylonian Chronicle* was largely impartial and accurate, reporting reverses as well as successes. It covered events in Babylonia, dated by regnal year, but also mentioned some things that took place in neighboring Elam and Assyria. The *Babylonian Chronicle* was begun in 747 B.C.E. under Nabonassar and continued into the Seleucid period, although there are many gaps in the sequence. Texts were usually labeled as extracts from a more comprehensive record. Reference on one tablet to it being copied from a waxed writing board suggests that day-to-day records were kept on ephemeral media and were subsequently collated and copied onto the more permanent medium of clay tablets.

Astronomy

Determining the will of the gods and their intentions for the future was of key importance; this information was communicated in various ways that could be interpreted by those with the requisite knowledge. Omens and portents were therefore collected and recorded, along with information on the events that followed them. A major source of such portents, and one that became increasingly important in the first millennium, was the movement of heavenly bodies. In observing and recording these phenomena Mesopotamian sages, and particularly those of Babylonia, became extremely knowledgable about the regular courses of the stars, planets, moon, and sun. Some celestial events, particularly eclipses, were seen as boding ill: In a number of recorded instances, a substitute king was enthroned to deflect the danger of the eclipse from the real monarch.

A number of astronomical texts survive, the earliest dating from around 1700 B.C.E. These contained celestial observations and calculations to enable the patterns of the heavens to be predicted. The second-millennium *Enuma Anu Enlil* ("When Anu and Enlil"), a compilation of astronomical observations and the events that they presaged, was the most popular work, known in numerous Neo-Assyrian copies. It was in seventy tablets, covering various phenomena: phases of the moon, lunar eclipses, and conjunctions of the moon with planets and fixed stars; the sun, including solar eclipses and coronas; meteorological portents, including thunderstorms and clouds; and a compendium of stellar and planetary movements.

Other important texts included "Astrolabe," concerned with the heliacal rising of three fixed stars over the course of the year, and *MUL.APLIN* "Plough Star," a two-tablet compendium of all the movements of celestial bodies known in the seventh century B.C.E. when it was compiled. These included the paths of three major constellations of fixed stars, associated respectively with Anu, Enlil, and Ea. These texts also gave arithmetic information for calculating when intercalary months should be inserted into the calendar and establishing the variation in daylight hours, month by month, throughout the year.

Cartography and "The Babylonian Map of the World"

Among the clay tablets from the later third millennium onward are a number of maps and plans giving designed layouts for houses or temples, with written measurements. A seated statue shows Gudea with a temple plan and architect's rule on his knees. Others are land survey plans, setting out measured arrangements of fields, with information on the quality of the soil and their current use. One tablet of particular interest shows a scale plan of the city of Nippur, dated around 1500 B.C.E. It is carefully labeled, with measurements, and shows the city's walls and gates, the river Euphrates and canals, and a number of temples including the Ekur, temple of Nippur's patron god Enlil.

The "Babylonian Map of the World," showing Babylon, Mesopotamia, the surrounding ocean, and the lands beyond, described in the text at the top of the tablet. (Zev Radovan/Land of the Bible Picture Archive)

One large area is labeled "garden in the city." Another map gives details of royal and temple properties around Nippur, and there are area maps on which the Euphrates, canals, roads, and a city are marked, including one of the Akkadian period showing mountains and cultivated land near Nuzi and labeled with compass directions.

The most ambitious map ("the Babylonian Map of the World") schematically represents the world as known to the Babylonians around 700 B.C.E., surviving in a later copy. Two concentric circles surround the mapped area, representing the ocean, and two parallel vertical lines represent the Euphrates, running down to the marshes in the south, which are identified with a label. Another label placed across the river marks the location of Babylon. At the top a semicircle indicates the mountains and around the right side Urartu, Assyria, and Der are named, with Susa at the bottom. Outside the ocean captions identify strange lands inhabited by fabulous creatures. This is the earliest known attempt to map the world.

SCIENCE

Medicine

Although the treatment of medical problems included spiritual and magical practices as well as medical intervention, Mesopotamian doctors seem to have enjoyed considerable success in dealing with disease and other medical problems. A number of letters praise individual doctors or recommend remedies that have been efficacious, although others express anxiety about conditions that had failed to respond to treatment.

The city of Isin, whose tutelary goddess Ninisin (Gula) was associated with healing and midwifery, was a center of medical learning. In several texts individuals seeking to prove their medical credentials claimed to have trained in Isin.

Diagnosis. Because ill health was considered to have an external cause, whether due to punishment by the gods or bewitchment by an unquiet spirit, demon, or sorcerer, a major part of diagnosis lay in divination and magical ways of ascertaining the reason behind the illness. Compilations were made of observed signs and prognoses: the largest, *Enuma ana bit marsi ashipu illiku* ("When the exorcist is going to the house of the patient"), consisted of forty tablets, with some three thousand entries. Nevertheless there were also texts listing physical symptoms with instructions on preparing the appropriate medication and usually the observation that the patient "will get well," although in some cases death is said to be the expected outcome. Common recorded medical troubles included toothache, ear and eye problems, impotence, gastrointestinal ailments, skin diseases, incontinence, and respiratory disorders. Diagnosis could involve taking the patient's temperature and pulse, observing his skin color, looking for inflammations, and examining his urine.

Treatment. Two specialists dealt with illness. The *ashipu* (exorcist) used incantations and ritual actions to placate displeased gods and persuade them to turn away their wrath, drive away demons, lift curses, reverse spells, or lay troubled spirits responsible for an illness—but he might also prescribe a medical preparation. Conversely, the *asu* (physician), who dealt mostly with the physical symptoms, would probably administer his medicine with a charm or incantation. Physicians included women as well as men. Problems could be treated by either specialist, although from the mid-first millennium, there was more frequent recourse to the ashipu than the asu. One Neo-Assyrian court doctor, Urad-Gula, is listed at different times as an ashipu and as an asu: It is not known if his was a special case.

The story *The Poor Man of Nippur* gives a picture of the physician: clad in ordinary clothes but with a shaven head, and equipped with a libation jar and censer, he advertises his skills, saying that he comes from Isin, the city of medical learning. (In this irreverent tale, however, the Poor Man uses this disguise to create an opportunity for revenge: He beats up his patient, the Mayor, who has previously behaved badly toward him.) Other references show doctors also carried a bag containing herbs and sometimes incantation texts. Physicians like the disguised Poor Man of Nippur might seek private custom, but many were attached to royal courts.

Many of the treatments used were folk remedies, composed of herbs, animal material, or minerals, and administered as potions, enemas, or suppositories or used as ointments or poultices. Collections of prescriptions are known from Neo-Assyrian sources, particularly from Assur, but Sumerian medical texts from the Ur III dynasty also survive. These specified the injury or ailment and followed it with details of the appropriate treatment. Treatments involving incantations and the performance of rituals were often recorded in the same compendia as those using drugs. The three-tablet pharmacopoeia *uru.an.na / mashtakal* listed several hundred medicinal ingredients, including leaves, roots, seeds, and other plant material, salts, alum, and various types of powdered rock, and animal products such as blood, milk, fat, and bone. Many of the plants used probably had antibacterial properties. Often, however, the ingredients, particularly plants, are difficult to identify from their ancient names, making it impossible to assess how effective they would have been.

An Ur III–period tablet gives recipes for poultices and plasters, which contained ingredients such as mud, beer or wine, juniper, myrrh, honey, fat, and various plants. Resins were also a common ingredient, particularly terebinth. Beer and hot water were used to wash the affected area, which might then be rubbed with oil before the healing or soothing paste was applied. Oil could also be used as a wound dressing, applied on a fine linen bandage: This would have helped protect the wound from bacterial infection. Some recipes mention "essence of cedar," introducing the possibility that the Mesopotamians knew how to distil volatile oils.

One Neo-Assyrian text, compiled by the physician Nabu-le'u, gives a rare more detailed insight into treatment, listing medicinal plants, the complaints they should be used to treat, and the way they should be taken, including how often and at which time of day and whether the patient should take them on an empty stomach.

Prophylaxis. Epidemic disease and the dangers of dirty water were known. The possibility of contagion was recognized, and sometimes whole villages were evacuated to prevent the spread of disease. A royal letter from Mari spoke of one of the palace women having an infectious illness and advised that a cup, seat, and bed should be kept for her exclusive use to avoid the other palace women catching the disease from her.

A midwife attended women in labor. Both during pregnancy and after giving birth, mother and child were often protected by amulets to shield them from the baleful attentions of Lamashtu, the demonness responsible for miscarriage, death in pregnancy or labor, stillbirth, and death in infancy. Amulets worn as protection against demons often depicted the demon on one side and a text exorcising it on the other.

Surgery. The asu dressed wounds, set limbs, and performed simple surgical interventions such as lancing boils. A basic knowledge of human anatomy was probably acquired from the study of animal anatomy (important in divination) and from practical experience of treating war casualties and accident victims. Hammurabi's law code refers to setting a broken nose and healing a sprained tendon. Some more serious operations might be performed, but, according to Hammurabi's code, if the patient did not recover the surgeon was liable to have his hand cut off. Two types of surgery were listed in Hammurabi's inscription: a major operation by which the patient's life would be saved and "opening the eye socket," both performed using a bronze lancet. An incomplete tablet from Ashurbanipal's library hints at an operation in which the chest was opened to allow an abscess to drain. In another, better-preserved text, an abscess under the scalp was to be lanced and, if necessary, infected bone scraped away; if the abscess had not ripened, heat was to be applied to bring it to a head. One OB legal text may refer to a cesarean section performed on a dead woman. Surgical techniques were probably passed down from teacher to pupil: There are no texts discussing surgical practice.

Natural Sciences

The people of Mesopotamia had a good practical knowledge of the properties of clay, sand, metal ores, bitumen, stone, and other natural materials, using them to manufacture pottery, faience, glass, soap, metals, lime plaster, waterproofing, and other useful things. Metallurgy involved scientific skills such as smelting and cupellation; textile manufacture, the chemical treatment of hides and the manipulation of various dyes and mordants; the creation of glass required particular skills and knowledge; and extraction and distillation may also have been practiced. Surviving literature, however, suggests the Mesopotamians had little intellectual interest in the pure investigation of the physical and chemical properties of materials, which had no place in the school curriculum, and the emphasis in learning was on copying and repetition rather than investigation and enquiry. Technological knowledge seems largely to have been transmitted orally and by example, from practitioner to pupil (and often from father to son). Only doctors, astronomers, exorcists, and other ritual specialists have left volumes of observational data concerning their disciplines. The rare exceptions to this were recipes, for alloying metals, for making glass in various colors, for mixing dyes, and for making perfumes, generally with a colophon urging the initiated reader to keep the information from unauthorized eyes.

The Mesopotamians were, however, deeply interested in the way the world was ordered by the gods. Many different versions of the Creation story were current: Literary accounts generally included a section on the creation of humanity and the organization of the world. Among the earliest texts, when writing was still in its infancy, are classificatory word lists, which are a form of taxonomy, and which were to become a regular part of education in school. These divided the world up into categories such as domestic and wild animals, birds, fish, trees, plants, and minerals. Within each category the entries were listed in an ordered or hierarchical fashion: for example, the body parts started with the head and worked down. Technical terms and chemical substances were also listed. Another popular literary form was the disputation, in which two opposing parties discuss their contribution to a particular activity or field of operation, boasting of their own achievements and denigrating their rival. For instance, Hoe and Plough dispute their relative importance in agriculture (see chapter 5); other disputations take place between Sheep and Grain, Bird and Fish, Ploughman and Shepherd, and Ox and Horse.

Biology was generally written about only insofar as it had a bearing on the accepted forms of scholarship. Animal physiology was studied in minute detail for divination, with attention focused on particular organs, notably the liver. Animal behavior was also relevant to divination. One practical text deals with training horses. Again, it is probable that there was a great body of knowledge transmitted orally: Those who worked with animals, such as shepherds, would have had practical expertise in treating the ailments of their charges, gaining knowledge that was only occasionally recorded in veterinary medical texts.

LANGUAGES AND SCRIPTS

The Languages of Mesopotamia and Their Speakers

In remote times many different languages were probably spoken in the Near East, particularly in mountain areas where formidable natural barriers separated communities. Trade, transhumance, and population movement brought groups speaking different languages into contact with each other, and the growth of larger communities—city-states, intercity leagues, and eventually empires—brought some languages to prominence, while others died out. Only those languages used in writing are known in detail, although some words from other languages were also recorded. The first writing that can be read was in the Sumerian language. The script was borrowed by the Akkadian language, which overtook Sumerian in everyday use: This was one of the large Semitic language family that dominated, and still dominates, the Near East.

The mountains that ring the north and east of Mesopotamia and the lands beyond held speakers of languages with different affiliations, as did the lands of Egypt and the rest of Africa beyond the deserts to the west. To the south lay Dilmun and Magan, whose languages are unrecorded, and beyond them Meluhha, whose tongue required the services of an interpreter.

Southern Substrate.   A handful of words with no affinity to any known language occur in Sumerian texts. These include the names of some plants, animals, and natural features, and a few other words, including some associated with date cultivation. It is thought that these words belong to a substrate language spoken by the indigenous pre-Sumerian inhabitants of southern Mesopotamia.

Sumerian.   An agglutinative language with generally monosyllabic roots, Sumerian is not related to any surviving language family. It was spoken by the (literate) inhabitants of Sumer by the third millennium B.C.E. and presumably earlier. It was also understood over a wide area: Many texts written in Sumerian by local scribes are known from late-ED Ebla, far to the northwest. How early Akkadians and Sumerians were present in southern Mesopotamia is unknown, but by the time that written records allow us to distinguish Akkadian from Sumerian speakers, around 2600 B.C.E., both were to be found throughout the region, albeit with Sumerians concentrated in the south and Akkadians in the north.

Sumerian is the language for which the first script was devised, and it persisted in literature and royal inscriptions long after Akkadian became the main language of Babylonia, although it ceased to be spoken by the early second millennium. A humorous tale, *Why Do You Curse Me?*, relates how a doctor from Isin was invited to visit a grateful patient in Nippur and had difficulty obtaining directions to the latter's house because he could not understand the Sumerian speech of a street vendor. The story ends with a scornful comment on the ignorance of a supposedly educated man.

In addition to the standard Sumerian language *(emegir)* there was also an unusual dialect, *emesal* (Akkadian *luru*), used in some liturgical works, such as lamentations, and in love poetry: It was apparently spoken by women.

Akkadian.   The other main language of southern Mesopotamia, Akkadian, was spoken predominantly in the northern part where an early form of the language is attested from written names by 2600 B.C.E. Closely in contact over the centuries, Akkadian and Sumerian influenced each other. Akkadian gained greater currency when it became the language of officialdom in the Sargonic Empire. It was used also for literary works and by the early second millennium was the main language of Babylonia.

A form of Akkadian was probably also spoken in the north during the third millennium. From the early second millennium onward, two dialects of Akkadian are attested, Babylonian over much of Mesopotamia and Assyrian in the region of Assur, becoming later the languages, respectively, of the Babylonian and Assyrian Empires. Akkadian, and particularly Babylonian, became the lingua franca of the Near East and Egypt, used in diplomatic correspondence, for example between Egypt and its vassals in the Levant; often this was a hybrid language (Peripheral Akkadian) using Akkadian vocabulary with local linguistic forms and syntax. Akkadian was widely read: Many surviving cuneiform literary texts in Akkadian come from neighboring realms, including Egypt and the Hittite kingdom of Anatolia. An archaic and consciously literary dialect of Akkadian, Standard Babylonian, was used for literary works by both the Babylonians and the Assyrians in the later second and first millennia.

Old Akkadian and its descendants were part of the eastern branch of the large Semitic language group of which the only other known member was Eblaite, a language known from a few late-ED texts from Ebla, perhaps a dialect of Akkadian.

Other Semitic Languages.   The languages of the Semitic group (a subsection of the wider Afro-Asiatic language family) were widely spoken in the Near East by both nomadic pastoralists and settled farmers, probably from time immemorial. In the third millennium, groups of West Semitic speakers inhabited the Levant: Southern Mesopotamians were particularly aware of people they knew as Amorites (*martu / amurru*—"westerner"), nomads and raiders who moved around in the desert area between Mesopotamia and the settled communities of the Levant coast. The Amorites were succeeded by other tribal groups, also speaking Semitic languages. Aramaic, attested from the ninth century B.C.E., was a group of dialects spoken by the Aramaeans, tribal groups in Syria, and in some of the northern coastal city-states of the Levant, which became widespread and was used as an official language by the Assyrians.

Hurrian.   In the region north of the Diyala and east of the Euphrates dwelled speakers of the Hurrian language. They were known on the upper Khabur by the time of the Akkadian Empire and thence spread southward down the Tigris and Zagros foothills as far as the Diyala and west into the middle Euphrates and Cilicia. In the mid-second millennium Hurrian was the language of the Mitanni Empire. The area in which Hurrian was spoken rapidly contracted after the fall of Mitanni, and by the first millennium Hurrian speakers were probably confined to the foothills of the north. Beyond the Hurrian area was Urartu, where a related language was spoken, part of the Caucasian family, whose many languages are spoken in the small area between the Black Sea and the Caspian. Hurrian and Urartian probably diverged from a common ancestor in the third millennium B.C.E.

Kassite.   Contemporary with Mitanni, Babylonia was ruled by Kassites, a group whose antecedents are disputed but who probably came originally from the Zagros. Gradually settling in central Mesopotamia during the early centuries of the second millennium, they became thoroughly integrated with the Babylonians, and almost nothing is known of their language: just royal names in inscriptions and a few lists giving some Kassite words and names with their Babylonian equivalents. From these it seems that this also was a language without known relatives.

Neighbors. The Mesopotamians encountered speakers of other languages in the course of trade, international diplomacy, and war. An Akkadian-period seal refers to the owner as an interpreter of the Meluhhan language. Although the subject is still controversial, many scholars believe the language of the Indus civilization was an early member of the Dravidian language family, to which languages now spoken in southern India and pockets elsewhere belong. Evidence shows this to have been far more widespread in the second millennium, when Dravidian strongly influenced the (Indo-European) Indo-Aryan languages that predominate in the subcontinent today.

Indo-European-language speakers were known by the early second millennium to Assyrian traders in Anatolia. In this region a number of Indo-European languages, including Hittite, Luwian, Lydian, Lycian, and Phrygian, are attested in the second and first millennia. Earlier, non-Indo-European, languages were also spoken here, notably Hattic, the language of the people whom the Hittites eventually replaced. The Medes and Persians, first-millennium inhabitants of the western Iranian plateau, were also Indo-European speakers. Still a bone of considerable contention, the original home of the Indo-European languages is thought by many scholars to have been in the Caucasus region north of the Black Sea and Caspian. Speakers of these languages spread into Europe, Anatolia, and the Iranian plateau, eventually reaching India and Central Asia.

In Iran they entered a region inhabited by the speakers probably of many different languages. Khuzestan and the adjacent highlands, the closest neighbors of the Babylonians, were home to many disparate and independent groups, of which only some spoke the language known as Elamite. The earliest written records from this area, the "Proto-Elamite" texts, dating from the late fourth into the third millennium, have not been deciphered, and it is not certain what language they render. From around 2200 B.C.E., however, the cuneiform script was used and the language has been identified as Elamite. It continued to be spoken in the region into the Achaemenid period. Elamite has no known relatives, with the possible exception of Dravidian, with which it may have shared a common ancestor, Proto-Elamo-Dravidian. Mountain regions are well known as areas where contacts are difficult and languages therefore proliferate, so it is likely that many of the mountain tribesmen who perennially plagued the Mesopotamians, such as the Guti and Lullubi, spoke separate languages. Only the names of a few Guti kings are known, and of the Lullubi, nothing except this name itself.

The Development of Writing Systems

Writing was invented first in Mesopotamia, and the idea probably spread from there to Elam, other parts of the Near East, and Egypt. In the Sumerian story

Enmerkar and the Lord of Aratta, King Enmerkar of Uruk claimed the invention (although in reality it had developed over a period of time half a millennium earlier). Not surprisingly, the newly invented letter was a puzzle to the king of Aratta: "The lord of Aratta looked at the tablet. The transmitted message was just nails . . ." (Electronic Text Corpus of Sumerian Literature "Enmerkar and the Lord of Aratta," ca. lines 538–539).

Antecedents. Recent work, particularly by Denise Schmandt-Besserat, suggests that the Mesopotamian script, the world's first writing system, had its roots in a simple recording mechanism widely used across the Near East from the eighth millennium onward, using clay tokens as counters. By the fourth millennium a regular system existed in which a considerable number of different shapes consistently stood for particular things: a tetrahedron for a measure of grain, a sphere for a larger quantity of grain, a disc with a cross on it for a sheep, and so on. While some, generally abstract, shapes had great antiquity, others were devised in the fourth millennium to deal with the increasing complexity of accounting and often clearly depicted the thing that they stood for: a handled jar for sheep's milk, for instance.

Many tokens were pierced and were originally threaded on a string attached to a bulla (a solid lump of clay bearing stamped seal impressions) or enclosed in a hollow ball of clay, again with seal impressions (also often referred to as a bulla but more properly called an envelope). Once sealed inside an envelope, the tokens representing a transaction were safe from tampering. On the other hand, they were also invisible, so it was impossible to ascertain the envelope's contents without breaking it open. To get around this problem, a copy of the contents might be impressed on the outside.

At some point it occurred to people that the record on the outside of the envelope rendered its contents superfluous: The same information could more simply be recorded as pictures of the tokens on a piece of clay, without the tokens themselves—and thus the written clay tablet was invented, around 3300 B.C.E. in Uruk in Sumer.

The beginning of writing was probably more complicated than this in reality. Clay tablets bearing signs interpreted as numbers, and sometimes also a seal impression, are known from fourth-millennium sites across a broad area, including Nineveh in the north, Tell Brak and Habuba Kabira in the northwest, and Susa, Choga Mish, and Godin Tepe in western Iran as well as Uruk, and two tablets from Tell Brak bear both a circle, interpreted as the sign for ten, and a picture of an animal (one a goat, the other a sheep). The initial stages of the development of writing, therefore, probably took place over a wide area. Nevertheless, it was probably in Sumer that the value and potential of written recording was appreciated and that improvements and extensions of the idea were very rapidly developed. Certainly it is evidence from Uruk, where more than 5,000 tablets of Late Uruk date have been found, that allows the story of early writing to be followed. By around 3000 B.C.E. not only Uruk but also Jemdet Nasr, Eshnunna, and Uqair were providing evidence; and in the Iranian plateau at the same time, a somewhat different form of writing, proto-Elamite, was also developing, as evidenced at Susa and Iranian sites as far east as Shahr-i Sokhta. Knowledge of subsequent development depends on the rather patchy finds of early texts, including two substantial archives from Shuruppak and Abu Salabikh.

From Pictures to Script.   The Late Uruk and Jemdet Nasr–period tablets were generally accounts, listing quantities of particular commodities, although around 15 percent were lexical texts (word lists). Each item, usually a number and some other information, was arranged in a separate box drawn on the surface of the tablet, often with the total for the tablet given on the reverse. Many of the signs used at first closely matched the tokens and their representations on the outside of clay envelopes, and many other new pictorial signs were also used. But during the ED period the limitations of pictorial representation stimulated the development of less straightforward signs, to stand for verbs, for example. A sign in the form of a human head, standing for "head," for instance, was combined with the sign for bread to form the verb "to eat." A number of related meanings could be signified by a single sign: A triangle of three semicircles represented not only "mountain" but also "foreign land," since the mountains of the Zagros were Sumer's nearest neighbor, and "captive" or "slave," because this region held Sumer's closest enemies, too. Other things difficult to depict could be represented by an attribute: a star to stand for a deity, for example.

Up to this point the signs had been used as logograms: representations of words. Logographic signs (like internationally recognized traffic signs or chemical hazard warnings today, for example) are read with the same meaning but different sound values by the speakers of different languages. Another step forward in the development of the script, therefore, (attested in ED I-II tablets from Ur) was the use of a sign to represent a sound instead of an idea. This made it possible to extend meaning by punning (the rebus principle): Thus the sign for *dug* "pot" was also used to represent *dug* "good" and *dug* "to say." Some sounds were represented by a number of different signs (there were fourteen different signs for *gu,* for example), and some signs were used with several different meanings and therefore several different sound values (polyphony), for example the sign for mouth (KA) could be read as *ka* (mouth), *gu* (shouting), *zu* (tooth), *du* (to speak), and *inim* (word). To reduce confusion, a determinative was often added to words: a sign that indicated what category the word belonged to, which was not itself read. Such categories included deity (represented by a star), animal, man, woman, place-name, stone, river, and so on. Through the earlier centuries of the third millennium, signs came increasingly to represent syllabic sounds rather than words, enabling grammatical elements and syntax, previously supplied by the reader from the context, now actually to be represented. By later ED III, the script was able faithfully to transcribe words and sentences as they would be spoken, text was written in the word order of the spoken language, and there was a broad range of written material, including literary works.

Beyond Sumerian.   The cuneiform script had been devised to render Sumerian, an agglutinative language that used monosyllabic roots and affixes: It was therefore easy to string together signs representing segments of words. Akkadian, also spoken in southern Mesopotamia, was very differently structured, using roots made up of three consonants, with grammatical elements indicated by variations in their combination with vowels: The devices employed to write Sumerian words did not work well in Akkadian. From around 2600 B.C.E., adaptation of the script to write Akkadian, therefore, further encouraged phonetic rather than logographic sign use and completed the development of a complete writing system, which became largely syllabic, although logograms were never completely discarded. Individual signs could be used in any of three ways, as syllabic signs conveying sound, as logograms conveying meaning (and therefore read as different sounds in different languages), and as determinatives, aiding the understanding of the text without contributing any sounds: Only experience and context could tell the scribe how to interpret each sign.

The script came into widespread use in southern Mesopotamia during the earlier third millennium and spread to Assyria and the northwest where it was used at Ebla to write Sumerian and Eblaite in ED III. Assyria and Babylonia developed their own, quite similar, versions of the script. The script was modified to write the Hurrian, Urartian, and Hittite languages, and by the mid-second millennium was in use even in Egypt for international correspondence. Cuneiform was introduced into Elam where the Proto-Elamite script had fallen into disuse. Most texts in Elam were written in the Sumerian or Babylonian languages until the late second millennium when Elamite began to be used; this continued into the Persian period when a syllabic cuneiform script was also devised to write Old Persian.

Tablets and Writing.   The signs were originally pictographic, but it was difficult and slow drawing curved lines, and so signs began to be written in a series of wedge-shaped straight lines of various thicknesses and lengths. By ED II the signs became increasingly stylized and soon bore little resemblance to their original form. They also became fewer in number and standardized, the same signs being used in widely separated cities. Although each sign now needed a larger number of impressions, these were impressed in a restricted range of directions, making them faster to write than before.

At first the signs were written randomly within boxes arranged in columns (see photo p. 66) going from top to bottom and from right to left. At some time, possibly as early as 2900 B.C.E. but more probably toward the end of ED III, the tablets were rotated ninety degrees to the left, perhaps making it easier for the scribe to hold the tablet and write: The direction of writing now ran in horizontal lines from left to right, starting at the top. The wedge strokes were now almost always impressed with the head either at the top (vertical strokes) or on the left side (horizontal strokes). The stylus was also used to mark lines on the tablet, sometimes dividing larger texts into columns.

Tablets were made of specially prepared clay, presumably kept soft by being moistened during the writing process, although a loss of clarity in the later part of some longer texts shows that the writing surface had become drier as

An Assyrian clay tablet (above) and a tablet encased in a clay envelope (below). (Library of Congress)

the task of writing proceeded. Clay used for practice work in schools or as "scrap paper" during tasks could be returned to the general clay store for reuse, but if left to dry in the sun a tablet would become hard and durable. Tablets intended as a permanent and immutable record, however, (including literary and other works kept in libraries) were often fired.

From late in the ED III period some tablets began to be enclosed in envelopes, made of a thin skin of clay. This gave added protection to a tablet that had to be carried over a distance or kept as a record. The text of the tablet could be repeated on the envelope, as it often was for legal documents, along with the witnesses' seals. Envelopes could also be used to keep the contents of the document secret, for example in private or sensitive correspondence. In this case, the envelope would probably be marked only with a seal and the name of the person to whom the letter was addressed. This played a pivotal role in the legendary early career of Sargon of Akkad. His master, King Ur-Zababa, sent Sargon to Lugalzagesi of Uruk with a letter "about murdering Sargon." However, "In those days, although writing words on tablets existed, putting tablets into envelopes did not yet exist" (Electronic Text Corpus of Sumerian Literature, "The Sargon Legend," lines 53–54), so Sargon read the text and saved himself.

Media. Although most surviving Mesopotamian written material is on clay, other media were also used. By ED II legal documents such as records of land and house sales were cut into stone or inscribed on clay wrapped around pegs driven into the wall of the house. Writing was widely used on stone, including royal votive statues and vessels, land grants such as Kassite kudurrus, Assyrian reliefs, and stelae such as Hammurabi's famous law code and Assyrian triumphal obelisks (see photos pp. 80, 99, 213, 246). Seals, made generally of stone, were very common. Objects of metal, glass, pottery, and ivory were also sometimes inscribed, and bricks might bear stamped inscriptions.

The remains of several books were found at Kalhu, dated to the seventh century: These each consisted of a set of hinged rectangular tablets of walnut wood or ivory that had originally contained a writing surface made of wax mixed with orpiment. The ivory title page of one showed that it had been a copy of the astronomical text *Enuma Anu Enlil.* Written references show that these writing tablets were extensively used. Papyrus and parchment were employed as writing media and ostraca for ephemeral writing in the Levant and Egypt; an ostracon with Aramaic writing was found at Assur, and reliefs show a flexible writing surface, parchment or papyrus, in use by Assyrian scribes. Environmental conditions mean that these have not survived in West Asia (although their clay labels often have).

The Alphabet. From around 1700 B.C.E. in Sinai and the Levant a script (Proto-Sinaic / Proto-Canaanite) was developed based on Egyptian uniconsonantal hieroglyphs. Each sign was given a single consonantal value, the initial sound of the word represented by the sign in the Canaanite West Semitic language (the acrophonic principle): Thus, for example, the Egyptian hieroglyph for a snake, a sinuous line with the Egyptian sound value "dj," was read as

One of the earliest Proto-Canaanite inscriptions, from Gezer. It is believed that the Proto-Canaanite script was the precursor of the alphabet. (Zev Radovan/Land of the Bible Picture Archive)

"nahashu" in the Canaanite language and therefore had the sound value "n." The structure of Semitic languages made the representation of vowels seem unnecessary (although ways of representing them were later developed in the Near East): The original consonant-only alphabet became established in the Levant where it was ancestral to the Phoenician, Hebrew, and Aramaic scripts; the latter emerged around 1000 B.C.E. The Levantine alphabet spread widely to the east and south: The early script provided the basis for the southern Arabian script and its descendants in Ethiopia, and Aramaic was the ancestor not only of most of the alphabetic scripts of the Near East, including Arabic, but also of the early Indian script, Kharoshthi. The syllabic Brahmi script of South Asia, from which the later Indian scripts descend, also derives from a Semitic alphabetic script.

Around the fourteenth century another alphabetic script, this time using cuneiform signs, was devised in Ugarit, probably inspired by the Proto-Sinaic / Proto-Canaanite script. It survived until the destruction of Ugarit around 1200 B.C.E. but did not find wide acceptance.

The alphabet was a convenient tool, because it could be used to render the sounds of any language with relative faithfulness, and in this respect was much more flexible than the cuneiform script; it was also easier to write, using ink on papyrus, parchment, or ostraca (potsherds). A number of Assyrian reliefs show a pair of scribes, taking notes on the events of war or the gathering of booty afterward: One writes with a stylus on clay or writing tablets, the other with a pen on papyrus or parchment. Opinions are divided on what the latter is doing: writing a parallel record in Aramaic or making on-the-spot sketches for the relief illustrations of the campaign? Many Assyrian cuneiform texts have marginal notes in Aramaic, probably to identify the content of tablets for filing clerks who could only read Aramaic.

Seals. Stamp seals had been used since the late fifth millennium to mark ownership of property. The strings of tokens were generally fastened with a bulla bearing the stamped impressions of a seal, and envelopes containing tokens also generally bore seal impressions. The seal had a unique design representing the individual or institution responsible for the record, authenticating it and making it proof against tampering. The design was cut into the surface of a small square or rectangular seal, which was stamped into the wet clay.

The surface of stamp seals provided a limited area for the design, and during the Uruk period they gave way to the more practical cylinder seal. The design was carved around this and was rolled across the wet clay, producing an impression that could cover any surface area with no loss of clarity: It was far better suited for use on the administrative clay balls holding tokens and on the tablets that succeeded them. The large area of a cylinder seal gave scope for the construction of complex designs, often small scenes featuring animals or people and gods (see photos pp. 63, 90, 92, 208). To the design was often added a written inscription, identifying the owner by name and giving other information such as the name of the ruler of the time, the owner's occupation and parentage, and the name of the deity or master he or she served. In the first millennium, however, stamp seals were revived though cylinder seals also continued in use.

Seals were impressed into the clay sealing jars, on ropes "locking" doors, and on the fastenings of packages. Personal names began to be engraved on seals in the ED II period. From the Akkadian period onward, seals were used by officials to show that they had witnessed legal documents and to authorize transactions. In later times individuals could use a seal to "sign" documents, such as loan or sale deeds: Those without a personal seal could affix their mark by pressing a fingernail or the hem of their garment into the wet clay.

The History of Decipherment. By the third century C.E. cuneiform scripts had gone out of use and were subsequently forgotten. From the seventeenth century onward, when Western explorers and antiquaries began to take an interest in Persia and the Near East, a number of cuneiform inscriptions were copied and pored over by scholars interested in deciphering them. Achaemenid inscriptions from Persepolis and Behistun in Persia, written in cuneiform scripts in three different languages (Old Persian, Elamite, and

Babylonian) were particularly useful. Attempts at decipherment of the Old Persian inscriptions, by Georg Friedrich Grotefend and others, focused on the known royal titles "Great King, King of Kings" and the personal names of the monarchs, couched in the form "X, son of Y." Success was achieved by the separate efforts of Eugene Burnouf, Christian Lassen, a German professor, Edward Hincks, an Irish clergyman, and Henry Creswicke Rawlinson, a British army officer, scholar, and diplomat. The script was found to be syllabic.

Scholars, particularly Hincks, Edwin Norris, librarian and secretary of the Royal Asiatic Society, and Rawlinson, then began work on deciphering the Elamite and Late Babylonian scripts, using the Old Persian texts as a bilingual and the proper names and titles as the starting point. Related material was available in the form of the cuneiform tablets and monumental inscriptions that were being recovered from excavations in the Assyrian cities of Nineveh, Nimrud, and Khorsabad, written in the allied Assyrian language and script. Different ways of spelling the same formulaic expressions were an important key to the sound values of the cuneiform signs. Slowly the scholars were able to read the different signs, recognizing that some could be used with more than one pronunciation, and they identified other features, such as determinatives and grammatical elements. The language was unknown to them, but they had a knowledge of other Semitic languages akin to Akkadian and were therefore able eventually to work out the meaning of the texts. The moment of triumph came in 1855 when four scholars, Hincks, Rawlinson, Fox Talbot, and Julius Oppert, independently translated a newly discovered text of Tiglath-Pileser I. The strong similarities among their translations proved convincingly that the code of Akkadian cuneiform had been cracked.

Once Akkadian texts could be read, the numerous Sumerian-Akkadian word lists (in effect dictionaries) revealed a new language, quite unlike Akkadian or any Semitic language or, indeed, any known language. For a while it was thought that it was not a language at all but a sacred code used by Mesopotamian priests. Its grammatical analysis by Paul Haupt in the 1870s, however, demonstrated that it was a fully developed language, and the Sumerian texts discovered in the 1880s at Lagash, which dealt with a great range of mundane as well as sacred matters, supported this, leading to its acceptance. The dictionaries often included not only Akkadian translations of Sumerian words, but often also a pronunciation guide. But whereas the Akkadian use of the script was largely phonetic, in Sumerian signs were often used logographically and there were many homophones—and in some cases even today the sound value associated with particular signs in certain contexts is unknown.

A more recent decipherment was of the Ugaritic script discovered in 1929. Its location suggested that it rendered a Semitic language, and the number of its signs implied that it was an alphabetic script. The decipherers used words that could be guessed from their context to build up a set of probable sound values for the various signs, and the script had been cracked by 1933. Not all scripts have been successfully deciphered, however. The Proto-Elamite script still defies attempts to decipher it, as does the script of the more distant land of

Meluhha. Elamite, although it can be transliterated because it is written in cuneiform, is still incompletely understood. This is also true of Urartian.

LITERATURE

It was not until around 2500 B.C.E. that the Mesopotamian script came fully to represent the sounds of speech and could be read without the need to interpret signs and construct meaning. Nevertheless already by this stage the script was being used to write a wide range of different things: not just accounts, personal names, and titles, but also dedicatory inscriptions, word lists, records of military achievements, royal inscriptions and other historical material, legal documents, and works of literature, such as proverbs and epic poems.

Survival

Most of the earliest written tablets come from Uruk, where out-of-date records had been discarded and incorporated as rubble into the constantly restructured buildings of the Eanna precinct. It became common for temples and palaces to store archives of current records during their period of relevance, usually no more than three generations—although some documents were kept for as many as two hundred years—and to discard or destroy them when they ceased to be of interest. Many of the surviving archives, therefore, come from buildings or settlements that were destroyed by fire: In the conflagration, the clay tablets became baked, turning them into permanent and extremely durable documents. This is true, for example, of the tablets from Ebla, Kanesh, and Mari. The huge volume of material that has resulted from these rare destructions gives some indication of the vast quantity of written material that was around in Mesopotamian times. Clay tablets, baked and unbaked, are known from almost every site investigated, and some, such as Ur, Nippur, and Abu Salabikh, have yielded substantial collections.

Archives and Libraries

Archives were often stored in a dedicated room or set of rooms, secured by a seal on the rope fastening the door, although smaller archives might be kept within ordinary rooms in houses. Tablets might be arranged side-by-side in rows on wooden shelves, or organized in containers, such as baskets, wooden boxes, or pottery jars, carefully labeled with a clay tag describing the contents. In the first-millennium Shamash temple at Sippar, the tablets were filed in pigeonholes of plastered brick built along the walls of the archive room. Copious official archives contained material such as tax records, official correspondence, records of materials issued and finished goods received, and legal records. There were also private libraries, often the property of professional people such as doctors, singers, and astronomers, who had copies of compendia of vocational information, such as the exorcists' collection *Enuma Anu Enlil.* Literate individuals might also own literary works, and such volumes were also included in temple and palace collections. The library of the Shamash temple at Sippar was largely made up of literary works, including religious and astronomical texts, royal inscriptions, and classic compositions such as *Enuma elish.* Examples of libraries are known from Kalhu, Nippur, Ur, and other cities. The finest and most comprehensive was the library assembled by the last Assyrian king, Ashurbanipal, who attempted to collect copies of every work extant at the time, around 1,500 volumes: Part of this library, preserved by the destruction of Nineveh, has been recovered by archaeologists. A smaller royal library was collected by Tiglath-Pileser I at Assur. Both kings seem to have derived most of their texts from sources where there was a long tradition of scholarship. Texts often had a colophon at the end, giving such information as the title of the work or a summary of its contents, the date, details of the source of the original from which it was copied, the name of the author, or other pertinent data; those on Ashurbanipal's volumes also stated that they were the property of the king and often cursed anyone who might steal them. If the text was long and ran over more than one tablet, the colophon would say so and give the first line of the next tablet in the series.

Education and Literacy

Much early material has survived in later copies because the Babylonian education system involved learning by copying and tradition was strongly respected. Although Sumerian died out as a spoken language, many of the Sumerian literary works of the third millennium were preserved in later copies. Ashurbanipal boasted of being able himself to read texts written before the Flood. The Ur III king Shulgi was also proud of his own scholarship; he took a keen interest in education, establishing academies in Ur and Nippur.

Scribes were an important part of the labor force, because their services were required in many activities: making records of goods coming into and going out of temples, palaces, merchant houses, and private establishments; keeping track of personnel; undertaking land surveys and field records; writing accounts of royal achievements; recording wills and legal judgments; committing hymns and oral literature to writing; composing royal inscriptions; and so on. They were also employed to write letters, wills, deeds of sale, and other documents for people who could not themselves read, who made up the majority of the population. The epilogue to Hammurabi's law code implies that the text was publicly read out, and it may have been a common practice for royal inscriptions to be read aloud to the citizens.

The proportion of the population that was literate varied with place and time, probably reaching its peak in the OB period and generally being greater in Babylonia than in the north. In the Assyrian Empire literacy was probably largely confined to scribes attached to the temple or palace. There were also probably differences in the degree of literacy—that required by a merchant to keep accounts and write letters being far less than the high level of education achieved by scholars. It has been suggested that literacy in cuneiform was probably never high since the script was complex and required a lengthy education to master, and that the advent of the alphabet increased literacy since it was easier to learn, although this has not been demonstrated. Some kings were literate, others not; in merchant houses it might be expedient for all family members to be literate; exorcists, doctors, and other specialists also needed to be able to read and write. The Ur III bureaucracy required many literate officials, but in some later regimes, literacy was confined to the relatively limited number of scribes. Records at Mari refer to the employment of female as well as male scribes, and a number of texts mention literate female slaves.

History of Literature

Because what we have of Sumerian and Akkadian literature depends on accidents of preservation and discovery the record is very patchy, with some periods producing a wealth of material and others very little; and the kinds of material preserved vary, giving an unbalanced picture of development.

From Uruk to the Old Babylonian Period.   The earliest written materials, from the late Uruk and Jemdet Nasr periods, were economic and administrative documents, along with some lexical texts. ED I-II texts are few but substantial archives were recovered from early ED III Shuruppak and Abu Salabikh, and from Ebla in the northwest, and a small number from other cities, scattered from Uruk and Ur in the south to Mari in the central Euphrates. The script had not yet reached the stage where the writing mirrored speech, so these early texts are hard to understand, but they included incantations to ward off illness, hymns, and poems, including one about Lugalbanda and others on mythological subjects. Most of the texts were in Sumerian, but one hymn was probably in early Akkadian, and some of the Ebla archive texts were in Eblaite. Kings were beginning to dedicate inscribed vessels in the temples and set up inscribed stelae. Already, therefore, the repertoire of written materials included administrative, lexical, historical, religious, and mythological texts.

By the time of the Akkadian Empire, the script was closely reproducing the spoken word, but unfortunately few literary texts are known from this period. From the Ur III Empire, as well as a huge volume of administrative documents, recording economic and personnel matters in meticulous detail, there are a few poems and hymns, and other compositions of this period survive as later copies. These include epic texts, some looking back to the Akkadian dynasty, such as the *Curse of Agade*, others glorifying the Uruk dynasty of Gilgamesh to whom the Ur III kings claimed to be successors.

The bulk of Sumerian texts, composed from late ED onward, survive as copies made in the OB period, the peak of Mesopotamian literary creativity, found particularly in private houses in Nippur and Ur. These included school exercises in mathematics and writing, accounts of school life, hymns and lamentations, mythological and historical poems, law codes, disputation poems, love songs and lullabies, proverbs and riddles, formal letters, and incantations.

The contemporary cities of northern Babylonia have also yielded literary materials in Sumerian, particularly hymns, some of them in *emesal*. Sumerian was by now a dead language, used only by scholars, and contemporary texts were written in Akkadian. A large number of letters and records, dealing with economic and administrative but also personal matters, survive from the burned ruins of the Assyrian trading station at Kanesh in Anatolia and the palace of Mari on the central Euphrates.

From the Mid-Second Millennium Onward. A substantial gap in the literary record occurred after the fall of Hammurabi's dynasty. The destruction of the Hurrian town of Nuzi in the fourteenth century preserved a large number of public and private records, including legal documents, letters, and administrative records. Many letters sent by kings and officials to the pharaoh are preserved in the Egyptian city of Akhetaten (Amarna), and the archives of many Near Eastern cities and states included copies of Akkadian literary works, such as epic, mythological, and semihistorical poems, supplementing those recovered from Mesopotamia itself. A growing body of literature, composed now in Akkadian instead of Sumerian, accumulated through the later second and first millennia. These included new versions of earlier stories, such as *Ishtar in the Netherworld*, and new stories, such as *Enuma elish* and *The Story of Erra*, as well as new compositions in old and new genres of religious literature and other branches of literary composition such as disputations, fables, and love poems, and the time-honored Sumerian lexical texts, now translated and greatly expanded and developed. Epic poems about historical monarchs began to appear, including fictive "autobiographies." On the practical side, there was a growing body of "scientific" literature: compilations of omen and divination observations, treatments for illnesses, recipes and other treatises, as well as mathematical tables and exercises.

Toward the end of the second millennium and into the first, extant Sumerian literature was collected and the texts standardized in editions with Akkadian translations, generally alternating line-by-line with the Sumerian version. These included lexical texts, hymns and other religious compositions, and a few epic and mythological poems. Considerable effort was made by scholars to produce definitive versions of classic texts by studying and collating manuscripts from different sources. After the fall of Mesopotamia to the Persians, such scholarly work continued for many centuries: A few Sumerian incantations, with Greek phonetic transcriptions, survive from the first and perhaps second century C.E.

Records and Other Nonliterary Texts

The first written texts were economic and administrative records of the receipt and disbursement by the temple of various commodities, such as grain, textiles, and oil. Later texts from temples and palaces were similarly concerned with goods and materials coming into the establishment as taxes, tribute, gifts, the produce of estates, and the proceeds of trade and investment, and being issued from them in rations and wages or as raw materials and goods for trading, manufacture, and construction. Records were also required to manage and monitor the deployment of personnel.

Writing was used in a number of other nonliterary contexts: on seals, giving some details of the owner, and on votive offerings giving some information about who presented them and to which deity, although royal gifts bore increasingly long dedicatory texts. From the Akkadian period onward bricks incorporated into public buildings were often stamped with the name of the king who had commissioned them and information about the structure such as the names of the temple, the deity to whom it was dedicated, and the city in which it was built. Votive clay nails inscribed with the name of the king and a dedication or a longer text were also incorporated into temples. Early Sumerian texts already known before 2500 B.C.E. included magical charms to ward off disease. Often such spells would be written on amulets for individuals to wear.

Law Codes and Legal Documents.   Tablets recording details of legal matters included wills, adoption documents, marriage contracts, records of loans, rental documents, and house and land-sale deeds. Beginning with Uru-inimgina of Lagash in the twenty-fourth century B.C.E., there were also occasional texts that now go by the name of law codes, in which some rules of conduct and appropriate punishments for crime were laid down by the king as a policy statement, although these were probably rarely followed in ordinary legal rulings. Many records of legal proceedings and the results of court cases are among the surviving documents. While most legal documents were written on clay, records of land transfers could be inscribed in stone, such as the kudurrus of the Kassite period. Stone versions of Hammurabi's law code were set up in Babylon and Sippar, and copies on clay tablets were distributed to other cities.

Legal documents also included international agreements, treaties, tribute lists, and other texts devoted to relations between states. Tablets recovered from Ezida, the temple of Nabu, at Kalhu included a number of Vassal Treaties, in which the rulers of nine subject states swore to uphold the succession of Ashurbanipal to the throne of his father, Esarhaddon—a measure that the latter took to avoid the kind of conflict he had suffered on his own accession.

Letters.   Letters exchanged between Ibbi-Sin, the last Ur III king, and the governor of Isin, Ishbi-Erra, survived as OB school texts. Many thousands of letters have been found in palaces and other archives, dealing with official matters such as international relations or diplomatic gifts, or business concerns such as prices and commodities, but also events like the capture of a lion. The extensive Assyrian palace archives at Nineveh included letters on a wide range of subjects such as omens, military and diplomatic matters, and domestic concerns. Some of the most interesting are personal letters, preserved, for example, in the palaces at Mari and Karana and in the Old Assyrian trading station of Kanesh: They show individuals worrying about their health and personal relationships, sending each other gifts, or complaining about poor-quality slaves. Queen Iltani of Karana received a letter from her sister in Assur reporting her failure to obtain a lapis lazuli necklace that Iltani desired; another sister wrote asking for new slaves and sent some wool and a container of shrimps as a sweetener with her request. Zimri-Lim of Mari and his wife,

Shibtu, exchanged many letters while he was absent, on business matters and private concerns: from the birth of twins to Shibtu's request that Zimri-Lim wear the coat and tunic she had made him. An earlier Mari ruler, the ne'er-do-well Yasmah-Addu, received many admonitory letters from his father, Shamshi-Adad, and those from his "perfect" brother, Ishme-Dagan, were scarcely more conciliatory.

Word Lists and Other Scribal Exercises

Many early texts survive as OB teaching materials from the scribal quarter of Nippur and from private houses in Ur. Once the basic skills had been mastered, education proceeded mainly by copying, learning, and applying model and traditional material in subjects such as law, the forms of diplomacy, and mathematics. A wealth of literary texts were also copied by the student.

By the OB period, although Sumerian had become a dead language, it was still an important part of the curriculum. The student therefore also had to copy and learn long lists of Sumerian words and their Akkadian equivalents; these were also important reference tools for working scribes. The first sign lists showing how to write and read individual signs come from the ED period and contained only Sumerian logograms and their pronunciation. Later versions also gave a translation of the Sumerian word: These are known in Eblaite, Akkadian, Hittite, Kassite, Hurrian, Ugaritic, and even Egyptian, and often also showed how to pronounce the Sumerian signs. One major list, which became the main "textbook" in the later second millennium, started in the early OB period as less than 1,000 lines of text but was added to over the years, eventually running to forty-four tablets and having around 14,400 entries. A concise version of this (*Ea A = naqu*) was also used: It had most of the same Sumerian single-cuneiform signs but gave only the main translation into Akkadian, whereas the complete version (*A a = naqu*—"A pronounced 'a' means complain") listed all known translations. Different forms of lexical lists existed, some dealing with etymology, some with themes, some with phonology, some giving synonyms; one gave standard Sumerian equivalents for *emesal* words and their Akkadian translation.

Thematic lists began in the late Uruk period and included the earliest version of what became known as the Standard Professions List. These lists were repeatedly copied, revised, and augmented over the following millennia. Those regularly used included the names of animals, trees, plants, gods, stars, wooden objects, pottery, food and drink, human kinship terms, and many others. The OB canonical version of these lists, *HAR-ra = hubullu*, covered twenty-four tablets and had around 10,000 entries. Originally these were only in Sumerian, but later they were also listed with Akkadian translations; finally, when many of the Akkadian words themselves had become unfamiliar, another column provided an up-to-date explanation of their meaning.

On a lighter level, a number of texts given to schoolchildren to copy were essays on their own condition: accounts of the ups and downs of a pupil's school day, or recitations of the scholarly accomplishments of a schoolboy.

Hymns and Other Religious Literature

A substantial part of Sumerian literature is made up of hymns, addressed to individual gods and to their temples. The earliest surviving hymns (and also the earliest literary work whose author is known) were composed by Enheduanna, daughter of Sargon of Akkad and entu-priestess of Nanna at Ur, who also edited a collection of hymns. In one Enheduanna paints a picture of the magnificence, power, awesomeness, and unpredictablility of the goddess Inanna, manipulating the great gods who dare not take a decision without her approval, controlling the lesser deities, ferocious in her wrath, raising the lowly and abasing the lofty. In another, *The Exaltation of Inana*, however, Enheduanna rages about her expulsion from the temple by Lugalane (leader of a revolt against Naram-Sin), exhorting the gods, Inanna, Nanna, Enlil, and An, to recognize Lugalane's impiety, turn their hearts toward her, and restore the status quo.

A number of Lamentations, poems dating mainly from the late third and early second millennia, were also concerned with the way the will of the gods was reflected in human destinies. They began by painting a picture of desolation in a city forsaken by the god, the people dead in the streets, the buildings torn down or in flames, the empty fields choked with weeds, and foreign troops spreading carnage. Then the spirit of the poem lightened: The gods had relented, and the city and the land were being put to rights. The context of these poems was probably the restoration of temples and other sacred buildings after their destruction in warfare. The fate of the city was bound up with the will of the gods: Its fall reflected their displeasure, its restoration the return of their favor. Later compositions in this genre, not related to specific cities, became part of the liturgy, performed on certain days in the cultic calendar. Laments were also composed to mark the death of Dumuzi or the passing of kings, the latter perhaps modeled on the Sumerian poem lamenting the death of Gilgamesh.

Individual illness and misfortune were also seen as coming from the gods as punishment for known or unwitting faults. Medical treatment by the exorcist or the doctor involved the recitation of incantations and formulaic prayers, emphasizing the sufferer's piety, expressing contrition for any offense they might, knowingly or unknowingly, have committed, praising the gods, and begging for the punishment to be lifted. Sumerian and Akkadian literature contains many such prayers. These might also be addressed to the gods in the form of letters, written by a scribe and laid before the god's image.

In the later second millennium, scholars developed the philosophical train of thought of these prayers, exploring the inscrutability of the divine mind in a number of poems, including *Ludlul* (see chapter 8) and the *Babylonian Theodicy*. These are the major works in what is known as "Wisdom Literature," a genre of reflective writing that also includes collections of Sumerian proverbs, riddles, and fables, as well as disputations in which various materials, such as Copper and Silver, tools, plants, such as Datepalm and Tamarisk, animals, and other features of the natural world, such as Winter and Summer, debated their relative importance, putting forward their own merits and disparaging their rival. One collection of proverbs and wise advice, the *Instructions of Shuruppak,* couched in the form of a father's instructions to his son, was among the texts known from ED Shuruppak and Abu Salabikh.

Myths and Epics

The actions of the gods were explored further in a wealth of mythological poetry, retelling stories probably familiar to every Mesopotamian in oral form. Some dealt with how the world was created, ordered, and peopled (see chapter 8). These included *Enuma elish,* the great Babylonian poem composed in the late second millennium that tells how Marduk saved the gods from destruction and thereafter set the world in order and created humanity. In an earlier Sumerian poem, *Enki and the World Order,* it is Enki who allots to every part of the world its characteristics and to each deity his or her sphere of influence.

Other poems tell the story of individual deities. Many revolve around the seductive, capricious, and at times terrifying and merciless figure of Inanna: the adolescent courted by her future husband in a pastoral idyll, the calculating young goddess determined to win the benefits of civilization for her own city, the woman scorned exacting her vengeance, the greedy goddess demanding additional powers from Enki, the enthusiastic patronness of sexual indulgence in all forms, the magnificent tutelary deity of the glorious new city of Agade.

Gilgamesh. The deeds of heroic mortals were also the subject of many poems, and in these, too, the gods often make an appearance. The earliest surviving poem, dated before 2500 B.C.E., concerns the adventures of king Lugalbanda of Uruk. The stories of Lugalbanda's son Gilgamesh were particular favorites. Five Sumerian poems written down in the Ur III period recount episodes of Gilgamesh's heroic life: his defense of Uruk against Agga of Kish, his adventures with Enkidu, and his death. In the OB period these and other stories about Gilgamesh were collected and woven into a single epic, *Shutur eli sharri* "Surpassing all other kings," written in Babylonian Akkadian: The historical episode with Agga is dropped, and Gilgamesh's relationship with his friend Enkidu becomes the central narrative theme, from their initial conflict through their adventures together in perfect brotherhood to Enkidu's heartbreaking end and Gilgamesh's quest for immortality. This form was followed in the polished "Standard Version," *Sha naqba imuru* "He who saw the Deep," in eleven tablets revised and extended by an exorcist called Sin-liqe-unninni in the late second millennium. Copies have been recovered from Ashurbanipal's library and from places as far away as the Hittite capital Hattusas (Boghazkhoy), and clearly the story was popular with a wide audience for a long time.

When the epic opens, Gilgamesh is a very young man who is exasperating his citizens by exercising *doit de seigneur* with all the brides and exhausting the young men in competitive sport. The gods take a hand, creating the wild man Enkidu, who lives among the wild beasts. He is tamed and introduced to the ways of civilized urban life by a prostitute, and is encouraged to challenge

A tablet bearing part of the text of the Babylonian version of the Gilgamesh epic. (Zev Radovan/Land of the Bible Picture Archive)

Gilgamesh to a trial of strength. The two heroes are evenly matched, and after an epic bout of wrestling they become inseparable friends. To exercise their prowess Gilgamesh proposes an expedition to distant Cedar Mountain, where they slay the demon Humbaba (Huwawa).

Inanna (Ishtar) is overcome with desire for the glorious hero that Gilgamesh has become, but Gilgamesh scornfully rejects her advances, reminding her of her fickle treatment of former lovers. Inanna is furious; she approaches her father, An, and by shameless blackmail forces him to release the Bull of Heaven, which runs amok, destroying the lands of Uruk and killing hundreds of people. Gilgamesh and Enkidu in their pride slaughter the Bull and offer further insults to Inanna. Such impiety is too much for the gods: Enkidu must die

A broken tablet from Megiddo in the Levant, part of the Babylonian Epic of Gilgamesh. The findspots of copies of this text attest its widespread popularity in the ancient Near East. (Zev Radovan/Land of the Bible Picture Archive)

in punishment, which he does, miserably of a fever in his bed, a degrading death for a hero.

Gilgamesh goes mad with grief and, on reflection, with fear of his own death. He leaves Uruk in a vain quest for immortality, traveling through strange desert lands and mountains until he reaches the ocean and crosses to the island of Ut-napishtim, the immortal survivor of the Flood. Ut-napishtim criticizes Gilgamesh's foolish and irresponsible behavior and finally makes him aware of his limitations by challenging him not to sleep for seven days. Unsuccessful in this lesser feat, Gilgamesh accepts that he cannot conquer death and eventually returns to Uruk to achieve immortality by his public works, wisdom, and good governance.

Sargon and Naram-Sin.   Legends also accumulated around historical figures. Stories probably dating from the OB period recount the obscure birth of Sargon, son of a priestess and an unknown man from the mountains, who was cast adrift on the river in a basket and rescued by a palace gardener in Kish. Growing into a youth personally favored by Inanna, he becomes the king's cupbearer. The old sick king soon conceives a secret hatred for the golden youth and attempts to kill him by various means, but Inanna's advice saves Sargon every time. Eventually the king of Kish is deposed and Sargon's rise to power begins.

Sargon is the great heroic king, favored by the gods, and founder of the first empire in Babylonia: All that was considered good about this empire was being attached to him by the OB period and was being embellished by legend. In another poem, "King of Battle," he goes against the advice of his cautious advisers to mount an expedition, personally led by him, to rescue merchants in the Anatolian city of Burushkhanda. Here the heroic image of Sargon is polished up to support the activities of a later king, Shamshi-Adad.

In contrast, in the poem "The Curse of Agade," probably composed in the Ur III period, Sargon's grandson Naram-Sin is depicted as the antihero, sacrilegiously opposing the will of the gods. The Akkadian capital, Agade, is a glittering city in which Inanna establishes herself as patron. But something offends Enlil: He withdraws his favor, and the gods desert the city. Naram-Sin tries unsuccessfully for seven years to change Enlil's mind. In anger he launches a physical assault on Enlil's chief shrine in the holy city of Nippur, a deed that cannot go unpunished: Enlil causes the barbaric Guti to overrun and sack Agade.

Fragments of history are woven into these tales, but they are manipulated for the sake of the story and the moral it has to convey. The Guti did overrun parts of the south, but not for many years after Naram-Sin's reign. Naram-Sin was a pious monarch, whose offerings at Nippur are known and who was revered after his death. But he did proclaim himself to be divine, and it is perhaps this perceived impiety that in legend brought the eventual downfall of the dynasty.

Historical and Political Documents

Sifting the historical truth from a diverse range of sources is a task that has occupied many students of Mesopotamia's past. Literary compositions like *The Legend of Sargon* and *The Curse of Agade* are largely unhistorical although there may be fragments of historical information within them. More subtly, genuine contemporary historical records might also contain both truth and "spin," because they were often intended not only to record the achievements of rulers, individuals, or communities but also to present their actions in a favorable light to both human and divine audiences.

The first historical documents, known from the ED II-III period, were brief inscriptions on votive offerings and buildings, naming the royal donor. By the mid-third millennium, however, narrative texts were being written, explaining and justifying the king's actions and demonstrating that he was acting in accordance with divine will. Around 2400 B.C.E., Enmetena of Lagash gave an impassioned account of the long-running border dispute between Umma and Lagash. Some fifty years later Uru-inim-gina, also of Lagash, lauded his own efforts at reform and delivered a tirade against Lugalzagesi of Umma who had sacked Girsu.

The Akkadian kings produced rich propagandist inscriptions, describing their wide-ranging conquests and power and the prosperity of the land under their rule, with merchants coming to their city, Agade, from far across the sea. In contrast in the period following the fall of the Akkadian Empire, Gudea of Lagash was more concerned with recording his pious works. A two-cylinder poem describes Gudea's dream of Ningirsu's request that he construct a marvelous temple and his endeavors to bring together all the choice materials needed for the task: timbers from the Cedar Mountains, red stones (agate or carnelian) from Meluhha, gold, and silver. In their royal hymns the Ur III and later Babylonian kings were also more interested in proclaiming their efforts for the welfare of their people than their conquests. Many third-millennium inscribed monuments, stelae, and statues from the courtyard of the Ekur in Nippur were assiduously copied by OB scribes, complete with catalog details describing the monuments themselves.

In the north, kings such as Shamshi-Adad focused their inscriptions on their military achievements. Later Babylonian kings included fuller details of their conquests in their inscriptions but also celebrated praiseworthy aspects of their reigns, such as the construction of canals. Assyrian kings, from Adad-Nirari in the early thirteenth century, developed military inscriptions into longer first-person narratives of their achievements, those of Tiglath-Pileser I and of kings from the late eighth century onward being written because of their length on large clay prisms; stone stelae were also used in the ninth and eighth centuries. These records of conquests and triumphs were written with a dated section dealing with each campaign; later editions contracted the account of the king's earlier campaigns so as to make space for the most recent. Late in a long reign, the annals might omit some campaigns or run several together. These were written as dedicatory inscriptions to be placed in the foundations of buildings, a traditional practice. Royal texts were often written not for the human reader but for the deity to read and approve. The deeds of Assyrian kings were also celebrated in epic poems and in the inscriptions accompanying the forceful reliefs of the triumph of Assyrian might, carved on the palace walls to impress all who saw them. Kings boasted not only of military deeds but also of their feats of engineering, discovery, and magnificent construction.

Texts were also composed by scribes and scholars in imitation of earlier texts, drawing on and adapting earlier material for contemporary purposes.

The Sumerian King List was probably composed in the Ur III period to emphasize Ur's place in the divinely ordained scheme whereby from hoary antiquity a principal city was given rule over all the cities of Sumer and Akkad, an anachronistic fiction. One text, known now as the "Weidner Chronicle," was a piece of religio-political propaganda in the form of a letter to an OB king pointing out the disastrous fate of former kings who had failed to honor Marduk's temple in Babylon. Also composed by scribes following genuine earlier historic models was *Naru* literature (Akk. *stela*): spurious documents purporting to be copies of royal inscriptions that were produced by royal scribes for the purposes of propaganda, storytelling, or justifying current action or argument on the basis of falsified or misused ancient precedents.

TEXT REFERENCES

Alster, Bendt. 2000. "Epic Tales from Ancient Sumer: Enmerkar, Lugalbanda, and Other Cunning Heroes." Pp. 2315–2326 in *Civilizations of the Ancient Near East*. Edited by Jack M. Sasson. Peabody, MA: Hendrickson Publishers. (Reprint of 1995 edition. New York: Scribner.)

Bienkowski, Piotr. 2000. "Calendar" and "Law." Pp. 63 and 175–176, respectively, in *Dictionary of the Ancient Near East*. Edited by Piotr Bienkowski and Alan Millard. London: British Museum Press.

Bienkowski, Piotr, and Alan Millard, eds. 2000. *Dictionary of the Ancient Near East*. London: British Museum Press.

Bierbrier, M. L. 2004. "Hincks, Edward (1792–1866)." *Oxford Dictionary of National Biography*. Oxford: Oxford University Press. http://www.oxforddnb.com/view/article/13335 (cited November 21, 2004).

Biggs, Robert D. 2000a. "Medicine, Surgery, and Public Health in Ancient Mesopotamia." Pp. 1911–1924 in *Civilizations of the Ancient Near East*. Edited by Jack M. Sasson. Peabody, MA: Hendrickson Publishers. (Reprint of 1995 edition. New York: Scribner.)

———. 2000b. "Akkadian Literature: An Overview." Pp. 2293–2303 in *Civilizations of the Ancient Near East*. Edited by Jack M. Sasson. Peabody, MA: Hendrickson Publishers. (Reprint of 1995 edition. New York: Scribner.)

Black, Jeremy, and Alan Millard. 2000. "Hymns and Prayers." P. 151 in *Dictionary of the Ancient Near East*. Edited by Piotr Bienkowski and Alan Millard. London: British Museum Press.

Black, Jeremy, and W. J. Tait. 2000. "Archives and Libraries in the Ancient Near East." Pp. 2197–2209 in *Civilizations of the Ancient Near East*. Edited by Jack M. Sasson. Peabody, MA: Hendrickson Publishers. (Reprint of 1995 edition. New York: Scribner.)

Charpin, Dominique. 2000. "The History of Ancient Mesopotamia: An Overview." Pp. 807–830 in *Civilizations of the Ancient Near East*. Edited by Jack M. Sasson. Peabody, MA: Hendrickson Publishers. (Reprint of 1995 edition. New York: Scribner.)

Civil, Miguel. 1997. "Sumerian." Pp. 92–95 in *The Oxford Encyclopedia of Archaeology in the Near East*. Vol. 5. Edited by Eric M. Meyers. Oxford: Oxford University Press.

————. 2000. "Ancient Mesopotamian Lexicography." Pp. 2305–2314 in *Civilizations of the Ancient Near East.* Edited by Jack M. Sasson. Peabody, MA: Hendrickson Publishers. (Reprint of 1995 edition. New York: Scribner.)

Collins, Paul T. 2000. "Medicine." P. 193 in *Dictionary of the Ancient Near East.* Edited by Piotr Bienkowski and Alan Millard. London: British Museum Press.

Collon, Dominique. 1990. *Interpreting the Past. Near Eastern Seals.* London: British Museum Press.

Coulmas, Florian. 1999. *The Blackwell Encyclopedia of Writing Systems.* Oxford: Blackwell.

Crystal, David. 1987. *The Cambridge Encyclopedia of Language.* Cambridge: Cambridge University Press.

Dalby, Andrew. 1998. *A Dictionary of Languages. The Definitive Reference to More than 400 Languages.* London: Bloomsbury.

Dalley, Stephanie. 1984. *Mari and Karana. Two Old Babylonian Cities.* London: Longman.

————. 2000. *Myths from Mesopotamia.* Revised edition. Oxford: Oxford University Press.

Daniels, Peter T. 1997. "Writing and Writing Systems." Pp. 352–358 in *The Oxford Encyclopedia of Archaeology in the Near East.* Vol. 5. Edited by Eric M. Meyers. Oxford: Oxford University Press.

————. 2000. "The Decipherment of Ancient Near Eastern Scripts." Pp. 81–93 in *Civilizations of the Ancient Near East.* Edited by Jack M. Sasson. Peabody, MA: Hendrickson Publishers. (Reprint of 1995 edition. New York: Scribner.)

Davies, W. V. 1987. *Reading the Past. Egyptian Hieroglyphs.* London: British Museum.

Dean, Dennis R. 2004. "Smith, George (1840–1876)." *Oxford Dictionary of National Biography.* Oxford: Oxford University Press. http://www.oxforddnb.com/view/article/25806 (cited November 21, 2004).

Edzard, D. O. 2000. "The Sumerian Language." Pp. 2107–2116 in *Civilizations of the Ancient Near East.* Edited by Jack M. Sasson. Peabody, MA: Hendrickson Publishers. (Reprint of 1995 edition. New York: Scribner.)

Electronic Text Corpus of Sumerian Literature. "The Cursing of Agade." http://www-etcsl.orient.ox.ac.uk/ (cited January 30, 2002).

————. "Enmerkar and the Lord of Aratta." http://www-etcsl.orient.ox.ac.uk/ (cited January 30, 2002).

————. "The Exaltation of Inana." http://www-etcsl.orient.ox.ac.uk/ (cited January 30, 2002).

————. "A Hymn to Inana." http://www-etcsl.orient.ox.ac.uk/ (cited January 30, 2002).

————. "The Lament for Urim." http://www-etcsl.orient.ox.ac.uk/ (cited January 30, 2002).

————. "The Sargon Legend." http://www-etcsl.orient.ox.ac.uk/ (cited January 30, 2002).

Ferrier, R. W., and Stephanie Dalley. "Rawlinson, Sir Henry Creswicke, First Baronet (1810–1895)." *Oxford Dictionary of National Biography.* Oxford: Oxford University Press. http://www.oxforddnb.com/view/article/23190 (cited November 21, 2004).

Foster, Benjamin R. 1995. *From Distant Days. Myths, Tales and Poetry of Ancient Mesopotamia.* Bethesda, MD: CDL Press.

————. 1997. "Akkadians." Pp. 49–54 in *The Oxford Encyclopedia of Archaeology in the Near East.* Vol. 1. Edited by Eric M. Meyers. Oxford: Oxford University Press.

Gentili, Paolo. *"Sargon, re senza rivali."* http://www.helsinki.fi/science/saa/ sargon.html (cited September 11, 2002).

George, A. 1999. *The Epic of Gilgamesh. A New Translation.* London: Allen Lane, Penguin Press.

Glassner, Jean-Jacques. 2000. "Progress, Science, and the Use of Knowledge in Ancient Mesopotamia." Pp. 1815–1824 in *Civilizations of the Ancient Near East.* Edited by Jack M. Sasson. Peabody, MA: Hendrickson Publishers. (Reprint of 1995 edition. New York: Scribner.)

Gragg, Gene B. 2000. "Less-Understood Languages of Ancient Western Asia." Pp. 2161–2179 in *Civilizations of the Ancient Near East.* Edited by Jack M. Sasson. Peabody, MA: Hendrickson Publishers. (Reprint of 1995 edition. New York: Scribner.)

Hallo, William W. 2000. "Lamentations and Prayers in Sumer and Akkad." Pp. 1871–1882 in *Civilizations of the Ancient Near East.* Edited by Jack M. Sasson. Peabody, MA: Hendrickson Publishers. (Reprint of 1995 edition. New York: Scribner.)

Healy, John F. 1990. *Reading the Past. The Early Alphabet.* London: British Museum Press.

Huehnergard, John. 1997. "Akkadian." Pp. 44–49 in *The Oxford Encyclopedia of Archaeology in the Near East.* Vol. 1. Edited by Eric M. Meyers. Oxford: Oxford University Press.

———. 2000. "Semitic Languages." Pp. 2117–2134 in *Civilizations of the Ancient Near East.* Edited by Jack M. Sasson. Peabody, MA: Hendrickson Publishers. (Reprint of 1995 edition. New York: Scribner.)

Kramer, Samuel Noah. 1981. *History Begins at Sumer. Thirty-Nine Firsts in Recorded History.* 3rd revised edition. Philadelphia: University of Pennsylvania Press.

Liverani, Mario. 2000. "The Deeds of Ancient Mesopotamian Kings." Pp. 2353–2366 in *Civilizations of the Ancient Near East.* Edited by Jack M. Sasson. Peabody, MA: Hendrickson Publishers. (Reprint of 1995 edition. New York: Scribner.)

Majno, Guido. 1975. *The Healing Hand. Man and Wound in the Ancient World.* Cambridge, MA: Harvard University Press.

Mallory, J. P. 1898. *In Search of the Indo-Europeans. Language, Archaeology and Myth.* London: Thames and Hudson.

Melchert, H. Craig. 2000. "Indo-European Languages of Anatolia." Pp. 2151–2159 in *Civilizations of the Ancient Near East.* Edited by Jack M. Sasson. Peabody, MA: Hendrickson Publishers. (Reprint of 1995 edition. New York: Scribner.)

Melville, Duncan J. "Mesopotamian Mathematics." http://it.stlawu.edu/ %7Edmelvill/mesomath/index.html (cited November 24, 2004).

Meyers, Eric M., ed. 1997. *The Oxford Encyclopedia of Archaeology in the Near East.* 5 Volumes. Oxford: Oxford University Press.

Michalowski, Piotr. 1997. "Sumerians." Pp. 95–101 in *The Oxford Encyclopedia of Archaeology in the Near East.* Vol. 5. Edited by Eric M. Meyers. Oxford: Oxford University Press.

———. 2000. "Sumerian Literature: An Overview." Pp. 2279–2291 in *Civilizations of the Ancient Near East.* Edited by Jack M. Sasson. Peabody, MA: Hendrickson Publishers. (Reprint of 1995 edition. New York: Scribner.)

Millard, Alan. 2000. "Amorites," "Annals and Chronicles," "Aramaeans," "Archives," "Lexical Texts," and "Maps and Plans." Pp. 16, 21–22, 28–30, 181, and 188, respectively, in *Dictionary of the Ancient Near East*. Edited by Piotr Bienkowski and Alan Millard. London: British Museum Press.

Moran, William. 2000. "The Gilgamesh Epic: A Masterpiece from Ancient Mesopotamia." Pp. 2327–2336 in *Civilizations of the Ancient Near East*. Edited by Jack M. Sasson. Peabody, MA: Hendrickson Publishers. (Reprint of 1995 edition. New York: Scribner.)

Nagle, D. Brendan, and Stanley M. Burstein. 1995. *The Ancient World: Readings in Social and Cultural History*. Englewood Cliffs, NJ: Prentice Hall.

Nissen, Hans J. 1988. *The Early History of the Ancient Near East*. Chicago: University of Chicago Press. (Paperback edition 1990.)

Oates, Joan. 1986. *Babylon*. Revised edition. London: Thames and Hudson.

O'Connor, J. J., and E. F. Robertson. "A History of Zero." http://www-history.mcs.st-andrews.ac.uk/HistTopics/Zero.html (cited November 24, 2004).

Oppenheim, A. Leo, and Erica Reiner. 1977. *Ancient Mesopotamia. Portrait of a Dead Civilization*. Revised edition. Chicago: University of Chicago Press.

Parpola, Asko. 1994. *Deciphering the Indus Script*. Cambridge: Cambridge University Press.

Pearce, Laurie E. 2000. "The Scribes and Scholars of Ancient Mesopotamia." Pp. 2265–2278 in *Civilizations of the Ancient Near East*. Edited by Jack M. Sasson. Peabody, MA: Hendrickson Publishers. (Reprint of 1995 edition. New York: Scribner.)

Postgate, J. Nicholas. 1994. *Early Mesopotamia*. London: Routledge.

Potts, D. T. 1999. *The Archaeology of Elam. Formation and Transformation of an Ancient Iranian State*. Cambridge: Cambridge University Press.

Powell, Marvin A. 2000. "Metrology and Mathematics in Ancient Mesopotamia." Pp. 1941–1957 in *Civilizations of the Ancient Near East*. Edited by Jack M. Sasson. Peabody, MA: Hendrickson Publishers. (Reprint of 1995 edition. New York: Scribner.)

Reade, Julian. 1983. *Assyrian Sculpture*. London: British Museum Publications.

Roaf, Michael. 1990. *Cultural Atlas of Mesopotamia*. New York: Facts on File.

Rochberg, Francesca. 2000. "Astronomy and Calendars in Ancient Mesopotamia." Pp. 1925–1940 in *Civilizations of the Ancient Near East*. Edited by Jack M. Sasson. Peabody, MA: Hendrickson Publishers. (Reprint of 1995 edition. New York: Scribner.)

Saggs, H. W. F. 1995. *Peoples of the Past. Babylonians*. London: British Museum Press.

Sasson, Jack M., ed. 2000. *Civilizations of the Ancient Near East*. 4 Volumes. Peabody, MA: Hendrickson Publishers. (Reprint of 1995 edition. New York: Scribner.)

Schmandt-Besserat, Denise. 1996. *How Writing Came About*. Austin: University of Texas Press.

Sigrist, Marcel, and Peter Damerow. "Mesopotamian Year Names." http://www.cdli.ucla.edu/dl/yearnames/yn_index.htm (cited February 26, 2003).

Simpson, R. S. 2004. "Norris, Edwin (1795–1872)." *Oxford Dictionary of National Biography*. Oxford: Oxford University Press. http://www.oxforddnb.com/view/article/20268 (cited November 21, 2004).

Van de Mieroop, Marc. 1997. *The Ancient Mesopotamian City.* Oxford: Oxford University Press.

———. 1999. *Cuneiform Texts and the Writing of History.* London: Routledge.

———. 2004. *A History of the Ancient Near East. ca. 3000–323 BC.* Oxford: Blackwell.

Vanstiphout, H. 2000. "Memory and Literacy in Ancient Western Asia." Pp. 2181–2196 in *Civilizations of the Ancient Near East.* Edited by Jack M. Sasson. Peabody, MA: Hendrickson Publishers. (Reprint of 1995 edition. New York: Scribner.)

Von Soden, Wolfram. 1985. *The Ancient Orient. An Introduction to the Study of the Ancient Near East.* Translated by Donald G. Schley. Grand Rapids, MI: William B. Eerdmans Publishing Company.

Walker, Christopher B. F. 1987. *Reading the Past. Cuneiform.* London: British Museum Press.

Whitt, William D. 2000. "The Story of the Semitic Alphabet." Pp. 2379–2397 in *Civilizations of the Ancient Near East.* Edited by Jack M. Sasson. Peabody, MA: Hendrickson Publishers. (Reprint of 1995 edition. New York: Scribner.)

XI

Mesopotamian Civilization Today

After nearly two centuries of investigation, much is known about Mesopotamian civilization, but much still remains unknown, poorly understood, or uncertain. Many of the texts recovered from excavations have yet to reveal their secrets: Their volume is great, their condition often poor, their language challenging, and the number of scholars who can read them small—but the task is infinitely rewarding. A great recent advance has been the use of computer graphics programs to redraw cuneiform texts from photographs of tablets. Much other excavated material also remains to be studied: Finds like the thousands of ivory fragments recovered from Nimrud take years to conserve, piece together, and analyze. Although many excavations have taken place, often they have concentrated on monumental architecture—palaces, temples, and city walls—and comparatively little is known about urban domestic architecture and even less about rural settlements and land use, although research has increasingly focused on all of these areas of interest in recent years. In addition, there are many controversies about the significance of particular archaeological discoveries or historical texts, and changing archaeological theory has also focused new attention on interpretations of the archaeological and documentary evidence. There is much to do. But the prospects for Mesopotamian archaeology are not good: Warfare, intercommunity violence, sanctions, and looting have devastated many sites, seriously reduced the resources available for funding archaeology, and made the region a dangerous place in which to work, for locals and foreigners alike.

FIELDWORK

Archaeology, once focused almost exclusively on "sites," and particularly on the most substantial structures within the most substantial settlements, has moved in recent decades toward a much more holistic approach to the remains of the past. Several projects have attempted to map the entire layout of a major settlement, such as the investigation at Abu Salabikh. This site has also been the testing ground for a micromorphological study, providing new clues to the activities that had taken place in parts of the settlement. Many new scientific techniques of analysis are now available to archaeologists; some such as micromorphology give new insights into the function and use of structures and areas within them, and others such as microwear analysis and the analysis of residues on or in objects provide new information about the uses to which artifacts were put.

Settlements are now generally not viewed and investigated as isolated entities but as a part of a landscape that has many aspects: the natural environment, which provided resources and opportunities but also imposed constraints; a superimposed economic environment of human exploitation and land management, such as farming practices, forestry, agricultural infrastructure (including facilities for irrigation and water control), industry, and mineral extraction; the human landscape, including both the distribution and hierarchy of settlements and the networks of communications; and the ritual landscape.

Aerial photography has for many decades provided an important tool for investigating the landscape and human activity at all levels; aerial reconnaissance has seen tremendous advances in recent years. As well as conventional photography, there are now infrared photography, high-resolution satellite photography, and radar scans, among others. The political situation in Iraq since 1991 means that the area has been exceptionally well covered by aerial reconnaissance (although it could be some time before the resulting material becomes available for archaeological scrutiny). The resolution that can be achieved with satellite sensors can be as good as 60 centimeters, allowing features of the size of people to be identified. Using satellite imaging, ancient watercourses have been traced in several parts of the Near East, including Mesopotamia; space imaging radar even allows the detection of former rivers buried under several meters of sand. Computers play a major role as tools for handling this data: enhancing images, filtering out noise, converting information to a form that can be easily transferred to maps, and allowing other types of manipulation. The latter includes use within GIS (Geographical Information Systems), which enable information on a range of aspects of the natural and human environment, such as topography, settlement patterns, industrial activity, communications networks, and vegetation, to be combined and considered in relation to each other.

Floods, Marshes, and Coastlines

The marshland of the south has always been a place that has harbored refugees, fugitives, and rebels (see photo p. 9), as well as the indigenous peoples who more than 8,000 years ago developed a way of life adapted to the region. After the Shi'ite uprising in 1991, Saddam Hussein attempted to deal with this refuge area by draining it. Since his overthrow in 2003, work has begun on restoring the marshes, regarded by many as the original Garden of Eden. Before the area is once again inundated, there is a window of opportunity to investigate and map traces of early settlement, extinct watercourses, and the changing coastline along the head of the Gulf. The interplay of rising sea levels, sedimentation, and changing river channels means that the coastline and the distribution of watercourses, marshes, and dry land have been constantly changing throughout prehistoric and historic times. These have had a major impact on human settlement patterns, and human interference has also shaped the landscape, redistributing water via canals, dykes, and other works for irrigation and water conservation. Much has still to be learned of the detail of these changes, and even the general picture is still debated.

The Great Flood

Fieldwork in this region could shed new light on a related topic of absorbing interest: the Flood. Familiar to children from the biblical story of Noah, an earlier Mesopotamian version of the story has been known since the nineteenth century C.E. The Sumerian King List, composed around 2100 B.C.E., refers to the Flood, and a fragment of a Sumerian version of this story is also known, although the earliest surviving full account is *Atrahasis,* in a version dated around 1700 B.C.E. The hero of this tale was a legendary king of Shuruppak, known in different versions as Ziusudra, Atrahasis, or Ut-napishtim. Chronological data derived from various sources suggests a date of around 2900 B.C.E. for the origin of the Flood story. Deposits composed of alluvial silt consistent with a major flood have been excavated at Shuruppak, dated around 2900 B.C.E., and at Kish around the same time, and significant changes in the course and number of channels of the Euphrates River have been documented in the period 3000–2800 B.C.E. At present, however, this is far from being evidence of a universally destructive inundation, rather than a number of separate episodes affecting different cities. Personal experience of recent localized floods in Britain shows how quickly the sufferings of different regions in separate years can be conflated in popular memory: How much easier it would have been before the days of global communications and a universally used calendar for a series of such local floods to be seen later as one single catastrophic deluge.

Another suggestion less plausibly links the Flood to global postglacial changes in sea levels, rivers, and lakes, on the grounds that this would account for the widespread currency of the story. One recent theory moves the Flood away from Mesopotamia to the Black Sea. Here underwater reconnaissance has revealed that the Mediterranean and the Black Sea were once separated by a narrow land bridge between Asia and Europe. Rising sea levels in the Mediterranean caused this to be breached around 5500 B.C.E., pouring water into the much lower basin of the Black Sea and drowning a huge area of land around the Black Sea shores, with catastrophic effects. Those who did not lose their lives would have fled to inland areas of Europe and Anatolia. To suggest, however, that this event gave rise to a Flood myth in southern Mesopotamia strains credulity.

The Lost City of Agade

When Sargon of Akkad created his empire, he established a new city, Agade, to be his capital. The poem "The Curse of Agade" describes the new city in glowing colors: its warehouses filled with grain, gold, and precious stones; the convivial and festive life of its inhabitants, well furnished with food and drink; its cosmopolitan feel, with exotic animals rubbing shoulders with flocks of wooly sheep and colorful foreigners with the healthy, happy, and fulfilled locals; its quays overflowing with goods from every land. After Sargon's dynasty fell, the city was never again of national importance, but it was still known and visited in the first millennium B.C.E.; Nabonidus investigated and restored temples here. Like most other Mesopotamian cities it was later forgotten, but unlike most it has not been rediscovered, despite many attempts to find it.

Clues to its location can be gleaned from textual references, but they are not unambiguous. The city lay in the alluvial plain north of Kish. Ships from Meluhha, Magan, and Dilmun moored at its quays; these were probably substantial seagoing vessels, and so this must imply that they had sailed up a major river. One text speaks of ships traveling from Agade to Nippur, implying that both were on the same river, the Euphrates. The heartland of the Akkadian Empire, the region in the center of Mesopotamia where the Tigris and Euphrates most nearly approach each other, has not been extensively surveyed. Many scholars believe that the evidence suggests Agade was situated somewhere between Babylon, Kish, and Sippar. Agade could lie partially beneath the city of Babylon, where later deposits would have prevented it from being detected. Before the Iraq war a Japanese team were investigating a site on the outskirts of Kish that they hoped might prove to be Agade. Other scholars, however, locate Agade well toward the east, on the Tigris, perhaps near its confluence with the Diyala or perhaps within the area of modern Baghdad. This long-lived and extensive metropolis could well overlay and hide the remains of an ancient city, but if so there must have been a canal system linking the Tigris and Euphrates: Aerial reconnaissance could shed light on this.

CONTINUING CONTROVERSIES

Few interpretations of archaeological remains endure unchallenged. New data and new understandings of the way that societies operate lead scholars constantly to revise and refine their explanations of the past. Mesopotamia's archaeology is no exception: There are lively debates on topics such as the origins of agriculture, the beginning of writing, and the development of civilization, in which Mesopotamia features prominently, and other more local subjects from the prehistoric period, such as the significance of the Uruk phenomenon and the origin of the Sumerians, are also of absorbing interest to archaeologists.

Chronology

In the historical period, one of the major problems is with chronology, because, as outlined in chapter 3, although the sequence of development is generally well established, there are major areas of uncertainty. For the later third and second millennia, there is a difference of more than a century between the High and Low Chronologies: Each can be supported by pieces of convincing evidence, but only one can be correct.

The fabric of Mesopotamian chronology is draped like a curtain from a few secure hooks, and like curtain hooks, some of these are moveable. Between them there are lengths of solid fabric whose substance remains the same wherever they move along the rail, but the material between them is less solid and can be stretched or contracted. As a result, for example, the length of the period between the fall of the Akkadian dynasty and the accession of Ur-

Nammu, the first king of the Ur III dynasty, is uncertain, although the duration of these dynasties themselves is well known. One hundred and sixty-seven and a half years, as the Sumerian King List says? Sixty-six years, a revised version based on the probability that some of the intervening dynasties were contemporary? Thirty years, the duration of the longest-lasting of these dynasties, that of Uruk? None, and in fact a small overlap, with the shadowy latest kings of Akkad contemporary with the early years of Ur-Nammu?

A huge volume of written data, such as royal inscriptions, offical documents, letters, omen texts, and chronicles, provide the raw material from which the historical framework has been constructed. Well-documented periods, often those that had strong rulers and were politically stable, form the strong fabric of the curtain; anarchical or poorly documented periods are the gauzy patches between. Independently datable events that were recorded are the hooks on which the fabric hangs: the eclipse that occurred on June 15, 763 B.C.E., provides a secure hook on which to hang the strong fabric of first-millennium chronology, although even here there are gauzy patches, such as the ill-documented years 630–627 B.C.E., when it is unclear whether Ashurbanipal was still alive. In contrast, in the second millennium the moveable hook provided by the observations of Venus in the reign of Ammi-saduqa places that king's accession in three or even four possible places: 1702, 1646, 1582, or perhaps 1550 B.C.E.

Most scholars opt to use the Middle Chronology (dating Ammi-saduqa's accession at 1646 B.C.E.), not because it is most convincing but because it is a convenient temporary fixed point until the correct date is finally established: Scholarly consensus on the historical framework greatly facilitates discussion of other issues. Work to establish a firm chronology, however, continues, each little piece of evidence that can be discovered or deduced making the picture a little clearer.

The Royal Cemetery at Ur

When Leonard Woolley uncovered sixteen ED tombs at Ur full of rich grave goods and bodies, he was in no doubt that he was seeing the remains of royal burials accompanied by sacrificed retainers. The orderly arrangement of the bodies and the presence beside each one of a goblet from which, he surmised, they had drunk poison, led him to believe that these were voluntary sacrifices, lovingly accompanying their master or mistress to the netherworld. The persuasive and eloquent language in which all Woolley's reports are written has entranced generations of readers, archaeologists and non-archaeologists alike, and for a long time his interpretation remained the accepted view. There was even textual evidence to support it. In the fragmentary Sumerian poem "The Death of Gilgamesh," a large number of servants and family, including not only his wives but also his children, seem to have been laid in the grave along with the dead man. But the text is incomplete, and the meaning is not entirely clear. In the years since Woolley uncovered this cemetery, only one further instance of apparent human sacrifices has come to light in Mesopotamia, an ED cemetery at Kish (Cemetery Y), where several graves furnished with a cart and draught oxen contained a number of individuals: In this case, however, it is possible that these were family graves in which the bodies of family members were successively interred, a common practice. Human sacrifice, therefore, was not a general Sumerian custom, although on occasion a slave (seen as a chattel rather than a person) was included among the grave goods.

In more recent years, doubts have been cast both on the royal identity of the sixteen principal burials within the Ur tombs and on the sacrificial nature of the other burials. Inscribed seals have been found in some of the graves, but their position in the grave makes it possible that they were gifts from the living rather than certainly possessions of the deceased. Of the named individuals, only two, Akalamdug and Meskalamdug, are known from other sources to have been rulers of Ur. Meskalamdug's burial differs from the sixteen "royal" interments: He was placed in an ordinary grave, distinguished only by the richness of its grave goods and its association with the name of a known king. Among the several thousand ordinary graves in the cemetery there were a number that were richly furnished. What distinguish the "royal" graves from these are the stone or brick-built vaulted tomb chambers in which the principal burial was laid and the associated "sacrifices."

Clearly these individuals were special in some way, but they need not have been royalty. Another plausible theory is that they were priests and priestesses of Nanna, the tutelary deity of Ur; in later times the temple precinct at Ur included a crypt in which Nanna's priestesses were buried. A further suggestion is that they were individuals who had acted as substitute king when omens predicted the monarch's death. To avert this disaster the chosen individual would assume the role and duties of the king during the crisis period and would thereafter be killed along with his queen and his retainers. Although in principle this seems to match the burials at Ur, the practice was rare, and it seems unlikely that as many as sixteen such episodes should have occurred at Ur in as little as a century.

Archaeologists are divided in their opinions on the supposed sacrifices. Some suggest that these graves were the mausolea of important people, kings, queens, priests, or priestesses, beside whose revered corpses were laid the bodies of those who wished or were entitled to be buried with them, including their relatives and servants. In this scenario the bodies of those who predeceased their lord or lady would have been stored up in a mortuary place, awaiting the latter's burial. Woolley's "poisoned chalices" can easily be explained, for burials of the period are often furnished with a cup. Other archaeologists are still convinced by Woolley's theory of voluntary suicide or at least accept that these people were sacrificed. Either way, the cemetery remains unique in Mesopotamian history, an enduring mystery.

The Hanging Gardens of Babylon

By the third century B.C.E., the Hellenistic Greeks controlled the lands of many ancient civilizations, including Egypt and Mesopotamia. It was an age of cultural, scientific, and philosophical enquiry and technological inventiveness, in which the achievements of the older civilizations were critically compared with those of the Greeks and with contemporary works. Some were singled out as exceptional feats of architecture, craftsmanship, and engineering, a changing list that became known as the Seven Wonders of the World. Among these were the Hanging Gardens of Babylon.

The earliest surviving mention of these gardens is around 270 B.C.E. by the Babylonian author Berossus: He wrote of a palace built by Nebuchadrezzar II in just fifteen days, in which a "hanging garden" was constructed to please the king's Median queen, an edifice resembling a mountain with stone terraces planted with trees. An inscription of the king himself described this palace as being high as a mountain and partially constructed of stone, although he did not mention a garden. Later Greek writers furnish more details of the gardens: They were built on stone foundations with brickwork above and layers of reeds and bitumen, all standard features of Mesopotamian architecture. A hidden mechanism fed the terraces with water to support the trees, and there were pavilions among the vegetation. Pleasure gardens stocked with exotic trees and plants were often part of Babylonian and Assyrian palaces, an extension of the common shade-tree gardens (see chapter 5). What made those of Babylon a Wonder of the World was probably their magnificence, their tiered arrangement, and the engineering feat involved in supplying them with water.

Water-lifting devices were well known to the Mesopotamians. The simplest was the shaduf, used for lifting water from canals for irrigation, and for raising water from a lower to a higher watercourse or reservoir. To supply the hanging gardens with water in this way would have required an army of gardeners and, more importantly, would have been visible. The Greek texts refer to a hidden mechanism: This could have been an Archimedes screw, a device that seems to be described in the inscriptions of the Assyrian king Sennacherib, centuries before Archimedes.

Can the Hanging Gardens be identified? Babylon has been thoroughly plundered by brick robbers, and only the foundations of its buildings remain. Following the texts, those of the Hanging Gardens should be of stone, massive enough to support a substantial tiered superstructure, and situated close to the river from which the water was raised. A possible candidate for this is the series of structures that lies between the river and the North and South Palaces. The Western Outwork is a walled enclosure built of baked bricks set in bitumen, with walls 20 meters thick. To its north lies an unexcavated area, west of the North Palace. Perhaps here there was once an arrangement of terraces supporting gardens planted with trees and irrigated with water drawn from the Euphrates: Detailed investigation of this area is needed to further this suggestion, which many scholars find unconvincing.

Some doubt that the Hanging Gardens of Babylon ever existed. Herodotus, who may have visited Babylon in the fifth century B.C.E., made no mention of the gardens, although he accurately described many of the city's most impressive features. Coupled with the difficulty of identifying a convincing location for the gardens in Babylon, this seems strong grounds for dismissing the Hanging Gardens as merely a legend.

Another theory, however, has recently been proposed. Herodotus, writing only a century after the fall of the Babylonian Empire, often did not distinguish between the Babylonians and the Assyrians, whose cities had fallen into decay after the Babylonians sacked them in 612 B.C.E. Babylon, however, continued to flourish for many centuries. Suppose the Hanging Gardens had been located not in Babylon, but in the now-ruined Assyrian capital, Nineveh, and the tale of their glories transferred to Babylon, famous for its magnificence?

There is much to support this view, first suggested in the 1850s, forgotten, and recently proposed anew by Stephanie Dalley. The Assyrians constructed magnificent gardens in their palaces, described in royal inscriptions. Scenes from the palace walls at Nineveh often depict these gardens: One, for example, shows Ashurbanipal and his queen picnicking beneath a grapevine, laden with fruit, among the trees of their garden whose diverse varieties the sculptors have been careful to depict. Significantly, another of Ashurbanipal's palace reliefs shows the gardens of his grandfather Sennacherib's vast "Palace without a Rival:" They rise up over tree-clad slopes to a terrace with a pillared pavilion, and through them run streams fed by an aqueduct. Sennacherib took a keen interest in civil and hydraulic engineering and the creation of artificial landscapes. His inscriptions describe and his reliefs show a nature reserve outside Nineveh, a swamp created for water management, stocked with wild boar, deer, and fish, and attracting heron and other birds. The aqueducts, weirs, dams, and tunnels he constructed to bring water to Nineveh from the Zagros, some of which are still in use today, watered a huge area of arable land and orchards around the city as well as parks and gardens within it, of which the most sumptuous was the royal pleasure park beside his palace. This he described as "A park, the image of Mount Amanus, in which all kinds of spices, fruit trees and timber trees, the sustenance of the mountain and Chaldea, I had collected and I planted them next to my palace" (quoted in Leick 2001: 228).

THE DESTRUCTION OF OUR COMMON HERITAGE—
WILL MESOPOTAMIA SURVIVE?

A wave of looting followed the Gulf War in 1991 and the subsequent uprising in the south. The sanctions imposed after the war and the air strikes on Iraq seriously affected economic conditions in the country, already undermined by the crippling expense of Iraq's war against Iran in the 1980s. This drastically reduced the funding available for archaeology and the contacts between Iraqi scholars and their international colleagues. The overthrow of Saddam in 2003 has made it possible for Iraqi scholars to travel and catch up on new developments in the discipline, but this is a small gain in comparison with the devastating results of the breakdown of law and order in the country. The sacking of the National Museum immediately after the Coalition seizure of Baghdad made headline news: Many of the best-known pieces lost at that time, including the Warka Vase (see photo p. 69), seem to have been taken by ordinary Iraqis in the heat of the moment and have since been returned. Around eight thousand objects from the museum, including the treasures from the queens' tombs at Nimrud and from the Royal Cemetery at Ur, had been safely deposited in the vaults of the Central Bank and in secure storage facilities by museum staff before the war. But many of the smaller pieces from the museum, including thousands of seals, were looted, apparently to order by professional thieves: They have disappeared without a trace and have probably now found their way into private collections in the Western world. The accepted total of objects taken from the museum stands at around 15,000, of which around 8,000 had been recovered by November 2004. Other museums also suffered similar depredations: The museum at Babylon was heavily looted; important remains including thirty panels from the Balawat Gates were taken from the Mosul Museum; and others were also targeted or have been looted since then.

But the most desperate casualty of the conflict and its aftermath has been the archaeological sites. Private collectors' buying power and their interest in antiquities from civilizations around the world have grown exponentially over recent decades. While many ancient objects are legitimately bought and sold, their supply falls far short of demand, fueling a trade in illegally acquired pieces. These are often obtained by poor peasants in countries like Peru who take the frequently high risks involved in breaking the law by looting known archaeological sites in return for generally quite small sums of money; but the international market in illegally obtained artifacts is big business, often operated by criminal organizations. These criminal dealers and the private individuals (and, regrettably, sometimes also publicly owned institutions) who encourage their activities by buying antiquities that lack a legal pedigree are those truly responsible for the wanton destruction of our shared human heritage. In most countries, including the United States, it is against the law to trade in or possess antiquities that were not legally acquired, and those who do so risk penalties from confiscation to imprisonment (or worse—in some countries, notably in East and Southeast Asia, dealers in illegal antiquities can be executed). Illegal digging not only removes valuable antiquities from the public domain where they can be studied; far more seriously, in the process of tearing these objects from the ground their context is destroyed, wiping out all the information that can be learned from the association between the objects, their place of deposition, and other artifacts, and the latter, moreover, are often damaged or destroyed in the process of digging out the saleable pieces—a process analogous to cutting a book up into its individual words and throwing most of them away: The meaning is lost and can never be recovered.

Iraqis have always been proud of their heritage and of their unique position as guardians of the Cradle of Civilization. Until recently they zealously preserved their ancient sites and cherished their antiquities, and most still maintain this attitude. However, in the 1990s, when ordinary Iraqis were squeezed between the tyranny of Saddam and the terrible deprivations caused by the international sanctions, Iraq began to leak antiquities. In 1989–1990, Professor John Russell had documented the reliefs that had decorated the palace of Sennacherib at Nineveh; in 1995 he was horrified to recognize a fragment of one of the relief-decorated slabs offered for sale on the international antiquities

A guard at the ancient city of Kalhu (Nimrud) walks past an alabaster bas-relief. Thieves under orders from foreigners allegedly chipped the head away from this figure in an attempt to make money during the years of international sanctions in the 1990s, a crime repeated in a number of well-known Iraqi sites. This vandalism, however, is nothing compared to the scale of the destruction to ancient sites and illegal export of antiquities that has occurred since the fall of Saddam Hussein's regime. (Lynsey Addario/Corbis)

market. Over the following two years he identified a number of others, fragments often smashed from the center of what had still been intact slabs in 1990. Photographs taken of the throne room by Muayad Said Damerji in 1997 confirmed that the reliefs had been reduced to rubble and the saleable fragments removed. This is but one well-documented example of the looting of Iraqi sites and smuggling of Mesopotamian antiquities that took place during the international sanctions that reduced many inhabitants of a once-prosperous nation to destitution. Saddam himself became concerned about the situation, executing looters and sponsoring heavily guarded archaeological rescue excavations by the Iraq Department of Antiquities in a number of southern sites, particularly Umma, to protect them from the attention of looters. Despite the attacks on a number of sites, the situation was kept relatively under control by a network of site guards who could call out support from the army and police force at any signs of trouble.

Desperate as this situation was, matters have become infinitely worse since the fall of Saddam Hussein in 2003. The Iraqi army and police force were disbanded, and the Coalition forces and the nascent new Iraqi police force have been unable to establish law and order in the country; in this situation the preservation of antiquities is very low on the list of priorities. Whereas in the 1990s looters operated on a small scale and risked serious legal penalties if caught, since spring 2003 looters have been operating with impunity and on a vast scale, in well-armed bodies of two to three hundred men. When challenged by military personnel or police they generally run away but return as soon as the threat has passed. By May 2003 senior archaeologists of the Coalition nations were reporting numerous holes in the important Sumerian cities of Larsa, Umma, Adab, Isin, Bad-Tibira, Nippur, Zabalam, and a number of smaller settlements including Ubaid: At least thirty sites had suffered. From the air Umm al-Hafriyat "looked like a waffle" (Gibson 2004a). Some sites had not sustained damage: Uruk survived because it was strongly protected by the local tribe which has been involved with the meticulous German excavations conducted there since the 1920s; Ur, Babylon, Kish, Nimrud, Nineveh, and Khorsabad were largely unaffected because they were either military camps or had been given military protection, although Nimrud and Nineveh had suffered recent looting and the U.S. forces in Babylon had themselves inflicted an unacceptable and unnecessary amount of damage by constructing security fences, driving heavy military vehicles over ground within the city, thereby causing the destruction of buried material, and bulldozing areas to create helicopter landing sites. Some attempted looting of the glazed bricks by American soldiers is also reported to have taken place. In addition, the American presence here has drawn insurgent attacks upon the city. In May 2003 the region around Nasiriyyah was being well protected by the Italian forces responsible for Dhi Qar province. Eight months later when John Russell overflew southern Iraq in a helicopter, the Italians were still managing to protect Nasiriyyah, despite the brutal murder of a number of them in November 2003; but the destruction on sites including Maskan Shapir, Nippur, Drehem, and particularly Isin was continuing unabated. In the spring of 2004 Dutch forces were helping local guards to protect Uruk and had captured some looters; Italian *carabinieri* had captured others. But by September of 2004, reports put the number of sites that had suffered serious damage at around one hundred, showing that the problem has been escalating.

Some of the material taken from these sites and from museums has been offered for sale in the bazaar in Baghdad and elsewhere; but much of it has been smuggled across the border into neighboring countries and thence into the international antiquities market where most material has now disappeared. To the best of their ability under the difficult circumstances, international agencies operating in Iraq, and in particular the Italians, have been active in policing the routes by which the smuggling takes place and have seized a quantity of looted material. Coalition forces and Iraqi police are also actively combatting smuggling, and there has been cooperation from the neighboring countries, particularly Jordan, in monitoring border crossings, seizing antiquities, and arresting the smugglers; customs officials in a number of countries, including the United States, France, and Switzerland, have also seized a considerable number of items and returned them to the Iraqi authorities; but despite the successes, only a small fraction of the looted material is being retrieved. The lack of security presents a major obstacle: For example, a collection of antiquities seized in October 2004 was lost again when the party of guards responsible for it were ambushed by bandits and murdered. Some of those managing the looting operations are thought to be members of the old regime, but very many foreigners are also involved: probably the majority of those financing the operations, supplying equipment and weapons, and handling the smuggling and sale of the looted antiquities; and it is likely that many are members of international criminal organizations. In October 2004 John Russell estimated the number of tablets being smuggled out of Iraq at 3,000 per week and reported that the sites from which they had been looted had been *totally* destroyed.

Although some measures are being taken to bring the situation under control (1,272 guards are supposed to be in place to watch over 3,232 sites by the end of 2004—that is about one guard for every three sites), as of December 2004 the situation shows no signs of improving. Security is still a problem throughout the country, with kidnappings, murders, and suicide bombings in Baghdad and other cities, bandits in the desert regions, and a number of areas where the Iraqi Authority and Coalition forces have no control. In this climate the bands of looters flourish and their destruction goes unchecked in many sites. The security situation must (God willing) eventually settle down and Iraq must once more become a stable, safe, and prosperous country. But for the Mesopotamian cities that have survived the vicissitudes of the past 5,000 years this will probably come too late. As John Russell said (1998: 51) we are looking at "the destruction of a fundamental part of our common heritage and once it is gone, it is gone forever."

TEXT REFERENCES

Adams, Robert McCormack, and Hans J. Nissen. 1972. *The Uruk Countryside. The Natural Setting of Urban Societies.* Chicago: The University of Chicago Press.

Al-Gailani-Werr, Lamia. "Antiquities in Iraq." *British School of Archaeology in Iraq Newsletter* 3, May 1999.

"Archeological Site Protection Discussed in Al-Hilla in Coalition Provisional Authority (Iraq), January 6, 2003." http://www.cpa-iraq.org/pressreleases/20040110_Archeology-Hillah.htm (cited 14 January 2004).

Atwood, Roger. 2004. *Stealing History. Tomb Raiders, Smugglers, and the Looting of the Ancient World.* New York: St.Martin's Press.

Bahrani, Zainab. "Days of plunder." *Guardian,* Tuesday, August 31, 2004. http://www.guardian.co.uk/Iraq/Story/0,2763,1294027,00.html (cited September 1, 2004).

Crawford, Harriet. 1991. *Sumer and the Sumerians.* Cambridge: Cambridge University Press.

Cryer, Frederick. 2000. "Chronology: Issues and Problems." Pp. 651–664 in *Civilizations of the Ancient Near East.* Edited by Jack M. Sasson. Peabody, MA: Hendrickson Publishers. (Reprint of 1995 edition. New York: Scribner.)

Dalley, Stephanie. 1994. "Nineveh, Babylon, and the Hanging Gardens: Cuneiform and Classical Sources Reconciled." *Iraq* 56: 45–58.

Deblauwe, Francis. Continuously updated 2003. Iraq War and Archaeology site. http://iwa.univie.ac.at.

Edens, Chris. 2001. "Babylon. The Mystery of the Hanging Gardens." Pp. 162–165 in *The Archaeology Detectives. How We Know What We Know about the Past.* Edited by Paul G. Bahn. Lewes: The Ivy Press.

Electronic Text Corpus of Sumerian Literature. "The Cursing of Agade." http://www.etcsl.orient.ox.ac.uk/ (cited January 30, 2002).

———. "The Death of Gilgamesh." http://www-etcsl.orient.ox.ac.uk/ (cited December 2, 2002).

———. "The Flood Story." http://www-etcsl.orient.ox.ac.uk/ (cited December 2, 2002).

Farchakh, Joanne. 2004. "The Massacre of Mesopotamian Archaeology. Looting in Iraq Is Out of Control." *Daily Star,* Tuesday, September 21, 2004. http://www.dailystar.com.lb/article.asp?edition_id=10&categ_id=4&article_id=8536 (cited September 21, 2004).

George, Andrew. 1999. *The Epic of Gilgamesh. A New Translation.* London: Allen Lane, Penguin Press.

———. "A Visit to Baghdad in September 1999." *British School of Archaeology in Iraq Newsletter* 4, November 1999.

Gibson, McGuire. 2004a. "Nippur and Iraq at Time of War." Updated article from *Oriental Institute Annual Report 2002–2003.* Circulated via Iraq crisis list April 15, 2004.

———. 2004b. "Comment on Lauren Sandler, 'The Thieves of Baghdad.'" (A misleading article published in *Atlantic Monthly.*) Circulated via Iraq crisis list October 2, 2004.

Hallo, William W., and William Kelly Simpson. 1998. *The Ancient Near East. A History.* 2nd edition. Belmont, CA: Wadworth / Thomson Learning.

Herrmann, Georgina. "A Visit to Baghdad, April 2000." *British School of Archaeology in Iraq Newsletter* 5, May 2000.

Kolin'ski, Rafal. "10 Weeks in Babylon." *British School of Archaeology in Iraq Newsletter* 13, May 2004. http://www.britac.ac.uk/institutes/iraq/newsnews13.htm(babylon (cited November 12, 2004).

Kuniholm, Peter Ian, Bernard Kromer, Sturt W. Manning, Maryanne Newton, Christine E. Latini, and Mary Jayne Bruce. 1996. "Anatolian Tree Rings and the Absolute Chronology of the Eastern Mediterranean, 2220–718 B.C.E." *Nature* 381: 780–783.

Leick, Gwendolyn. 2001. *Mesopotamia. The Invention of the City.* London: Allen Lane, Penguin Press.

McDonald, Helen. "Report from Iraq (June–August 2003)." *British School of Archaeology in Iraq Newsletter* 12, November 2003. http://www.britac.ac.uk/institutes/iraq/newnews12.htm (cited November 12, 2004).

Nissen, Hans J. 1988. *The Early History of the Ancient Near East.* Chicago: University of Chicago Press. (Paperback edition 1990.)

Oates, Joan. 1986. *Babylon*. Revised edition. London: Thames and Hudson.

Reade, Julian. 1983. *Assyrian Sculpture*. London: British Museum Publications.

———. 1999. "The Hanging Gardens of Babylon." Pp. 27–29 in *Seventy Wonders of the Ancient World*. Edited by Chris Scarre. London: Thames and Hudson.

———. 2000. *Mesopotamia*. 2d edition. London: British Museum Press.

Renfrew, Colin, and Paul Bahn. 2000. *Archaeology*. 3d edition. London: Thames and Hudson.

Robson, Eleanor. "Iraq: The History of Mathematics and the Aftermath of the War." *British Society for the History of Mathematics Newsletter* 49 (Autumn 2003): 1–9. http://www.dcs.warwick.ac.uk/bshm/Iraq/iraq-wartext.htm (cited December 4, 2004).

Russell, John Malcolm. 1998. *The Final Sack of Nineveh. The Discovery, Documentation, and Destruction of King Sennacherib's Throne Room at Nineveh, Iraq*. New Haven, CT: Yale University Press.

Saggs, H. W. F. 1995. *Peoples of the Past. Babylonians*. London: British Museum Press.

Scarre, Chris. 1999. *Seventy Wonders of the Ancient World*. London: Thames and Hudson.

Scurlock, JoAnn. 2000. "Death and the Afterlife in Ancient Mesopotamian Thought." Pp. 1883–1895 in *Civilizations of the Ancient Near East*. Edited by Jack M. Sasson. Peabody, MA: Hendrickson Publishers. (Reprint of 1995 edition. New York: Scribner.)

Sullivan, R. E. "Iraq Journal: Grave Robbers' Looting Spree." Fox News, January 16, 2004. http://www.foxnews.com/story/0,2933,108684,00.html (cited January 16, 2004).

Van de Mieroop, Marc. 2004. *A History of the Ancient Near East. ca. 3000–323 BC*. Oxford: Blackwell.

Wiseman, Donald J. 1991. *Nebuchadrezzar and Babylon. The Schweich Lectures of the British Academy 1983*. Oxford: Oxford University Press.

Woolley, Leonard. 1982. *Ur "of the Chaldees."* The final account, *Excavations at Ur*, revised and updated by P. Roger and S. Moorey. London: Book Club Associates / Herbert Press.

Wright, Henry T., T. J. Wilkinson, Elizabeth C. Stone, and McGuire Gibson. "The National Geographic Society's Cultural Assessment of Iraq." http://news.national-geographic.com/news/2003/06/0611_030611_iraqlootingreport.html (cited June 14, 2003).

Glossary

AKK. = Akkadian
SUM. = Sumerian

ABU SALABIKH A city occupied in the Early Dynastic period, possibly to be identified as ancient Eresh. An archive of ED IIIa tablets were found here.

ABZU (Akk. Apsu) 1. God of the primordial freshwater. 2. The realm of freshwater after the Creation, the responsibility of the god Enki (Ea). The term is particularly associated with the extensive freshwater around Eridu, where a shrine developed.

ACHAEMENID PERIOD From 539 B.C.E. when Babylon fell to the Persians, Mesopotamia was part of the Achaemenid (Persian) Empire. This was founded by Cyrus II in 550 B.C.E. after defeating the Median king, Astyages.

ADAB (Modern Bismaya) A Sumerian city 30 kilometers southeast of Nippur, allied with Shuruppak in the Early Dynastic period, when it features in the Sumerian King List.

ADAD (Sum. Ishkur) Akkadian name for the storm god, revered for his gift of rain and water from mountain streams, bringing vegetation for pasturing animals. Son of the sky god An (or, in earlier traditions, of Enlil), with whom he shared a twin shrine at Assur (see photo p. 187).

AGADE Capital of the Akkadian Empire, founded by Sargon of Akkad and described in the poem "The Curse of Agade." Probably situated in the area between Babylon, Kish, and Sippar, its location was still known to first-millennium Mesopotamians, but it has yet to be identified by archaeologists.

AKITU Southern Mesopotamian rural festivals, celebrated from third millennium onward, also the name given specifically to the Babylonian New Year festival (*see also* New Year festival; *bit akitu*).

AKKAD The northern part of Babylonia, known as *ki-uri* in Sumerian.

AKKADIAN The eastern branch of the Semitic language family. The earliest known form, Old Akkadian (2600–2000 B.C.E.), gave rise to the Assyrian and Babylonian dialects.

AKKADIAN EMPIRE First state uniting the lands of southern Mesopotamia (Sumer and Akkad), founded by Sargon of Akkad in 2334 B.C.E. The empire's influence stretched from eastern Anatolia to western Iran and endured until 2193 B.C.E., when it succumbed to internal problems and external attacks, especially by the Guti.

AKKADIAN PERIOD The period of the Akkadian Empire, 2334–2193 B.C.E.

AKKADIANS Speakers of the Akkadian language who in the third millennium B.C.E. lived particularly in Akkad but were also present in Sumer.

ALALAKH (Modern Tell 'Atchana) A city on the Amuq plain east of the Orontes, often a dependent of its more powerful neighbors.

ALLUVIUM Fertile silt deposited by rivers over their floodplains. The alluvium of the Euphrates provided the agricultural prosperity of southern Mesopotamia, but few natural resources other than plants, date palms and a few other trees, mud and clay, and animals.

ALPHABET A script in which signs represent individual phonemes. The first alphabet was devised by Canaanites around 1700 B.C.E. Two alphabets are known at Ugarit in the fourteenth century B.C.E. One, using cuneiform characters, was used only briefly; the other, based on Egyptian hieroglyphs with Canaanite phonetic values, is ancestral to most of the alphabets of the later world. The original alphabet rendered only consonants; signs for vowels were added by the Greeks when they modified the script to write their own language.

AMARNA LETTERS Remains of the royal archive in the short-lived Egyptian capital, Akhetaten (modern Tell el-Amarna), were rediscovered in 1887. It contained correspondence received from, and copies of a few letters sent to, contemporary Near Eastern rulers, including Mitanni and Kassite kings. It therefore constitutes a major source of information on international diplomacy and politics in the fourteenth century B.C.E. Most of the letters were written in Akkadian cuneiform, the internationally used script and language.

AMORITES (Sum. *martu*, Akk. *amurru*) Semitic-speaking pastoralists living in the Syrian steppe in the later third millennium B.C.E., when they posed a threat to Babylonia, leading to the construction of a defensive wall against them. They gradually settled in Babylonia and had merged with the Babylonian population before the middle of the second millennium B.C.E. The Mari royal house in the eighteenth century B.C.E. were Amorites. Tribes in parts of the Levant in the second millennium B.C.E. were also known as Amorites (*see also* Martu).

AN (Akk. Anu) 1. The Sumerian god of the sky, sometime patron of Uruk, where the Kullaba precinct was dedicated to his worship. Father of the gods and creator of the universe after the separation of heaven and earth, in some versions of the Creation myth. 2. "On High," the upper region of the cosmos, contrasted with Ki, "Below," the Earth, including the underworld.

ANATOLIA Asiatic Turkey.

ANNALS Dated royal records of campaigns, which are a major source of historical information. They begin with simple inscriptions in the ED III period that mention campaigns along with royal titles and range from brief sentences to the clay prisms of Neo-Assyrian kings inscribed with hundreds of lines of text.

ANSHAN The region around the city of Anshan (modern Tell-i Malyan) in Iran, often associated with Elam as a unified kingdom.

ANU *see* An.

ANUNNAKI (Anuna, Anunnaku) An early Sumerian term for the gods, especially the mass of nameless gods who were first created. By the second millennium, however, the term generally refers more specifically to the gods of earth and the underworld, contrasting with *igigi.*

ANZU (Sum. Imdugud) A monstrous lion-headed bird, the flapping of whose wings created whirlwinds and sandstorms. It features in a number of traditional tales and legends.

ARABS A general term used for nomads in the first millennium B.C.E. and as a specific ethnic term for the nomadic inhabitants of Arabia from the fourth century C.E. Like most of the inhabitants of the Levant they spoke a Semitic language. Arabs riding camels were among the enemies depicted in the reliefs of King Tiglath-Pileser at Nimrud but they also collaborated with the Assyrians as allies of Esarhaddon in his conquest of Egypt. Tribes operating from oases in northeast Arabia were traders, particularly in incense from the kingdoms of southwest Arabia, and enjoyed generally good relations with the Babylonians.

ARAMAEANS Inhabitants of the region west of the middle Euphrates around 1000 B.C.E. who subsequently settled in the Euphrates bend, forming tribal kingdoms known by the title "Bit" ("House"). They occupied settled villages and practiced mixed farming, with a strong emphasis on pastoralism.

ARAMAIC 1. A western Semitic language current from the ninth century B.C.E., the language of the Aramaeans. 2. An alphabetic script that was in widespread use in the Near East in the first millennium and which was ancestral to many later scripts.

ARATTA A city and region, probably in eastern Iran, that features in the early-third-millennium B.C.E. story of Enmerkar as the source of exotic materials including lapis lazuli and precious metals. The story claims Inanna, goddess of Uruk, was also worshipped in Aratta. Recent discoveries of a large cemetery and associated settlement near Jiroft on the Halil River in Kerman province, southeast Iran, indicate the presence there in the third millennium of a civilized society, which is being tentatively identified with Aratta. More than a hundred other sites have been located along the Halil River. The manufacture of chlorite vessels seems to have been a major local industry.

ARCHIVES Collections of texts stored together, especially in temples and palaces and mainly made up of official documents such as tax records and royal correspondence.

ARD A primitive form of plough that cut through the soil, breaking it up and creating a furrow, but not turning the soil.

ASAG (Akk. Asakku) A monstrous demon born of the union of An and Ki. He and his allies, the stones of the mountains, were defeated by the storm god Ninurta (or Adad in another version). The Asag was also seen as a magical demon responsible for death by disease.

ASHIPU *(Sum. lu.mash.mash)* Exorcist.

ASHUR Patron god of the city of Assur and of Assyria. His importance grew with the power of the Assyrians. Indefinite in his original attributes, he gradually appropriated those of other major gods, particularly the Sumerian god Enlil and the Babylonian deity Marduk.

ASHURBANIPAL King of Assyria (668–627 B.C.E.). He completed the conquest of Egypt and extended the empire, also fighting a series of campaigns against the Elamites and their ally, his brother, Shamash-shum-ukin, king of Babylon. He decorated the palace at Nineveh with reliefs and established a library containing all the extant works of Mesopotamian literature (see photos pp. 20, 104, 106).

ASHURNASIRPAL II King of Assyria (883–859 B.C.E.). He was responsible for greatly extending the empire and built the North-West Palace at Kalhu.

ASSUR (Ashur; Modern Qalat Sherqat) Capital city of the Assyrians in the second millennium B.C.E. and an important religious center thereafter when the capital was shifted to other cities. Kings were generally buried here.

ASSYRIA Northern Mesopotamia. The area around the city of Assur and the center of an empire of fluctuating extent, ranging from the heartland along the upper Tigris to an empire stretching from Egypt to Elam, including the Levant and Babylonia. The rain-fed plains of Assyria enjoyed agricultural prosperity. The region was dominated by Mitanni in the mid-second millennium B.C.E. but regained its independence under Ashur-uballit I and thereafter grew to become a major power in the first millennium B.C.E.

ASSYRIANS The inhabitants of Assur and its region, or of Assyria; speakers of Assyrian, a language derived from Old Akkadian.

ASU Doctor.

ATRAHASIS 1. "Very wise," king of Shuruppak, hero of the Old Babylonian poem recounting the Flood story. In other versions he is known as Ziusudra or Utnapishtim. 2. The title by which this poem is usually known in English.

BABYLON Probably founded in the early or mid-third millennium B.C.E., Babylon rose to prominence in the eighteenth century B.C.E. when the earlier southern cities were in decline; thereafter it remained the centre of Babylonia and one of the greatest cities of the ancient world. The most spectacular remains date to the Neo-Babylonian period and include the temple and ziggurat of Marduk, Nebuchadrezzar's palace, the great Processional Way to the *akitu* temple, and the city walls and gates. Controversy surrounds the location of the famous Hanging Gardens. The city's importance survived its fall to the Persians in 539 B.C.E.

BABYLONIA Southern Mesopotamia, composed in the third millennium B.C.E. of Sumer and Akkad. Babylonia rose to power under the dynasty of Hammurabi, experiencing periods of expansion and decline. Political, economic, and geographical considerations brought it frequently into conflict with Assyria to its north and Elam to its east, and it was periodically ravaged by nomads from the adjacent mountains and deserts, who were frequently later assimilated into the Babylonian population.

BABYLONIANS The inhabitants of Babylonia. Speakers of Babylonian, which developed from Old Akkadian in the early second millennium B.C.E.

BALA (Akk. palu) 1. The divinely ordained "turn" at holding supreme kingship in Sumer, according to the Sumerian King List. 2. The tax (offerings) paid by the core provinces of the Ur III Empire, consisting of a proportion of their produce.

BALAWAT (Ancient Imgur-enlil) A palace built by Shalmaneser III 16 kilometers northeast of Nimrud. A pair of massive wooden gates sheathed in bronze and decorated with reliefs show Shalmaneser's campaigns; two other pairs were erected by Ashurnasirpal II (see photos pp. 31, 168).

BAN (Sum.) A measure of volume, around 10 liters, equivalent to 10 *sila*.

BARIGA (Sum.) A measure of volume, around 60 liters, equivalent to 6 *ban*.

BARU Diviner.

BERU *see* stage.

BILTU *see* talent.

BIT, BITU (Sum. *E*) "House." Broad term with many extension meanings. 1. Temple, temple household. 2. Clan. 3. Province in later Babylonia, reflecting clan-based political organization. 4. Clan-based regional division in the desert region between Mesopotamia and the Levant.

BIT AKITU The shrine used in the *akitu* festival in a number of cities; situated outside the city, it was approached by a processional way.

BITANNU The inner courtyard and private portions of the palace.

BIT HILANI A pillared portico giving access to a large chamber or throne room, a feature of northern Syrian architecture. The portico was adopted by Sargon II and incorporated into his palace at Dur-Sharrukin.

BORSIPPA (Modern Birs Nimrud) A town near Babylon whose ziggurat was often mistakenly identified by early travelers as the Tower of Babel. Its patron deity was Nabu, the son of Marduk.

BRAK, TELL (Probably ancient Nagar or Nawar) A tell occupied from the Ubaid period to around 1200 B.C.E.; the city was at its height around 2500 B.C.E., before it was incorporated into the Akkadian Empire, when Sargon built a frontier fortress here. One of its most impressive monuments is the Eye Temple of the Uruk period, where numerous eye idols were found.

BULLA 1. A solid clay tag usually bearing a seal impression attached to a string of tokens. 2. A hollow clay ball used as an envelope to contain tokens: This is a loose use of the term *bulla*, and it should more properly be called an envelope.

BUR (Sum.) A measure of area, equivalent to 3 *eshe*—around 6.48 hectares.

BURUSHKHANDA (Purushkhanda; Akk. Purushhattum; modern Acem Hoyuk or Karahuyuk-Konya) An Anatolian town in which the Assyrians opened a trading colony (karum) in the nineteenth century B.C.E. A Sumerian story, *King of Battle*, preserved in a text found at fourteenth-century B.C.E.

Amarna, recounts how Sargon of Akkad mounted an expedition to rescue Akkadian merchants who were suffering oppression in Burushkhanda: This may have been written as propaganda in the reign of Shamshi-Adad when the Assyrian trading colony at Kanesh was revived.

BUSHEL *see* gur.

CANAANITES Inhabitants of the region bordering the Mediterranean between Egypt and Anatolia in the second millennium B.C.E. and inventors of the alphabet.

CARCHEMISH (Modern Jerablus) A major town in the second and first millennia, situated on the west bank of the Euphrates. Ruled by Assyria from 717 B.C.E., it was the scene of the Babylonians' defeat of Assyria and Egypt in 605 B.C.E.

CHALDAEANS Tribes who settled in southern Mesopotamia around 1000–900 B.C.E. They formed several independent kingdoms in conflict with Babylonian and Assyrian rulers. In 626 B.C.E. a Chaldaean dynasty seized the Babylonian throne, founding the Neo-Babylonian Empire.

CHLORITE A form of steatite (soapstone) found at various places, including near Tepe Yahya on the Iranian plateau where fine chlorite bowls were manufactured and widely exported.

CIMMERIANS Central Asian nomads who made troublesome raids on northern Near Eastern states during the ninth to seventh centuries B.C.E.

CIRE-PERDUE "Lost-wax"—a technique of casting metal where a full-scale model of a desired object is made in wax, which is then coated in clay and fired. The wax runs out leaving a mould in which metal objects in complex shapes can be cast.

CONE MOSAICS Colored wall decorations, usually in geometric patterns, made by pushing clay cones with painted heads (or occasionally cones of colored stone) into wall plaster.

CUBIT Sumerian *kush*, Akkadian *ammatu*: a measure of length, around 50 centimeters.

CUNEIFORM Wedge-shaped, a term used to describe the Mesopotamian writing formed by impressing a wedge-shaped reed stylus into soft clay.

CYLINDER SEAL A cylinder usually of stone inscribed with a design and written text that could be endlessly reproduced by rolling it across wet clay. Cylinder seals began to replace the simpler and less useful stamp seals in the fourth millennium B.C.E. (see photos pp. 63, 90, 92, 208, 247).

DAGAN A West Semitic grain god extensively worshipped in the Near East including Mari. He was assimilated into the Mesopotamian pantheon in a subordinate position.

DAMGULNUNA (Akk. Damkina) A mother goddess, wife of Enki and mother of Marduk. Probably another name for Ninhursaga. City goddess of Malgum, she was also worshipped in early times at Umma and Lagash. Like Enki, she received offerings of fish.

DANNA *see* stage.

DECIPHERMENT Breaking the code of ancient scripts. In order for decipherment to be possible there have to be substantial texts in the script; a knowledge of the underlying language is necessary unless there are bilingual inscriptions; scripts using the same or similar characters may be helpful but should not be relied on. Many Near Eastern scripts, including cuneiform, have been deciphered since their discovery in the last few centuries, but some still defy decipherment, notably Proto-Elamite.

DENDROCHRONOLOGY A method of physically dating wood that can produce accurate and precise calendar dates. It has been little used in the Near East but has had a vital secondary impact by providing data for calibrating radiocarbon dates.

DER (Modern T. Aqar) A city-state east of the Tigris in northeastern Babylonia, capital of Emutbal.

DILMUN (Akk. Tilmun) Referred to in legend as the paradise land and as the home of the immortal couple who survived the great Flood, Dilmun was known to Sumerians from the fourth millennium B.C.E., when it may be identified as Tarut Island and adjacent areas of the Arabian mainland. In the third millennium B.C.E., the name referred to the island of Bahrain as well, and around 2000 B.C.E., Failaka was also incorporated within its realms. Dilmun was an important trading state, possessing abundant freshwater, pearls, and excellent dates of its own and acting as a major entrepôt for goods from farther southeast (Magan and Meluhha).

DIYALA A major river flowing down from the Zagros to join the Tigris, which acted as a main artery of trade. Its middle reaches, the Hamrin basin, were an important area of dry farming, occupied from Samarra times, whereas irrigation agriculture was practiced on the plains of the lower Diyala by the Ubaid period. The latter region formed the territory of the city of Eshnunna.

DUMUZI (Tammuz) The divine shepherd and husband of the goddess Inanna. Dumuzi was also the "élan vital" of the date palm and by extension of the vegetation that grew annually, his death coinciding with the end of the growing season for crops and birthing season for animals.

DUR-KURIGALZU (Modern Aqar Kuf) The Kassite capital founded by Kurigalzu I in the late fifteenth or early fourteenth century. It was abandoned after the fall of the Kassites. The main religious complex, including the ziggurat, was dedicated to Enlil. A substantial palace with painted walls has also been uncovered.

DUR SHARRUKIN (Modern Khorsabad) "Sargon's fortress," a city built in 717 B.C.E. by the Assyrian king Sargon II as his capital but abandoned after his ill-omened death in 706.

EA *see* Enki.

EANNA Name of a district of Uruk and more specifically the precinct of Inanna; possibly a separate village in Ubaid times (see photo p. 82).

EARLY DYNASTIC PERIOD (ED) The period of historical and legendary kings and emerging city-states in southern Mesopotamia, from around 2900

B.C.E. to the beginning of the Akkadian Empire. It was divided into three phases, I ca. 2900–2750 B.C.E., II ca. 2750–2600, and III ca. 2600–2334 B.C.E., subdivided into IIIa and IIIb.

EBLA (Modern Tell Mardikh) The city was capital of a small independent kingdom in the Orontes valley during the Early and Middle Bronze Age. A massive wall and a number of palaces have been excavated here. It is famous for its archive of around 1,200 tablets, preserved when the city was burned down in the twenty-third or twenty-second century B.C.E. The city was abandoned after it was again fired around 1600 B.C.E.

ED Early Dynastic period *q.v.*

EGYPT Apart from little-understood links in the late fourth millennium (Pre-Dynastic period), Egypt and Mesopotamia did not have much contact until the later second millennium B.C.E. when they were among the powers vying for control of the Levant and engaging in international diplomacy. In the seventh century B.C.E., Assyria briefly conquered Egypt.

EKAL MASHARTI Review Palace. Part of the royal establishment developing from the ninth century B.C.E. as a base for the ordnance, animals, and supplies for the increasingly large professional armies of the Assyrian kings. The complex also included a parade ground where the troops could be drilled and inspected, and storerooms for booty taken on campaign. "Fort Shalmaneser" at Kalhu is the best-known example.

EKALLATUM A small kingdom north of Assur, ancestral home of the eighteenth-century king, Shamshi-Adad.

EKUR "Mountain house," the temple of the supreme god Enlil in the city of Nippur, regarded as the paramount shrine by the ED and later people of southern Mesopotamia, where kings dedicated inscribed vessels and stelae to the god. Regarded as the seat of the gods' assembly, it was probably the place where the alliance of southern Mesopotamian city-states met to elect their leader.

ELAM The region to the east of Babylonia, in southwestern Iran, comprising both highland and lowland zones. The main cities were Susa and Anshan, capitals of the regions of Susiana and Anshan. From early times Elam was strongly linked culturally with its western neighbor, Mesopotamia, enjoying periods both of cooperation and of hostility. Elam also had important links with towns to the east on the Iranian plateau. Initially home to many disparate and independent groups, of which only some spoke the language known as Elamite, Elam came to denote a polity of variable size, often known locally as Susa and Anshan.

ELAMITE A language spoken by the people of southwestern Iran, the inhabitants of Elam, although other languages were also spoken there. Elamite is not related with certainty to any other known language.

EMAR (Modern Meskeneh) A town strategically situated at the main crossing of the Euphrates on routes linking Mesopotamia to the Levant, Anatolia, and the Mediterranean. Emar was important from the third millennium B.C.E. until its fall in 1185 B.C.E.

EMESAL (Akk. *luru / ummisallu*) A Sumerian dialect with some differences in sound and vocabulary, used by women. It was also used in some liturgical songs.

EMUTBAL An Amorite kingdom in the east of Mesopotamia, whose rulers gained control of Larsa in 1834 B.C.E.

EN 1. Sumerian: "lord." The main religious and political leader of early Sumerian cities. Later his function probably became purely religious. 2. (Akk. *entu*) The title used for high priestesses, such as that of Nanna in Ur.

ENHEDUANNA Daughter of Sargon and *entu*-priestess at Ur. She both collected sacred texts and herself composed hymns, and is the first author in the world to whom we can give a name.

ENKI (Akk. Ea) God of the freshwater ocean (Abzu) and of wisdom and magic, who was well disposed toward humanity and helped them on a number of occasions. His main shrine, E-abzu ("house of the Abzu"), was at Eridu, and dates back into the Ubaid period. Enki played a leading role in the Creation, shaping lesser gods and everything the gods might need including, eventually, humanity from clay softened with the water of the Abzu.

ENLIL (Akk. Ellil) "Lord Air," the god of the wind, particularly the life-giving winds of spring. Also known as Nunmanir. Usually portrayed as the son of An, but sometimes seen as the son of two earlier offspring of primordial ocean. He was the ruler of the gods until supplanted by Marduk during the second millennium B.C.E.

ENMERKAR Legendary king of Uruk, said to be the son of Utu, father of Lugalbanda and grandfather of Gilgamesh. He is the protagonist of a poem "Enmerkar and the Lord of Aratta," in which he attempts to gain precious materials from Aratta to build a temple for Inanna, and features in several other poems that also deal with relations between Aratta and Mesopotamia, including "Enmerkar and En-suhgir-ana."

ENMETENA King of Lagash ca. 2404–2375 B.C.E. He defeated Umma and restored the disputed boundary between the two states, and he built a canal linking the Euphrates to the Tigris.

ENSI Originally a steward, an official responsible for supervising the cultivated land of a settlement, but later the governor of a city or the king of a minor city.

ENTU see *en*.

ENUMA ANA BIT MARSI ASHIPU ILLIKU "When the exorcist is going to the house of the patient . . . ," a medical collection of some forty tablets listing omens, symptoms, and aspects of the patient to be observed along with some prognoses and a few magical treatments.

ENUMA ANU ENLIL "When Anu and Enlil . . . ," the first words and title of the principal collection of astronomical observations and their interpretation as omens.

ENUMA ELISH "When on High . . . ," the first words and title of the Babylonian Epic of Creation, composed around 1100 B.C.E. This polished work recounts the emergence of the gods and Marduk's creation of the world, justifying the political preeminence of Marduk and his city, Babylon.

EPIC OF ERRA Composed in Akkadian around 1000–800 B.C.E. by Kapti-ilani-Marduk after it was revealed to him in a dream, the epic tells the story of a disastrous period when Marduk leaves control of the world in the hands of Erra, god of strife. This reflects the period of international disturbance around the end of the second millennium B.C.E.

EPONYM A year known by the name of an Assyrian official, the *limmu.* By the first millennium these formed a regular pattern: The second year in a king's reign took his name, followed by five years named after the chief state officials, and the names of provincial governors were used thereafter. Careful eponym lists were kept, as they were vital for various recording purposes.

ERESH An ancient Sumerian city, possibly to be identified with modern Abu Salabikh.

ERESHKIGAL (Akk. Allatu) Daughter of Nanna and ruler of the netherworld. By her first husband Gugulanna, she bore Ninazu, father of Ningishzida, both underworld deities; later she was courted by Nergal who became her co-ruler in the underworld.

ERIDU (Sum. Eridug) One of the earliest Sumerian cities, and in myth the first city created by Enki when he brought order to the world. It was located on an island of higher ground in the southern Mesopotamian marshland and was believed to sit within the Abzu, the freshwater ocean underlying the Earth, the realm of Enki whose principal shrine was located here. This existed by Ubaid times and was venerated, renovated, and embellished by monarchs long after the settlement itself had been abandoned.

ERRA (Sum. Nergal) Originally a separate deity, Erra later became syncretized with Nergal. God of strife, pestilence, and destruction, he was the protagonist in a late-second-millennium poem "The Epic of Erra" that reflected the political, military, and economic chaos of the times.

ESAGILA The temple of Marduk at Babylon.

ESHE A measure of area, equivalent to 6 *iku*—around 2.16 hectares.

ESHNUNNA (Modern Tell Asmar) A city on the Diyala in northeast Babylonia, capital of the state of Warium. The city existed in the ED period but expanded greatly in the later third millennium when large temples and palaces were built here. It was one of the cities that vied for power in the Isin-Larsa period but was conquered by Hammurabi in 1763 and abandoned a few years later.

ETANA A legendary king of Kish, whose story survives in incomplete Akkadian texts. The childless king prays to Shamash for an heir. Following the god's advice, he rescues an injured eagle from a pit where it has been cast, without its feathers, as punishment for betraying its sworn friendship with a snake. Etana cares for the eagle until its feathers regrow, when it takes him on its back and flies with him to Heaven to obtain the Plant of Birth (a scene illustrated on cylinder seals). The end of the story is lost, but the Sumerian King List shows that Etana eventually had a son (see photo p. 208).

ETEMENANKI "Foundation of Heaven and Earth": the ziggurat of Marduk (the "Tower of Babel") in Babylon.

EUPHRATES The more amenable of the two rivers that watered Mesopotamia. The majority of Babylonian cities were built along its many branches.

FAIENCE A paste of silica grains such as quartz sand, lime, and an alkali such as soda or potash, mixed with water and heated to around 800–950 degrees centigrade (1440–740 Fahrenheit) when the grains sinter and the surface melts to form a glaze. Ash made by burning desert plants supplied the lime, soda, and potash. Copper oxide was added to the mixture, colouring the faience blue, turquoise or green. Faience was made in Mesopotamia from the mid-fifth millennium.

"FORT SHALMANESER" The *ekal masharti* of Kalhu, built by Shalmaneser III.

GAGUM (Akk.) Sacred household of *naditums* dedicated to the worship of particular gods (such as Shamash and Aya at Sippar), and including a range of personnel, from administrators and scribes to laborers and slaves.

GALA (Akk. *kalum*) Lamentation priest, a post possibly held by a homosexual, transvestite, or eunuch.

GESHTINANNA A rural goddess, sister of the fertility god Dumuzi and his chief mourner when he was taken to the netherworld. She became a substitute for him there to allow him to return to Earth for six months of the year, and acted as a scribe to the queen of the underworld, Ereshkigal.

GILGAMESH Legendary king of Uruk, who may have lived around 2600 B.C.E., although some scholars place him up to 200 years earlier. Many stories were told of him, from his conflict with the historical king Agga of Kish to his wanderings in search of immortality; these enjoyed wide popularity in the ancient Near East. After his death he became a judge in the underworld.

GILGAMESH EPIC The story of Gilgamesh is known from five Sumerian poems of the Ur III period, which recount separate episodes in his life; from an epic poem of the eighteenth century B.C.E., *Shutur eli sharri* "Surpassing all other kings," preserved only as fragments, and its successor, *Sha naqba imuru* "He who saw the Deep," known also as the Standard Version, composed in the late second millennium B.C.E.

GIN *see* shekel.

GIPARU (Sum.) The residence of the moon god Nanna, his wife Ningal, and the important *entu*, priestess who served him, located within the precinct of Nanna at Ur.

GIRSU (Modern Telloh) Located in the territory of Lagash, it rose to the position of the principal city during ED times, eclipsing Lagash city. The city deity was Ningirsu (identified with Ninurta); records from the temple of his wife, Bau (or Baba), were for a long time the main source of information on the organization of early temple estates. The city has also yielded many fine stone statues and stelae such as the "Stele of the Vultures" and many statues of Gudea. It declined from the late third millennium.

GLACIS A steep artificial mound of earth over a mudbrick or stone core, faced with clay or lime, on which a city's walls were erected. A glacis slowed and hampered attacks and made it more difficult for the attackers to set up scaling ladders.

GUN *see* talent.

GUR A Sumerian measure of volume (bushel), equivalent to 5 *bariga*—around 300 liters.

GUTI (Gutians) The inhabitants of Gutium, a mountainous region in the Zagros, whose raids troubled the latter years of the Akkadian Empire. They seized control of part of Sumer and Akkad until expelled by Utu-hegal of Uruk around 2120.

HAMMURABI King of Babylon 1792–1750 B.C.E. who extended his small kingdom into a great empire by military campaigning, diplomacy, and ruthlessness, driving out the Elamites and Guti, and conquering the cities of Babylonia and the middle Euphrates. He took a keen interest in administration and justice (see photos pp. 88, 246).

HARRAN A city on the Balikh in northern Mesopotamia, an area associated with the Aramaeans and with biblical figures, including Abraham and Jacob. The moon god Sin was its patron deity. It was the last stronghold of Assyrian resistance to the Babylonians, falling in 610. Thereafter it was controlled by the Medes until the conquest by the Persians in the reign of the Babylonian king Nabonidus, a native of the city and devotee of Sin. He restored the temples neglected by the Medes.

HATTUSAS (Modern Bogazkhoy) An Anatolian town containing an Assyrian karum in the nineteenth century B.C.E., it later became the capital city of the Hittite Empire.

HITTITES The Indo-European-speaking inhabitants of Anatolia, whose empire began to develop around 1700 B.C.E., reaching its peak around 1400–1200 B.C.E. when it controlled much of the Euphrates region and the northern Levant, bringing it into conflict with Egypt and Mitanni.

HUMBABA *see* Huwawa.

HURRIAN A language of the Caucasian family. Individuals with Hurrian names are mentioned in texts from at least the time of the Akkadian Empire.

HUWAWA The demon of the Cedar Mountain, the guardian appointed by Enlil, who was slain by Gilgamesh and Enkidu after they deprived him of his "auras" by trickery. In the Standard Version of the Gilgamesh epic he is called Humbaba.

IGIGI (Igigu) Originally in OB times a collective term for the chief gods, it later came to mean all the gods of Heaven, contrasted with Anunnakki, the gods of the Earth and the underworld.

IKU A measure of area, equivalent to 100 *sar*—around 0.36 hectares.

IMDUGUD *see* Anzu.

INANNA (Akk. Ishtar) Variously portrayed as the daughter of An, Nanna, Enlil, or Enki. Goddess of love, war, rain and storms, the morning and evening star, and various more minor responsibilities. The goddess of prostitutes and carnal love, she had no connection with motherhood and little with matrimony, the Sacred Marriage in which she took part being essentially a fertility ritual, rapidly followed in mythology by the death of her spouse, Dumuzi. She was one of the most important deities, playing a leading role in many myths. Inanna was the patron deity of Uruk, and initially of Agade, and was worshipped in Kish as the wife of the city's deity, Zababa, and, according to the poem "Enmerkar and the Lord of Aratta," in distant Aratta in eastern Iran.

ISHKUR Sumerian name for the storm god, called Adad in Akkadian. Revered in the north as a source of life-giving rain, in the south he was more feared as the bringer of storms, hail, and floods.

ISHME-DAGAN Son of Shamshi-Adad I, and his viceroy in Ekallatum. He spent much time campaigning against the Elamites and Eshnunna. After succeeding his father in 1776, he gradually lost lands, becoming a vassal of Hammurabi from 1764 until his death in 1741.

ISHTAR Patron goddess of Nineveh and Arbil, among other cities, and Assyrian goddess of war. Probably originally a separate goddess but early syncretized with Inanna.

ISIN Capital city of the eponymous state that gained control of most of southern Babylonia after the fall of the Ur III Empire. Its territories shrank in competition with other emerging states, and it was conquered by Larsa around 1794 B.C.E.

ISIN-LARSA PERIOD The period from the fall of the Ur III Empire in 2004 to the creation of Hammurabi's empire in the 1760s. Many states vied for power during this period, with Isin initially dominant and Larsa becoming the major power after 1794.

ISRAEL A kingdom that emerged in the early first millennium in the southern Levant. Traditionally, after the death of Solomon it was partitioned into Israel in the north with its capital at Samaria and Judah in the south. Until its fall to Assyria in 720 B.C.E., it was constantly at the mercy of its powerful neighbors, Egypt and Assyria, and in conflict with Judah and other local kingdoms.

JEMDET NASR A settlement north of Kish occupied from the later Uruk to early ED periods, which has given its name to the intervening Jemdet Nasr (JN) period. A large number of tablets with early writing were excavated here in a building that was probably a palace.

JIROFT *see* Aratta.

JN Jemdet Nasr period, ca. 3100–2900 B.C.E.

JUDAH The southern kingdom after the traditional partition of Israel in the late tenth century, it retained control of the capital, Jerusalem. It suffered periodic attacks by Israel and Assyria, and finally fell to the Babylonians in 586 B.C.E., when many of its leading people were deported.

KALAM "The Land"—the Sumerian name for Babylonia.

KALHU (Modern Nimrud, biblical Calah) Originally a small administrative centre, Kalhu was the Assyrian capital from 863 to 707 B.C.E. and remained an important city thereafter. Palaces were built here by Ashurnasirpal II, who also transformed the original settlement into a magnificent city, Shalmaneser III, Adad-Nirari III, Tiglath-Pileser III, and Esarhaddon. In 1990 the lavishly furnished tombs of three Assyrian royal ladies were discovered in Ashurnasirpal's palace. The city was sacked in 612 B.C.E. when the Assyrian Empire crumbled.

KANESH (Modern Kultepe) An Anatolia town with a substantial foreign merchant quarter (karum) in its lower town. Merchants from a number of cities operated here, including Assur. The destruction of the town by fire preserved the merchants' archive of tablets, mainly dealing with their trade but alluding also to personal matters.

KAR-TUKULTI-NINURTA A new capital 3 kilometers north of Assur built by Tukulti-Ninurta I but abandoned after his death in 1207.

KARANA A trading city in northern Mesopotamia, often identified with Tell al-Rimah where an extensive OB archive was discovered.

KARUM Literally "quay"—a trading colony or commercial center, such as that established in the nineteenth-century Anatolian town of Kanesh; many cities had a karum outside their walls.

KASSITE The language spoken by the Kassites, apparently unrelated to any known language. Only a few words in the Kassite language survive, mostly names, although there are also two short Akkadian-Kassite word lists.

KASSITE PERIOD The Kassite king Agum II seized power in Babylonia around 1570 B.C.E. and the dynasty survived until 1155.

KASSITES A tribal group probably originally from the Zagros, who gradually settled in Babylonia as laborers and mercenaries in the early second millennium B.C.E. After the fall of Hammurabi's dynasty, Kassites seized control. Their reign was a time of peace, prosperity, and cultural development.

KHORSABAD *see* Dur Sharrukin.

KI (Akk. Irsitu) 1. The goddess of Earth, also known as Urash. From her union with An came all plants. 2. The Earth, with the Abzu, the Ocean, and the Netherworld; contrasted with An, "On High."

KING LIST A list of kings giving their length of reign and often city and parentage, sometimes with other information. The earliest is the Sumerian King List, running from before the Flood to the fall of Isin; others list Babylonian and Assyrian kings from the early second millennium onward.

KISH (Modern Tell Ingharra and Tell Uhaimir) An important northern Sumerian city, occupied from the Ubaid period into Achaemenid times. Excavated remains of the ED city include a large administrative building, a cemetery with chariot burials, and two ziggurats. By the late ED period the title "King of Kish" implied some form of authority over the cities of Sumer (see photo p. 72).

KUDURRU A land grant record, particularly applied to stone examples from the Kassite period, which were carved with relief designs of gods or their symbols and sometimes of the king. They bore details of land grants and tax exemptions from kings to their loyal followers. Later kudurrus were often humbler records in the form of tablets and could refer to private transfers of land (see photos pp. 94, 213).

KUSH *see* cubit.

LAGASH (Modern Al-Hiba, Sum. Urukug) One of the major Sumerian city-states in ED times, frequently in conflict with Umma over disputed border territory. It enjoyed a period of prominence after the fall of the Akkadian dynasty, particularly under Gudea. Its first city, Lagash, was eclipsed by the city of Girsu during the ED period.

LAMASHTU Evil she-demon, daughter of the god Anu, who attacked unborn children and young babies and brought disease more generally.

LAND, THE *Kalam,* the Sumerian name for Sumer and Akkad.

LAPIS LAZULI A beautiful and highly valued blue stone; the only source known to the people of the ancient Near East was Badakhshan in Afghanistan.

LARSA (Modern Senkereh) A city south of Uruk that gained control over much of Babylonia in the early second millennium B.C.E. Under the Amorite dynasty founded by Kudur-Mabuk in 1834 and particularly under Rim-Sin I Larsa's power grew, defeating its main rival Isin in 1794. It succumbed to Hammurabi in 1763, after a six-month siege.

LAW CODES Royal statements of social, economic, and legal policy or reforms, expressed in the form of a code of practice; these probably did not determine day-to-day legal practice.

LEVEE A riverbed and surrounding banks raised above the level of the plain through which the river flows. Levees are formed in regions of low gradient like southern Mesopotamia where periodic floods cause the river to overtop its banks. The resulting reduction in the velocity of the river's flow causes much of the silt it was carrying to be deposited in its bed and on its banks, progressively raising them.

LIMMU *see* eponym.

LOGOGRAM A sign representing a word: This has the same meaning in different languages but a different spoken form.

LOST-WAX CASTING *see* cire-perdue.

LUDLUL The "Poem of the Righteous Sufferer," an Akkadian lamentation of 500 lines spread over four tablets, recounting the sufferings of a virtuous individual, his attempts to understand his misfortunes, and eventual resignation to the situation where the gods may have to cause an individual suffering while maintaining the greater good of the world.

LUGAL (Akk. *sharrum*) "Great Man." A title given to war leaders that later came to mean king. His duties included leading the army in defense of the city and acting as judge.

LUGALBANDA Legendary king of Uruk, son of Enmerkar and father of Gilgamesh. Taken ill in the journey to Aratta, he was left to recover and experienced a number of supernatural adventures.

LUGALE A poem recounting the myth of Ninurta's defeat of the monster Asag.

LUGALZAGESI Governor of Umma from ca. 2349 B.C.E., conqueror of Lagash, and king of Uruk from 2340. He gained control of Ur and the approval of Nippur and went on to create an empire in Sumer with influence through much of the north. He was defeated around 2316 B.C.E. by Sargon.

LULLUBI People from the mountains to the east who were referred to in Akkadian times.

MAGAN A name probably applied to the Makran coast of Iran but mainly to the Oman peninsula where substantial deposits of copper ore were mined. Its inhabitants traded with Mesopotamia and Dilmun, Meluhha, and probably southern Arabia and East Africa.

MANA *see* mina.

MANNAI A state in northwest Iran, east of the Zagros.

MANU *see* mina.

MARDUK Son of Enki and Damgalnuna, Marduk was the patron deity of Babylon and rose to prominence in the pantheon as his city gained in importance. The Babylonian Creation story, *Enuma elish*, written down around 1100 B.C.E., provides a mythological justification for his achievement of supreme divine power. Marduk was often referred to as Bel, meaning "Lord."

MARI A city in the middle Euphrates region, founded in the ED period. The royal palace is well preserved and has been completely excavated, giving a detailed picture of the layout and functioning of royal households. Mari controlled a city-state in the early second millennium, when much is known about public and royal private life here from letters and other documents preserved in the palace archive when the town was sacked by Hammurabi in 1757 B.C.E.

MARTU (Akk. *amurru*) 1. The Amorites *q.v.* 2. A nomadic shepherd god associated with the Amorites; he was depicted in art dressed in nomad garb, carrying a shepherd's crook and sometimes with a gazelle under his arm. When the Amorites began to settle in Babylonia, Martu was incorporated into the Babylonian pantheon: He married the daughter of the god Numushda, despite the latter's warnings that Martu and his people were uncivilized savages who ate raw meat and did not live in houses or bury their dead.

MASHKAN SHAPIR (Modern Tell Abu Dhuwari) Second city of the kingdom of Larsa during the nineteenth and eighteenth centuries B.C.E. Its layout has been recorded by surface survey with limited excavation. The city was traversed by at least six canals, with two large harbors. The southern sector of the city housed the temple of Nergal and other religious buildings. Administrative buildings and a walled cemetery lay in the southwest. Industrial activity was found throughout the settlement although there were also concentrations of pottery making, copper, and stone working in particular sectors of the walled city.

ME (Akk. *parsu*) A key Sumerian religious concept, the *ME* were the divine powers behind all the features of civilization, encompassing not only the benefits such as kingship, peace, justice, crafts, writing, and the arts, but also the less attractive aspects such as slander, perjury, and prostitution. Generally they were held by the supreme gods, An, Enlil, or Enki.

MEBARAGESI A king of Kish mentioned in the Sumerian King List (where he is called Enmebaragesi—lord Mebaragesi), father of Gilgamesh's opponent Agga. His historical reality is attested by two early ED inscriptions bearing his name.

MEDES An Indo-European-speaking people, who created a kingdom in western Iran in the eighth century B.C.E. and spread westward, allying with the Babylonians to bring about the downfall of Assyria.

MELUHHA 1. The Indus civilization that flourished between ca. 2600 and 1800 B.C.E. in the valleys of the Indus and Saraswati Rivers and adjacent areas. Traders from Meluhha were present in Sumer and Akkad, bringing many important raw materials, but there is no evidence that the Sumerians ventured as far afield as Meluhha. 2. In the first millennium B.C.E. the name Meluhha was transferred to Nubia.

MICROMORPHOLOGY The study of a thin section of a soil sample under the microscope, which can yield data on formation processes and composition that can reveal information on the environment and human effects upon it, and on the activities that took place in parts of a settlement.

MINA Sumerian *mana*, Akkadian *manu*, a measure of weight, equivalent to 60 shekels—around 500 grams.

MITANNI The Hurrian kingdom that flourished in northern Mesopotamia ca. 1600–1100 B.C.E., controlling Assyria and other neighboring smaller states, and rivaling the Hittites and Egyptians.

MUSHHUSSSHU "Furious snake," a dragon with horns on its forehead, a snake's head, body, and tail, the forelegs of a lion and hindlegs of a bird of prey. Principally known as the attendant of Marduk, this creature was also associated with Enlil and Marduk's son Nabu and became associated with Ashur when the Assyrians under Sennacherib conquered Babylonia.

MUSHKI A region and its people probably identifiable as Phrygia in Anatolia. In the eighth century it was initially hostile to Assyria but later allied with it.

NABONIDUS Last king of Babylonia 555–539 B.C.E. He spent ten years of his reign in the oasis of Taima, outside Babylonia; his son Belshazzar acted as his viceroy in Babylon.

NABU God of scribes and writing and, by extension, wisdom; minister, and later son, of the Babylonian supreme deity Marduk; his wife was Nisaba who had earlier been the patron deity of writing. Beautifully written texts were often deposited as votive offerings from scribes in the shrines of Nabu.

NAMMU The mother of creation. In one version of the Mesopotamian Creation myths she was the primordial water from which all creation arose; in others she was the wife of An and mother of Enki. Jacobsen suggests she was the power in the riverbed to produce water.

NANNA (Also known as Suen or Nanna-Suen; Akk. Sin) God of the moon, patron deity of the city of Ur. Nanna was the father of a number of major deities, notably Utu, Inanna, and Ereshkigal (see photo p. 223).

NARAM-SIN Fourth king of the Akkadian dynasty, 2254–2218 B.C.E. He campaigned widely and was made a god during his lifetime.

NEBUCHADREZZAR II King of Babylonia 604–562 B.C.E. As crown prince he completed the conquest of Assyria and brought peace to the united realm. He undertook major building work in Babylon and other cities.

NEO-ASSYRIAN PERIOD The period of Assyria's greatest expansion, from the accession of Tiglath-Pileser II in 966 to its fall to the Babylonians and Medes in 609 B.C.E.

NEO-BABYLONIAN PERIOD The period in Babylonia contemporary with the rise and fall of the Assyrian Empire, and particularly the period from the expulsion of the Assyrians in 626, when Babylonia became the major power in the Near East, to the fall of Babylon in 539 B.C.E.

NERGAL (Akk. Erra) A son of Enlil and his wife Ninlil or Belet-ili, Nergal was a warlike deity who violently courted Ereshkigal, Queen of the Underworld, and became her co-ruler. Originally a separate deity he became closely identified with Erra, both being associated with plague and other forms of disaster and violent or sudden death.

NEW YEAR FESTIVAL Also known as *akitu*, this was the principal festival in Babylon, celebrating both the beginning of the year and the supreme role of Marduk, the city's patron deity, and reaffirming the responsibilities of the king. The New Year began around the spring equinox, the time of the barley harvest, the celebration of which was also marked by the festival.

NIMRUD *see* Kalhu.

NIMRUD IVORIES A huge assemblage of thousands of ivories, mainly decorations from furniture, excavated from various parts of Nimrud, notably Fort Shalmaneser, the Burnt Palace, and wells in the North-West Palace, where they had been abandoned by looters in 612 B.C.E. Originally the ivory objects and the furniture decorated with ivory had been either in use in the palaces or stored in Fort Shalmaneser: They were acquired as royal gifts, tribute or booty by Assyrian kings from Ashurnasirpal II to Ashurbanipal.

NINDAN (Akk.) A measure of length, equivalent to 12 cubits—about 6 meters.

NINEVEH (Ancient Ninua) A settlement on the Tigris established in the seventh millennium B.C.E. and already substantial by the Ninevite 5 period (the regional equivalent to the ED period in the south). Shalmaneser I and later kings built palaces here, and Sennacherib made it the Assyrian capital. Prominent mounds, now called Kuyunjik and Nebi Yunus, attracted the attention of early excavators: The former was the citadel, where Sennacherib's "Palace without a Rival" and Ashurbanipal's palace have yielded magnificent reliefs and Ashurbanipal's library; the latter held the royal arsenal.

NINGAL A goddess, wife of the moon god Nanna and worshipped along with him at Ur and Harran. Mother of Utu (Shamash).

NINGIRSU Patron deity of Girsu, the capital of Lagash state, and identified with Ninurta, god of storms. On the "Stele of the Vultures," an ED victory stele, he is shown gathering the defeated enemy from the rival state of Umma into a net.

NINHURSAGA (Akk. Belit-ili) "Lady of the Foothills." Also known as Damgalnuna, Nintur, and Ninmah. She was the principal mother goddess, involved in the various versions of the creation of humanity. Sometimes depicted as the wife of Enlil to whom she bore Ninurta and the gods of Summer and Winter, she is alternatively his sister or the wife of Enki. She was worshipped as Ninmah in the city of Adab and also had connections with Kish.

NINISINA (Akk. Gula) "Lady of Isin," daughter of An, and patron deity of the city of Isin. She became a Great Goddess during that city's period of power, usurping Inanna's position as goddess of war. Goddess of healing and divine midwife, she became identified with the Semitic goddess Gula in the late OB period.

NINLIL Also known as Sud. A goddess, wife of Enlil, and mother of Nanna. She was probably a mother goddess and a goddess of grain.

NINMAH Another name for the mother goddess, Ninhursaga, and patron deity of the city of Adab.

NINURTA The god of storms, the spring flood, and warfare, Ninurta was often associated with the mountain foothills, realm of his mother Ninhursaga. Inventor of the plough and of irrigation, he was particularly associated with agriculture, whereas Ishkur, another storm god, was associated with pastoralism. His principal shrine was at Nippur.

NIPPUR (Sum. Nibru) One of the principal cities in ED and later times, Nippur was never the political center of a larger entity but instead enjoyed spiritual authority as the home of the ruling god Enlil, until this role was usurped by Marduk and Babylon. Here the gods met in assembly, possibly mirroring an assembly of ED kings. In addition to Enlil's shrine, Ekur, the city had temples to Inanna, Ninurta, and other deities. Excavations uncovered many OB texts in what was probably the scribal quarter of the city.

NUZI (Modern Yorgan Tepe) A settlement east of the Tigris, occupied from the Ubaid period. It was a provincial town of the kingdom of Arrapha in the Mitanni Empire, mainly occupied by Hurrian speakers. Extensive archives give a very full picture of life here.

OBSIDIAN Volcanic glass, highly prized for its appearance and the sharpness of its flaked edge, traded in the Near East by the beginning of the Holocene Epoch.

OB Old Babylonian period *q.v.*

OLD AKKADIAN The Semitic language spoken in the third millennium, ancestral to Assyrian and Babylonian.

OLD BABYLONIAN PERIOD Strictly this refers to the period from the fall of Isin in 1787 to the fall of Babylon in 1595 B.C.E., but it is also used more loosely to refer to the whole period from the fall of the Ur III empire in 2004 until 1595.

ONAGER The wild steppe ass, *Equus hemionus.* This intractable beast was never fully domesticated, but crossing it with the domestic donkey produced an animal that was both strong and docile. References to onagers pulling vehicles generally mean this hybrid.

OSTRACON (pl. ostraca, *also* ostrakon, ostraka) The Greek word for potsherd (sherd), referring specifically to a piece of pottery used as a writing medium and frequently as "scrap-paper."

OSTRAKA *see* ostracon.

'OUEILI, TELL EL- The solitary seventh-millennium settlement currently known in southern Mesopotamia.

PAZUZU A first-millennium demon, god of the winds. Despite his grotesque and forbidding appearance, he was benevolent, warding off harmful winds and driving away the demoness Lamashtu who threatened infants and unborn children. Amulets of Pazuzu were often worn by pregnant women.

PERSIANS Indo-European speakers living in western Iran by the first millennium B.C.E. and including both the tribes known as Medes *(q.v.)* and those referred to as Persians in antiquity. The latter achieved hegemony under Cyrus II from 550 B.C.E., founding the Persian or Achaemenid Empire (*see also* Achaemenid Period).

PHOENICIANS First-millennium descendants of the Canaanite inhabitants of the Levant coast, renowned as traders and seafarers (see photos pp. 141, 239).

PICTOGRAPH A pictorial sign used in writing.

POOR MAN OF NIPPUR A humorous folk tale about a poor man, Gimil-Ninurta, who is badly treated by the local mayor and exacts his revenge by creating three opportunities to beat him up.

POTSHERD *see* sherd.

PROCESSIONAL WAY A paved road leading from the city's sacred precinct to the extramural *akitu* temple. A processional way has been uncovered at Assur and is known from literary sources to have existed at Uruk. The best known is that of Babylon, where it ran from the Esagila, Marduk's shrine, leaving the city through the imposing Ishtar Gate. It was flanked by walls with monumental decoration showing lions. Known to the Babylonians as *ai-ibur-shabu*, "may the proud not flourish," this was the route taken not only by the New Year festival procession but also at the ceremonial departure and return of the army led by the king.

PROTO-ELAMITE The script devised in Elam in the late fourth millennium that died out during the ED period. Although it is assumed to render an early form of the Elamite language, this has not been demonstrated since it has not been deciphered.

PUABI A queen buried in the Royal Cemetery at Ur and named on an inscribed seal found in her tomb.

PUZRISH-DAGAN (Modern Drehem) Livestock depot under the Ur III kings, situated near Nippur. All livestock paid in taxes were brought here before being distributed to centers such as Ur and Nippur.

QARQAR A place on the Orontes where a battle was fought in 853 B.C.E. between the Assyrians and a combined force including Israel, other Levantine states, and Egyptian and Arab contingents, under the leadership of the king of Damascus.

QATNA A city in Syria, capital of an important kingdom in the early second millennium B.C.E., linked to Mesopotamia via the desert route that ran from Mari through the oasis of Tadmor (Palmyra).

QU *see sila.*

REBITU A public place belonging to a city ward, next to the gate inside the city wall, where the assembly met and the garrison was stationed; it was perhaps also the scene of market activities.

RIM-SIN I Second king of the Amorite dynasty of Isin, who enlarged the kingdom to include most of southern Mesopotamia. Ruling from 1822, he was finally defeated by Hammurabi in 1763 B.C.E.

SAR (Sum.) A measure of area, around 36 square meters.

SARGON II King of Assyria 721–705 B.C.E. He fought long and hard against Babylonia, gaining control of it in 709, and also campaigned against Urartu and states in the north, where he was killed in battle. He shifted Assyria's capital to Dur-Sharrukin, a new foundation, which was abandoned after his death.

SARGON OF AKKAD Founder of the city of Agade and creator of the Akkadian empire. He ruled from 2334 to 2279 B.C.E., but it is not clear how early in his reign he gained control of the city-states of Sumer.

SCYTHIANS Central Asian horse-riding nomads who attacked northern Near Eastern and Iranian states during the first millennium B.C.E. The Assyrians fought against them but also made alliances with them.

SEA PEOPLES A collective term for aggressive groups from a number of sources in the eastern and central Mediterranean, often accompanied by women and children, and therefore probably refugees from problems in their homelands. They attacked coastal states in the Near East and Egypt during the thirteenth and twelfth centuries B.C.E. Some, like the

Philistines (Peleset), settled in the regions they entered, and some found service as mercenaries.

SEALAND The marshy southern lands of Babylonia around the head of the Gulf, which offered a place of refuge for those forced to flee enemies or justice. In the second millennium two Babylonian dynasties arose here and during the first millennium it was the home of Chaldaean tribes.

SEMITIC LANGUAGES The group of languages spoken by most of the peoples of the Near East, ancient and modern.

SENNACHERIB King of Assyria 704–681 B.C.E. He campaigned for most of his reign against Babylonia and the Elamites, sacking Babylon in 689, an impious act that may have precipitated his assassination. He also fought in the north and east. He moved Assyria's capital to Nineveh where he constructed his "Palace without a Rival" (see photos pp. 169, 180).

SEVEN SAGES Seven wise men (*apkallu*) who lived before the Flood, representatives of seven cities. Enki selected and instructed them, entrusting them with the task of introducing the arts of civilization to humanity. They were also credited with laying the foundations of Uruk's first city walls, which Gilgamesh rebuilt. Eventually they angered the gods and were banished to the Abzu, taking on a fishy appearance: It is as men-fish that they are often depicted in Assyrian art. They are also shown as griffin-demons, with birds' heads and wings, purifying with pine cone and bucket.

SEXAGESIMAL Base-sixty (counting system).

SHADUF A simple device for lifting water from rivers or reservoirs, devised by the Mesopotamians in or before the third millennium B.C.E. This consisted of a horizontal beam fixed to an upright but able to pivot, with a bucket on one end that was pulled down and dipped into the water. When released, a counterweight on the other end of the beam raised the bucket, which could then be emptied into a trough or irrigation channel.

SHALMANESER III King of Assyria 858–824 B.C.E. He extended the Assyrian realms to the Euphrates and campaigned over an area from the southern Levant to Babylonia and western Iran; he also constructed the Review Palace at Kalhu (see photos pp. 31, 98, 99, 168).

SHAMASH (Sum. Utu) God of the sun and divine patron of justice; sometimes regarded as the son of Anu or Enlil, unlike his Sumerian counterpart. He shared a temple with Sin (Nanna) in Assur (see photo p. 246).

SHAMSHI-ADAD I A member of the Amorite ruling house of the kingdom of Ekallatum. Shamshi-Adad (1836–1781 B.C.E.) carved out an empire on the upper Tigris and Euphrates, which he ruled from Shubat-Enlil. He adopted the title *Shar kishshatim* "King of the Universe."

SHA NAQBA IMURU "He who saw the Deep," known also as the Standard Version of the Gilgamesh epic, a poem in eleven tablets. Substantial portions of the text are missing. A twelfth tablet, tacked on at the end, is a line-by-line translation of the Sumerian account of the netherworld.

SHEKEL Sumerian *gin*, Akkadian *shiqlu*, a measure of weight equivalent to 180 *she* (barleycorns), around 8 grams.

SHERD (potsherd) A piece of broken pottery, generally invaluable to the archaeologist: if distinctive, as an indication of the date of the context in which it was found; as a clue to networks of communication and trade; and as a source of information on technology and economic, domestic, and public activities; sometimes informing on art and aesthetics; sometimes carrying decoration that gives other insights into the life of the people who made the vessel from which it came.

SHIQLU *see* shekel.

SHUBAT-ENLIL (Modern Tell Leilan) A city north of the Khabur River chosen by Shamshi-Adad I for his capital.

SHULGI Second and greatest king of the Ur III dynasty, 2094–2047 B.C.E. He spent the first part of his reign organizing his realm and thereafter extended the empire north and east.

SHUMMA ALU "If a city is situated on a hill . . . ," a collection of omens from observed phenomena running to 107 tablets, of which few have survived and only the titles are known. These omens included the behavior of all sorts of animals, encounters with particular animals in certain places, and particular occurrences.

SHUMMA IZBU "If a newborn animal . . . ," the major reference collection of types of abnormal births among sheep, other animals, and people, understood to be omens. Comprising at least twenty-four tablets, copies of the compendium have been found not only in Mesopotamia but also in the Hittite capital, Hattusas, and at Ugarit.

SHURUPPAK A major Sumerian city in the ED period and home of the hero of the Flood story, Ziusudra.

SHUTUR ELI SHARRI "Surpassing all other kings," the Akkadian epic of Gilgamesh written down in the eighteenth century B.C.E., and possibly composed by a single author from the traditional stories. Only small fragments of this survive, both from Babylonia and from cities as distant as Hattusas, but they are enough to determine that the Standard Version, written down in the late second millennium, was extensively, though not slavishly, based on this text.

SILA (Akk. *qu*) A measure of volume, around 1 liter.

SIN (Sum. Nanna) The god of the moon, son of Enlil and Ninlil and patron deity of Ur, Harran, and the Arabian oasis town of Taima where his devotee, the Babylonian king Nabonidus, resided for ten years.

SIPPAR (Modern Abu Habbah, Biblical Sepharvaim) A city on the Euphrates in the north of Babylonia. The temple of its patron deity, Shamash, had an attached *gagum,* where the daughters of many royal houses lived as *naditums.* The city, which was a major trading center, had a number of tented suburbs visited or lived in by nomadic groups. A very large number of texts have been excavated from Sippar, including a Neo-Babylonian library in the Shamash temple.

STAGE Sumerian *danna,* Akkadian *beru,* a measure of length, around 10.8 kilometers.

"STANDARD OF UR" A wooden object inlaid with shell, red stone, and lapis lazuli, found in the Royal Cemetery at Ur. Woolley believed it to have been a standard, carried on a long wooden pole, but it was more probably the sounding box of a musical instrument.

STANDARD VERSION *see Sha naqba imuru.*

STELE (pl. stelae) An inscribed monolith.

SUBSTITUTE KINGS When omens predicted death or disaster to the king, the dire consequences of this might be averted by installing a temporary substitute king who ruled until after the foretold danger had passed, when he and all his temporary court were killed and his symbols of office (throne, scepter, table, and weapon) burned on his grave. This practice was known throughout Mesopotamian history but rarely invoked.

SUMER The southern part of Babylonia, home of the first city-states, known as *ki-engi* in Sumerian.

SUMERIAN The language of the Sumerians, spoken in Sumer, although not exclusively, and identified as the language of the earliest readable script.

SUMERIANS The inhabitants of Sumer and speakers of Sumerian; how early they settled in the region is unknown.

SUSA An ancient city, capital of Elam, situated on plain of the Ulai River east of Sumer.

SUTU (Suti, Sutaeans) Nomads living in the second millennium in the desert regions west of the middle Euphrates, a constant scourge on their settled neighbors to east and west, including Mari.

TABLET OF DESTINIES A tablet written in cuneiform and impressed with seals that conveyed authority over the gods. It was taken by the Imdugud (Anzu) bird, which was killed by Ninurta who restored the tablet to Enki, and was stolen from Enlil by Tiamat and recovered by Marduk, who then wore it.

TALENT Sumerian *gun*, Akkadian *biltu*, a measure of weight, around 30 kilograms, equivalent to 60 minas.

TELL A settlement mound formed by the gradual accumulation of debris from demolished or decayed mudbrick buildings.

TEMENOS Sacred enclosure or precinct.

THERMOLUMINESCENCE A radiometric dating technique most commonly used on fired clay such as pottery.

THRESHING SLEDGE A heavy wooden board set with stone chips, used to thresh harvested grain by being drawn over it repeatedly by a team of oxen. The operator may lead the team or control it from a seat on the back of the board.

TIGLATH-PILESER III King of Assyria 744–727 B.C.E., responsible for rebuilding the empire after several decades of decline and for many reforms and improvements to the army, the communications network, and the organization of the state.

TIGRIS One of the two rivers upon which Mesopotamia depended for its existence, the Tigris was favored for settlement in its upper reaches in northern Mesopotamia, but few cities were located on its lower reaches, where its waters were difficult to harness.

TOWER OF BABEL One of the Wonders of the World, the ziggurat of Marduk at Babylon.

UGARIT (Modern Ras Shamra) A settlement on the Levantine coast, occupied from early Neolithic times, and an important town in the third and second millennia B.C.E.

UMMA (Modern Tell Johka) An early city north of Uruk and often allied with it or under its influence. For a long time in the ED period it was locked in a border dispute with Lagash. Around 2340 B.C.E. under Lugalzagesi it conquered Lagash, becoming part of Lugalzagesi's unified Sumer before the region fell to Sargon of Akkad.

UR (Modern Tell al-Muqayyar, Sum. Urim) Settled by the Ubaid period, Ur developed into one of the principal cities of Sumer. Now situated well inland, in the third millennium it was a major port. Excavations uncovered the ED Royal Cemetery and Ur III–period mausoleums; the precinct of the city's god Nanna, including the *giparu,* the establishment of his priestess, and the ziggurat of Ur-Nammu, reconstructed by Nabonidus; and an area of OB housing in which many tablets were found.

URARTU State in what is now Armenia, the mountainous region north of Assyria and southeast of the Black Sea. It adopted the cuneiform script and a number of other aspects of Mesopotamian culture but was inimical to Assyria. The latter often campaigned against Urartu but with little lasting effect.

UR "OF THE CHALDEES" The home of the biblical patriarch Abraham around 1800 B.C.E., generally taken to be the Sumerian city of Ur, but more probably to be identified with the small town of Ur near Harran in northwestern Mesopotamia.

UR III EMPIRE Established by Ur-Nammu in 2112 B.C.E., the Ur III Empire incorporated Sumer and Akkad and a larger area to the east, reaching its peak under Shulgi (2094–2047), and declining under later kings until 2004 when the Elamites sacked Ur. The state was highly bureaucratic.

UR-NAMMU Founder of the Ur III dynasty in 2112 B.C.E., Ur-Nammu united the cities of Sumer and constructed ziggurats in a number of them. He was killed in 2095 while campaigning against the Guti.

URU-INIM-GINA (formerly transcribed as UruKAgina) King of Lagash ca. 2351–2342. A reformer who was defeated but probably not deposed by Lugalzagesi of Umma.

URUK (Modern Warka, biblical Erech, Sum. Unug) Occupied by the Ubaid period, Uruk was one of the earliest cities to develop in the world. The Eanna and Kullaba precincts, dedicated respectively to Inanna and An, were the scene of frequent and dramatic experimentation in monumental architecture in the Uruk period, and the city also saw the birth of writing. Uruk continued to be one of the leading cities in Sumer in the ED period, during which it was ruled by legendary kings including Gilgamesh, but declined thereafter (see photos pp. 69, 82, 151).

URUK PERIOD Roughly coincident with the fourth millennium (4100–3100 B.C.E.), the Uruk period was a time of strong international communications and of major innovation, which saw the invention of the potter's wheel, animal traction and wheeled transport, writing, and other key developments.

UT-NAPISHTIM (Akk.) "He found life," the immortal hero of the Flood story (known in other versions as Ziusudra or Atrahasis) whom Gilgamesh visits in quest of immortality.

UTU (Akk. Shamash) God of the sun and of truth, justice, and righteousness. Like Enki, Utu took a benevolent interest in human affairs. Utu traveled across the sky during the daytime, and at night he passed through the underworld where he administered justice. In Sumerian mythology he was the son of Nanna and affectionate brother of Inanna. His principal shrines, called E-babbar, were in Larsa and Sippar; in the latter there was also a *gagum* (cloister), which housed *naditum,* votaresses of Shamash.

WARKA VASE A large alabaster vase from Uruk, with several registers of relief decoration showing a religious procession. One of the treasures of the Iraq museum, it was stolen when the museum was sacked in 2003 during the fall of Baghdad but has been returned (see photo p. 69).

WASHSHUKANNI The Mitanni capital. This has yet to be located: Several possible sites have been suggested, but none convincingly.

YAMHAD A state in Syria, with its capital at Aleppo. It enjoyed considerable power in the early second millennium.

YASMAH-ADDU Son of Shamshi-Adad I and his ineffectual viceroy in Mari from 1788 until 1776 when his father died and he was rapidly ousted by Yahmud-Lim of Yamhad and the latter's son-in-law Zimri-Lim.

ZAGROS Mountain range to the east of Mesopotamia, source both of minerals and other resources and of enemy tribes.

ZIGGURAT A temple platform constructed in tiered stages. The first ziggurats were erected by Ur-Nammu, but had antecedents in earlier temples on platforms, such as the temple of An at Uruk. Ur III ziggurats had three stages; those of the later second and first millennia up to seven, each painted in a different color. Of the latter the most famous was Etemenanki, the "Tower of Babel" (see photos pp. 82, 201).

ZIMRI-LIM The last king of Mari (1775–1757) before its sack by Hammurabi, his former ally. Son-in-law of the important king of Yamhad, Yahmud-Lim. Tablets preserved when the Mari palace was torched include many personal and official letters and other documents from his reign, which give an unusually full picture of palace life in the eighteenth century B.C.E.

ZIUSUDRA (Zi-ud-sura) "Life of long days." A king of Shuruppak, the Sumerian hero of the Flood story; known in the Akkadian version of the story as Atrahasis and as Ut-napishtim in the account in the Standard Version of the Gilgamesh cycle.

TEXT REFERENCES

Bienkowski, Piotr, and Alan Millard, eds. 2000. *Dictionary of the Ancient Near East.* London: British Museum Press.

Black, Jeremy, and Anthony Green. 1992. *Gods, Demons and Symbols of Ancient Mesopotamia. An Illustrated Dictionary.* London: British Museum Press.

Bottero, Jean, ed. 2001a. *Everyday Life in Ancient Mesopotamia.* Translated by A. Nevill. Edinburgh: Edinburgh University Press.

———. 2001b. *Religion in Ancient Mesopotamia.* Chicago: University of Chicago Press.

Charpin, Dominique. 2000. "The History of Ancient Mesopotamia: An Overview." Pp. 807–830 in *Civilizations of the Ancient Near East.* Edited by Jack M. Sasson. Peabody, MA: Hendrickson Publishers. (Reprint of 1995 edition. New York: Scribner.)

Covington, Richard. "What Was Jiroft?" Saudi Aramco World 55: 5 (September/October 2004). http://www.saudiaramcoworld.com/issue/200405/what.was.jiroft.htm.

Cryer, Frederick. 2000. "Chronology: Issues and Problems." Pp. 651–664 in *Civilizations of the Ancient Near East.* Edited by Jack M. Sasson. Peabody, MA: Hendrickson Publishers. (Reprint of 1995 edition. New York: Scribner.)

Dalley, Stephanie. 1984. *Mari and Karana. Two Old Babylonian Cities.* London: Longman.

———. 2000a. *Myths from Mesopotamia.* Revised edition. Oxford: Oxford University Press.

———. 2000b. "Ancient Mesopotamian Military Organization." Pp. 413–422 in *Civilizations of the Ancient Near East.* Edited by Jack M. Sasson. Peabody, MA: Hendrickson Publishers. (Reprint of 1995 edition. New York: Scribner.)

Farber, Walter. 2000. "Witchcraft, Magic, and Divination in Ancient Mesopotamia." Pp. 1895–1910 in *Civilizations of the Ancient Near East.* Edited by Jack M. Sasson. Peabody, MA: Hendrickson Publishers. (Reprint of 1995 edition. New York: Scribner.)

Grayson, A. Kirk. 2000. "Assyrian Rule of Conquered Territory in Ancient Western Asia." Pp. 959–968 in *Civilizations of the Ancient Near East.* Edited by Jack M. Sasson. Peabody, MA: Hendrickson Publishers. (Reprint of 1995 edition. New York: Scribner.)

Green, Anthony. 2000. "Ancient Mesopotamian Religious Iconography." Pp. 1837–1856 in *Civilizations of the Ancient Near East.* Edited by Jack M. Sasson. Peabody, MA: Hendrickson Publishers. (Reprint of 1995 edition. New York: Scribner.)

Green, Anthony, and Jeremy Black. 2000. "Sacrifice and Offering." Pp. 247–248 in *Dictionary of the Ancient Near East.* Edited by Piotr Bienkowski and Alan Millard. London: British Museum Press.

Greengus, Samuel. 2000. "Legal and Social Institutions of Ancient Mesopotamia." Pp. 469–484 in *Civilizations of the Ancient Near East.* Edited by Jack M. Sasson. Peabody, MA: Hendrickson Publishers. (Reprint of 1995 edition. New York: Scribner.)

Hallo, William W. 2000. "Lamentations and Prayers in Sumer and Akkad." Pp. 1871–1882 in *Civilizations of the Ancient Near East.* Edited by Jack M. Sasson. Peabody, MA: Hendrickson Publishers. (Reprint of 1995 edition. New York: Scribner.)

Hallo, William W., and William Kelly Simpson. 1998. *The Ancient Near East. A History.* 2d edition. Belmont, CA: Wadworth / Thomson Learning.

Jacobsen, Thorkild. 1976. *The Treasures of Darkness. A History of Mesopotamian Religion.* New Haven, CT: Yale University Press.

Kramer, Samuel Noah. 1981. *History Begins at Sumer. Thirty-Nine Firsts in Recorded History.* 3rd revised edition. Philadelphia: University of Pennsylvania Press.

Kuhrt, Amelie. 1995. *The Ancient Near East. c. 3000–330 BCE.* 2 Volumes. London: Routledge.

Leick, Gwendolyn. 1991. *A Dictionary of Ancient Near Eastern Mythology.* London: Routledge.

———. 1999. *Who's Who in the Ancient Near East.* London: Routledge.

———. 2001. *Mesopotamia. The Invention of the City.* London: Allen Lane, Penguin Press.

Liverani, Mario. 2000. "The Deeds of Ancient Mesopotamian Kings." Pp. 2353–2366 in *Civilizations of the Ancient Near East.* Edited by Jack M. Sasson. Peabody, MA: Hendrickson Publishers. (Reprint of 1995 edition. New York: Scribner.)

Lloyd, Seton. 1980. *Foundations in the Dust.* Revised edition. London: Thames and Hudson.

Maidman, Maynard Paul. 2000. "Nuzi: Portrait of an Ancient Mesopotamian Provincial Town." Pp. 931–947 in *Civilizations of the Ancient Near East.* Edited by Jack M. Sasson. Peabody, MA: Hendrickson Publishers. (Reprint of 1995 edition. New York: Scribner.)

Millard, Alan. 2000. "Eponyms," "Kudurru," "Shulgi," and "Taxation." Pp. 106–107, 171–172, 270–271, and 284, respectively, in *Dictionary of the Ancient Near East.* Edited by Piotr Bienkowski and Alan Millard. London: British Museum Press.

Oates, Joan. 1986. *Babylon.* Revised edition. London: Thames and Hudson.

Oates, Joan, and David Oates. 2001. *Nimrud. An Assyrian Imperial City Revealed.* London: British School of Archaeology in Iraq.

Oller, Gary H. 2000. "Messengers and Ambassadors in Ancient Western Asia." Pp. 1465–1473 in *Civilizations of the Ancient Near East.* Edited by Jack M. Sasson. Peabody, MA: Hendrickson Publishers. (Reprint of 1995 edition. New York: Scribner.)

Oppenheim, A. Leo, and Erica Reiner. 1977. *Ancient Mesopotamia. Portrait of a Dead Civilization.* Revised edition. Chicago: University of Chicago Press.

Pearce, Laurie E. 2000. "The Scribes and Scholars of Ancient Mesopotamia." Pp. 2265–2278 in *Civilizations of the Ancient Near East.* Edited by Jack M. Sasson. Peabody, MA: Hendrickson Publishers. (Reprint of 1995 edition. New York: Scribner.)

Pollack, Susan. 1999. *Ancient Mesopotamia. The Eden that Never Was.* Cambridge: Cambridge University Press.

Postgate, J. Nicholas. 1994. *Early Mesopotamia.* London: Routledge.

———. 2000. "Royal Ideology and State Administration in Sumer and Akkad." Pp. 395–411 in *Civilizations of the Ancient Near East.* Edited by Jack M. Sasson. Peabody, MA: Hendrickson Publishers. (Reprint of 1995 edition. New York: Scribner.)

Potts, D. T. 1997. *Mesopotamian Civilization. The Material Foundations.* London: The Athlone Press.

———. 1999. *The Archaeology of Elam. Formation and Transformation of an Ancient Iranian State.* Cambridge: Cambridge University Press.

Powell, Marvin A. 2000. "Metrology and Mathematics in Ancient Mesopotamia." Pp. 1941–1957 in *Civilizations of the Ancient Near East.* Edited by Jack M. Sasson. Peabody, MA: Hendrickson Publishers. (Reprint of 1995 edition. New York: Scribner.)

Roaf, Michael. 1990. *Cultural Atlas of Mesopotamia.* New York: Facts on File.

Robertson, John. 2000. "The Social and Economic Organization of Ancient Mesopotamian Temples." Pp. 443–454 in *Civilizations of the Ancient Near East.* Edited by Jack M. Sasson. Peabody, MA: Hendrickson Publishers. (Reprint of 1995 edition. New York: Scribner.)

Roux, Georges. 1992. *Ancient Iraq*. 3d edition. Harmondsworth: Penguin.

Sasson, Jack M., ed. 2000a. *Civilizations of the Ancient Near East*. 4 Volumes. Peabody, MA: Hendrickson Publishers. (Reprint of 1995 edition. New York: Scribner.)

————. 2000b. "King Hammurabi of Babylon." Pp. 901–916 in *Civilizations of the Ancient Near East*. Edited by Jack M. Sasson. Peabody, MA: Hendrickson Publishers. (Reprint of 1995 edition. New York: Scribner.)

Stol, Marten. 2000. "Private Life in Ancient Mesopotamia." Pp. 485–499 in *Civilizations of the Ancient Near East*. Edited by Jack M. Sasson. Peabody, MA: Hendrickson Publishers. (Reprint of 1995 edition. New York: Scribner.)

Stone, Elizabeth. 2000. "The Development of Cities in Ancient Mesopotamia." Pp. 235–248 in *Civilizations of the Ancient Near East*. Edited by Jack M. Sasson. Peabody, MA: Hendrickson Publishers. (Reprint of 1995 edition. New York: Scribner.)

Van de Mieroop, Marc. 1997. *The Ancient Mesopotamian City*. Oxford: Oxford University Press.

Veenhof, Klaas R. 1977. "Some Social Effects of Old Assyrian Trade." Pp. 109–118 in *Trade in the Ancient Near East. Papers Presented to the XXIII Rencontre Assyriologique Internationale*. Edited by J. D. Hawkins. London: British School of Archaeology in Iraq.

————. 2000. "Kanesh: An Assyrian Colony in Anatolia." Pp. 859–872 in *Civilizations of the Ancient Near East*. Edited by Jack M. Sasson. Peabody, MA: Hendrickson Publishers. (Reprint of 1995 edition. New York: Scribner.)

Yoffee, Norman. 2000. "The Economy of Ancient Western Asia." Pp. 1387–1399 in *Civilizations of the Ancient Near East*. Edited by Jack M. Sasson. Peabody, MA: Hendrickson Publishers. (Reprint of 1995 edition. New York: Scribner.)

Zettler, Richard L. 1997a. "Nippur." Pp. 149–152 in *The Oxford Encyclopedia of Archaeology in the Near East*. Vol. 4. Edited by Eric M. Meyers. Oxford: Oxford University Press.

Chronology

This chronology uses calibrated radiocarbon dates and Middle-Chronology historical dates; for discussion of Mesopotamian chronology, see chapters 3 and 11.

APPROX. DATES	CULTURES AND CULTURAL DEVELOPMENTS; KINGS
11,500–9000	Growing number of sedentary hunter-gatherer communities, based on exploitation of cereals and nut-bearing trees.
9000–8500	Hunter-gatherer communities; some sedentary communities and agriculture in the Levant and northern Zagros.
8500–7000	Aceramic Neolithic: spread of agricultural communities throughout most of the areas of the Near East where rain-fed agriculture was possible. Some domestic animals.
7000–6000	Beginning of pottery making and metallurgy. Arable farming and animal husbandry were now well established.
	Northern Mesopotamia: Hassuna—rain-fed agriculture.
	Central Mesopotamia: Samarra—simple irrigation agriculture.
	Southern Mesopotamia: probably hunter-fisher-gatherer communities although much of the region was probably marshland.
6000–5000	Northern and Central Mesopotamia: Halaf replacing Hassuna and Samarra.
	Southern Mesopotamia: Appearance of farming communities (Ubaid 0) by ca. 6200; fishing, hunting, and gathering still important; Ubaid 1–2—farming communities practicing simple irrigation and building shrines.
5000–4100	Southern Mesopotamia: Ubaid 3–5—pottery made on the tournette; some economic specialization.
	Northern and Central Mesopotamia: Ubaid replacing Halaf by ca. 4500.
4100–3400	Early Uruk period—Great increase in number of settlements in southern Mesopotamia. Major innovations and developments including wheel-made pottery, the wheel, animal traction and transport, and wool.

3400–3100 Southern Mesopotamia: later Uruk period—emergence of writing; economic specialization and administrative control; developing urbanism and substantial temple complexes. Close links with Elam.

Northern Mesopotamia: culturally and economically less developed and politically more fragmented than southern Mesopotamia; trade and cultural links with the south.

3100–2900 Southern Mesopotamia: Jemdet Nasr period—emergence of first cities. Burgeoning social and political complexity. Writing becoming more sophisticated.

Northern Mesopotamia: Ninevite 5 pottery associated with developing towns.

2900–2750 Southern Mesopotamia: Early Dynastic I—first city-states with kings, warfare, and city walls. Population now mainly concentrated in cities. Cuneiform script developing.

2750–2600 Southern Mesopotamia: Early Dynastic II—proliferation of city-states. Dynasties enumerated in Sumerian King List.

__Kish__	__Uruk__	__Ur__
	Meskiaggasher	
	Enmerkar	
Mebaragesi	Lugalbanda	Meskalamdug
	Dumuzi	
Agga	Gilgamesh	Akalamdug

2600–2334 Southern Mesopotamia: Early Dynastic III—historical kings. ED IIIa—spectacular graves in Royal Cemetery at Ur. Writing system fully developed. Larger political units emerging and region briefly united by Lugalzagesi.

__Kish__	__Uruk__	__Ur__	__Lagash__
		First Dynasty	
		Mesanepada	En-hegal ca. 2570
Uhub ca. 2570		ca. 2560–2525	Lugal-shag-engur
Mesalim ca.			ca. 2550
2550			Ur-Nanshe ca.
			2494–2465
		A-anepada ca.	King of Kish
		2525–2485	
		Meskiagnunna ca.	
		2485–2450	Akurgal ca.
			2464–2455
		Elili ca. 2445	
			Eannatum ca.
			2455–2425
			King of Kish
	En-shakush-anna	Balili	Enannatum I
Enbi-Ishtar ca.	ca. 2430–2400		ca. 2424–2405
2430			

Kish	Uruk		Lagash
Ku-baba	Lugal-kineshe-dudu (Lugal-kigine-dudu) ca. 2400 King of Kish; Uruk, Ur, Umma		Enmetena (Entemena) ca. 2404–2375
Puzur-Sin			Enannatum II ca. 2374–2365
			En-entarzi ca. 2364–2359
	Lugalkisalsi Lugalzagesi (governor of Umma from ca. 2349)		Lugalanda ca. 2358-2352
Ur-Zababa ca. 2340	ca. 2340–2316 king of Kish, Umma, Uruk, Ur and Lagash		Uru-inim-gina (UruKAgina) ca. 2351–2342

2334–2193   Akkadian Empire—After defeating Lugalzagesi, Sargon united Sumer and Akkad. The empire's influences stretched to the northern Levant, eastern Anatolia, and the Zagros, and through the Gulf. Centralized authority maintained by military force and economic success. Standardization of many aspects of public life.

Akkadian Empire	Elam	Guti
Sargon (Sharru-kin) 2334–2279	Hishibrashini	
Rimush 2278–2270	Emahsini	
Manishtushu 2269–2255	*Akkadian regents*	
	Eshpum	
	Ilshu-rabi	
Naram-Sin 2254–2218	Epirmupi	
	Ili'ishmani	
	kings of Awan	
	Hita	Imtaa
Shar-Kali-Sharri 2217–2193	Kutir-Inshushinak	Erriduwazir
		Sarlagab

2193–2154   Collapse of Akkadian Empire—individual city-states regained their independence although some dominated others. Raids by the Guti nomads.

Agade	Guti	Lagash
period of anarchy 2192–2190		Lugal-ushumgal
Igigi		
Nanium		Puzur-Mama
Imi	kings (total of dynasty = 21)	Ur-Utu
Elulu		
realm reduced to Agade area		
Dudu 2189–2169		Ur-Mama
Shu-turul 2168–2154		

2153–2113 Revival in Sumer. Guti threatened many settled communities and for some decades controlled part of southern Mesopotamia before being driven out by Utu-hegal.

Uruk	Guti	Lagash
Ur-nigina 2153–2147	kings	Ur-Bau (Ur-Baba) 2155–2142
Ur-gigira 2146–2141		Gudea 2141–2122
Utu-hegal 2123–2113	Tirigan ?–2120	Ur-Ningirsu 2121–2118
		Pirig-me 2117–2115
		Ur-gar (Ur-ni) 2114
		Nam-mahazi (Nammahani) 2113–2111

2112–2004 Third Dynasty of Ur (Ur III): Ur-Nammu reunited Sumer and Akkad. His son Shulgi created a close-knit highly bureaucratic state and gained control of the western part of Iranian plateau. Foreign trade highly developed. Ziggurats constructed in major cities. Growing economic and political decline under pressure from the Amorites in the west culminated in the sack of Ur by the Elamites from the east.

Sumer and Akkad	Elam
Ur III (Third Dynasty of Ur)	
Ur-Nammu 2112–2095	Puzur-Inshushinak ca. 2100
Shulgi 2094–2047	*Elam under Ur III control*
	Elamite Shimashki kings
Amar-Sin 2046–2038	Girnamme
	Tazitta
Shu-Sin 2037–2029	Ebarti I ca. 2040
	Tazitta
Ibbi-Sin 2028–2004	Kindattu—*sacked Ur 2004*

2004–ca. 1780 Old Babylonian period: After the sack of Ur, Elam remained closely involved with southern Mesopotamia (Babylonia). Isin became the dominant city-state, challenged from ca. 1925 by Larsa and eventually conquered in 1794. The independent kingdoms in the west, such as Mari, enjoyed prosperity under Amorite rulers. Assur in northern Mesopotamia (Assyria) involved in lucrative trade with Anatolia. Under Shamshi-Adad much of the north was united.

ca. 2000–1895

Isin	Larsa	Eshnunna	Assur	Elam
First Dynasty of Isin	*Dynasty of Larsa*	Ituriya (II)shu-iliya	*Old Assyrian*	*Shimashki dynasty*
Ishbi-Erra 2017–1985	Naplanum 2025–2005	ca. 2028 Nur-ahum	*kings* Sulili ca. 2015	Kindattu Iddadu I
Shu-ilishu 1984–1975	Emisun 2004–1977	Kirikiri Bilalama		Tan-ruhurater ca. 1970
Iddin-Dagan 1974–1954	Samium 1976–1942	Ishtar-ramashshu	Kikkiya	*Sukkalmah*
Ishme-Dagan 1953–1935		Usur-awassu Azuzum		*(Grand Regents)*

Isin	Larsa	Eshnunna	Assur	Elam
Lipit-Ishtar 1934–1924	Zabaya 1941–1933	Ur-Ninmar Ur-Ningizzida Ipiq-Adad I	Akkiya	Ebarat (Ebarti II) Idaddu II
Ur-Ninurta 1923–1896	Gungunum 1932–1906		Puzur Ashur I	Shilhaha Atta-hushu fl.1916–1894 *usurper supported by Gungunam of Larsa?*
	Abi-sare 1905–1895			

ca. 1895–1820

Isin	Larsa	Babylon *First dynasty*	Eshnunna	Assur	Elam
Bur-Sin 1895–1874	Sumu-El 1894–1866	Sumu-abum 1894–1881	Abdi-Erah	Shallim-ahhe Ilu-shuma	Pala-ishshan
Lipit-Enlil 1873–1869		Sumu-la-El 1880–1845	Shiqlanum		Kuk-Kirmash
Erra-imitti 1868–1861	Nur-Adad 1865–1850		Sharriya Belakum (Warassa?)	Erishum I	
Enlil-bani 1860–1837				Ikunum Sharru-kin I (Sargon)	Kuk-Nashur I
	Sin-iddinam 1849–1843	Sabium 1844–1831	Ibal-pi-El I		
	Sin-eribam 1842–1841		Ipiq-Adad II	Puzur-Ashur II	
Zambiya 1836–1834	Sin-iqisham 1840–1836				
Iterpisha 1833–1831	Silli-Adad 1835		Naram-Sin 1830?–1815		
Urdukuga 1830–1828	Warad-Sin 1834–1823	Apil-Sin 1830–1813			
Sin-magir 1827–1817					

ca. 1820–1780

Isin	Larsa	Babylon	Eshnunna	Assur	Mari
	Rim-Sin I 1822–1763			Naram-Sin (*of Eshnunna*) 1819–1815	Yaggid-lim ca. 1820
Damiq-ilishu 1816–1794			Dannum-takhaz	Erishum II 1814–1811?	Yahdun-lim ca. 1810–1798
		Sin-muballit 1812–1793		Shamshi-Adad I (Samsi-Addu) (1836) 1813–1781	Sumu-Yaman 1797
1794 conquered by Larsa and 1787 by Hammurabi			Dadusha ca. 1805–1780		*(under Shamshi-Adad I 1796–?1788)*
		Hammurabi 1792–1750			Yasmah-Addu ?1788–1776

ca. 1780–1595 After the death of Shamshi-Adad, Hammurabi forged an empire encompassing all of Babylonia and much of Assyria. Babylon from now onward was the main center of the south. After Hammurabi's death the Babylonian Empire gradually crumbled. Babylon was sacked by the Hittites in 1595.

ca. 1780–1750

Elam	Larsa	Babylon	Eshnunna	Assur	Mari
Shiruk-Tuh ca. 1785	Rim-Sin I 1822–1763	Hammurabi 1792–1750	Ibal-pi-El II 1779–1762	Ishme-Dagan I 1776–1741	Zimri-Lim 1775–1757
Simut-wartash I ca. 1772	*1763 conquered by Hammurabi*				
Siwe-palar-huppak ca. 1770			*1762 conquered by Hammurabi destroyed by Samsu-Iluna*	*reduced realm became vassal to Hammurabi*	*Destroyed by Hammurabi 1757*
Kuduzu-lush I ca. 1765	Rim-Sin II 1741–1736				

ca. 1750–1595

Sealand	Babylon	Assur	Elam
First Dynasty of the Sealand	Hammurabi 1792–1750	Mutu-Ashkur Rimush Asinum	
Iluma-ilum (Ilumael) ca. 1732	Samsu-iluna 1749–1712		Kutir-Nahhunte I ca. 1730
	Abi-eshuh 1711–1684	*Anarchy—8 usurpers*	Lila-irtash ca. 1700
Itti-ili-nibi		Belu-bani 1700–1691	Temti-Agun ca. 1698
	Ammi-ditana 1683–1647	Libaia 1690–1674	
Damiq-ilishu 1677–1642		Sharma-Adad I 1673–1662	Kutir-Shilhaha
	Ammi-saduqa 1646–1626	Iptar-Sin 1661–1650	
Ishkibal 1641–1617	Samsu-ditana 1625–1595	Bazaia 1649–1622	Kuk-Nashur II ca. 1645–1600
		Lullaia 1621–1616	
		Kidin-Ninua (Shu-Ninua) 1615–1602	
Shushshi 1616–1590	*1595 Babylon sacked by Hittites*	Sharma-Adad II 1601–1599	

1600–1155   Kassite period in Babylonia. The Kassites, settlers here from the eighteenth century B.C.E., gained control around 1570, introducing an era of peace and prosperity in which Gulf trade was reestablished. Assyria was conquered by the Hurrian kingdom of Mitanni, its neighbor in the west, regaining its independence around 1350 after Mitanni's collapse. Egypt's campaigns in the Levant brought it into direct contact, peaceful and otherwise, with the Mesopotamian states. Border disputes between Assyria and Babylonia led to outright warfare by the late thirteenth century, in which Babylonia was often allied with Elam. Nevertheless, Elam brought down the Kassite dynasty, sacking Babylon in 1155.

Babylonia	Sealand	Assyria	Elam
(local Kassite kings from Gandash ca. 1729 to 1570)	*First Dynasty of the Sealand* Gulkishar 1589–?— 55 years *controlled*	Erishum II 1598–1586 Shamshi-Adad II 1585–1580	*Sukkalmah* Kudu-zulush II Kuk-Nashur III Tan-Uli
Kassite dynasty	*Babylon*	Ishme-Dagan II 1579–1564	
Agum II ca. 1570	GISH-EN	Shamshi-Adad III 1563–1548	Temti-halki
	Peshgaldaramash	Ashur-nirari I 1547–1522	Kuk-Nashur IV
		Puzur-Ashur III 1521–1498	*Kidinuid dynasty* ca. 1500–1400
	Adarakalamma Ekurduanna	*Under Mitanni*	
Burnaburiash I ca. 1530–1500	Melamkurkurra	Enlil-nasir I 1497–1485	Kidinu
Kashtiliash III ca. 1490 (Ulamburiash)	Ea-gamil *ca. 1475 conquest by Kassites*	Nur-ili 1484–1473	

Babylonia	Mitanni	Assyria	Elam
	Parrattarna ca. 1480	Ashur-shaduni Ashur-rabi I	Tan-Ruhurater II Shalla
Agum III ca. 1465	Kirta Shuttarna I (Parsatatar)	Ashur-nadin-ahhe I ca. 1440 Enlil-nasir II 1430–1425	Tepti-Ahar
	Saushtatar ca. 1430	Ashur-nirari II 1424–1418	Inshushinak-sunkir-nappipir (Inshushinak-shar-ilani)
Karaindash ca. 1415	Parrattarna II?	Ashur-bel-nisheshu 1417–1409	
Kadashman-harbe I		Ashur-rim-nisheshu 1408–1401	Hurpatila
Kurigalzu I fl. 1390	Artatama I ca. 1400	Ashur-nadin-ahhe II 1400–1391	*Elam defeated by Kurigalzu I*
Kadashman-Enlil I ca. 1374–1360			*Igehalkid dynasty* Igehalki 1400–1380
	Shuttarna II ca. 1380	Eriba-Adad I 1390–1364	Pahir-ishshan I ca. 1375
	Artashumara Tushratta and Artatama II	*Middle Assyrian period*	Attar-kittah

(Continues)

1600–1155

	Babylonia	Mitanni	Assyria	Elam
	Burnaburiash II 1359–1333	Tushratta and Shuttarna III ca. 1350 *Under Hittites* Shattiwaza	Ashur-uballit I 1363–1328 *restored Assyrian independence ca. 1350*	Humban-numena I ca. 1350–1340
	Karahardash 1333			Untash-napirisha ca. 1340-1300
	Nazi-bugash 1333		Enlil-nirari 1327–1318	
	Kurigalzu II 1332–1308	Shattuara I	Arik-den-ili	
	Nazimaruttash 1307–1282	(Shutatarra) ca. 1300	1317–1306	
		Wasashatta ca. 1280	Adad-nirari I 1305–1274	
	Kadashman-Turgu 1281–1264	*Annexed by Assyria* Shattuara II	Shalmaneser I (Shalmanu-ashared)	Unpahash-napirisha
	Kadashman-Enlil II 1263–1255		1273–1244	Kidin-Hutran I Kidin-Hutran II

Babylonia	Assyria	Elam
Kudur-Enlil 1254–1246	Tukulti-Ninurta I 1243–1207	Napirisha-Untash
Shagarakti-Shuriash 1245–1233		
Kashtiliash IV 1232–1225		Kidin-Hutran III ca. 1235–1210?
1225 conquered by Assyrians		
Tukulti-Ninurta I 1225		
Enlil-nadin-shumi 1224		*Shutrukid dynasty* ca. 1200–1100
Kadashman-Harbe II 1223		
Adad-shuma-iddina 1222–1217	Ashur-nadin-apli 1206–1203	Hallutush-Inshushinak 1205–1185
restoration of Kassite line		
	Ashur-nirari III 1202–1197	
Adad-shuma-usur 1216–1187	Enlil-kudurri-usur 1196–1192	
Melishipak 1186–1172	Ninurta-apil-Ekur 1191–1179	Shutruk-nahhunte I 1185–1155
Marduk-apla-iddina I (Merodach-Baladan) 1171–1159	Ashur-dan I 1178–1133	Kutir-nahhunte II 1155–1150
Zababa-shuma-iddina 1158		
overthrown by Elamites		
Kutir-nahhunte 1158–1157?		
Enlil-nadin-ahhe (Enlil-Shuma-usur) 1157–1155		
Babylon sacked by Elamites 1155		

1150–ca. 950 The whole Near East in the period 1200–900 suffered a recession, possibly related to climatic deterioration. After Babylonia declined, a succession of strong kings maintained relative prosperity in Assyria. The death of Tiglath-Pileser I in 1076 heralded decline in Assyria also.

Babylonia	Assyria	Elam
Second Dynasty of Isin	*Middle Assyrian period continued*	Shilhak-Inshushinak 1150–1120
Marduk-kabit-ahheshu 1157–1140	Ashur-dan I 1178–1133	
Itti-Marduk-balatu 1139–1132		
Ninurta-nadin-shumi 1131–1126	Ashur-resha-ishi I 1132–1115	
Nebuchadrezzar I 1125–1104	Ninurta-tukulti-Ashur 1115	Hutelutush-Inshushinak 1120–1110
	Mutakkil-Nusku 1115	
Enlil-nadin-apli 1103–1100	Tiglath-Pileser I (Tukulti-apil-esharra)1114–1076	
Marduk-nadin-ahhe 1099–1082		*Neo-Elamite period 1000–750/700*
Marduk-shapik-zeri 1081–1069	Ashared-apil-Ekur 1075–1074	*period poorly known— no texts—links to Mesopotamia at a minimum*
	Ashur-bel-kala 1073–1056	
Adad-apla-iddina 1068–1047	Eriba-Adad II 1055–1054	Shilhina-hamru-lagamar early 11th century
Aramaean usurper	Shamshi-Adad IV 1053–1050	
Marduk-ahhe-eriba 1046		
Marduk-zer-x 1045–1034	Ashurnasirpal I (Ashur-nasir-apli) 1049–1031	
Nabu-shumu-libur 1033–1026	*Assyrian domains reduced to heartland*	Humban-numena II mid-11th century
Second Dynasty of Sealand	Shalmaneser II 1030–1019	
Simbar-shipak 1025–1008		
Ea-mukin-zeri 1008	Ashur-nirari IV 1018–1013	
Kashshu-nadin-ahhe 1007–1005	Ashur-rabi II 1012–972	
Dynasty of Bazi		
Eulmash-shakin-shumi 1004–988		
Ninurta-kudurri-usur I 987–985		
Shirikti-Shuqamuna 985	Ashur-resh-ishi II 971–967	
Babylon VII— "Elamite Dynasty"		
Mar-biti-apla-usur 984–979		

ca. 950–780 Assyria began expanding from the late tenth century to become a dominant power under Ashurnasirpal and Shalmaneser in the ninth century, who created a more coherent empire than those of former times. Its new capital at Kalhu was richly endowed. Initially on good terms with its

ca. 950–780 powerful neighbor, Babylonia, Assyria turned against it under Shalmaneser's son Shamshi-Adad V, bringing about its collapse in the late ninth century, followed shortly by its own.

Babylonia	Assyria
Dynasty of E	*Neo-Assyrian kings*
Nabu-mukin-apli 978–943	Tiglath-Pileser II 966–935
Ninurta-kudurri-usur II 943	
Mar-biti-ahhe-iddina 942–?	Ashur-dan II 934–912
Shamash-mudammiq ?–ca. 900	Adad-nirari II 911–891
Nabu-shuma-ukin I ca. 895	Tukulti-Ninurta II 890–884
Nabu-apla-iddina ca. 870	Ashurnasirpal II 883–859
Marduk-zakir-shumi I ca. 854–819	Shalmaneser III 858–824
Marduk-balassu-iqbi ca. 818–813	Shamshi-Adad V 823–811
Baba-aha-iddina 812–	Adad-nirari III 810–783
anarchy	*decline*

ca. 780–609 Height of Neo-Assyrian period. Some decades of decline throughout Mesopotamia were brought to an end by Tiglath-Pileser III, who rebuilt and reorganized the Assyrian Empire. It was expanded by his successors, coming to dominate most of the Near East, including Babylonia, and even conquering Egypt for a time. For many years Babylonia resisted Assyrian domination, usually supported by Elam, which suffered significant defeats at Assyrian hands. After the death of Ashurbanipal Assyria fell to Babylonia and the Medes.

Babylonia	Assyria	Elam
	Shalmaneser IV	
5 unknown kings	782–773	
Ninurta-apla-x		
Marduk-bel-zeri		
Marduk-apla-usur	Ashur-dan III 772–755	
Eriba-marduk ca. 770		*Neo-Elamite II*
considered founder of		Huban-tahra ?760–743
Chaldaean dynasty		
Nabu-shuma-ishkun	Ashur-Nirari V	
ca. 760–748	754–745	
Nabu-nasir		Huban-Nukash I
(Nabonassar)		743–717
747–734		
Nabu-nadin-zeri	Tiglath-Pileser III	
733–732	744–727	
Nabu-shuma-ukin II		
732		
Babylon Dynasty IX		
Nabu-mukin-zeri		
731–729		
Babylonia conquered by	Shalmaneser V	
Assyrians	726–722	
Tiglath-Pileser III		
(Pulu) 728–727		

Babylonia	Assyria	Elam
Shalmaneser V (Ululayu) 726–722		Shutruk-Nahhunte II (Ishtar-nandi) ca. 717–699
Marduk-apla-iddina II (Merodach-Baladan) 721–710		Hallutush-Inshushinak (Hallushu) 699–693
Sargon II 709–705	Sargon II 721–705	Kutir-Nahhunte II 693–692
Sennacherib 704–703		
Marduk-zakir-shumi 703	Sennacherib (Sin-ahhe-eriba) 704–681	Humban-numena III 692–689
Marduk-apla-iddina II *(restored)* 703		Humban-haltash I 688–681
Bel-Ibni 702–700		Humban-haltash II 681–674
Ashur-nadin-shumi 699–694		
Nergal-Ushezib 693		
Mushezib-Marduk (Shuzubu) 692–689		Urtagu (Urtaki) 674–664
Sennacherib 688–681		Tepti-Huban-Inshushinak (Tempt-Humban-Inshushinak / Te-Umman) 664–653
Nabu-zer-kitti-lishir 680		
Esarhaddon 680–669	Esarhaddon (Assur-ahhe-iddina) 680–669	
Ashurbanipal 668	Ashurbanipal (Ashur-ban-apli) 668–627	*Assyrian interference in succession*
Shamash-shuma-ukin 667–648		Humban-Nikash III (Ummanigash) 653–652 (and Tammaritu I as subordinate king)
		Tammaritu II 652–649
		Indabibi 649
		Humban-haltash III (Ummanaldash) 648
		Tammaritu II *(restored)* 648
		Humban-haltash III *(restored)* 647–644
Kandalu (= Ashurbanipal?) 647–627		*646 Assyrians raze Susa*
Assyrians expelled— interregnum 626	Ashur-etil-ilani 626–623?	*626 Assyrian domination replaced by Babylonian?*
	Sin-shuma-lishir 623	
	Sin-shar-ishkun ca. 623–612	Shutur-Nahhunte III
	Ashur-uballit II 611–609	Hallutash-Inshushinak
	Assyria conquered by Babylonians and Medes 612–609	Atta-hamiti-Inshushinak
Chaldaean Dynasty— Babylon X		*Elam conquered by Babylonians and Medes sometime between 597 and 586*
Nabopolassar (Nabu-apla-usur) 625–605		

609–539 Neo-Babylonian period. After the collapse of Assyria in 609, Babylonia seized control of its erstwhile dominions, briefly enjoying control of a vast empire. Under Nebuchadrezzar II Babylon was extensively rebuilt and embellished. But the Persian Empire, growing in might, overcame Babylonia after less than a century, in 539.

Babylonia	Medes	Persians
Chaldaean Dynasty	(Dayaukku ca. 700 Kashtaritu 673–652)	(Achaemenes)
Nabopolassar (Nabu-apla-usur) 625–605	Cyaxares 625–585?	Teispes I ca. 635–610
		Cyrus I ca. 610–585
Nebuchadrezzar II (Nabu-kudurri-usur) 604–562		
Amel-Marduk (Evil-Merodach) 561–560	Astyages 585–550	Cambyses I ca. 585–559
Nergal-shar-usur (Neriglissar) 559–556		Cyrus II the Great
Labshi-Marduk 556		*559–530 became king*
Nabonidus (Nabu-na'id) 555–539		*of Medes 550*
Belshazzar (Bel-shar-usur) *(regent 549–544/540)*		
Persians conquer Babylon 539		

1550–1295	EGYPTIAN 18TH DYNASTY
Years	King
1550–1525	Ahmose
1525–1504	Amenhotep I
1504–1492	Thutmose I
1492–1479	Thutmose II
1479–1425	Thutmose III
1473–1458	Hatshepsut
1427–1400	Amenhotep II
1400–1390	Thutmose IV
1390–1352	Amenhotep III
1352–1336	Akhenaten (Amenhotep IV)
1338–1336	Smenkhkare
1336–1327	Tutankhamun
1327–1323	Ay
1323–1295	Horemheb

(after Shaw and Nicholson 1995: 311)

747–656	EGYPTIAN 25TH DYNASTY
Years	King
747–716	Piy (Piankhy)
716–702	Shabaqo
702–690	Shabitqo
690–664	Taharqo
664–656	Tanutamani
664–525	**EGYPTIAN 26TH DYNASTY**
Years	King
[672–664	Nekau I]
664–610	Psamtek I (Psammetichus)
610–595	Nekau II
595–589	Psamtek II
589–570	Apries
570–526	Ahmose II
526–252	Psamtek III

(after Shaw and Nicholson 1995: 311)

TEXT REFERENCES

*=main sources

Baines, John, and Jaromir Malek. 1996. *Atlas of Ancient Egypt.* Oxford: Andromeda.

*Bienkowski, Piotr, and Alan Millard, eds. 2000. *Dictionary of the Ancient Near East.* London: British Museum Press.

Bottero, Jean. http://mesopotamie.chez.tiscali.fr/Site-reduction/l.htm. (cited September 6, 2002).

*Brentjes, Burchard. 2000. "The History of Elam and Achaemenid Persia: An Overview." Pp. 1001–1021 in *Civilizations of the Ancient Near East.* Edited by Jack M. Sasson. Peabody, MA: Hendrickson Publishers. (Reprint of 1995 edition. New York: Scribner.)

*Brinkman, J. A. 1977. "Appendix: Mesopotamian Chronology of the Historical Period." Pp. 335–348 in *Ancient Mesopotamia. Portrait of a Dead Civilization.* Revised edition. Edited by A. Leo Oppenheim and Erica Reiner. Chicago: University of Chicago Press.

*Charpin, Dominique. 2000. "The History of Ancient Mesopotamia: An Overview." Pp. 807–830 in *Civilizations of the Ancient Near East.* Edited by Jack M. Sasson. Peabody, MA: Hendrickson Publishers. (Reprint of 1995 edition. New York: Scribner.)

Cryer, Frederick. 1995. "Chronology: Issues and Problems." Pp. 651–664 in *Civilizations of the Ancient Near East.* Edited by Jack M. Sasson. Peabody, MA: Hendrickson Publishers. (Reprint of 1995 edition. New York: Scribner.)

Curtis, John, ed. 1982a. *Fifty Years of Mesopotamian Discovery.* London: British School of Archaeology in Iraq.

*Hallo, William W., and William Kelly Simpson. 1998. *The Ancient Near East. A History.* 2nd edition. Belmont, CA: Wadworth / Thomson Learning.

*Kuhrt, Amelie. 1995. *The Ancient Near East. ca. 3000–330 BCE.* 2 Volumes. London: Routledge.

Leick, Gwendolyn. 1999. *Who's Who in the Ancient Near East.* London: Routledge.

———. 2001. *Mesopotamia. The Invention of the City.* London: Allen Lane, Penguin Press.

Meyers, Eric M., ed. 1997. *The Oxford Encyclopedia of Archaeology in the Near East.* 5 Volumes. Oxford: Oxford University Press.

Nissen, Hans J. 1988. *The Early History of the Ancient Near East.* Chicago: University of Chicago Press.

*Oates, Joan. 1986. *Babylon.* Revised edition. London: Thames and Hudson.

Pollack, Susan. 1999. *Ancient Mesopotamia. The Eden that Never Was.* Cambridge: Cambridge University Press.

Postgate, J. Nicholas. 1994. *Early Mesopotamia.* London: Routledge.

*Potts, D. T. 1999. *The Archaeology of Elam. Formation and Transformation of an Ancient Iranian State.* Cambridge: Cambridge University Press.

Quirke, Stephen and Jeffrey Spencer. 1992. *The British Museum Book of Ancient Egypt.* London: British Museum Press.

Reade, Julian. 2000. *Mesopotamia.* 2d edition. London: British Museum Press.

Reichel, Clement. "Political Change and Cultural Continuity in Eshnunna from the Ur III to the Old Babylonian Period." http://www-oi.uchicago.edu/OI/DEPT/RA/DISPROP/Reichel_diss.html (cited January 27, 2003).

*Roaf, Michael. 1990. *Cultural Atlas of Mesopotamia.* New York: Facts on File.

*Roux, Georges. 1992. *Ancient Iraq.* 3d edition. Harmondsworth: Penguin.

Sasson, Jack M., ed. 2000a. *Civilizations of the Ancient Near East.* 4 Volumes. Peabody, MA: Hendrickson Publishers. (Reprint of 1995 edition. New York: Scribner.)

Sasson, Jack M. 2000b. "King Hammurabi of Babylon." Pp. 901–916 in *Civilizations of the Ancient Near East.* Edited by Jack M. Sasson. Peabody, MA: Hendrickson Publishers. (Reprint of 1995 edition. New York: Scribner.)

*Shaw, Ian, and Paul Nicholson. 1995. *British Museum Dictionary of Ancient Egypt.* London: British Museum Press.

Vallat, Francois. 2000. "Susa and Susiana in Second-Millennium Iran." Pp. 1023–1033 in *Civilizations of the Ancient Near East.* Edited by Jack M. Sasson. Peabody, MA: Hendrickson Publishers. (Reprint of 1995 edition. New York: Scribner.)

*Van de Mieroop, Marc. 2004. *A History of the Ancient Near East. ca. 3000–323 BC.* Oxford: Blackwell.

Villard, Pierre. 2000. "Shamshi-Adad and Sons: The Rise and Fall of an Upper Mesopotamian Empire." Pp. 873–884 in *Civilizations of the Ancient Near East.* Edited by Jack M. Sasson. Peabody, MA: Hendrickson Publishers. (Reprint of 1995 edition. New York: Scribner.)

Bibliography

GENERAL

Bienkowski, Piotr, and Alan Millard, eds. 2000. *Dictionary of the Ancient Near East.* London: British Museum Press.

Bottero, Jean. *An Online Encyclopedia of the Near East.* From http://mesopotamie.chez.tiscali.fr/Site-reduction/a.htm *to* http://mesopotamie.chez.tiscali.fr/Site-reduction/z.htm (cited September 6, 2002).

Meyers, Eric M., ed. 1997. *The Oxford Encyclopedia of Archaeology in the Near East.* 5 Volumes. Oxford: Oxford University Press.

Sasson, Jack M., ed. 2000a. *Civilizations of the Ancient Near East.* 4 Volumes. Peabody, MA: Hendrickson Publishers. (Reprint of 1995 edition. New York: Scribner.)

HISTORY OF DISCOVERY

Larsen, Mogens T. 1996. *The Conquest of Assyria: Excavations in an Antique Land. 1840–1860.* London: Routledge.

Lloyd, Seton. 1980. *Foundations in the Dust.* Revised edition. London: Thames and Hudson.

Matthews, H. C. G., and Brian Harrison. 2004. *Oxford Dictionary of National Biography.* Oxford: Oxford University Press. http://www.oxforddnb.com.

HISTORY, HISTORIOGRAPHY, AND ARCHAEOLOGY

Cooper, Jerrold S. 1983. *Reconstructing History from Ancient Inscriptions: The Lagash-Umma Border Conflict.* Malibu: Undena.

Cooper, Jerrold S., and Glenn M. Schwartz, eds. 1996. *The Study of the Ancient Near East in the 21st Century.* Winona Lake, IN: Eisenbrauns.

Crawford, Harriet. 1991. *Sumer and the Sumerians.* Cambridge: Cambridge University Press.

Kramer, Samuel Noah. 1971. *The Sumerians. Their History, Culture, and Character.* Chicago: University of Chicago Press.

———. 1981. *History Begins at Sumer. Thirty-Nine Firsts in Recorded History.* 3rd revised edition. Philadelphia: University of Pennsylvania Press.

Liverani, Mario, ed. 1993. *Akkad. The First World Empire.* Padua: Sargon.

Matthews, Roger. 2003. *The Archaeology of Mesopotamia. Theories and Approaches.* London: Routledge.

Oates, Joan. 1986. *Babylon.* Revised edition. London: Thames and Hudson.

Oppenheim, A. Leo, and Erica Reiner. 1977. *Ancient Mesopotamia. Portrait of a Dead Civilization.* Revised edition. Chicago: University of Chicago Press.

Parpola, Simo, and R. M. Whiting, eds. 1997. *Assyria 1995.* Helsinki: Helsinki University Press.

Pollack, Susan. 1999. *Ancient Mesopotamia. The Eden that Never Was.* Cambridge: Cambridge University Press.

Postgate, J. Nicholas. 1994. *Early Mesopotamia.* London: Routledge.

Reade, Julian. 2000. *Mesopotamia.* 2d edition. London: British Museum Press.

Roux, Georges. 1992. *Ancient Iraq.* 3d edition. Harmondsworth: Penguin.

Saggs, H. W. F. 1984. *The Might that Was Assyria.* London: Sidgwick and Jackson.

———. 1988. *The Greatness that Was Babylon.* Revised edition. London: Sidgwick and Jackson.

———. 1995. *Peoples of the Past. Babylonians.* London: British Museum Press.

Schmandt-Besserat, Denise, ed. 1976. *The Legacy of Sumer.* Malibu: Undena.

Van de Mieroop, Marc. 1999. *Cuneiform Texts and the Writing of History.* London: Routledge.

MESOPOTAMIA IN WEST ASIA

Akkermans, Peter M. M. G., and Glenn M. Schwartz. 2003. *The Archaeology of Syria. From Complex Hunter-Gatherers to Early Urban Societies (ca. 16,000–300 BC).* Cambridge: Cambridge University Press.

Algarze, Guillermo. 1993. *The Uruk World System. The Dynamics of Expansion of Early Mesopotamian Civilization.* Chicago: University of Chicago Press.

Charvat, Petr. 2002. *Mesopotamia before History.* Revised edition. London: Routledge.

Hallo, William W., and William Kelly Simpson. 1998. *The Ancient Near East. A History.* 2d edition. Belmont, CA: Wadworth / Thomson Learning.

Kuhrt, Amelie. 1995. *The Ancient Near East. c. 3000–330 BCE.* 2 Volumes. London: Routledge.

Liverani, Mario. 2001. *International Relations in the Ancient Near East, 1600–1100 BC.* New Haven, CT: Palgrave.

Matthiae, Paolo. 1981. *Ebla: An Empire Rediscovered.* Garden City, NY: Doubleday.

Moran, William L. 1992. *The Amarna Letters.* Baltimore, MD: Johns Hopkins University Press.

Nissen, Hans J. 1988. *The Early History of the Ancient Near East.* Chicago: University of Chicago Press. (Paperback edition 1990.)

Pettinato, Giovanni. 1991. *Ebla: A New Look at History.* Baltimore, MD: Johns Hopkins University Press.

Roaf, Michael. 1990. *Cultural Atlas of Mesopotamia.* New York: Facts on File.

Rothman, Mitchell S., ed. 2001. *Uruk, Mesopotamia and Its Neighbors. Cross-Cultural Interactions in the Era of State Formation.* School of American Research Advanced Seminar Series. Santa Fe, NM: School of American Research Press.

Stein, Gill, and Mitchell Rothman, eds. 1994. *Chiefdoms and Early States in the Near East.* Madison, WI: Prehistory Press.

Van De Mieroop, Marc. 2004. *A History of the Ancient Near East. ca. 3000–323 BC.* Oxford: Blackwell.

Wilhelm, Gernot. 1989. *The Hurrians.* Warminster: Aris and Phillips.

Wilkinson, T. J. 2003. *Archaeological Landscapes of the Near East.* Tucson: University of Arizona Press.

ECONOMY, TRADE, AND FOREIGN RELATIONS

Archi, A., ed. 1984. *Circulation of Goods in Non-Palatial Context in the Ancient Near East.* Rome: Edizione dell'Ateneo.

Bulletin on Sumerian Agriculture. Cambridge: Sumerian Agriculture Group.

Crawford, Harriet. 1998. *Dilmun and Its Gulf Neighbours.* Cambridge: Cambridge University Press.

Diakonoff, Igor M. 1969. *Ancient Mesopotamia: Socio-Economic History.* Moscow: Nauka.

Gibson, MacGuire, and Robert Biggs, eds. 1987. *The Organization of Power: Aspects of Bureaucracy in the Ancient Near East.* Chicago: University of Chicago Press.

Hawkins, J. D., ed. *Trade in the Ancient Near East. Papers Presented to the XXIII Rencontre Assyriologique Internationale.* London: British School of Archaeology in Iraq.

Larsen, Mogens Trolle. 1976. *The Old Assyrian City-State and Its Colonies.* Copenhagen: Akademisk Forlag.

Lipinski, Edward, ed. 1979. *State and Temple Economy in the Ancient Near East.* 2 Volumes. Louvain: Departement Orientalistiek.

Potts, D. T. 1990. *The Arabian Gulf in Antiquity.* Oxford: Clarendon Press.

———. 1999. *The Archaeology of Elam. Formation and Transformation of an Ancient Iranian State.* Cambridge: Cambridge University Press.

Powell, M. A., ed. 1987. *Labor in the Ancient Near East.* Winona Lake, IN: Eisenbrauns.

Ratnagar, Shereen. 1981. *Encounters. The Westerly Trade of the Harappa Civilization.* Delhi: Oxford University Press.

Snell, Daniel. 1982. *Ledgers and Prices: Early Mesopotamian Merchant Accounts.* New Haven, CT: Yale University Press.

Yoffee, Norman. 1982. *Explaining Trade in Ancient Western Asia.* Malibu: Undena.

INDUSTRY, TECHNOLOGY, AND SCIENCE

Barber, Elizabeth J. W. 1991. *Prehistoric Textiles.* Princeton, NJ: Princeton University Press.

Dilke, O. A. W. 1987. *Mathematics and Measurement.* London: British Museum.

Moorey, P. R. S. 1994. *Ancient Mesopotamian Materials and Industries. The Archaeological Evidence.* Oxford: Clarendon Press.

Nissen, Hans J., Peter Damerow, and Robert K. Englund. 1993. *Archaic Bookkeeping.* Chicago: University of Chicago Press.

Photos of objects from the Iraq Museum. http://the.iraq.museum.

Potts, D. T. 1997. *Mesopotamian Civilization. The Material Foundations.* London: The Athlone Press.

DAILY LIFE

Bahrani, Zainab B. 2001. *Women of Babylon. Gender and Representation in Mesopotamia.* London: Routledge.

Bottero, Jean, ed. 2001a. *Everyday Life in Ancient Mesopotamia.* Translated by A. Nevill. Edinburgh: Edinburgh University Press.

Dandamaev, Muhammed A. 1984. *Slavery in Babylonia.* Revised edition. DeKalb: Northern Illinois University Press.

Lesko, Barbara S., ed. 1989. *Women's Earliest Records from Ancient Egypt and Western Asia.* Atlanta, GA: Scholars Press.

Nemet-Nejat, Karen Rhea. 2002. *Daily Life in Ancient Mesopotamia.* Westport, CT: Hendrickson Publishers.

Snell, Daniel C. 1997. *Life in the Ancient Near East. 3100–332 B.C.E.* New Haven, CT: Yale University Press.

Veenhof, R., ed. 1996. *Houses and Households in Ancient Mesopotamia.* Leiden: Nederlands Historisch-Archaeologisch Instituut te Istanbul.

SETTLEMENT AND SETTLEMENTS

Adams, Robert McCormack. 1965. *The Land behind Baghdad.* Chicago: University of Chicago Press.

———. 1981. *Heartland of Cities.* Chicago: University of Chicago Press.

Adams, Robert McCormack, and Hans J. Nissen. 1972. *The Uruk Countryside.* Chicago: University of Chicago Press.

Curtis, John, ed. 1982. *Fifty Years of Mesopotamian Discovery.* London: British School of Archaeology in Iraq.

Dalley, Stephanie. 1984. *Mari and Karana. Two Old Babylonian Cities.* London: Longman.

Ellis, Maria Dejong, ed. 1992. *Nippur at the Centennial.* Philadelphia, PA: University Museum.

Foster, Benjamin. 1982. *Umma in the Sargonic Period.* Hamden, CT: Archon.

Gibson, MacGuire. 1972. *The City and Area of Kish.* Miami, FL: Field Research Projects.

Harris, R. 1975. *Ancient Sippar.* Leiden: Nederlands Historisch-Archaeologisch Instituut te Istanbul.

Huot, J.-L., ed. 1989. *Larsa. Travaux de 1985.* Paris.

Leick, Gwendolyn. 2001. *Mesopotamia. The Invention of the City.* London: Allen Lane, Penguin Press.

Liverani, Mario. In press. *Uruk: The First City.* Translated by Z. Bahrani and Marc Van de Mieroop. Chicago: University of Chicago Press.

Martin, Harriet P. 1988. *Fara: A Reconstruction of the Ancient Mesopotamian City of Shuruppak.* Birmingham, UK: Chris Martin and Associates.

Moorey, P. R. S. 1978. *Kish Excavations 1923–1933.* Oxford: Clarendon Press.

Oates, Joan. 1986. *Babylon.* Revised edition. London: Thames and Hudson.

Oates, Joan, and David Oates. 2001. *Nimrud. An Assyrian Imperial City Revealed.* London: British School of Archaeology in Iraq.

Owen, David I., and Gernot Wilhelm. 1999. *Nuzi at Seventy-Five.* Bethesda, MD: CDL Press.

Russell, John Malcolm. 1991. *Sennacherib's Palace without a Rival at Nineveh.* Chicago: University of Chicago Press.

———. 1998. *The Final Sack of Nineveh. The Discovery, Documentation, and Destruction of*

King Sennacherib's Throne Room at Nineveh, Iraq. New Haven, CT: Yale University Press.

Safer, Fuad, Mohammed Ali Mustafa, and Seton Lloyd. 1981. *Eridu.* Baghdad: State Organization of Antiquities and Heritage.

Site Photos from Iraq Web page. http://oi.uchicago.edu/OI/IRAQ/sites/sitesintro.htm

Starr, R. F. S. 1939. *Nuzi.* 2 Volumes. Cambridge, MA: Harvard University Press.

Stone, Elizabeth. 1987. *Nippur Neighborhoods.* Chicago: Chicago University Press.

Van De Mieroop, Marc. 1992. *Society and Enterprise in Old Babylonian Ur.* Berlin: Berliner Beitrage zum Vorderen Orient 12.

———. 1997. *The Ancient Mesopotamian City.* Oxford: Oxford University Press.

Westenholz, Joan Goodnick, ed. 1996. *Royal Cities of the Biblical World.* Jerusalem: Bible Lands Museum.

Wiseman, D. J. 1991. *Nebuchadrezzar and Babylon. The Schweich Lectures of the British Academy 1983.* Oxford: Oxford University Press.

Woolley, Leonard. 1982. *Ur "of the Chaldees."* The Final Account, *Excavations at Ur,* revised and updated by P. Roger and S. Moorey. London: Book Club Associates / Herbert Press.

RELIGION

Black, Jeremy, and Anthony Green. 1992. *Gods, Demons and Symbols of Ancient Mesopotamia. An Illustrated Dictionary.* London: British Museum Press.

Bottero, Jean. 1992. *Mesopotamia: Writing, Reasoning, and the Gods.* Chicago: University of Chicago Press.

Jacobsen, Thorkild. 1976. *The Treasures of Darkness. A History of Mesopotamian Religion.* New Haven, CT: Yale University Press.

Leick, Gwendolyn. 1991. *A Dictionary of Ancient Near Eastern Mythology.* London: Routledge.

ART AND ARCHITECTURE

Amiet, Pierre. 1980. *Art of the Ancient Near East.* New York: Harry N Abrams.

Frankfort, Henri. 1996. *The Art and Architecture of the Ancient Orient.* 5th edition. New Haven, CT: Yale University Press.

Gunter, Ann, ed. 1990. *Investigating Artistic Environments in the Ancient Near East.* Washington, DC: Smithsonian Institution Press.

Moorgat, A. 1969. *The Art of Ancient Mesopotamia.* London: Phaidon.

Reade, Julian. 1983. *Assyrian Sculpture.* London: British Museum Publications.

Strommenger, E., and M. Hirmer. 1964. *The Art of Ancient Mesopotamia.* London: Thames and Hudson.

LANGUAGE, WRITING, AND SEALS

Collon, Dominique. 1987. *First Impressions. Cylinder Seals in the Ancient Near East.* London: British Museum Publications.

———. 1990. *Interpreting the Past. Near Eastern Seals.* London: British Museum Press.

Glassner, Jean-Jacques. 2003. *The Invention of Cuneiform: Writing in Sumer.* Translated by Zainab Bahrani and Marc Van de Mieroop. Baltimore, MD: Johns Hopkins University Press.

Healy, John F. 1990. *Reading the Past. The Early Alphabet.* London: British Museum Press.

Nissen, Hans J. Peter Damerow, and Robert K. Englund. 1993. *Archaic Bookkeeping.* Chicago: University of Chicago Press.

Schmandt-Besserat, Denise. 1992. *Before Writing: From Counting to Cuneiform.* 2 Volumes. Austin: University of Texas Press.

———. 1996. *How Writing Came About.* Austin: University of Texas Press.

Veenhof, K., ed. 1986. *Cuneiform Archives and Libraries.* Leiden: Netherlands Instituut voor het Nabije Oosten / Netherlands Institute for the Near East.

Walker, Christopher B. F. 1987. *Reading the Past. Cuneiform.* London: British Museum Press.

LITERATURE

Cagni, L. 1977. *The Poem of Erra.* Malibu, FL: Undena.

Cooper, Jerrold. 1983. *The Curse of Agade.* Baltimore, MD: Johns Hopkins University Press.

Dalley, Stephanie. 2000. *Myths from Mesopotamia.* Revised edition. Oxford: Oxford University Press.

Electronic Text Corpus of Sumerian Literature. http://etcsl.orient.ox.ac.uk/index.html.

Foster, Benjamin R. 1993. *Before the Muses: An Anthology of Akkadian Literature.* 2d edition. Bethesda, MD: CDL Press.

George, A. 1999. *The Epic of Gilgamesh. A New Translation.* London: Allen Lane, Penguin Press.

Grayson, A. Kirk. 1975. *Assyrian and Babylonian Chronicles.* New York: J. J. Augustin Publisher.

Hallo, William W., and J. J. van Dijk. 1968. *The Exaltation of Inanna.* New Haven, CT: Yale University Press.

Jacobsen, Thorkild. 1987. *The Harps that Once. . . . Sumerian Poetry in Translation.* New Haven, CT: Yale University Press.

Lambert, W. G. 1960. *Babylonian Wisdom Literature.* Oxford: Clarendon Press.

Michalowski, Piotr. 1989. *The Lamentation over the Destruction of Sumer and Ur.* Winona Lake, IN: Eisenbrauns.

Oppenheim, A. L. 1967. *Letters from Mesopotamia.* Chicago: University of Chicago Press.

Pritchard, J. B., ed. 1969. *Ancient Near Eastern Texts.* 3d edition. Princeton, NJ: Princeton University Press.

Reiner, Erica. 1985. *Your Thwarts in Pieces, Your Mooring Rope Cut: Poetry from Babylonia and Assyria.* Ann Arbor: University of Michigan.

Sandars, Nancy K. 1971. *Poems of Heaven and Hell from Ancient Mesopotamia.* Harmondsworth: Penguin.

THE THREAT TO MESOPOTAMIA'S PAST

Atwood, Roger. 2004. *Stealing History. Tomb Raiders, Smugglers, and the Looting of the Ancient World.* New York: St. Martin's Press.

Russell, John Malcolm. 1998. *The Final Sack of Nineveh. The Discovery, Documentation, and Destruction of King Sennacherib's Throne Room at Nineveh, Iraq*. New Haven, CT: Yale University Press.

A number of regularly updated Web sites provide information on the current state of archaeological sites and museums in Iraq and other related matters of interest.

Francis Deblauwe. The 2003 Iraq War and Archaeology Web site.

http://iwa.univie.ac.at

http://iwa.univie.ac.at/academic.html

http://writing.deblauwe.org/writing.html

Juan Cole's Web log

www.juancole.com

A regular e-mail update on the situation can be obtained by subscribing (free) to Iraqcrisis, a moderated Web list administered by Professor Charles Jones of the University of Chicago. To subscribe consult https://listhost.uchicago.edu/mailman/listinfo/iraqcrisis

"Lost Treasures from Iraq" Web site maintained by the Oriental Institute, University of Chicago.

http://oi.uchicago.edu/OI/IRAQ/iraq.html

"Heritage of Iraq" Web site on Iraq's museums maintained by Dr. Helga Trenkwalder at the University of Innsbruck (in German).

http://info.uibk.ac.at/c/c6/c616/museum/museum.html

USEFUL WEB PAGES

www.gatewaystobabylon.com/

www.sumerian.org/sumerian.htm

Two sites with many links to useful pages.

http://www.etana.org/abzu/

Research archive maintained by Chicago Oriental Institute / American Schools of Oriental Research.

http://oi.uchicago.edu/OI/PROJ/SUM/Sumerian.html

Sumerian Lexicon Project.

http://www.fordham.edu/halsall/ancient/asbook03.html

Internet history sourcebook site—links to many useful texts.

JOURNALS

Bulletin of the American Schools of Oriental Research Iraq

Journal of the American Oriental Society

Journal of Cuneiform Studies

Journal of the Economic and Social History of the Orient

Journal of Near Eastern Studies

Mesopotamia

Orientalia

Sumer

Index

About the Author

Jane McIntosh is a native of Scotland. She studied archaeology at the University of Cambridge, in England, from which she also received her doctorate and where she taught for a number of years. She has traveled widely, taking part in excavations and other fieldwork in Iraq, Cyprus, India, and Britain. Since 1995 she has worked full time as a writer of books, articles, and multimedia on a range of archaeological subjects. She is a widow, with one son.